The Lost Children

The Lost Children

RECONSTRUCTING EUROPE'S FAMILIES

AFTER WORLD WAR II

Tara Zahra

Harvard University Press

Cambridge, Massachusetts, and London, England

2011

Library of Congress Cataloging-in-Publication Data
Zahra, Tara.
   The lost children : reconstructing Europe's families after World War II / Tara Zahra.
      p. cm.
   Includes bibliographical references and index.
   ISBN 978-0-674-04824-9 (alk. paper)
   1. Refugee children—Europe—History. 2. War victims—Europe—History. 3. Families—
Europe—History. 4. World War, 1939-1945—Social aspects. I. Title.
   HV640.4.E8.Z34 2011
   362.87083'094—dc22   2010052246

To Debbie and Marc Zahra

Contents

Preface

In 2007, 4,317,000 babies were born in the United States, breaking the 1957 record. We are enmeshed in a deeply maternalist culture, one that celebrates maternal self-sacrifice, often pits the needs of mothers against those of their children, and demands more commitment than ever of parents. One source of the present-day vogue for what has been called "intensive parenting" among middle-class parents in the United States is a set of assumptions about children's psychological "best interests." While these "best interests" are presumed to be timeless, inscribed in the deepest structures of human nature, they can in fact be traced back to the unlikely setting of European orphanages, displaced person camps, and war nurseries during and after the Second World War.

Contemporaries often described the Second World War as a "war against children." The plight of Europe's so-called "lost children" during World War II—children who were hungry, displaced, orphaned, murdered—will be familiar to anyone who has seen images of children in contemporary zones of crisis. The political controversies that erupted over the custody of Europe's lost children at mid-century will also resonate with today's readers. From Haitian orphans to celebrity adoptions, the movement of children across national frontiers continues to ignite political and cultural conflict.

World War II was not only a moment of unprecedented violence against children, however. It also spawned ambitious new humanitarian movements to save and protect children from wartime upheaval and persecution. Through their work with displaced children, these child-savers generated new psychological theories, child-rearing methods, and social welfare programs. Many of our fundamental ideas about the nature of childhood trauma first developed in the context of World War II and its aftermath. The same can be said for contemporary notions of what makes for a happy childhood or a "healthy" family environment. The reconstruction of war-torn families after 1945 ulti mately entailed more than a simple restoration of prewar "normality." It was a moment in which basic ideals of family and childhood were reinvented. As the reconstruction of families was linked to the reestablishment of peace and stability in postwar Europe, these lessons in child development echoed well beyond the nursery. They went on to shape postwar ideas about the very na ture of the family, democracy, and human rights in the shadows of Nazism and Communism.

Archival resources on displaced persons are incredibly rich, but accessing them has required a fair amount of personal displacement and the assistance of many individuals and institutions. I could not have completed the research for this book without the support of a Milton Fund Research Grant from Harvard University, a Charles A. Ryskamp Fellowship from the ACLS, the Woodrow Wilson Center's East European Studies Program, and the Univer sity of Chicago Division of Social Sciences. I am grateful to the Harvard Society of Fellows, the University of Chicago, and the Institute for Advanced Study in Paris for providing me with crucial fellowship support and leave from teaching. I also thank the *Journal of Modern History* for permission to reprint parts of my March 2009 article, "Lost Children: Displacement, Family, and Nation in Postwar Europe."

Many colleagues and friends helped shape and improve this book. Larry Wolff and Robert Moeller both read the entire manuscript with great care, and provided generous and constructive ideas for revision. Atina Grossmann's work on displaced persons first brought this topic to life for me. I am grateful for her judicious and insightful feedback on draft chapters, as well as her sup port and enthusiasm. My friends and colleagues Alison Frank, Edith Sheffer, and Alice Weinreb also provided valuable suggestions on parts of the manu script. I am particularly indebted to my friend and colleague Daniella Doron, who generously shared archival tips, ideas, and hours of conversation about displaced children in Paris, New York, and Chicago.

I have been extremely lucky to find an intellectual home at the University of Chicago since beginning this book. I am particularly grateful to my colleagues Leora Auslander, Sheila Fitzpatrick, and Michael Geyer, for welcoming me and surrounding me with intellectual stimulation, collegiality, and support. My research assistants Rachel Applebaum and Natalie Belsky deserve special ac knowledgment for their valuable assistance tracking down sources and secondary materials. Emily Osborn and Jennifer Palmer supported me tremendously with their editorial and intellectual guidance, culinary skills, and friendship.

I thank my editor Joyce Seltzer at Harvard University Press for her confidence in this book, and for helping me to make my ideas and writing more clear and accessible. I also thank Jeannette Estruth and everyone else at Harvard who contributed to the editing and production of *The Lost Children*.

I am particularly grateful to Laura Lee Downs, whose inspiring work on the history of childhood first led me to think about the political meaning of family separation. She nurtured *The Lost Children* through many revisions, and kept my spirits high as I completed this book in Paris.

Writing and teaching history would be very lonely work without my friend, colleague, and role model Pieter Judson. His wisdom, wit, and historical imagination sustain and inspire me. I am indebted to him for his insight on countless drafts, his empathy and support, and his steadfast friendship.

I dedicate this book to my parents, Debbie and Marc Zahra. I thank them for teaching me to read, driving me to ballet, supplying me with meat, swimming in cold water, and beating me at Scrabble. I owe everything to their constant love, support, and confidence in me.

Introduction: Civilization in Disarray

In May of 1951, Ruth-Karin Davidowicz, age 13, was desperate to leave Germany. Ruth-Karin had the misfortune of being born in Berlin to Jewish parents in 1938. When she was still an infant, her family attempted to escape Nazi Germany to go to Palestine. They were caught and interned in Romania en route, and her father was deported to the Majdanek concentration camp, where he died. The rest of the family—grandparents, aunts, uncles, and cousins, perished in Auschwitz. Ruth-Karin and her mother managed to remain in Romania, where they survived the war. After their liberation, they illegally traversed the frontiers of Romania and Austria, eventually reaching the American zone of occupied Germany. In Bavaria, they found refuge in the Displaced Persons camps run by the United Nations Relief and Rehabilitation Administration (UNRRA) and the International Refugee Organization (IRO).

By 1951, Ruth-Karin had grown to be a healthy girl with long, brown braids and a bright smile, "well-built for her age, with a strong and firm handshake," according to Mrs. Roch, the American social worker assigned to her case. Ruth-Karin was chosen to immigrate to the United States under the U.S. Displaced Persons Act of 1948 (DP Act). However, since her mother was too sick to make the journey, Ruth-Karin would have to go alone. An organization called European-Jewish Children's Aid had already planned to place her with previously chosen American foster parents. But Ruth-Karin's mother had not yet signed the necessary release forms. Mrs. Roch explained to Mrs. Davidowicz that she could no longer postpone her decision. The lifetime of the DP Act was limited, and the children's program was ending soon.

Ruth-Karin did not hide her impatience with her mother. "When in America, can I keep in letter contact with my mother?" she asked Mrs. Roch. Her mother responded bitterly that she would surely forget to write. Mrs. Roch explained to Ruth-Karin that her foster parents would probably not mind if she wrote to her mother, but they would expect her to obey them and not her mother. She should not expect her American parents to send money to her mother, nor to sponsor her for immigration to the United States later on. Ruth-Karin agreed to these conditions. When she was 21, she promised, she would get a job and bring her mother to the United States herself. Mrs. Davidowicz was skeptical. She replied, "By then I'll be dead and you'll be married and have forgotten all about your mother."

Things had become tense between the teenager and her mother over the past few months. Every day Ruth-Karin asked her mother if she had signed the release form yet. The document stated that Mrs. Davidowicz fully relinquished her parental rights and agreed to her daughter's adoption in the United States. Ruth-Karin talked incessantly about her future in America: attending an American High School and living with a Jewish family there. But Mrs. D. felt that Ruth-Karin was all she had left. Once her daughter was gone, she confided, there would be nothing left to do but "poison herself." She knew she would probably never see her daughter again. Besides which, once Ruth-Karin was gone, her mother would no longer receive the orphan's pension of 70 DM a month that supported them both.

On the other hand, Ruth-Karin's prospects in Germany were dismal. Mrs. Davidowicz was in poor health. She had recently fainted on the street and been taken to the hospital. She couldn't work, and considered her remaining life in Germany to be "vegetative." Mrs. D. did not anticipate living much longer, she confessed, and knew that none of her friends would take care of her daughter when she was gone. But she continued to waver. It was clear to Mrs. Roch that Ruth-Karin could no longer stand her mother's indecision, and so she asked Ruth-Karin to leave the room during the rest of the interview. With Ruth-Karin outside, Mrs. Roch counseled Mrs. D. to consider the matter "with a cool head." By focusing on her fears of being alone, the social worker advised, she was selfishly putting her own emotions ahead of her daughter's best interests. Did she want her daughter to grow up in a German orphanage? Mrs. D. finally agreed to sign the release form and Ruth-Karin was free to travel to the United States to live with her new parents. With her departure, all traces of her and her mother disappear from our view.[1]

Ruth-Karin's story was hardly atypical in postwar Europe. During and after the Second World War, an unprecedented number of children were separated from their parents due to emigration, deportation, forced labor, ethnic cleansing, or murder. As the Nazi empire crumbled, millions of people roamed the continent in search of lost family members. They placed ads in newspapers, waited on train platforms, and wrote letters to new international agencies and government officials. During the war, many Europeans sustained themselves with fantasies of reunion with their loved ones. After the war, they waited and hoped, often in vain, for signs of life. As Ruth-Karin's story suggests, even when families managed to stick together during the war, they often did not survive the peace intact.

Germany, divided into four zones of occupation by the Allies after the Nazi defeat, boasted the largest number of so-called "unaccompanied children." Red Cross posters in Germany featured rows of children's photos under the headline, "Who Knows our Parents and our Origins?" The German Red Cross received over 300,000 requests to trace missing children between 1945 and 1958, while the new International Tracing Service (ITS) registered 343,057 missing children between 1945 and 1956.

The separation of families was more than a challenging logistical problem. So-called "lost children" held a special grip on the postwar imagination. They stood at the center of bitter political conflicts as military authorities, German foster parents, social workers, Jewish agencies, East European Communists, and Displaced Persons (DPs) competed to determine their fates. These battles were linked to the reconstruction of European civilization at large in the aftermath of total war. In the words of Vinita A. Lewis, a social worker with the International Refugee Organization (IRO) in Germany in 1948, "The lost identity of individual children is *the* Social Problem of the day on the continent of Europe."[2]

Lewis drew attention to the lost identities of children in a context in which there was no shortage of "social problems" in Europe. The Continent appeared to be in ruins in 1945. American and British relief workers typically disembarked at French ports and traveled eastward, marveling at the spectacle of human and physical destruction.[3] They linked the physical ruin of European cities to the psychological disorientation of their residents. Traveling through Cologne in July 1945, British official and writer Stephen Spender reported, "My first impression on passing through the city was of there being not a single house left. There are plenty of walls, but these walls are a thin mask in front of the damp, hollow, stinking emptiness of the gutted interiors . . . The ruin of the city is reflected in the internal ruin of its inhabitants, who, instead of being lives that can form a scar over the city's wounds, are parasites sucking at a dead carcass, digging among the ruins for hidden food."[4]

For millions of Europeans, homelessness was a bitter fact of life in 1945. At least 14 million Germans had no place to call home at the end of the war, thanks to the massive flight of Germans from Eastern Europe and the complete destruction of 4.1 million apartments. More than half of the homeless in Germany were children. Since most German men (and increasingly, boys) had been mobilized in the Wehrmacht by 1945, the majority of the 12 million ethnic German refugees who fled the Red Army or were expelled from Eastern Europe in the final months of the war and its aftermath were women and children. UNESCO (the United Nations' Educational, Scientific, and Cultural Organization), founded in 1945, estimated that 8,000,000 children in Germany (including both German citizens and displaced persons), 6,500,000 in the Soviet Union, and 1,300,000 children in France were homeless in 1946.[5]

Those lucky enough to have a roof over their heads often lacked furniture, heat, electricity, running water, and any means of transportation. Women stood in long lines for food and supplies and scavenged abandoned buildings. In liberated German and Austrian cities, they faced the likelihood of being raped by Red Army soldiers. In Vienna, "There was virtually no transport; electric services were disrupted, and fuel of all sorts was almost entirely lacking. Hospital services were in a state of confusion. The streets were full of rubble . . . Families were widely separated, and children had often been evacuated long distances away by the Nazis," reported UNRRA worker Aleta Brownlee in the summer of 1945.[6]

The tragic physical and mental state of Europe's children, in particular, spawned dystopian fears of European civilization in disarray. In 1946, the British-American writer Alice Bailey alerted the American public about "those peculiar and wild children of Europe and of China to whom the name 'wolf children' has been given. They have known no parental authority; they run in packs like wolves; they lack all moral sense and have no civilized values and know no sexual restrictions; they know no laws save the law of self-preservation."[7] Her words reflected a widespread consensus that the Second World War had destroyed the family as completely as Europe's train tracks, factories, and roads.

Whereas interwar humanitarian efforts had focused primarily on meeting children's material needs, Europeans were particularly obsessed with restoring the psychological stability of youth after World War II. They disagreed violently, however, about the best means for achieving that stability. Educators and policymakers debated whether children's psychological needs could best be served in foster families or children's homes, by returning to their nations of origin or starting new lives abroad. But they all claimed to defend children's psychological "best interests," at the same time they sought to restore political and social stability to Europe.

The breakdown of the family was more than a social problem of the highest magnitude. Many European children had experienced the total collapse of the values and hierarchies that had traditionally structured family life. Jewish families were subject to particularly extreme pressures, as they were forced into tighter living spaces, harassed on the streets, and stripped of their jobs, property, and citizenship. As Jews were progressively excluded from public life, they spent more time at home in the company of their family members and Jewish friends. Many saw the family as a welcome refuge from a hostile outside world. But family relationships were also severely tested by persecution and material deprivation.[8]

Ruth Kluger of Vienna was seven years old when the Third Reich annexed Austria in 1938. She witnessed her family straining to the breaking point under Nazi rule. "When I tell people that my mother worried about my father's possible love affairs when he was a refugee in France, and that my parents had not been a harmonious couple in their last year together . . . or that I feel no compunction about citing my mother's petty cruelties toward me, my hearers act surprised, assume a stance of virtuous indignation, and tell me that, given the hardships we had to endure during the Hitler period, the victims should have come closer together and formed strong bonds," she reflects. "In our heart of hearts, we all know the reality: the more we have to put up with, the less tolerant we get and the texture of family relations becomes progressively more threadbare. During an earthquake, more china gets broken than at other times."[9] Ruth gradually came to realize that the grown-ups in her orbit had no superior knowledge or protection to offer her, that they were in fact "entirely flummoxed by the turn of events, and that, in fact, I was learning faster than they."[10]

Ruth and her mother were eventually deported to the Theresienstadt ghetto near Prague, and then to Auschwitz, where they managed to remain together. But the breakdown of parent-child relations continued in the camp. Their first night, as they lay in the middle row of a three-tiered bunk, Ruth's mother suggested the unthinkable. "My mother explained to me that the electric barbed wire outside was lethal and proposed that she and I should get up and walk into that wire. I thought I hadn't heard correctly . . . I was twelve years old, and the thought of dying, now, without delay, in contortions, by running into electrically charged metal on the advice of my very own mother, whom

God had created to protect me, was simply beyond comprehension."[11] Her mother accepted Ruth's refusal with a shrug, and they never discussed the incident again.

The first thought of those liberated from the daily terror of the concentration camps—after finding food and water—was typically to locate surviving family members. But an estimated 13,000,000 children in Europe had lost one or both parents in the war. Even those family members who were reunited could not simply pick up where they had left off. European children returned to families that lacked adequate housing, clothing, and food. Many Jewish and East European children, who had survived the war in hiding or in exile abroad had acquired new names and sometimes new religious beliefs, languages, and national loyalties during the war. Very young children often had no memory of their parents at all. They returned "home" to strangers, relatives who had been pushed to the brink of physical and emotional collapse during the war.[12]

In this context, Europeans began to build orphanages. Almost as soon as the shooting stopped, ad-hoc liberation committees and humanitarian agencies began to gather children up from concentration camps, streets, and hiding places. They assembled them in chateaus seized from Germans, military barracks, the dormitories of summer camps, and requisitioned hotels. In Bielsko, Poland, the Education Department of the Central Committee of Jews in Poland was charged with caring for surviving Jewish orphans and youth. The Central Committee's Dom Dziecka in Bielsko opened its doors to forty-five Jewish teenagers on June 7, 1945. Their new home was a "bombed-out, dilapidated, ruin of a building, lacking any kind of furniture, kitchen equipment, or tableware," reported orphanage director Dr. P. Komajówna. The youths, mostly concentration camp survivors, arrived in a state of severe distress. They exhibited an "absolute lack of faith in their own strength or in a better future . . . huge distrust in the permanence of any social care for them . . . and an outstandingly negative attitude toward work, including even elementary care of personal hygiene," according to Komajówna.

Initially, counselors in the orphanage did not attempt any kind of psychological rehabilitation. They had more immediate concerns, such as the lack of beds and utensils. Their first priority was to make the orphanage habitable. "We embarked on the construction of our shared home—and it is necessary to remember that all of us were homeless, not only the children. The enormous zeal for construction that swept up the directors and educators hijacked the children too . . . Through our collective effort . . . we dragged in rubble, chopped wood, built frames, peeled potatoes, etc." The renovation project ultimately had its own pedagogical rewards. "We earned the recognition and respect of the children, saw the first signs of the rebirth of hope, the first post-camp smiles, the first signs of social feeling, born through collective labor—the feeling that we were living, that we were becoming a tight group, taking a liking to our new home, in which things were improving each day thanks to our common efforts."[13]

Komajówna's account of the first year in the Bielsko orphanage was typical of a widespread association between the material reconstruction of postwar Europe and the moral and emotional reconstruction of European youth. The ideological content of postwar initiatives to rehabilitate displaced youth varied as widely as the political visions that emerged from the war. The Bielsko orphanage, like most Central Committee children's homes in Poland, was led by educators with Socialist loyalties. But in contrast to efforts to rehabilitate youth after World War I, these initiatives were united across sharp geographical and political divides by a novel focus on the emotional consequences of wartime displacement.

As of September 30, 1945, the Supreme Headquarters Allied Expeditionary Force (SHAEF) and Soviet military forces estimated that they had provided assistance to an astounding 13,664,000 displaced persons in occupied Germany and Austria. Massive population displacement accompanied the Japanese defeat in the Pacific as well. Five million Japanese citizens returned to Japan at the end of the war, while allied authorities repatriated another one million former colonial subjects, including Koreans, Taiwanese, Chinese, and Southeast Asians. The Chinese National Relief and Rehabilitation Association reported that it had provided assistance to one million internally displaced persons by 1947.[14]

Within Europe, the majority of displaced persons, including children, were from Eastern Europe. Military authorities and UNRRA had assisted some 7,270,000 displaced Soviet laborers and POWs; 1,610,000 Poles; 1,807,000 French citizens; 696,000 Italians; 389,000 Yugoslavs; 348,000 Czechs; and 285,000 Hungarians by September 1945. During the spring and summer of 1945, over 10,000,000 displaced persons journeyed home, at a rate of 10,500 people a day. Almost all of the 1,000,000 refugees who remained on German soil a year after the liberation were East Europeans who could not or would not board the repatriation trains. Out of the 773,248 DPs receiving UNRRA assistance in June 1946, over half were registered as Poles—though many of these "Poles" were probably Soviet Russians, Ukrainians, or Baltic refugees trying to avoid repatriation to the Soviet Union. Many of these so-called "hard core" refugees hailed from the Polish territory east of the Curzon line that was annexed by the USSR at the end of the war.[15]

Children under the age of fourteen represented only a small percentage of the refugees entitled to assistance from the United Nations. Over 1.5 million children were among the Germans who fled or were expelled from Eastern Europe at the end of the war, but German children were considered "enemy nationals" and were therefore not UNRRA's responsibility.[16] The number of Allied children (so-called "United Nations' nationals") stranded in occupied Germany was relatively small by contrast. UNRRA estimated that it had only 153,000 children under the age of fourteen in its care as of July 1945. By the time UNRRA was replaced by the International Refugee Organization (IRO) in July 1947, it had provided assistance to 12,843 "unaccompanied children"— youth under the age of sixteen who were stranded in the western zones of Germany and Austria without a close family member. But displaced children and youth assumed an importance far beyond their numbers, as they became symbols of both wartime dislocation and postwar renewal.[17]

Simply defining a "child" was a serious challenge in postwar Europe. Technically, UNRRA and the IRO considered anyone under the age of seventeen to be a child. But establishing a legal age of majority did not fix a stable line between childhood and adulthood. For the sake of survival, many children learned to systematically lie about their ages during the war. In their encounters with postwar military officials and humanitarian agencies, they continued to strategically cross the boundary between childhood and adulthood. Austrian psychologist Ernst Papanek noted with frustration in 1946 that he could "never know how old a person really is . . . they 'adjust' age to purpose— when they believe children will go to Palestine first and they want to go, even men with beards say they are fourteen or fifteen, a girl that looked like a twenty-five year old said she was sixteen."[18] In other circumstances DP youth inflated their ages. East European officials typically insisted that all (non-Jewish) unaccompanied children under the age of seventeen be repatriated, by force if necessary. But many East European teenagers refused repatriation in the hope of settling abroad. They either lied about their ages or attempted to "mark time" in refugee camps until they reached the age of majority.[19]

A startling gap emerged between the representations of very young refugee children disseminated by the press and the demographic realities of liberated Europe. Many displaced "children," especially Jewish children, were in fact adolescents. But images of toddlers circulated widely in humanitarian appeals, inspiring couples in the United States and elsewhere to offer homes for adoption. They were disappointed upon discovering that blonde three-year-old girls were in short supply. In a typical request, Mrs. J. L. Young from Galveston, Texas wrote to the IRO in 1949 to place an order for "two little girls between the ages of four and ten. As for nationality I prefer French, Irish, Scottish. I would prefer them to be of Protestant belief."[20]

The war itself seemed to confuse the boundaries between childhood and adulthood. Years of malnourishment had robbed refugee children of inches and pounds, and they often appeared younger than their age. Most had missed out on years of schooling. But surviving Jewish youth in particular, also seemed to social workers to be disturbingly independent, mature, and unchildlike. French psychologist Simone Marcus-Jeisler concluded in 1947, "Precocious maturity, already favored on ethnic grounds, is particularly developed by the lives of adventure they have led. Their heavy responsibilities . . . do not encourage them to sit on the school bench and play innocent games once liberation arrives."[21] The alleged inability of refugee children to play became a familiar refrain of humanitarian appeals. In a widely published letter to Eleanor Roosevelt, Morris Troper, the European head of the American Joint Distribution Committee (JDC), described French refugee children arriving in Lisbon from France as "tired, wan, broken little old men and women . . . One of the most pathetic sights I have ever seen was that of these children, freed of restraints, trying to learn to play again."[22] One central goal of humanitarian workers after the war was to restore both children and adults to their traditional roles, to make children into children again.

Debates about who counted as a "child" nonetheless reflected an important political and social reality of wartime Europe: the category of the child was (and remains) deceptively universal. It obscures the extent to which differences of time, place, and geography have shaped both the definition of childhood and how childhood is experienced. During the Second World War, the wartime itineraries of displaced children were as varied as those of adult refugees, and depended heavily on nationality, race, religion, gender, social class, and age.

The first children to leave the Third Reich en masse without their parents had been Jewish children and adolescents who fled Nazi Germany, Austria, and Czechoslovakia with the Kindertransports during 1938–1939. By 1939, 82 percent of Jewish children under the age of fifteen had managed to escape Nazi Germany. Most emigrated with their parents, but approximately 18,000 Jewish children and youth left Germany on their own, with various child emigration schemes.[23] With the onset of the Second World War in September 1939, the doors to legal emigration slammed shut, even as the number of Jewish children threatened by Nazi persecution expanded with the Nazi empire.

At the same time that Jewish children fled Nazi persecution, British, French, German, and Soviet authorities implemented ambitious evacuation schemes for civilians as they mobilized to protect them from aerial bombardments. Throughout the war, civilian evacuations separated millions of children from their parents as they were ferried to safety in the countryside with school or youth groups. In Great Britain, the evacuations provoked widespread discussion about the effects of separating children from their mothers, generating new theories of child psychology and trauma.[24]

Tens of thousands of children in Europe were also uprooted or born in exile as a result of the Nazi system of forced labor. The Nazis imported millions of foreign workers during the war to replace men mobilized in the Wehrmacht—and to enable "Aryan" German women to stay out of the workforce. As of August 1944, 7,615,970 foreign workers and POWs toiled in the Reich. Although the regime introduced harsh penalties, including death, for illicit sexual relations between foreign laborers and Germans, such relations continued. Two or three death sentences per day were handed down to Soviet men accused of having intimate relations with German women in 1944, and up to 10,000 German women per year were sent to concentration camps for the crime of fraternizing with foreigners. But foreign workers and Germans lived and worked in close proximity, and the Nazi Sicherheitsdienst (SD, the Nazi intelligence service) estimated that foreign men had fathered at least 20,000 children with German women by 1942.[25]

Approximately one-third of the foreign workers in wartime Germany were women. Inevitably, many of them also became pregnant. Early in the war, pregnant laborers were sent home, but Nazi authorities began to suspect an epidemic of intentional pregnancies. After 1943, foreign workers who got pregnant in Nazi Germany were potentially subject to forcible abortion and sterilization. Those impregnated by German men were typically allowed to bring their babies to term, however. If the infant was deemed "Germanizable," it was seized and placed in a Lebensborn home (SS-run homes for single Aryan mothers and their babies) for eventual adoption by a German family. Those infants labeled racially "unworthy" were often condemned to a slow death by neglect and starvation in special institutions for foreign children.[26]

A significant number of East European children and youth were also among the forced laborers imported to Germany. In 1944, the Nazis had devised a plan, with the code name "Operation Hay," to deport 40,000–50,000 White Russian children between the ages of ten and eighteen to work in the Reich. At least 28,000 Soviet youth under the age of eighteen were conscripted for labor in the Luftwaffe and armaments industry by October 1944. Many remained adrift in Germany once the war ended.[27]

After the Nazi defeat, relations between Germans and foreign laborers continued. More children were born, and sometimes abandoned in Germany when their parents repatriated or emigrated. Displaced workers and their children were joined in refugee camps by millions of Germans who fled or were expelled from Poland, Czechoslovakia, Hungary, Romania, Yugoslavia, and the Baltic states after World War II. The tidal wave of refugees from the East had begun before the war even ended, as Germans fled the advancing Russian Army. The 1945 Potsdam agreements sanctioned the complete expulsion of Germans from East Central Europe. These expellees and refugees crowded into camps and rural villages in occupied Germany and Austria, comprising 5 percent of the total Austrian population in 1947 and a full 16 percent of the population in the Western (British, American, and French) zones of Germany.[28]

Many of the children swept up in the German flight and expulsion from the East were not actually German. As the Soviet army advanced, tens of thousands of Silesian, Polish-speaking, Czech-speaking, and Slovene-speaking children were evacuated from Eastern Prussia, Silesia, the Protectorate of Bohemia and Moravia, and Yugoslavia, where they had been living in German orphanages, Hitler Youth camps, and with German family members. An additional 20,000–50,000 East European children had been deliberately kidnapped for Germanization by the Nazi regime during the war. Nazi officials systematically changed the names of these children and destroyed their birth records. Now, at war's end, their origins and fates were contested.[29]

Jewish children initially represented one of the smallest groups of displaced youth after the war, since those too young to work had been systematically exterminated. In 1946, Jacques Bloch of the Oeuvre de Secours aux Enfants (OSE) estimated that only 175,000 European Jews under the age of sixteen had survived the war, out of a prewar population of 1.5 million. The survivors included 30,000 Jewish children who had endured a difficult wartime exile in the Soviet Union.[30] At least 200,000 Jews (along with between 350,000 and 1.5 million Poles) had been exiled in Siberia after Eastern Poland was annexed to the Soviet Union in 1939.[31] When the Hitler-Stalin pact dissolved with the Nazi invasion of the USSR in 1941, they were released. Many trekked toward Soviet Central Asia, following rumors of warm weather and abundant food (they instead found malarial conditions and persistent shortages). But even in these harsh conditions, most survived the war and typically returned to Eastern Europe after the war ended.[32]

These were rarely happy homecomings. The vast majority of Jews that returned from the USSR after the war did not remain in Eastern Europe for long, thanks to persistent anti-Semitism. Some 200,000 Jews, including many children, fled postwar anti-Semitism in Eastern Europe in a semi-organized underground movement toward Palestine (the *Bricha* or "flight") that began in the fall of 1945 and peaked in the spring and summer of 1946. Most of these Jews made their way through the American zone of Germany. Over 100,000 Jews fled Poland alone, including 33,600 youth who arrived in Germany in kibbutzim (collective settlements) and around 7,000 children unaccompanied by parents or relatives. Jewish babies were also a growing presence on German territory in 1946–1947, due to the skyrocketing birthrate of Jewish displaced persons, who were eager to begin families again. In November of 1946, there were reportedly 16.7 marriages and 14.1 births per 1,000 Jewish DPs in occupied Germany, compared to 3.7 births and 1.4 marriages among the German population in Bavaria. By 1946, Jewish children represented a full 60 percent of the unaccompanied children in UNRRA's assembly centers and children's homes.[33]

Amid the chaos and confusion of the war's end, UNRRA officials and Allied military authorities were intent on managing refugee movements in liberated Europe. As the above statistics suggest, they produced hundreds of pages of charts and graphs to document the number of refugees successfully "processed" and "disposed of": repatriated, resettled, or reunited with family members.[34] But these numbers were all estimates at best, as it was difficult to track the movement of displaced persons as they slipped in and out of camps, across borders, and between occupation zones. Many Displaced Persons did not live in camps at all. In August 1948, the IRO reported that 25 percent of refugees receiving assistance from the organization were so-called "free-livers." The number of free-living DPs may have been as high as 50 percent in Austria and Italy. Free-living DPs generally came into contact with humanitarian agencies only when in need of specific services, such as legal aid or help with emigration.[35]

The number of missing children was particularly difficult to establish, and was a matter of heated dispute between East European governments and UN officials. As Cold War divisions calcified, Czech, Polish, Soviet, and Yugoslav officials polemically inflated the number of children being illegally "seques-tered" by the Western allies in occupied Germany. The Polish Red Cross, for example, maintained that at least 200,000 Polish children had been kidnapped for Germanization during World War II, although the actual number was probably closer to 20,000. Sometimes these inflated numbers reflected wish-ful thinking. American and French Jewish agencies systematically overesti-mated the number of surviving "hidden" Jewish children that they expected to recover from Christian homes and institutions after the war. Most of these ostensibly "lost children" had of course been lost to the gas chambers and not to Christianity.[36]

*   *   *

World War II was not the first time that large numbers of European children left home alone. As European child savers mobilized on behalf of displaced children after World War II, previous experiences had already shaped their visions for reconstruction. The vast majority of children traveling solo in Eu-rope before the twentieth century journeyed to neighboring villages or regions rather than across oceans and continents, however. In many parts of Europe children of both genders left home at a young age: first to be nourished by a wet nurse (particularly in France), and then more definitively to be trained as apprentices, domestic servants, farm hands, and laborers. The average age of first employment for wards of the *Assistance publique* in France in the mid-1930s was thirteen and a half. In theory, young workers were to be treated as members of the households in which they worked. In practice, they were vulnerable to abuse, neglect, and homesickness. But however difficult the ad-justment, such separations were not necessarily experienced as traumatic rup-tures by these children. Nor were these separations denounced as harbingers of social or political disarray. Leaving home at a young age was a normal coming-of-age experience in societies in which childhood ended early and child labor was seen as a necessity.[37]

In the nineteenth century, however, romantic ideals of domesticity and childhood took hold among the European middle classes, promoted by phi-lanthropists, social workers, doctors, and educators. A long transition began, from a regime in which children were viewed as producers and laborers, to one in which they were considered future citizens. Childhood, in this new world, was to be reserved for learning, play, and freedom from adult respon-sibilities. Middle-class visions of domesticity in the nineteenth century also tended to valorize parental rights in an imagined private sphere. Along these lines, humanitarian, religious, and political organizations began to protest and politicize both (excessive) child factory labor and the forcible separation of children from their parents.[38]

One of the earliest examples of humanitarian action around the separation of families emerged in the United States in the mid-nineteenth century, when abolitionists began to protest the dissolution of slave families. Abolitionists depicted the separation of enslaved children and parents as a brutal abrogation of both religious and natural law. Between 1820 and 1860, at least 200,000 slave children were forcibly separated from their parents when they were sold from households in Maryland, Kentucky, and Virginia to plantations in the Deep South. In reality, the abolitionists' depiction of slaves stripped of all kinship relations was polemical. Particularly on large plantations, many slave children lived with their parents, and even those separated from family members typically forged strong kinship bonds in their new communities.[39] But slaves did live with the omnipresent threat of losing their children or parents on the auction block. Abolitionists aimed to expose slavery as a degrading assault on the integrity of the family, attacking the southern myth of slavery as a form of "benign domesticity."[40]

At around the same moment in history, a dramatic case of family separation scandalized Europe. In 1858 in Bologna, a Jewish child, six-year-old Edgardo Mortara, was secretly baptized by a Catholic servant in his household. Subsequently, he was kidnapped from his parents to be raised as a Catholic, with the blessing of Pope Pius IX. Jewish and anticlerical activists in Europe and the United States responded with outrage, depicting Edgardo's kidnapping as an affront to natural law, parental rights, and the Jewish community at large. The incident inspired the 1860 creation of the Alliance Israélite Universelle, the first international organization for the defense of Jewish rights. But Edgardo never returned to his parents or to his parents' faith. At the age of twenty-one, he became a monk with the support of a trust fund from the Pope.[41]

Almost a century later, the Mortara Affair would be invoked in debates about the fate of "hidden" Jewish children in Europe who had been baptized during World War II, particularly in the 1953 Finaly Affair in France. The separation of children from their parents was thus transformed into a humanitarian cause well before the total wars of the twentieth century. But these separations were depicted primarily as an infringement of parental rights, a crime against religious communities, or a violation of natural law. They were not perceived as a threat to children's psychological well-being. Nor were they linked to the survival of entire nations.

Even as abolitionists and Jewish advocates protested the dividing of families in the mid-nineteenth century, the emigration of unaccompanied poor children became a favored strategy for populating the British Empire and the American West. Philanthropic organizations such as the Dr. Barnardo's Homes, the Fairbridge Society, and even the Roman Catholic Church organized the resettlement of close to 100,000 British children in Canada beginning in the 1860s. Many of these children had living parents. In the view of these child-welfare advocates, British cities were crowded incubators of crime, disease, vice, and Socialism. The farmlands of the commonwealth, by contrast, were unpopulated and invested with moral and hygienic virtues that promised to offer "unfortunate" children a new start in life. Child migration continued to Canada until the late 1920s, when it ceased due in part to opposition by Canadian social workers. They objected to the institutional care of orphans and worried that the British were using Canada as a dumping ground for eugenically inferior children.[42]

In the United States, as many as 250,000 children were shipped westward on so-called "orphan trains" that carried children from New York and other East Coast cities to foster families in mid-western and western states. In one remarkable case, a group of forty Irish orphans from New York were placed with Catholic Mexican families in an Arizona mining town. Subsequently, local Protestant women abducted the children from their adoptive families. The resulting custody dispute eventually reached the U.S. Supreme Court, which ruled that the vigilante abductions had been legal. In its decision, the court equated the placement of "white" children in Mexican families to child abuse. The case was one of the first in a century rife with violent conflict over the transfer of children across national and racial lines.[43]

Unprecedented numbers of children were separated from their parents during World War I (1914–1918) and the 1915 Armenian genocide. The Great War was—not coincidentally—also the first war on European soil to directly target civilians, including children. The Armenian genocide also marked the first time in European history that the denationalization of children precipitated international legal intervention. In 1921, the League of Nations launched a campaign to rescue children who had been separated from their parents in the chaos of war, deportation, and genocide in the Ottoman Empire. The League's Commission for the Protection of Women and Children in the Near East operated branches in Constantinople and in Aleppo, Syria, between 1922 and 1927. Its official mission was to "reclaim" tens of thousands of Armenian women and children who had allegedly been abducted and Islamicized in Turkish families and institutions during the war. For the first but not the last time in the twentieth century, the "reclamation" of lost children became linked not only to international justice and humanitarianism, but also to national reconstruction in the aftermath of total war and genocide.

New international humanitarian organizations also carved out a wide sphere of action in Central Europe after World War I. Organizations such as Herbert Hoover's American Relief Administration (ARA) and the Save the Children Fund (SCF) campaigned to save millions of European and Russian children from famine and concurrently, to prevent the spread of Bolshevism in Europe. Hundreds of thousands of European children were sent away from their families in depleted cities to the more fertile countryside, in order to make up for the pounds and inches they had failed to gain during the war. Between the wars, the issue of family separation also appeared on the agenda of international social workers for the first time. The International Social Service, founded in 1924 in Geneva, was at the forefront of efforts to reunite families that had been "snapped in a dozen places" by international migration.[44] But these interwar organizations still focused primarily on providing material relief and legal aid to separated families, and not specifically on the emotional upheaval of wartime displacement.

Humanitarian efforts on behalf of children changed dramatically during the Spanish Civil War (1936–1939), which pitted supporters of Spain's nascent Second Republic against the nationalist forces of the authoritarian General Francisco Franco. The conflict eventually resulted in the evacuation of tens of thousands of unaccompanied Spanish children to France, Belgium, Great Britain, Mexico, and the Soviet Union, where they were safe from starvation, bombing, and Franco's troops. Displaced children increasingly stood at the center of polarizing diplomatic and political disputes. Franco's supporters in Spain and abroad accused Republican militants of brainwashing and denationalizing Spanish children in exile, and demanded their immediate repatriation. Partisans of the Republican cause, meanwhile, sought to cultivate the children's Republican and national loyalties abroad. Struggles over the custody of Spanish refugee children became an avenue through which the Spanish Civil War ballooned into a conflict that engaged much of Europe.

These interwar humanitarian campaigns served as both positive and negative models for international aid workers after World War II. During the Spanish Civil War, governments and a dizzying array of private, confessional, and explicitly political organizations competed to save Spanish refugee children and to secure their political, social, and religious loyalties. There was little coordination among these groups, which made no secret of their political goals:

to save children from the ravages of war, but also to transform them into the republican or nationalist militants of the future. After the Second World War, by contrast, humanitarian workers typically disavowed overtly political goals in favor of more universal ideals. Informed by the principles of "casework," a method of social work based on investigation of each "client's" individual circumstances, they claimed to uphold the "best interests of the child" rather than any particular political agenda. In the words of the Save the Children Fund's Edward Fuller, "Today, when a great part of the world is still smoking from the holocaust of war, and the achievements of generations of mankind have been cast on the rubbish heap, there is need for a new Universalism . . . In concern for the welfare of children may be found a common meeting ground for people who are at variance on most other subjects."[45] The wartime separation of families was now increasingly understood as a potential source of psychological trauma for the individual children concerned—and a cause of social upheaval that threatened entire nations. But even as Europeans defined the plight of children as a universal humanitarian cause after World War II, both the content and methods of rehabilitation defied consensus.

*   *   *

After the liberation, policymakers in both Eastern and Western Europe linked their activism on behalf of refugee youth to the reconstruction of European democracy and the repudiation of fascist values. But they disagreed about what democratization entailed, and about the precise relationships between democracy, the state, and the family. In the West, particularly in the United States, Austria, Germany, and Great Britain, liberal democrats, Christian leaders, and anti-Communists tended to define the evils of totalitarianism specifically in terms of its alleged destruction of the family. The United Nations itself proclaimed that the Nazis had waged a "war against children," elaborating, "Against their security in the family, against their education and general welfare, against their very lives, the fascists directed a deliberate campaign of destruction that has nothing to do with the incidental."[46] Western anti-Communists sought to strengthen the sovereignty of the family in the name of redressing Nazi crimes and thwarting the perceived threat of a Communist assault on the private sphere.

Socialists in liberated Eastern Europe also presented their efforts on behalf of lost children as means of redressing Nazi war crimes. In Germany's Soviet Zone of Occupation, for example, an SED (Socialist Unity Party, *Sozialistische Einheitspartei*) official suggested that the party advertise its efforts to bring displaced German children home in connection with upcoming elections, using slogans such as, "We are reestablishing the family ties that were dissolved by the Nazis!" As Cold War divisions solidified, East European Communist officials increasingly accused the Western Allies of perpetuating Nazi crimes by sequestering East European children in occupied Germany. They thereby translated the wartime struggle between Nazis and Slavs into a Cold War contest between East and West.

The centrality of the family to postwar reconstruction is already a familiar tale. The baby boom, the expansion of European welfare states, and the promotion of the so-called "nuclear family" in the name of a "return to normalcy," pervade popular images of Europe and the United States in the immediate postwar era.[47] Less familiar, however, is the extent to which new forms of expert knowledge about the family and child development emerged in the context of massive displacement during and after the Second World War. Europe's DP camps and orphanages became laboratories where psychologists, humanitarian workers, and policymakers tested ostensibly universal theories of child development through their observations of children uprooted by war and racial persecution.

To many postwar observers in Europe and America, the separation of families came to represent the quintessential Nazi transgression, an unparalleled source of social disarray. The principles of child welfare gleaned from wartime displacement quickly took on the aura of timeless facts. In reality, however, the notion that the separation of children from their parents produces a traumatic shock was first conceived in the crucible of Europe's refugee camps and orphanages in the mid-twentieth-century.[48] Between 1914 and 1945, humanitarian agencies intentionally separated children from their parents in order to solve a humanitarian crisis that they defined primarily in material and moral terms. Children were sent from Vienna to Amsterdam and from Madrid to Marseille in order to escape hunger, violence, and disease between the two World Wars. After World War II, by contrast, British and American psychologists tended to represent precisely such separations as humanitarian crises in their own right. In the words of Anna Freud (Sigmund's daughter) and Dorothy Burlingham, who studied children evacuated from London during the Second World War, "All of the improvements in the child's life may dwindle down to nothing when weighed against the fact that it has to leave the family to get them."[49] Freud and Burlingham's research was widely influential, particularly among the British and American social workers that later attempted to rehabilitate Europe's displaced children in postwar refugee camps.

At first glance, these international efforts appear to represent a chapter in a familiar story of Americanization and democratization in postwar Europe. British and American social workers descended on the European continent armed with the psychoanalytic theories and practices of social work that dominated Great Britain and the United States at mid-century. But their ideas were vigorously contested on the ground by continental pedagogues—and even by refugees—who often sought to rehabilitate Europe's lost children in collective settings, or flatly rejected family reunification for personal, social, or political reasons. Gradually, many relief workers responded to conditions on the ground in Central Europe, and began to legitimate collectivist, nationalist, and Zionist claims on refugee youth. The ideological opposition between the individualist ideals of Western humanitarian workers and the collectivist visions of East European and Jewish refugees and policymakers broke down in practice.

General accounts of the liberation of Europe tend to represent the Nazi defeat as a dramatic historical rupture: a moment of triumph for liberal democracy, internationalism, free markets, individualism, and human rights—at least in Western Europe.[50] Mark Mazower has observed that in the postwar West, "The struggle against Hitler had revealed the importance of human and civil rights. In the legal and political sphere, in other words, the trend was to reassert the primacy of the individual vis-à-vis the state."[51] United Nations' relief workers certainly framed their activism around displaced children using an individualist rhetoric of human rights and children's "best interests." But both international organizations and policymakers simultaneously upheld two collectives—the family and the nation—as the very basis for European reconstruction and as the recipe for individual psychological rehabilitation. In practice, moreover, humanitarian workers and child welfare experts did not aim to rehabilitate displaced persons as abstract individuals. They targeted refugees as children or adults, boys or girls, Jews, Germans, or Poles. In the process, they defined "human rights" and children's "best interests" in sharply gender-specific, nationalist, and familialist terms.

Nationalist and internationalist impulses were deeply intertwined in postwar reconstruction efforts. The rise of new international organizations after the Second World War was accompanied by the conviction that only the protection of national sovereignty and the creation of nationally homogenous nation-states could guarantee lasting peace. This logic was most dramatically expressed in the violent expulsion of twelve million Germans from Eastern Europe.[52] Pro-natalist policies, meanwhile, artfully blended nationalist and familialist concerns and found favor across the continent. In the wake of an obscene number of military and civilian casualties, European policymakers were anxious to repopulate. More than 16 million civilians and 8.6 million combatants did not survive World War II in the Soviet Union—one out of every eleven members of the 1939 population. Poland lost one-fifth of its population, while Yugoslavia lost one out of eight citizens.[53] Compensating for lost lives had particular significance and urgency for European Jews after the Holocaust, but every European government sought to replenish lost soldiers and civilians, recover missing children, and secure labor power for postwar reconstruction. These concerns fueled a spirited competition among European governments to claim displaced children as future citizens.

The resettlement of refugees and displaced persons after World War II ultimately represented a foundational moment in the development of postwar European migration policies. Both Eastern and West European authorities aimed to create homogenous nation-states in the name of national security after World War II. Migration policies—whether directed toward expelling "undesirables," repatriating exiled citizens, recruiting foreign labor, and even granting asylum to refugees—were all designed to serve this basic goal. Under such circumstances, nationalist ambitions to recruit "assimilable" migrants could trump the postwar humanitarian rhetoric of family reunification. This logic required that Ruth-Karin Dawidowicz leave her ailing mother behind in Germany in order to start a new life in the United States under the aegis of the DP Act, for example. Postwar American immigration authorities viewed Ruth-Karin as a young, healthy, and "assimilable" addition to the American population, but rejected her mother as an undesirable threat and burden.

Children were central objects of population politics, nation building projects, and new forms of humanitarian intervention in the twentieth century, as they represented the biological and political future of national communities. The rise of humanitarian activism around children and of ethnic cleansing in twentieth-century Europe were ultimately flip sides of the same coin. Children became a form of wartime plunder during the Armenian Genocide and the Second World War to the extent that they were perceived to be malleable. Such children represented valuable assets to nations desperate to expand their ranks. Humanitarian organizations and European immigration authorities shared these nationalist assumptions. As they assigned visas and distributed resources to refugees during and after the Second World War, they privileged children over adults. This was not simply because children were seen as more vulnerable or innocent than their parents. Children were favored in both child-rescue campaigns and migration policies because they were seen as more assimilable to homogenous nation-states than adults. An age-based hierarchy of children over adults both reflected and perpetuated the profound racial and nationalist hierarchies that underpinned migration policies in Europe between 1918 and 1951.

Humanitarian workers, child welfare activists, and government officials across Europe shared a general faith in the rehabilitative powers of both nation and family after World War II. But there was little consensus about what this meant in practice. More often than not, displaced children had some surviving family members, but they had also formed new kinship bonds during the war. They were torn between competing families, nations, and religions. Was a Jewish refugee child's rightful "family" an aunt in Cleveland, the French Catholic parents who had raised him since infancy, a Jewish children's home in France, or a Zionist kibbutz headed for Palestine? Should a Polish orphan remain in the care of the German farmers to whom her mother (perhaps a forced laborer) had abandoned her, be repatriated to a Polish orphanage, or resettled in Canada with adoptive parents? Disputes over such questions became important forums for defining the notions of home and homeland in postwar Europe.

The conflicted history of Europe's lost children was shaped by encounters between Polish slave laborers and German farmers; Wehrmacht soldiers and French women; American GIs and Jewish refugees; Vatican priests and Communist partisans. But these encounters did not precipitate the decline of nationalism or of national sovereignty. Instead, humanitarian agencies gradually reframed nationalist agendas and ideals in the more individualist language of children's "best interests" and human rights. Humanitarian workers were thus deeply implicated in the campaign to create homogenous nation-states after World War II. This was true not only because the "individual" implicit in the concept of human rights is a necessary abstraction. In concrete ways, nationalist ideals were absorbed into emerging visions of psychological stability, human rights, and democracy in post-fascist Europe.

The plight of refugees was central to postwar reconstruction in part because the confused identities of displaced persons paralleled a broader crisis of identity that confronted Europeans after the Second World War. This identity crisis had quite literal dimensions: forged birth certificates, passports, and identity papers were the currency of survival during the war. To cite just one prominent example, Pavel Friedländer, a German-speaking Jewish child from Prague, became a French Catholic named Paul-Henri Ferland when he spent

attributes responsibility to humanitarian workers

his days during World War II undercover in a Catholic boarding school near Vichy. After the liberation he changed his name again, and ultimately became an Israeli citizen and later, the Holocaust historian, Saul Friedländer. In his 1979 memoir, Friedländer confessed that even after forty years, it was still "impossible to know which name I am, and that in the final analysis seems to me sufficient expression of a real and profound confusion."[54] He was only one of approximately 10,000 Jewish children in occupied France whose lives depended on the ability to maintain a false identity.[55]

Impersonation continued under different circumstances after the war. The destruction of documents made it difficult to verify identities. Individuals seeking to escape a troubled past took advantage of the chaos. East Europeans who hoped to avoid repatriation or imprisonment for collaborating with the Nazis frequently resorted to imposture. Many posed as Poles, sometimes with a wink and a nod from military officials or translators. Jewish refugees heading toward Palestine pretended to be Greeks, counting on the linguistic and geographic ignorance of Allied GIs. German war criminals burned their SS uniforms and attempted to blend into the crowd.[56]

In an age before DNA testing, the process of identifying lost children was particularly daunting. In 1952, Johanna Müller of Wiesbaden even suggested to the German Red Cross (without irony) that all German babies and mothers should be tattooed with registration numbers. They would be more easily identified, she explained, in the event of a Third World War. Müller had firsthand experience of the German mass flight from the Prussian East at the end of the Second World War, during which thousands of children and parents had been separated in the chaos. She lamented the fate of an "unbelievably high number of children who in spite of good will cannot be returned to their parents, because there is no form of identification." Seven years after the armistice, many of these children languished in orphanages. Müller was convinced "that all citizens who . . . experienced the misery of the years after 1944 will have no objections to these security measures, which will protect the solidarity of the family."[57]

But the identity crisis that plagued European societies after World War II also operated on a more existential plane. This loss of identity represented both a menacing source of disorder and an enticing opportunity for reinvention. Fantasies of postwar reinvention were projected onto Europe's children. As they struggled to restore stability to Europe's displaced families, Europeans simultaneously crafted competing visions for the reconstruction of European democracy, and articulated Cold War ideologies that would define Europe for the next fifty years. They developed new theories about human development, the nature of emotional bonds within the family, and the value of familial and collective education. They aimed, above all, to reshape the confused identities of children in their own images. The campaign to rehabilitate Europe's lost children was at once an effort to define the legacy of the Nazi past and a bid to control the shape of Europe's future.

The Quintessential Victims of War

In July of 1946, the American branch of the Unitarian Service Committee (USC) created a colony for Spanish refugee children in France. By the end of that year, over a hundred children between the ages of five and twelve had passed through the villa La Garde in Saint Goin, nestled in the Pyrenees close to the Spanish border. Some, mostly orphans, became permanent residents at La Garde. All of the children's parents had fought against Franco during the brutal civil war in Spain (1936–1939) and since Franco won the war, returning to Spain would mean likely imprisonment or death for their militant parents. But social conditions in France were desperate at the end of the war. "After nearly a decade of suffering, civil strife and war . . . the new generation of the Spanish Community in France is in serious danger," a 1945 USC report warned. "Modern psychology stresses the fateful and lasting effect of the impact of such events in the formative period of the human soul . . . The physical and psychic effects of the civil war period appear to be . . . aggravated by the camp environment, the misery of the overcrowded and promiscuous barracks, of panicky men and hysterical women . . . This early experience will not fade out from the memories of the children who never saw harmonious family life and the 'sweet home' of childhood."[1]

Most of the children at La Garde had been displaced their entire lives. Many had lost their fathers. Jose Castro, nicknamed Pepito, was the son of a famous Republican lieutenant killed in battle against Franco. His mother did not earn enough as a seamstress to support her two children in France. Pepito was reportedly "as naughty as they come," but educators at St. Goin noted that he "has such a disarming personality that he is in a fair way of being spoiled by everyone he meets." Antonio Sanchez, born in 1939, was one of ten children of a republican guerilla. Both of his parents had survived the Civil War, but neither could work, as they suffered from tuberculosis. Eduardo Friemel was born in an internment camp in France in 1940. His father, a republican soldier, was captured by the Nazis in France and deported to Auschwitz, where he was executed for facilitating the escape of fellow prisoners. Eduardo spent most of the war hiding in dugouts in the mountains. He slept in a bed for the first time in his life at the age of eight when he arrived at La Garde.[2]

The director of the St. Goin colony until 1948 was J. M. Alvarez. Alvarez was typical of Spanish exiles in his determination to instill both nationalist and Republican values in his wards. In 1947, he described a typical lesson in the colony—a dialogue with his pupils. The lesson began innocently enough, with the question, "What do you want to be when you grow up?" The children responded with typical choices for 8–12 year olds in the 1940s: Pepito wanted to be a Sergeant in the Canadian Mounted Police, Conchita hoped to become a movie star, Juanito dreamed of fixing cars, Nina planned to become a secretary, Alberto a lion hunter, Lorenzo an airplane pilot.

One by one, Alvarez berated his pupils for their flights of fantasy. "Let's begin with Pepito. I thought that we all agreed about one thing that is perfectly clear: that our country, our beloved Spain, once so rich, has become a country of misery. We had agreed that we would help rebuild our Spain by working hard all together when conditions are such that we can return. But—here is Pepito who would turn his back on the memory of his father . . . He prefers to be a Canadian, it seems." Pepito lowered his head in shame. Carlos interjected, "I think that over there in Canada they don't need the services of Pepito, while in Spain there will be so much work for us all to do." Luis came to his friend's rescue, suggesting that Pepito should become a member of the Spanish Republican Police. Pepito, relieved, exclaimed, "That would be marvelous! I would go after the assassins of my father to deliver them to justice." "Well said," Alvarez praised him. "You had forgotten Spain. But it really isn't your fault. It is the fault of Franco because Spanish children are forced to languish in exile."

Alvarez was particularly hard on Ricardo, whose ambition was to become an "Avenger of the Far West, the celebrated masked cowboy." "My dear Ricardo," Alvarez lectured. "We are not living in a film world or dream world . . . Masked cowboys? That is fiction, pretty lies, and nothing more." Ricardo burst into tears. Only one child got it right: Radames, who announced proudly, "I am from Asturias. I am an orphan of the war in Spain, and I should like to be a miner as my father was, and my uncle. I think it is noble work to dig coal out of the bowels of the earth for all the factories and to warm the homes of the people." "Radames, that's spoken like a man," Alvarez praised. "I want to shake hands with you in front of your schoolmates, because you have understood."[3]

The pedagogy in the colony at St. Goin was not only intended to cultivate the nationalist and republican loyalties of Spanish refugee children. As the USC report makes clear, educators also intended to address the perceived psychological consequences of war and displacement. This focus on psychological rehabilitation represented a significant departure in twentieth-century relief work. In the late 1930s, at the height of the Spanish Civil War, Howard Kershner of the Quaker American Friends Service Committee had actually rejected offers of assistance from American psychologists. Kershner explained at the time that a child psychologist would not "have found much use for her talents" in Spanish refugee camps. "The problems we faced were elemental. Refugee children had been living on sand, in fields, abandoned buildings, in whatever shelter could be found for them. When the struggle is to get food, clothing, and warmth enough to keep life going, the immediate problem is not one for a psychological solution."[4]

Only ten years later, humanitarian organizations had radically changed their outlook. Increasingly, they were as concerned about the psychological aftershocks of war as about refugees' physical needs. As early as 1941, Lindsay Noble of the American Friends Service Committee became convinced that in spite of any potential material and educational advantages, keeping Spanish refugee children in France was a mistake. The dangers that concerned him were above all psychological in nature. Noble explicitly linked the confused national identities of refugee children with psychological dysfunction. "They grow up neither French nor Spanish, finding themselves in the sad situation of being nowhere, possessing no place of employment or home. In keeping them longer here in our colonies we are without a doubt doing more harm than good," he concluded.[5] By 1944, Charles Joy, the director of the USC, was also deeply concerned about the psychological dimensions of relief. "The problem of neurotic and psychotic children is a serious one. France has not made in the field of psychiatry the progress she has made in other fields," he maintained.[6]

This shift from providing bread and butter relief to psychological rehabilitation would have profound consequences—not only for Spanish refugee children, but also for the millions of families uprooted by the Second World War.

In order to understand this development, however, it is necessary to return to the moment when children were first cast into the international spotlight as the quintessential victims of war: the First World War and the Armenian Genocide and its aftermath. The humanitarian campaigns that followed World War I and developed between the two world wars were formative ventures for the architects of post-WWII humanitarian organizations who would draw both positive and negative lessons from their experiences. These interwar experiences set the stage for the development of more cultural, nationalist, and psychological solutions to wartime suffering after 1945.

As Europe's first total war, World War I had the distinction of being the first major conflict on European soil to target civilians. By the war's end, social conditions in Central and Eastern Europe were particularly catastrophic. The allies had imposed a naval blockade in 1914, choking food shipments to Germany and Austria-Hungary. The blockade continued after the armistice in 1918 in order to compel Germany to sign the Treaty of Versailles. Hunger, military defeat, and the collapse of the Wilhelmine, Habsburg, Romanov, and Ottoman empires were upheaval enough. But then a deadly flu epidemic ravaged Europe's population between 1918 and 1920, inflicting even more casualties than had the war. Vienna faced some of the most desperate conditions in Europe. Testifying to the Senate Foreign Relations Committee, Herbert Hoover, then Secretary of Agriculture, predicted, "I do not see what prospect there is [for Austrians] short of migration or death."[7]

Shortly after the outbreak of the Great War, charitable and religious organizations responded to the crisis, gathering forces and sending out their own troops—social workers and nurses whose official mission was to ease the suffering of children. British Quaker Francesca M. Wilson embarked on her first relief mission in Europe in 1916. Wilson would go on to follow the trail of misery across Europe in the twentieth century, attending to refugees in Serbia and Austria after World War I, in Spain and France during the Spanish Civil War, and in Europe after World War II with the United Nations Relief and Rehabilitation Administration (UNRRA). But Wilson began her career in humanitarianism during the First World War in the tiny village of Samoens in the French Alps, where she presided over the care of eighty women and children in a hotel converted into a refugee camp. Wilson was initially disappointed to be marooned in a sleepy Alpine village. When she signed up for relief work she had imagined being "just behind the front line with bombs falling all around." But she dutifully applied her skills to the tasks at hand: "changing babies, lifting up toddlers, washing napkins, consoling screaming children, separating scratchers and biters from their victims, making peace between angry mothers."[8]

Most of the women and children in Wilson's care had been evacuated from the overcrowded tenements of Paris. In Samoens they found a reprieve from food shortages and military violence. But Wilson saw the evacuation as an opportunity to civilize her charges as well as protect them from physical harm. She was optimistic that with proper attention, the psychological impact of the war would be minimal. "They forgot both the terror they had been through and their slum manners pretty rapidly, for children respond to civilized life almost as quickly as they do to barbarism," she proclaimed.[9]

In Samoens, Wilson participated in an unprecedented humanitarian experiment, delivering relief to civilians uprooted by the Great War. International humanitarian organizations, such as the International Committee of the Red Cross (founded in 1863), had offered assistance to victims of war since the mid-nineteenth century, but these earlier efforts had focused on soldiers and prisoners of war.[10] As the lines between battleground and home front radically blurred during World War I, an ever-greater number of civilians needed food, clothing, medical care, and shelter assistance.

The growing numbers and needs of refugees during World War I created a context for new forms of international action. War and migration had long divided families, but the First World War and its aftermath marked the birth of the modern refugee as a special legal category of migrant. In the nineteenth century, European government authorities typically did not distinguish between political or religious refugees and other migrants who crossed frontiers in search of employment or marriage. State borders largely remained open— at least to Europeans. Between 1823 and 1905, England did not expel a single refugee. In the United States, the Chinese Exclusion Act of 1882 was one of the first major laws to restrict immigration on explicitly xenophobic and racial grounds. But U.S. immigration authorities deported only a few hundred aliens a year between 1892 and 1907. Children were among these nineteenth-century migrants, but they were not typically targeted as specific objects of humanitarian or state intervention.[11]

All that changed during and after the First World War, which ushered in new practices of state control of migration and citizenship. At the same time millions of civilians were fleeing occupying armies during World War I, xenophobia reached new heights. Passports and visas were introduced across Europe and in the United States as an emergency security measure, but soon became a permanent requirement for crossing state borders. The 1917 Russian

Revolution and civil war, which culminated in the creation of the Soviet Union, generated widespread fears of a Bolshevik revolution across Europe. Immigrants from Eastern Europe, in particular, were viewed as portents of anarchy and social revolution. In 1917, the United States passed restrictive immigration legislation, requiring a literacy test for admission.[12] In France, beginning in April of 1917, all foreigners over the age of fifteen were required to carry identification cards.[13] All told, between 1914 and 1918, approximately 400,000 civilians found themselves behind barbed wire in Europe, mostly for the "crime" of being foreign.[14]

The refugee crisis intensified after the war's end. Approximately 9.5 million people in Europe were classified as refugees in 1926. Most were victims of the principle of national self-determination. Overnight, the collapse of the Russian, Ottoman, and Habsburg Empires had transformed citizens of the former multinational Empires into "minorities" in aggressively nationalizing states. Some 850,000 German-speakers left Western Poland for Prussia, 180,000 German-speaking Alsatians were forcibly expelled and relocated to Germany, and 120,000 Germans left the Soviet Union for Germany after the war. Another 860,000 political refugees from the Russian revolution and the Bolshevik regime emigrated throughout Europe in 1922.[15]

The crisis unleashed by the collapse of the Ottoman Empire inspired particularly radical solutions, uprooting millions of people from their homes. The Balkan Wars of 1912–1913 had already displaced several hundred thousand Muslims from the Balkans to the Ottoman Empire. In 1915, under cover of war, the Committee of Union and Progress (CUP), known popularly as the "Young Turks," began a secret campaign to eliminate the Armenian minority in the Ottoman Empire. Those Armenians who managed to escape the Genocide fled largely to the Russian Caucuses and to the Syrian and Lebanese regions of the Ottoman Empire. After the war, Armenia briefly became an independent Republic, but in 1920, Turkey and the USSR invaded the fragile state, and the Allies retreated from their initial commitment to protect its sovereignty. What remained of Armenia was transformed into a Soviet Socialist Republic in November of 1920. Armenians fled once again, forming a diaspora of approximately 205,800 refugees in the Balkans, the Middle East, and Europe. In Europe's first experiment with forced population exchanges, meanwhile, the 1923 Treaty of Lausanne mandated that 1,350,000 Greeks in Turkey be "peacefully" swapped for 430,000 Turks in Greece.[16]

The League of Nations' High Commission for Refugees, under the leadership of diplomat and arctic explorer Fridtjof Nansen, was established in 1921 as the first coordinated international effort to assist the unprecedented number of refugees. The Commission's original mandate to provide assistance to Russian refugees was extended to Armenians in 1923 and then later to Assyrian and Turkish refugees. The Nansen system provided stateless refugees with documents, so-called "Nansen passports," now critical to the establishment of a legal identity and the right to cross national frontiers. The "refugee" was born in international law.[17]

*　　*　　*

The First World War and the Armenian Genocide not only generated millions of refugees, it also inspired the first international effort to "reclaim" and rehabilitate children uprooted by wartime displacement and ethnic cleansing. Children were "lost" during the Armenian Genocide in many ways. Thousands simply starved and died along the routes of deportation. Other children were repeatedly raped, forced into servitude, sold into concubinage or marriage, or abducted. When caravans of Armenians stopped to rest in Turkish towns, groups of local Kurds and Turks often appeared to take the Armenian children away, sometimes by force. Albert, an Armenian survivor, recalled that his caravan was assembled in a field in one town. The town crier yelled, "whoever wants a woman or child, come and get them. . . . A man came and grabbed me. My mother began to cry and cry and would not let go of me. He slapped her and yanked me away." He was nine or ten years old at the time. He was taken to a Turkish family and put to work guarding sheep. Another survivor recalled that when her caravan stopped to rest, a Turkish man approached her grandmother and asked to take her away. The man said that all the Armenian children were going to die. He would give her a chance to survive. Her grandmother relented. The next day the man came to take her. "When he came, I remember my grandmother sitting like a dead person, crying and crying. The man took me and another Armenian girl away. He gave me to . . . a young woman who did not have a child." She lived with her foster mother for three years, forgot Armenian, and "became a Turk."[18]

Between 1921 and 1927, the League of Nations sponsored a mission to rescue the thousands of Armenian children alleged to be have been Islamicized in Turkish families and institutions during the Genocide. The League's Commission for the Protection of Women and Children in the Near East set a number of significant precedents. It took up the recovery of Armenia's lost children only as an urgent priority of the Armenian community, but also as an international (and "universal") humanitarian cause.[19]

The plight of Armenian children was first raised in the League of Nations General Assembly in 1920. There were several legal justifications for intervention. Article 23 of the League of Nations Covenant invested the League with the authority to supervise "the execution of agreements with regard to the traffic in women and children." In addition, article 142 of the Treaty of Sèvres, signed between the Allies and the Ottoman Empire on August 10, 1920, nullified conversions to Islam that had taken place during the war. The clause obliged the Turkish government to help search for and release individuals who had disappeared, were interned, or held in captivity.[20]

In February of 1921, the League Council established a Commission of Inquiry with Regard to the Deportation of Women and Children. The Commission consisted of three members, all experienced in relief work in the Ottoman Empire: Emma D. Cushman, an American affiliated with the Near East Relief Agency, Dr. W. A. Kennedy, a British doctor working with refugees near Constantinople, and Karen Jeppe, a Danish citizen with a missionary background stationed in Aleppo, Syria.

In its first report to the League in September 1921, the Commission estimated that 90,819 Armenian orphans had already been reclaimed from Turkish families and institutions, mostly through the efforts of private Armenian groups, Near East Relief, and the British High Commission. But another 73,000 women and children reportedly remained in captivity. Armenian authorities maintained that at least six thousand children were still being "detained in Muslim surroundings" in Constantinople alone, and that another 67,000 were hidden in Turkish families and orphanages in Anatolia.[21]

Officially, the Commission was supposed to remain politically, nationally, and religiously impartial. But its work clearly reflected the concerns of Western feminist organizations and Christian missionaries. Continuing a long tradition, Commission members interpreted the denationalization of Armenian women and children by Turkish or Islamic "barbarians" as an assault on Christian "civilization." In a report submitted to the League of Nations Second Assembly on September 21, 1922, Kennedy held the entire Turkish nation responsible for the abduction of "innumerable women, mostly young," who had been "rudely torn from their hearths and homes, compelled to perform the most degrading tasks" and "shut up in harems, into which it is almost impossible to penetrate." He elaborated, "Children torn from the Christian faith are often forced by ill treatment to disown even the little they remember of their past life. Their birth certificates are forged, and their true names are thus replaced by Turkish names ... It is almost impossible to get at them, as an entire people is an accomplice to this crime."[22] In a May 1922 report from Aleppo, Karen Jeppe likewise alleged that as Armenians fled or were deported during the 1915 Genocide, "the Muslims stole the women and children or bought them at a low price." Most of these children, she insisted, now "live in bondage, at the mercy of their masters, without any rights or protection, exposed to indignities and abuses of every kind."[23]

It is striking that these initial reports barely mention the circumstances of war, deportation, and genocide under which children changed hands. Instead, the kidnapping of Christian children is framed as an almost standard Turkish or Muslim practice. Many of the Armenian children and women who were reclaimed by the Commission had of course been violently abducted and suffered exploitation or abuse. But some were well integrated into Muslim families and treated well. Other children entered Muslim families through less nefarious channels. As they fled persecution, some Armenian parents sought to save their children by hiding them with Turkish families or institutions—just as Jewish families would attempt to hide their children among Christians several decades later. In other cases, Turkish charitable institutions gathered up abandoned Armenian children along the routes of deportation. A number of Armenian children had formed close bonds to their Turkish foster parents and had to be removed from them by force. A boy who had been adopted by a young Turkish couple recalled, "I was very happy there . . . The French announced that they would pay money to any family who has news of live Armenians. They came and found me too and wanted to take me away. You should have seen how this poor lady [his adoptive mother] cried and did not want to part from me. So I told her not to worry, I would run away and return."[24]

It is not coincidental that children and grown women were lumped together in the League's rescue effort. Both women and children were seen as a form of national property to be "reclaimed" after the war. Both were considered particularly vulnerable to abduction and abuse. And both were considered incapable of making rational decisions about their futures. At least half of the Armenian women who had allegedly been abducted or sold into slavery subsequently married Turkish men and had children with them, Jeppe reported. Whether or not these marriages were consensual, many of these women, she acknowledged, "are now so well accustomed to living in this milieu that they no longer desire to return to their former homes."[25]

In general, however, members of the League Commission were hard-pressed to acknowledge that either Armenian women or children might have formed genuine ties to the Turkish community or to Islam. Kennedy reported that many children vehemently insisted that they were Turks, in spite of evidence to the contrary. He explained "their persistence in the statement that they were Moslems" as a product of terror. "They had been threatened in many ways, and the older girls often state that, in such a case, they would be sent to houses of ill-fame." Other children, he reported, "openly state that they received or were promised gifts of various kinds to induce them to feel happy and remain Moslem. Some admit that they were happy and well treated. Some have actually for various reasons escaped to their Moslem homes . . . This is to be explained by the fact that they went from comfortable Turkish homes to Armenian institutions where no luxury exists or is possible."[26]

In a letter to the Secretary General of the League, Emma Cushman maintained that many Armenian children had been brainwashed by the Turks. She denounced the "unique and very clever manner in which the Turks contrive to conceal the identity of these children. They try to bring about not so much a change of name and locality, but rather a complete change of mind in the children. These children, for a period of time extending from one week to three months, will deny strenuously that they are Christians. Some, indeed, will go so far as to revile the Christians as infidels, and declare that they are loyal Moslems." Cushman, too, was reluctant to acknowledge the potential for genuine ties between Armenian children and their adoptive families. She insisted that most of the girls had been bribed to deny their origins "by gifts of clothing, personal adornments, such as beads, cheap jewelry, etc.," whereas the boys had generally been compelled to submit by force. Many children, she conceded, ran away to their Turkish families after being reclaimed by Armenian or British authorities. But she insisted that these runaways suffered from a "distorted mentality," and blamed "surreptitious visits or communication from the Turkish family, who either brought or sent some tidbits of food or a present of some kind."[27]

On September 23, 1921, in response to the first set of reports from the Commission of Enquiry, the League of Nations Assembly ordered the appointment of a League Commissioner for the Protection of Women and Children in the Near East. The League Commissioner was officially charged with the reclamation of trafficked women and children. The League also resolved to open a "Neutral House" for rescued women and children. Kennedy was appointed Commissioner, and he established a headquarters and League of Nations Neutral House in Constantinople with Cushman. Karen Jeppe led a branch of the League Commission and a second League home in Aleppo, Syria, a major area of settlement for Armenian refugees.[28]

In the Neutral House and in affiliated schools in Aleppo, Jeppe's branch aimed explicitly to renationalize, re-Christianize, and "re-civilize" lost Armenians. Jeppe reported in August 1924, "It is hard to believe your eyes when you compare the people in rags, dirty and of a savage bearing who arrive here, with the more or less civilized people who leave us a few months later. At first, our protégés often tend to try to run away if life here doesn't completely suit them; but soon 'the Armenian' within begins to reappear. Before they leave us, they are completely returned to their nationality."[29] Orphanages for Armenian children established by the Near East Relief and other private charities were also run in a nationalist spirit. The children were reeducated in the Armenian language and Christian religion, and learned Armenian nationalist songs and folk dances. Some survivors recalled that they were punished by their teachers or even beaten if they were caught speaking Turkish.[30]

Not surprisingly, the League's rescue campaign provoked an outcry from Ottoman and Muslim elites. Many saw the effort as an affront to the patriarchal privileges of Muslim men. One prominent Turkish feminist, Halide Edip Adivar, even insisted that Muslim children were the true victims of denationalization in the League's homes. In 1928, she alleged that "children brought to the [Neutral House] were left in the care of the Armenian women, and these Armenian women either through persuasion or threats or hypnotism, forced the children to learn by heart the name of an Armenian woman for their mother and an Armenian man for their father."[31]

The League's Commission operated for five years before falling victim to the reigning principle of national sovereignty in interwar Europe. The Treaty of Lausanne guaranteed Turkey's national sovereignty, hindering further action in Constantinople. In Syria, French mandatory authorities began to demand the termination of Jeppe's oeuvre in 1925, insisting that all humanitarian efforts in the mandate should be subject to the supreme authority of the French High Commissioner. At the very least, they wanted Jeppe to be replaced by a French citizen.[32] Robert de Caix, the French delegate to the League's Mandate Commission in Geneva, explained that "the work of liberating women and children who have entered into Muslim families voluntarily or by force can cause serious problems if one does not proceed discreetly and amicably ... Therein lies the danger for public order for which the Mandatory Power alone is responsible and which it alone has sacrificed to maintain." French authorities were particularly incensed by Jeppe's ambition to establish agricultural colonies for Armenian refugees in Syria. De Caix considered Armenian refugees "difficult people," and implied that the French government did not want them to become a permanent presence on Syrian soil. A year later, French Minister of Foreign Affairs Aristide Briand agreed that Jeppe's Commission "risks creating a lot of difficulties with the indigenous population, without responding to any real necessity." The French were, however, prevented from unilaterally terminating the Aleppo mission because of "the favor which this pro-Armenian charity enjoys with feminist and evangelical associations, who exercise a considerable influence in the milieu of the Secretariat of the League of Nations and in certain important delegations to the Assembly."[33]

The Commission finally ended its work in Constantinople in 1926 and in Aleppo in 1927. In her final report, Jeppe estimated that the Aleppo branch had successfully "reclaimed" 1,600 Armenians, 1,400 of whom had passed through the League's Neutral Home. Including those assisted by the Constantinople Commission, a total of some four thousand children and four thousand adults received aid from the League's Commission.[34] These were relatively modest figures compared to the number of children alleged to remain in Turkish hands—a numerical disparity that would surface again when the United Nations canvassed for lost East European and Jewish children after the Second World War. Jeppe explained this disparity with reference to the Commission's humanitarian ethic and restraint. The Commission had only mobilized to reclaim women and children who themselves wished to escape from the Turkish milieu, she insisted. "We were determined not to disturb friendly relations or to disturb family life in cases in which the women or children expatriated were treated well and considered members of the family . . . We only assisted those who could not resign themselves to their fate and who felt profoundly unhappy. . . . This is the reason the number of our protégés is relatively small. If we had been less scrupulous we would have been able to obtain, numerically, very different results."[35]

She estimated that only 6 percent of the Commission's wards ultimately chose to rejoin their Muslim families rather than the Armenian community. And while the goal of renationalizing and re-Christianizing Armenian women and children was never far from sight, Jeppe also insisted that the Commission's foremost goal had always been to reconstruct families torn apart by war. She thus celebrated the successful reunification of Armenian families as a triumph of the League's humanitarian principles, attesting, "I cannot describe the scenes which we have witnessed, when brothers and sisters are reunited by chance, or when fathers and mothers embrace a child that they believed they would never see again."[36]

The similarities between the League's mission to recover Armenian children and efforts to recover East European and Jewish children after World

War II are striking. They suggest the extent to which the loss and recovery of children were central to twentieth century experiences of war, genocide, and reconstruction more broadly. Whether it was Armenian children who became Turks, Czech children who became German, or Jewish children who became Christian, the transfer of children to a "foreign" nation or religion came to represent not only a humanitarian offense against individuals, but also a wartime assault against entire nations. After both World Wars, the recovery of lost children was tightly linked to national regeneration by communities decimated by genocide, war, and displacement.

These lost children were both victims and beneficiaries of the drive to create nationally homogenous states in Europe. In the first half of the twentieth century, European governments saw population as the highest measure of national power and prestige, the key to expanding economic and military might. The perceived ability of children to learn new languages, religions, and identities saved many of their lives during both the Armenian Genocide and the Second World War. But this ability to assimilate was a double-edged sword. In a world of warring nationalist movements and population politics, it also transformed children into a form of plunder, to be captured and remodeled by nations looking to expand their ranks.

*   *   *

In Central Europe as well, new humanitarian organizations found new terrain for action during and after World War I, setting a number of precedents for post-World War II relief work. Among the millions displaced by World War I and the collapse of the Ottoman, Russian, and Habsburg Empires were thousands of children evacuated from the path of occupying armies and starvation. These evacuations were small in scale in comparison to the massive civilian evacuations of the Second World War. But they represented a formative experience for child welfare experts who would later mobilize around displaced children during and after World War II. In 1918, Anna Freud led a group of Austro-Hungarian refugee children from depleted Vienna to the more fertile Hungarian countryside. (Twenty years later she would go on to author the most influential study of evacuated children during the Second World War). The Austro-Hungarian Ministry of Interior had organized the evacuation of nine hundred children from Vienna to Hungary in 1918, "in consideration of the fact that the uninterrupted, long-term stay of refugee children in Vienna . . . will negatively influence their development and health."[37] After the war, as Austria sunk into famine, the number of evacuees multiplied.

In 1920 more than 100,000 Austrian children traveled as far as Switzerland, Denmark, Holland, and Germany on holidays from hunger that lasted between eight weeks and a full year.[38]

In February 1920, an International Congress of Children's Aid Organizations in Geneva brought together delegates from all the major relief agencies in Europe and government representatives to discuss the progress of evacuation programs. There was little controversy at the Congress about the separation of children from their parents. In fact, representatives of the Austrian Ministry for Social Welfare praised the "moral and material benefits" of sending children abroad. A member of the Danish Committee for the Aid of Viennese Children even saw hungry Austrian children as potential ambassadors. Austrian children scattered across Europe were contributing to the development of "international understanding" in the aftermath of war, he proclaimed.[39]

Some evacuated children never returned home. Hermine Santrouschitz, an 11-year-old Viennese girl from a working-class family, was evacuated to Leiden in the Netherlands in December 1920. Her Dutch foster family gave her the nickname Miep and provided her with ample food and affection. She first returned to Vienna five years later and discovered that she no longer felt at home there. "I did not want to hurt my natural family's feelings, and I was still young and needed their consent. But I wanted desperately to return to the Netherlands. My sensibilities were Dutch, the quality of my feelings also Dutch." Miep Gies returned to the Netherlands and moved to Amsterdam with her foster family. Eventually she became a secretary of Otto Frank, Anne Frank's father, and was one of the Frank family's protectors during the Second World War.[40]

The occupation of Northern France and Belgium by German forces prompted equally ambitious schemes to protect children's safety and health. In the summer of 1918, during the Hindenburg offensive, the French government evacuated 75,000 Parisian children as the German army threatened to seize the capital. These children were typically taken in by peasant families in regions such as the Yonne and Nièvre, where the French *Assistance Publique* relied on long-established networks of foster parents, but they were sometimes sent as far away as Holland.[41] Far from worrying about the emotional effects of separating children from their parents, some French commentators speculated that the evacuees were better off in their new families, removed from their impoverished urban origins. A writer for the magazine *Débats* in 1919 even lamented the fate of children who "will have to leave behind a veritable family in the Netherlands" to return to their own parents. "Who knows," asked the magazine, "if their happiest days will not have been their days spent in Holland?"[42]

The central mission of international humanitarian organizations during and after the First World War was to protect European children from violence, starvation, and infant mortality. These threats did not diminish with the armistice. To this end, in May of 1919, Eglantyne Jebb founded the Save the Children Fund (SCF) in London. Jebb was moved by the plight of starving children in Central Europe during World War I. She protested the British Naval blockade in Central Europe in Trafalgar Square in London, distributing photographs of skeletal children with the caption, "Our Blockade has Caused This." A year after its founding, the SCF blossomed into an international organization, and the International Save the Children Union (SCIU) was born, headquartered in Geneva. Jebb drafted the Declaration of the Rights of the Child in 1923, the first international children's Bill of Rights, which was ratified by the League of Nations in 1924.[43]

On the other side of the Atlantic, Herbert Hoover's American Relief Administration emerged as the most important American effort to combat hunger in Europe. In October 1914, Hoover had organized the Commission for Relief in Belgium. The CRB distributed several billion dollars in relief aid to hungry children in German-occupied Belgium and Northern France during the First World War. After the war, Hoover turned his attention to Central and Eastern Europe, establishing the Child Feeding Program of the American Relief Administration (ARA). Officially, the ARA declared itself "impartially aloof from all politics, military, racial, or other controversial questions." In practice, its anti-Communism was never far from the surface. "Revolutions and political upheavals were of frequent occurrence and more than half of Europe, including Germany, tottered on the brink of anarchism, against which the only effective weapon was food," explained a 1922 ARA report.[44]

The success of the ARA and the SCF rested on creative fundraising strategies that fostered imagined affinities between American donors and Central European children. In one American suburb, the village green was transformed into a mock graveyard planted with two thousand white crosses, "each representing the grave of a child in Central Europe whose life might be saved by the immediate action of the residents of the village." A representative of the Hoover Commission stood by. Each time he received a ten-dollar bill, he lifted one cross out of the ground and replaced it with an American flag. Within a single week, the field of crosses had become a field of flags.[45]

The ARA penetrated the tiniest villages of Central and Eastern Europe through a network of local committees and soup kitchens. In March of 1919, at least 400,000 children in Austria received a daily meal courtesy of the ARA; along with 1,500,000 children in Poland; 600,000 children in Czechoslovakia; 400,000 children in Serbia; 500,000 children in Romania; and 200,000 children in Russian Armenia.[46]

The food crisis had begun during the war itself in Austria. Like the other Great Powers, Austria had anticipated a short war, and government officials made no plans to provision the population in a drawn-out conflict. By 1918, official rations allocated to the typical consumer in Vienna had plunged to 830 calories a day.[47] The situation did not improve when the war ended. Francesca Wilson, who left the French Alps to combat starvation in Vienna's working-class neighborhoods, described Vienna as "a city of the dead" in the summer of 1919.[48] The death rate among children aged 5 to 19 was up 50 percent from its pre-war level. The ARA estimated that 96.2 percent of Viennese children were undernourished in 1919.[49]

While theoretically focused solely on feeding starving children, the ARA embraced a pedagogical mission from the outset. Its representatives sought to deliver "American" values of self-help, efficiency, and cross-class solidarity along with surplus wheat and corn.[50] In a speech in October 1920, Hoover insisted, "it was essential that the problem of child life be made the responsibility of each community and that American charity should not become a pauperizing influence."[51] The psychological consequences of starvation were not a central concern of the ARA, however. Rather, Hoover believed that his soup kitchens could heal the festering wounds of class division in Europe and thereby prevent the Russian revolution from spreading west. "A princess stirring broth in a soup kitchen is the best argument for democracy that could possibly be found . . . It was through this kind of service that we were able to stave off anarchy," he explained to the *Saturday Evening Post*.[52]

American Relief Administration workers developed a distinctive method of delivering calories to needy children, intended to embody the values of efficiency and self-government. But in spite of the organization's emphasis on self-help, the agency was not particularly concerned about family solidarity. In fact, ARA policies were shaped by a profound mistrust of parents. Hoover assumed that if food were distributed to parents, the parents would simply eat it rather than share it with their children. So the organization mandated that children's plates must be cleaned on the spot in ARA cafeterias, under strict supervision. Clemens Pirquet of the University of Vienna, who devised this feeding program, explained, "One of the principles was that the children had to eat everything that was given them, and to the last crumb. Before leaving the place they are all inspected so that nothing is left in their dishes and that they do not take any bread or cake home, because the possibility would be that they would take it to their parents and other people." Disciplining picky eaters was essential for a society threatened by famine, in Pirquet's view. Force-feeding "means an education in eating, and such education is a very important thing for a poverty-stricken country, in whose interest it is that their inhabitants become accustomed to any kind of food available."[53]

Francesca Wilson was highly critical of ARA's methods, particularly their potential to undermine the family. "The policy of the Americans was to see the food down the children's throats . . . Hoover wanted to be certain that only children were fed, because he said that they had not, like their parents, been his enemies." The problem with this approach, she reasoned, was that "if mothers starve, there is no one to look after the children."[54] But throughout Europe, relief work centered on children, represented as the quintessential victims of the war. "The concern of the Save the Children Fund is solely with the children, the most innocent and deserving sufferers from the mistakes of mankind," declared Mrs. Philip Snowden of the British SCF in 1919.[55] Parents made less-compelling objects of sympathy—regardless of their politics.

In theory, the ARA intended to efficiently deliver rice and cocoa to Central European children. But the seeds of a more cultural approach were planted within this calorie-driven vision of relief. Along with American values and anti-Communism, ARA workers brought unspoken prejudices to Eastern and Central Europe, depicting the region and its people as inherently backward, violent, and corrupt—in imagined opposition to American modernity and efficiency.[56] These prejudices undercut their stated goals of facilitating self-help. ARA workers ultimately concluded that East Europeans did not have the capacity for self-government, that their backward culture, rather than war or material shortages, was the true source of hunger in Eastern Europe.

Encounters between relief workers and locals sometimes left humanitarian activists questioning whether East Europeans were even human. One SCF field worker reported that in the Sub-Carpathian Rus in Czechoslovakia in 1920, "The squalor is almost beyond belief. Six or seven people—if one can call them people—in one stuffy room, and a half-dozen hens or rabbits besides . . . Idiots and cretins abound."[57] At the same time that ARA workers claimed to promote class and national reconciliation, they scapegoated Jews, in particular, in order to explain their own failures. During another visit to the Sub-Carpathian Rus, ARA worker N. Leach blamed the limited success of ARA programs on Jewish sabotage. "With a ninety percent total illiteracy for Ruthenia and almost a hundred percent among the peasant class, the Jews find little difficulty in controlling the situation . . . One never sees a Jew doing hard manual labor," Leach reported.[58]

Perceived corruption also undermined the ARA's philosophy of self-help. The Chief of the Polish Mission, W. P. Fuller, lamented in 1920, "Unfortunately it is a fact that abuse is running rife and that an astonishing number of people in this country look upon our foodstuffs as something from which to derive personal benefit."[59] Lina Fuller, W. P. Fuller's wife, wrote a letter to her husband in January 1920 despairing of rampant corruption in the village of Parysów in Poland. She described her surroundings as a remote town of some five thousand souls, two-thirds Jewish, "all houses of mud and straw, and such poverty and dirt as you have never seen." Upon arrival, she reported, her car was greeted by "some 3,000 shrieking, howling wild humans who ran after the car wherever it went, like so many dogs. Picture the old Jew in that god-awful garment of rags, with flowing beard, barefooted in the snow and mud, running . . . falling down, and the crowd surging right over him . . . they were all crazed." After surveying the scene, Fuller interviewed the local priest, who informed her that "all the members of the committee were thieves, their fathers and grandfathers before them had been thieves; that they had stolen most of the food and had carted it away at night to the next town where they had sold it . . . that there were no honest men in the town (the three most honest had died of typhus the week before)." She concluded her visit with an inspection of the ARA soup kitchen, which turned out to be the apartment of the president of the local committee. Most of the food intended for distribution was stored under his bed. Outraged, Fuller stormed out and lectured the villagers, "telling them that they had failed to run their own show, and that now I was going to run it."[60] Her report reflects an emerging conviction among relief workers that the ARA's doctrine of self-government was ill suited to the "backward" conditions of Eastern Europe.

In Serbia, an ARA relief worker drew equally pessimistic conclusions. "The children are in a deplorable condition but as far as I can learn they always have been in bad shape . . . as soon as we withdraw the conditions will become the same as they were before the war. It seems a hopeless task as far as any permanent good is concerned."[61] And in Košice in Czechoslovakia, an ARA employee declared that the time had come to close the mission in 1920. The children there were still hungry, he conceded. But "I do not think they would look healthy after years of soup kitchens . . . There is doubtless in every town a considerable number of *poor* children, but their relief should surely not be undertaken by a foreign mission. We have had apparently little success in helping local committees to a more far-sighted view of the people's welfare."[62] W. P. Fuller ultimately concluded his mission in Poland with the concession that "the doctrine of independent control by the Polish has been a dire failure."[63]

These perceptions of failure shaped the development of later aid programs for refugees. The problems facing the new democracies of Eastern Europe, relief workers concluded, could not be solved with soup kitchens. Central and East European culture and psychology—judged through an anti-Semitic and orientalist lens—were the more fundamental obstacles to development. It was a lesson they carried to Europe after the Second World War, when humanitarian organizations devoted their efforts more explicitly to transforming refugees' psychological and cultural outlooks, rather than simply distributing goods. But by then, they would also have a new scientific language with which to express their concerns about refugees' "mentalities," grounded in the disciplines of child psychology and psychoanalysis.

At the same time that the First World War transformed Europe's starving children into objects of humanitarian intervention, new restrictions on immigration in Western Europe and the United States brought the plight of migrant families to the attention of international organizations. The restrictions on citizenship and mobility introduced during World War I had not been lifted after the war, for several reasons. In light of famine conditions in Central and Eastern Europe, West European and American officials feared that swarms of starving Europeans would rush toward their borders. And in the aftermath of the Russian Revolution, they also worried that refugees from the East would bring revolutionary ideas with them. In addition, as citizenship rights expanded in Europe's interwar republics—to include more generous welfare benefits and suffrage for women, for example, governments introduced new measures to prevent foreigners on their shores from accessing those rights. In the United States, the Johnson-Reed Immigration Act of 1924 introduced the infamous quota system, designed to choke immigration from Southern and Eastern Europe.[64] Only France, with its low birthrate and its shortage of agricultural and industrial labor, continued to welcome immigration in interwar Europe, until the Great Depression provoked a bitter reaction against foreigners there as well.[65]

These new restrictions on immigration created problems for families divided across national borders. The International Migration Service (IMS), which changed its name to the International Social Service (ISS) in 1946, was the first major international organization to focus exclusively on the problems facing families that had been "scattered in pieces all over the face of the globe" due to labor migration, persecution, or war.[66] Through counseling families toward promoting family solidarity, the IMS also contributed to a gradual shift from material to psychological forms of relief among international organizations.

The IMS developed from the activism of Anglo-Saxon Protestant women at the turn of the century. In 1914, women in the YWCA organized an international conference to discuss the pressing social issues faced by immigrant women and children. In 1920, the YWCA undertook a study of major ports and cities of emigration and immigration in Europe and the United States. The study foregrounded the need for an international organization to tackle the problems faced by transnational families. These women founded the IMS in 1922 with headquarters in London and Geneva. An American branch was established that same year, and a French office opened under the name Service Sociale d'Aide aux Émigrants (SSAÉ) in 1924.

Migration was on the rise between the wars, and by the eve of the Second World War, the agency employed 150 field officers in branches in France, Poland, Czechoslovakia, Greece, the United States, and Germany (until 1937).[67] In a publication celebrating its 25th anniversary, the IMS/ISS reflected, "Normal movement of population, displacement due to war, political, or religious oppression, international marriages, all of these create a need for people and agencies to work together across borders and frontiers to prevent the discouragement and suffering which contribute to the breakdown in family unity, waste of individual potentialities, and international ill-will."[68]

It was no coincidence that an international organization was born to attend to the "human problems" faced by migrant families at the same moment that many states closed their borders. In the 1920s and 30s, immigrants faced ever more complex legal barriers as they attempted to acquire citizenship, work, marry, divorce, and have children. These restrictions generally meant longer separations of husbands, wives, and children. The agency was particularly concerned with the moral and social risks that faced divided families. These concerns were also a legacy of the First World War. While the evacuation of children from war zones had not stirred much alarm in Europe, the extended absence of mobilized fathers generated a wave of anxiety about juvenile delinquency and adultery, a perceived consequence of a lack of male authority in the home.[69]

International Migration Service leaders hoped to bridge the gap between a labor market that propelled workers across state borders and a system of social protection based on principles of national citizenship and local responsibility.

In a 1931 speech to the National Council of Social Work, George Warren, director of the American Branch of the IMS, lamented that "the family, as it were, walks into a void because the country of departure and the country of destination immediately disclaim all responsibility for the social care of those forced to travel from one to the other."[70] In some countries, such as France, migrant social rights were protected through bilateral treaties. A 1920 treaty entitled Polish workers to the same status as French citizens with regard to pensions, workman's compensation, unemployment insurance, and family allocations, for example. Similar treaties protected the rights of Belgian and Italian workers in France. But in the United States, immigrants were generally left to the mercy of local and state authorities.[71]

While Warren promoted reform to bring the welfare state in line with the trans-Atlantic labor market, IMS workers adopted a more individualistic approach, using old-fashioned moral persuasion in their campaign to solidify family ties. An early IMS study, authored by Kenneth Rich and Mary Brant, examined the cases of the Immigrant Protective League in Chicago and outlined strategies for reunifying families. "There is an inexorable recurrence of the same obstacles in case after case, driving husbands and wives apart, and bringing family ruin," they lamented. The social worker's goal was to keep families intact through counseling. "The moderately simple problem which occurs at the beginning of a family break may be solved by various forms of persuasion."[72] The most common problem "type" identified by IMS social workers was the "Deserting Husband," who abandoned his wife and children in Europe. In general, Rich and Brant warned, "The man who has been away from his family for a number of years has become so accustomed to drifting about that he has forgotten the advantages of a home. He must be called in frequently and reminded of the goal toward which he is working, or his enthusiasm wanes and the family becomes permanently separated."[73]

While American social workers worried about deserting husbands, IMS representatives in Poland were equally concerned about the morality of women and children left in Europe without male supervision. Between 1918 and 1930, some 630,000 Poles left the European continent, while another 500,000 immigrated to other countries in Europe.[74] Adam Nagorski of the Polish Bureau of the IMS lamented to George Warren in February 1939, "The emigration country has to deal with a wife who is apt to lead an immoral life being abandoned by her husband and left behind without means."[75] Joan Kussak, Director of the IMS's Polish Branch in 1926, agreed that many Polish wives were "not worthy of our attention." But she also noted that the

Polish Branch was inundated with requests to trace husbands who left for America—never to be heard from again.[76]

Only when persuasion failed did the IMS consider legal action. There were cases, the agency lamented, in which men deserted their families in Europe, and "all the powers of persuasion, appeal, shame, and urging cannot arouse a spark of interest or cooperation." Caseworkers were not above exploiting their clients' fear of deportation in such cases. One social worker noted that "most of these men are . . . afraid of American institutions, and particularly of the power of American Women to enforce justice." When confronted with a deserting husband, she called him into her office and reminded him that "according to the laws of the United States, he is obliged to support his wife and children, that his consul will not uphold him as a lawbreaker . . . This is usually sufficient to gain his willingness to cooperate."[77]

In the wake of the Depression, the Spanish Civil War, and the Nazi seizure of power in Germany, the scope of IMS casework in Europe and America expanded. The organization shifted seamlessly from counseling delinquent husbands to aiding political refugees. The American caseload of the IMS more than doubled in the 1930s, from 1,734 families in 1927 to 3,590 families in 1939. "Practically all of the case situations reflected increasingly desperate need precipitated by the war in Europe," the IMS reported.[78] In 1939, the IMS coordinated a program to evacuate British children to the United States, and in 1940 it assisted efforts to resettle 100,000 German and East European Jews in the Dominican Republic. The IMS further expanded its authority after the Second World War, when it received a mandate to deliver casework services to refugees in Europe under the auspices of the United Nations High Commissioner on Refugees. Today the ISS continues to operate in nineteen countries worldwide, working largely in the field of international adoption.

Like the League of Nations and the American Relief Administration, the IMS contributed to the emergence of the divided family as an object of international intervention. IMS experts also accelerated a transition from material to psychological humanitarianism, delivering counseling rather than material assistance to migrant families. But the methods should not be confused with the goals of relief. Even as IMS workers used counseling and persuasion to encourage family solidarity, they were not typically concerned about the psychological well-being of individual children. Rather, IMS social workers aimed to reunify families because they feared that women and children would be left impoverished and demoralized without male support. These international social workers were pioneers in their efforts to "untangle the snarls in human lives that result from migration."[79] But the agency conceived of these snarls in social, economic, and moral terms. It would take the upheavals of the Second World War for social workers and child welfare experts to re-imagine displacement as a threat to children's mental health as well as to Europe's social and political stability.

*   *   *

The Spanish Civil War has often been called a dress rehearsal for the Second World War. It was a grim practice exercise not only for combatants, military planners, and European governments, but also for children. Tens of thousands of Spanish Republican children were separated from their parents and dispersed to foreign lands between 1936 and 1939, forming a diaspora in France, Belgium, the United Kingdom, the Soviet Union, and Mexico. When compared with the relatively short evacuations of the First World War, moreover, Spanish refugee children were typically exiled for years—if not permanently.

The conflicts surrounding displaced Spanish children echoed the League of Nations' movement to "reclaim" Armenian lost children, and prefigured the debates that would erupt after the Second World War about the denationalization of children in the Nazi empire. As in the Armenian case, child-savers were not only concerned about the material welfare of refugee children, but also about their national, political, and religious loyalties. More than ever, international organizations linked their work in soup kitchens and children's homes to the highest realms of international politics. In a speech to the directors of Quaker-run colonies for refugee children in France in 1942, Mr. Burritt Hiatt lectured, "You can no longer imagine that when you are in a school or an isolated children's colony that you have no relationship to the international situation."[80]

When people speak of the Spanish Civil War as a global conflict, they typically invoke the arms, money, and soldiers that crossed state borders—guns shipped from the Soviet Union to Republican guerillas, money and troops that flowed from Mussolini's Italy and Nazi Germany into Franco's hands, or volunteers in the International Brigade who enlisted in the struggle against fascism. But the movement of children across national borders also transformed the Spanish civil war into a European conflagration, creating transnational alliances and even kinship relations among Communists, social Catholics, Basque nationalists, Republicans, and fascist militants in far-flung lands.

Even as the plight of Spanish refugee children became a matter of international politics, however, contemporary observers still did not generally perceive children's suffering in psychological terms. They saw the separation of children from their parents as a political and national threat, not as a form of psychic trauma. Humanitarian workers thus continued to concentrate on providing calories, clothing, and medical care to refugee children. In the tradition of League of Nations' campaign to "reclaim" Armenian children from Turkish homes, they also continued to worry about sustaining children's national loyalties in exile.

The Spanish Civil War began in 1936, and the refugee crisis followed closely on the heels of Franco's conquests. Nationalist troops conquered the city of Guernica in April 1937, took the Basque capital Bilbao in June, and surged into Santander in August. As Franco's forces conquered growing swaths of Republican territory, Republican soldiers and their families fled to the shrinking zones under Republican control. By 1938, some two million Republican refugees were crowded in Catalonia. With the crushing Republican defeat in March of 1939, the crisis intensified. Close to 500,000 people pressed against the French border. They waited in bitter conditions, exposed to the cold, without adequate food or supplies. Finally French border guards relented, and the refugees rushed into France.[81] The French Interior Ministry estimated that 514,337 Spanish Republicans had found refuge on French soil by 1940, including 76,162 women and 78,629 children.[82]

Plans to evacuate Spanish children to France took shape not long after the Spanish Civil War began. In France, the Comité d'Accueil aux Enfants d'Espagne (CAEE) was formed in November of 1936 in cooperation with the Spanish Republican Ministry of Health and Social Assistance. The CAEE was an organ of the French Confédération Générale du Travail (CGT), which included all of France's major trade unions and was primarily controlled by Communists. The CAEE quickly recruited five thousand French families to open their homes to Spanish refugee children. This outpouring of support coexisted with sharp internal divisions over French involvement in Spain's civil war. Léon Blum, the Prime Minister of France's Popular Front government, which brought together France's left-wing Communist (PCF), Socialist (SFIO), and Radical parties in an alliance against the French Right, originally pledged to support the Republican army in its struggle against Franco. But under pressure from the French Right and British leaders, Blum signed a non-intervention agreement only three weeks after the war began. French supporters of Spain's Republican forces saw hosting Spanish refugee children as one of the few means by which they could demonstrate their solidarity with the Republican cause.[83]

The first group of 450 CAEE-sponsored evacuees departed for France on March 20, 1937. A year later, the CAEE reported that close to 9,000 Spanish children were in the organization's care, some 4,000 in collective colonies, and another 5,000 in private foster homes.[84] After the war, Franco's government estimated that a total of 34,037 children had been evacuated abroad during the Spanish Civil War—17,489 to France, 5,130 to Belgium, 3,291 to the Soviet Union, 4,435 to the United Kingdom, 807 to Switzerland, 430 to Mexico, 335 to French West Africa, and 120 to Denmark.[85] But these numbers are all vague estimates, because children moved constantly in and out of colonies and foster placements, and across the Pyrenees and back.[86] Between 7,000 and 11,000 unaccompanied Spanish children probably resided in French colonies and foster homes between October 1937 and January 1939.[87]

A veritable alphabet soup of overlapping and competing humanitarian organizations took charge of these children. In addition to the CGT, the American Friends Service Committee hosted 600 Spanish children in 16 colonies in France by 1941.[88] The Spanish Republican Ministry of Education also sponsored a own network of colonies and schools for evacuated children. Catholics and Basque nationalists, meanwhile, were often loath to send their children into the hands of "godless" Socialists and Communists, so they launched their own competing evacuation schemes. The Basque nationalist Partido Nacionalista Vasco (PNV) established colonies in France's Basque territories with the intent of guaranteeing the Basque loyalties of its charges. And the Comité National Catholique de Secours aux Réfugiés d'Espagne (CNC), established in 1937, created colonies in France with the support of the Vatican and French Catholics, pledging to sustain Spanish children's Catholic faith in exile.[89] Humanitarian workers would later denounce this overlapping, politicized tangle of humanitarian efforts as the antithesis of the rationalized, apolitical organization that they pledged to construct after World War II.

Spanish refugee children were highly vulnerable to the shifting tides of French immigration policies. In the 1920s the French government and employers had thrown open the gates to immigrant workers, as long as they fueled a growing economy and compensated for the low French birthrate. In 1931, France boasted the largest immigrant population in Europe, an estimated three million people. All that changed with the onset of the Great Depression. Initially, French officials continued to express sympathy for victims of Nazism, who were permitted to cross the border from Germany in the spring of 1933 without documentation. As the economic crisis deepened, however, and the persecution of Jews in Germany intensified, sympathy for refugees dissolved. In 1934–1935, the expulsion of illegal immigrants began in earnest.

Blum's Popular Front government, which came to power in the spring of 1936, initially brought some relief to refugees and immigrants in France. There was no formal change in immigration policy, but the pace of expulsions slowed. Since the Popular Front came to power just as Republican refugees began to pour across the Pyrenees, many Spanish refugees initially received a warm welcome, especially in traditionally red regions of southern France. During the Second Popular Front government of Camille Chautemps, however (June 1937– January 1938), the French economy sank further into the Depression, public funds to support Spanish refugees were exhausted, and some 150,000 refugees (especially Basques from the northern zones of Spain) were deported. When the Popular Front collapsed in 1938, official attitudes toward refugees hardened further. Claiming that France was "saturated," Édouard Daladier's center-right government began efforts to repatriate and intern unwanted refugees. The arrival of close to 350,000 Spanish refugees in early 1939 inflamed passions on the right. The right-wing and Catholic press denounced Republican asylum seekers as "terrorist hordes" and accused them of fomenting anarchism.

The French government had been unprepared for the influx of Spanish refugees, and conditions in refugee camps were appalling. Refugees were poorly sheltered from the elements, undernourished, and subject to harsh discipline by French authorities.[90] Daladier's government was not inclined to improve conditions. The French government was paying some 200 million francs a month to support refugees, and hoped to secure an agreement with Franco to guarantee Spain's neutrality in the (increasingly likely) event of a French war with Germany. Though repatriation was technically "voluntary," by the end of 1939 close to 200,000 Republican refugees had returned to Spain, under considerable pressure.

In spite of these conditions, children placed in foster homes by the CAEE retained mostly warm memories of their experiences in France. "My adoptive family was Communist, extraordinary people, unfailingly kind to me," recalled one former evacuee. Another *niña* remembered enjoying luxuries beyond her wildest imagination. "They bought me beautiful clothes, and for the first time in my life, I was taken to a beauty parlor," she recalled. "They treated me like their own daughter, maybe even a little better."[91]

The children evacuated by the PNV and the Catholic Church were sometimes less warmly received, particularly those who landed in the French-Basque provinces in the summer of 1937. Local Catholics suspected the refugees of harboring anti-Catholic loyalties. One former refugee child recalled that "all the French in the little towns were hostile: they called us 'Little Basque Pigs,' 'Scum of Spain,' 'Red-Separatists,' or simply 'Refugees' in such a tone I would cringe and want to hide." Another remembered being ostracized at church. "We even had to sit in a separate section at Mass in the village, and take Communion after everyone else, as though we children would somehow contaminate the good French families." In regions unsympathetic to the Republican cause, Spanish children encountered hostility from local officials as well. "The mayor was pro-Franco and despised us. He always complained of the amount of water our little colony used, saying the pigs they raised deserved it more than we did," recalled one former refugee.[92]

Spanish children in the USSR also recalled their early experiences in exile in mostly positive terms. These testimonies, collected in Spain forty years later, reflect the difficult transitions experienced by Spanish refugees who repatriated to Spain from the Soviet Union in the 1950s. Following the Second World War, during which Spanish children shared many of the ordeals of their Soviet compatriots, the early years of exile in the 1930s may have acquired a rosy glow. But even in the late 1970s, many children recalled their experiences in Soviet institutions with a surprising dose of nostalgia.

Refugee children hosted by the Soviet Union during the Spanish Civil War occupied a privileged position in a society strained by scarcity. They were greeted as heroes, celebrated with parades, flowers, and caviar. Their children's homes became showpieces for the Soviet regime, intended to advertise the magnificence of Soviet humanitarianism, internationalism, and culture to the world. In letters home, the children described banquets of white bread and chocolate, films, concerts, ballet lessons, and the loving attention of their teachers. The daughter of one worker from Bilbao recalled, "Our own parents only gave us slaps on the cheek and complaints, but the teachers there were so incredibly patient and helpful and loving to us." Other former evacuees were grateful for the educational and cultural opportunities on offer. "We arrived in Russia more savage than civilized . . . The experience in Russia changed our lives. We became educated, thinking persons." Women were often grateful for the career opportunities they enjoyed in the USSR.[93] Araceli Sánchez-Urquijo simply recalled her years in exile in the Soviet Union as "the happiest of her life."[94]

Many things changed with the onset of the Second World War, and especially with the Hitler-Stalin pact, which made the ongoing presence of Spanish refugees on Soviet soil embarrassing for Stalin. Some Spanish teachers who accompanied the children were rumored to fall victim to the purges. Conditions took another turn for the worse with the onset of the war against Nazi Germany in 1941. Spanish children were integrated into Russian schools, since it was clear that they would not immediately (or ever) return to Spain. They shared hardships endured by their Soviet peers, including evacuation, hunger, and German occupation. Many were transplanted from luxurious children's "palaces" to cold and shabby barracks. But even after 1941, Spanish refugee children enjoyed privileged treatment, receiving significantly higher bread rations than Soviet children.[95]

*   *   *

Forces within Spain began to lobby for the repatriation of Spanish refugee children before the Civil War even ended. While Franco's emissaries insisted on the repatriation of Spanish refugee children in the name of parental and national rights, exiled Republicans were equally opposed to the children's return to a nationalist Spain. To complicate matters, many of the children's parents were missing, imprisoned, dead, or themselves in exile, courtesy of Franco.

Jean Herbette, the French ambassador to Spain, was among the most ardent advocates of repatriation. Herbette, who served as Ambassador to Spain between 1931 and 1937, was a complex figure. While he supported Spain's Republican, left-wing government in the early 1930s, he was ultimately recalled by the Popular Front for his manifest sympathies for Franco. He was particularly concerned about the contagion of Basque nationalism on French soil. "As the department knows, last week two British torpedo boats transported 450 children from Bilbao to Saint-Jean-de-Luz . . . It has come to my attention that the people who are accompanying these children unloaded a voluminous shipment of propaganda literature, a large part of which was printed in Basque, onto our soil at the same time. One must fear that this abuse of our hospitality will encourage Basque nationalism in our own country, to the detriment of our national unity," he wrote in a 1937 missive to the Quai d'Orsay. Herbette warned of the thin line between humanitarian aid and political agitation, insisting, "Every colony of Spanish children risks becoming a source of foreign propaganda and political agitation on our territory."[96]

His fears were well justified. The presence of Spanish refugee children in France became a focal point of ongoing domestic and international conflicts throughout the 1930s and 1940s. On March 20, 1937, a group of right-wing French women wrote to the editors of the Basque nationalist newspaper *Diario Vasco* to "express, in the name of all French women, our energetic opposition to the loathsome sequestration of children by the Spanish Reds, who have torn these children from their mothers and shipped them to Russia."[97] Proponents of repatriation were supported by the Vatican and by a right-wing international press campaign that claimed that exiled children had been kidnapped, denationalized, and de-Christianized by Communist militants. France's relatively conservative diplomatic corps, meanwhile, locked horns with the Ministry of the Interior, which remained firmly in the hands of Socialist ministers throughout the Spanish Civil War. Some 10,000 Spanish children were directly in the hands of the CGT-controlled CAEE, which obstructed all attempts to repatriate them. The CAEE, in turn, received aid from a network of Socialist and Communist prefects in southern France, who hindered repatriation efforts.[98] The Spanish Civil War, and increasingly a civil war between the French Right and Left, was fought in microcosm over exiled Spanish children. As disputes over the children's education and repatriation transcended national frontiers, refugee children became a vehicle through which the Spanish Civil War escalated into a conflict that engaged much of Europe.

Bilbao, the capital of the autonomous Basque region established by the Spanish Republic in 1931, fell to Franco's forces on June 18, 1936. Two months later, Franco launched a crusade to repatriate all Basque children abroad. Monsignor Hildebrand Antoniutti, deployed by the Vatican to lobby French authorities for repatriation, assisted Franco's forces. In a meeting with French diplomats in August, Antoniutti insisted that a large number of the children had been trafficked to France and were being detained against their parents' will. He reported "mothers coming to say that they have had no news from their children and that they don't even know where they are." It was not a question of politics, Antoniutti insisted, but rather "of humanity" to return these children to their parents "without further delay." Herbette agreed, "A return to the family is normal, while the separation of families is an aberration from the most legitimate of traditions."[99]

But in spite of these appeals to "humanity" and to family unity, conflicts over repatriation often pitted family members against one another. In another memo to the Minister of Foreign Affairs dated June 25, 1937, Herbette noted that many children themselves refused repatriation, but dismissed this fact. "The refusal of the children should not supersede the formal desire expressed by their fathers or mothers to see them return to the midst of the family. Nor should we take account of disagreements between the parents, unless we possess authentic proof that the father is opposed to the children's return ... Keeping Spanish children in France against their families' will can only be interpreted as an effort to convert them to ideas that are incompatible with those they will encounter in their familial milieu," he claimed.[100]

Some adolescent girls in exile, in particular, grew accustomed to the independence they enjoyed in France. They chafed against their relatives' insistence that they return to the patriarchal strictures of family life. In November 1937, Victor Echave from Bilbao demanded the repatriation of his nieces, orphans residing in the French department of the Ain. The girls, aged 18 and 15, stubbornly refused, informing the prefect that they "will never agree to the demands of their relative, an uncle by marriage, whose authority over them they do not recognize." The two young women were both employed, financially independent, and had an older sister in France. But the age of majority in France was 21.[101] Cecilia Vera Gandul, age 18, also resisted her family's calls to duty. Cecilia lived with her uncle in France and worked as a seamstress. In a letter in December 1938, her sister in Spain exhorted her to return home, writing, "Cecilia ... You must understand how much we need your help. If all of us acted like you did, leaving and abandoning our mother, what would she have done? If you think that you are going to earn your living by knitting you have lost your mind." Cecilia also refused to heed the call of familial duty.[102]

Women and children were ultimately more vulnerable to forcible repatriation due to their legal status as dependents. Under the Vichy regime, French police sought more effective means of removing unwanted refugees from French soil. Increasingly, they deported women and children whose husbands or fathers resided in Spain. Mercédès Ferrer, age 13, lived with her mother in France in 1942 when French police officials in Gers tried to deport both mother and child on the grounds that "the head of the family is in Spain." Even when the women concerned were employed, French authorities insisted that they risked becoming a burden to the state when separated from their husbands or fathers. The humanitarian trope of "family reunification" thereby became a means of reinforcing the patriarchal authority of husbands and fathers over their "dependent" wives and children, and of protecting the French state from financial obligations toward foreign women and children.[103]

In both Spain and France, the right-wing press supported the repatriation campaign, alleging that refugee children in France were being denationalized and neglected. In 1940, following the repatriation of more than 6,000 Spanish children from France to Spain, L'Ideal in Granada claimed that many returning children "don't know how to speak Spanish and almost none of them know their parents." The children arrived from France "in deplorable conditions . . . clothed in rags, infected with parasites, malnourished," the paper reported. The French consul in Malaga refuted these claims, attesting, "I have received several visits from parents accompanied by their recently repatriated children . . . These children have not only testified to their gratitude and regret that they were obliged to leave our territory, but have also complained of the miserable regime that they have encountered on Spanish territory." Many Spanish parents, he added, lamented having "given in to their feelings of affection, which had the consequence of putting their children in deplorable material conditions that are very inferior to those which they experienced in France."[104]

But records show that some Spanish parents were indeed frustrated in their efforts to reclaim their children. In September 1938, Angela Fernandez requested the department of the Isère to repatriate her 15-year-old daughter Josefa. Josefa had complained to her mother that she was obliged to do excessive farm labor and was receiving unwanted sexual attention from her foster brother. French consular officials quickly wrote to the Minister of Foreign Affairs in Paris requesting that the girl be repatriated, but noted with dismay that out of 55 requests for the repatriation of Spanish children from the department, only one had actually been satisfied.[105]

In another case in January 1938, Vinancio Pinedo-Saez addressed a heartfelt letter to the Prefect of Tarn requesting the repatriation of his children Jose Luis and Angel. "The children are my only reason for living in this world . . . I have no doubt that you . . . will do everything possible so that someday soon I will be able to embrace these beings who I love so much."[106] His pleas received little sympathy from the CAEE. Roux Zola replied, "Don't think that your letter scares us, because we will assume the necessary responsibilities toward your children as long as necessary, and our consciences are at ease."[107] It was not until February 20, 1939 that the Ministry of Interior finally ordered the Prefect of Bouches-du-Rhône to expedite the repatriation of Pinedo-Saez's children—a week before the French government officially recognized Franco's government.[108]

Thanks largely to the obstruction of the Ministry of the Interior and local Socialist prefects, only 95 Basque children were repatriated in 1937 and only 43 returned to Spain in 1938.[109] But in April 1939, after the Republican defeat, Henri-Philippe Pétain, the future head of state of France's collaborationist Vichy regime, was named French ambassador to Franco's Spain. And after the French defeat in the Second World War, the Vichy regime's Interior Minister Marcel Peyrouton agreed to Spanish demands to conduct a census of all Spanish orphans on French soil and to repatriate them "in the interest of France" and in recognition of Spain's "rights" to its children.[110]

Repatriations accelerated dramatically after 1939. The number of civilian refugees in France had dropped to 86,776 (including approximately 52,272 children) by April 1940. Over half of the unaccompanied Basque children returned home. But the Franco regime remained dissatisfied.[111] Many exiled children did not return home willingly. In 1938, Franco's government formed an Extraordinary Delegation for the Repatriation of Minors. Beginning in 1941, this body fell under the jurisdiction of the Servicio Exterior de Falange, the Spanish Secret Service.[112] After France's defeat by the Nazis, the Servicio Exterior enjoyed free reign in all of France. When legal means failed, the Service did not hesitate "to resort to extraordinary measures through which, in one way or another, we almost always succeeded in capturing the minor."[113]

The Service developed creative tactics to reclaim Spanish children from France. In 1942, an organization called Social Services for Foreign Workers distributed coupons for clothing, toys, and food in order to gain access to the homes of exiled Spaniards—and then to seize Spanish children and repatriate them by force. When French foster families refused to relinquish their wards, Spanish agents dug up compromising information about their political backgrounds and then blackmailed them, threatening to report them to the police if they did not turn over the children. Other children were simply snatched off the street.[114] "It was a true hunt for red children. The only thing missing were shotguns and pellets," recalled Eduard Pons Prades, who had been evacuated to France with his brothers and mother.[115] Out of some 17,849 children exiled in France, 12,831 were repatriated by 1949, according to the statistics of the Servicio Exterior. By comparison, only 34 out of 5,291 children had returned from Russia.[116]

Once repatriated, refugee children were supposed to be reunited with their families, but this often proved impossible. Many evacuees had forgotten their names, or learned that their parents in Spain were now dead, imprisoned, or missing. A law passed in 1941 stipulated that children whose parents were missing were to be assigned new names. Their official documents and identity papers were altered to prevent their relatives from tracing them. The children were then placed in orphanages or in the homes of families friendly to the Franco regime for "reeducation."[117]

Maria and Florencia Calvo were among the Spanish children forcibly repatriated by the Servicio Exterior. Maria had been adopted by an American Quaker couple in France, while Florencia had been living with a French family. "The family treated me very well, looked after me wonderfully. A moment arrived when it was necessary to hide me ... They changed my clothes every day so that no one would recognize me. Every day we went to school via a different route." But eventually Franco's agents captured both girls and repatriated them by force to Spain, where they were placed in orphanages. Their mother had died when the girls were young, and their father was missing. Maria's last name was changed to Exposita in accordance with the 1941 law. A Spanish couple adopted her and pretended that she was their biological daughter. The sisters were first reunited twenty years later.[118]

Franco's supporters, however, did not monopolize the concern over denationalized Spanish children. Spanish Republicans also aspired to nurture Spanish loyalties in their wards so that these children would one day return to lead a victorious Republic. An initial agreement between the Spanish (Republican) Ministry of Education and the CAEE/CGT specified that Spanish refugee children would be placed with workers' families in France. The CAEE preferred family placement because it was the least expensive way to care for the evacuated children. But four months later, the Spanish Republican government demanded that refugee children be placed in collective colonies, where Spanish teachers would provide their instruction. In August 1937, the Spanish Republican government of Valencia issued a decree placing all children's colonies abroad under the authority of the Republican Ministry of Education. "The government has the firm desire that the children evacuated abroad . . . receive as much as possible an education from Spanish teachers," so that they would "conserve the values of the culture of their country, in particular the use of their language," the decree stipulated.[119]

Children hosted by the CAEE in France typically attended French public schools. But other French colonies, especially those for Basque children, were animated by an explicitly nationalist pedagogy. The largest colony for Basque children was La Citadelle at St.-Jean-Pied-de-Port, directed by Vicente Amezaga. At its peak, 800 people lived in the colony's cramped quarters. In spite of rustic conditions (the residents had to eat in shifts because there was not enough silverware) one former resident recalled a familial and fiercely nationalist environment: "We had a full program for our religious, cultural, and educational formation, in a totally Basque atmosphere. All our teachers were more than mere educators; they were like fathers and mothers to all of us."[120]

The conflicts that surrounded the young refugees of the Spanish Civil War prefigured the diplomatic wrangling around children during and after World War II. The international humanitarian workers, child welfare experts, and diplomats who took up the cause of refugee families during and after the Second World War would draw heavily on their experiences and perceptions of the war in Spain. Many organizations that mobilized on behalf of children during the Spanish Civil War, including the American Friends Service Committee and the Unitarian Service Committee, shifted their resources, infrastructure, and expertise seamlessly from the children of Spain to the children displaced by the Nazi occupation of Europe.

Even as the plight of Spanish refugee children was intensely politicized, nonetheless, contemporary observers did not typically understand children's suffering in psychological terms. Humanitarian workers in interwar Europe, as during the First World War, concentrated on providing for the material needs of refugee children. And yet humanitarian activists during the Spanish Civil War simultaneously set the stage for a shift toward a more psychological approach to relief. Like the League of Nations' Commission to "reclaim" Armenian children, these activists were deeply concerned about the threatened national and religious loyalties of displaced children. Increasingly, moreover, they represented the denationalization of children not only as a threat to the future of the Spanish nation, but also as a menace to children's individual welfare.

Alfred Brauner, a French literary scholar and humanitarian worker, was one of the first experts to promote nationalism as a form of psychological rehabilitation for refugees. As a doctoral student, he worked with children in refugee camps in Spain during the Civil War. He documented intense national and Republican loyalties among children in these camps. Brauner praised this nationalism as a productive coping mechanism: "In spite of the privation and the bombardments, they possessed a healthy nationalism that could aid our pedagogical work," he reported.[121] Brauner ultimately became a prominent child welfare expert in France, where he continued to write about children's emotional responses to war. During and after the Second World War, other humanitarian activists would follow his lead. Preserving children's health and their national loyalties in exile remained a priority in Europe's displaced person's camps and orphanages after World War II. But as the "lost child" became the face of victimhood during World War II, a larger community of experts began to reimagine relief in more explicitly psychological terms. The Unitarian Service Committee's colony in St. Goin was only one of hundreds of children's castles, colonies, and homes that sprouted up across Europe after World War II, all devoted to assuaging the psychic as well as the physical scars of war.

This shift toward guarding children's national loyalties and psychological health would have profound and ambiguous consequences during and after World War II. On the surface, humanitarianism seemed to become more ambitious through the psychological turn, more attentive to the needs of the "whole child." But when humanitarian workers began to worry about the psychological dangers of alienating Spanish children from their culture, they simultaneously took a more conservative approach to relief. As postwar humanitarian workers began to define their mission in both psychological and nationalist terms, insisting that children's well-being could only be served in their families and nations of origin, they suggested that the "trauma" of crossing frontiers of kinship, class, nation, or culture was so great that children were better off consigned to the milieu into which they were born. Such claims had long been made by nationalist politicians and movements, who feared the dangerous malleability of children's loyalties. But now humanitarian workers justified nationalist claims on children in a language of individual psychological well-being. If the worst threat to a child was familial separation or a confused national identity, "rescuing" children from poverty, abuse, war, or political persecution had become a risky venture indeed.

Saving the Children

Early in the morning on March 12, 1938, the German Wehrmacht marched into Austria. While the Spanish Republic went down in flames, the twenty-year-old Austrian Republic was wiped off the map of Europe without a single shot being fired. As Nazi tanks rolled into Austria, they were showered with flowers and cheered on by jubilant crowds of Austrians waving swastika flags. Seven-year-old Ruth Kluger lay in bed with strep throat when the revelry reached Vienna. "Below the window men were yelling in chorus . . . During the next days the first German uniforms appeared on the street. These soldiers spoke German, but with a funny, harsh accent, not like us, and initially I believed they didn't belong here as much as I did."[1]

Over the next several years Ruth would be painfully disabused of this notion. She was in first grade in 1938. Shortly after the Anschluss, the school principal came to her class and demonstrated how to use the Hitler salute, informing the children that the salute was not to be used by Jewish children. "Because the principal was friendly and the teacher visibly embarrassed, I was unsure at first—such is the touching optimism of the young—whether our special status was a privilege or an insult."[2]

Exclusion soon took more hurtful forms. Ruth was expelled from her school and sent to a new school for Jewish children. Her father, a doctor, was arrested by the Nazis. He was eventually released, but he quickly fled to Italy and then France, leaving Ruth and her mother behind in Vienna. Ruth and her mother were forced to leave their sunny apartment for a crowded, dark tenement that they shared with several Jewish families. They lived in a single room infested with bedbugs. As Jewish adults were deprived of their jobs, their property, and their civil rights, Jewish children lost their friends to emigration. They were barred from schools, universities, youth groups, playgrounds, swimming pools, ice cream parlors, and movie theaters. Vienna became "a city that hated children," Kluger recalled, "Jewish children, to be precise."[3]

Jewish emigration from Nazi Germany and Austria intensified in the aftermath of the Kristallnacht pogroms on November 11, 1938. The unabashed violence of Kristallnacht forced many Jews to abandon any illusion that they could outlive the Nazi regime in peace. But the financial and bureaucratic obstacles to emigration were immense by 1938. And few countries were willing to accept Jewish refugees, thanks to widespread anti-Semitism that had been exacerbated by the Great Depression.[4]

A growing number of German-Jewish parents made the excruciating decision to send their children abroad on their own. Refugee children did not threaten to compete with adults on the labor market, and they were therefore more readily accepted by potential host countries. After Kristallnacht, several emigration schemes emerged—called Kindertransports—to usher Jewish children to safety in England, Palestine, and the United States without their parents.

Some parents could not tolerate the pain of separation. One day a man at the Jewish Community Center suggested that Ruth's mother sign her up for a Kindertransport. "It was a last chance he said, just in the nick of time. Very advisable. My heart pounded, for I would dearly have loved to leave Vienna, even if it meant betraying my mother. But she didn't ask me and didn't even look at me as she answered in an even voice: 'No. A child and its mother belong together.' On the way home I fought down my disappointment without mentioning it . . . I never forgot that brief glimpse of another life which would have made me a different person."[5] But most parents seized the opportunity to save their children if they could. By the beginning of the Second World War, a full 82 percent of children under 15 had left the Third Reich. Still, some 25,000 children and youth under the age of 25 were trapped in Germany in July 1941.[6] Hundreds of thousands more remained in Austria and occupied Western and Eastern Europe. Ruth Kluger recalled that "there came a point where nothing could be done." She was deported with her mother to the ghetto-concentration camp of Theresienstadt/Terezín in September 1942, on one of the last transports out of Vienna.[7]

*   *   *

Ruth's story reflects the particular experiences of a Jewish child growing up under Nazi rule. As Hitler's armies engulfed Europe, an ever greater number of young Jews discovered that they lived in cities that "hated children." At the same time, parents, educators, and humanitarian organizations mobilized to extract children from Hitler's grasp, with or without their parents. Along with armies, tanks, soldiers, and supplies, the onset of the Second World War set an unprecedented number of children into flight. As Europeans and Americans attempted to rescue children from persecution and violence, they simultaneously confronted fundamental questions about child development. They engaged in fierce debates about the value of collective and familial education, and about the best methods to heal children from wartime suffering.

For Jewish children, the psychological upheaval of displacement began before they left home. As the Nazi regime inflicted greater hardships on German Jews, many children overheard their fathers and mothers arguing over whether, where, and how to escape. "Our bags were always packed, we were always on the brink of moving to another country, and we were never comfortably settled, not even for the near future," Ruth recalled.[8] Most Jewish children fled Germany with their parents, often in a string of successive displacements as the Nazi empire expanded. But tens of thousands of children boarded trains and ocean-liners on their own, traveling to new families and new lives in Palestine, Britain, and the United States.[9] They were met in distant ports by foster parents and social workers, who had their own ideas about how best to help refugee children cope with persecution and separation from their parents.

The vast majority of Jewish children in Nazi-occupied Europe did not make it onto a Kindertransport, however. Most Jewish children from Eastern Europe (with the exception of 669 children from Czechoslovakia) never even had the opportunity to escape.[10] But even under the most extreme conditions of Nazi occupation, Jewish educators in ghettos and concentration camps organized on behalf of children and youth. Ruth herself landed in the Theresienstadt/ Terezín camp-ghetto, the site of one of the most ambitious child-welfare programs behind ghetto walls. Educators in Terezín could not whisk Jewish children to safety outside the Nazi empire, nor could they save them from deportation to the death camps. But they did their best in extreme conditions to safeguard children from physical and material deprivation, as well as from the perceived moral degradation of camp life.

Many non-Jewish children were also uprooted by the Second World War. Across Europe, hundreds of thousands of children were evacuated from cities threatened by German and Allied bombs to the more sheltered countryside. These children were not typically threatened by racial persecution. But the British evacuations, in particular, became a key moment in the development of theories of child psychology and child welfare in Britain and America, shaping plans for the rehabilitation of Europe's families after World War II.

Not surprisingly, in the radically different contexts of civilian evacuations, the Kindertransports, and the Terezín ghetto, child-savers came to very different conclusions about how best to protect children in wartime. These differences reflected the structural limitations imposed by the war, immigration laws, finances, and Nazi policies. But they also reflected distinctive local traditions of child welfare and diverging visions for the postwar future. The competing philosophies of rescue that emerged during World War II set the stage for debates about how best to rehabilitate displaced families after the war ended.

One of the most forceful debates raged over the issue of whether displaced children needed a familial context, or whether some kind of collective solution might better meet the children's emotional needs. In both the British evacuations and the American Kindertransports, social workers typically derived proof of psychoanalytic principles and of the importance of family solidarity through their encounters with refugee children. In the Terezín ghetto, by contrast, Zionist and Socialist pedagogical activists became equally convinced of their collectivist methods and ideals. Their pedagogical program was intended to save Jewish youth from the perceived threat of "moral corruption" in the Darwinian environment of the ghetto, and to prepare for the postwar regeneration of the Jewish community.

In spite of substantial differences, however, all of Europe's wartime child-rescue schemes were animated by a common educational principle. Even as American and British social workers claimed to uphold "individualist" principles of child welfare, refugee children in New York and internees in Terezín alike encountered a strongly nationalist pedagogy. In the United States and Britain, social workers were determined to transform young refugees into assimilated immigrants, model members of the American and British national communities. In Terezín, by contrast, pedagogues were more intent on forging a self-consciously Jewish nation. But in both cases, child-savers linked national integration not only to the survival and rebirth of the Jewish community, but to children's mental health under conditions of extreme insecurity.

*　　*　　*

In Britain, operation "Pied Piper" began at the dawn of the German invasion of Poland. Between September 1 and 3, 1939, 47 percent of all English schoolchildren set out for the countryside carrying backpacks and gas masks. Upon arrival, evacuees were typically gathered in a central location such as the town square, where prospective host parents were invited to select their wards. In Bedford-Midland, one schoolteacher reported that "the scene which ensued was more akin to a cattle—or slave-market than anything else. The prospective foster-mothers . . . just invaded us and walked about the field picking out what they considered to be the most presentable specimens . . . those that felt that they were going to get left behind dissolved into tears."[11]

The evacuations became an important symbol of the trauma of the civilian experience in wartime Britain. Massive civilian evacuations took place in Great Britain, France, Nazi Germany, the Soviet Union, and elsewhere in Europe during the Second World War, but left the deepest imprint in the U.K. In France, the Soviet Union, and in Germany itself, the experience of German occupation (or defeat), military casualties, hunger, and deportations overshadowed evacuation as the defining wartime cataclysms. In a comparison of the evacuations in Britain and France, Laura Lee Downs locates diverging perceptions of the evacuations in distinctive cultures of family and childrearing. In France in the early twentieth century, children of the popular classes often left home at a young age while their mothers worked outside the home. By the 1930s, hundreds of thousands of French working-class children spent summers away from home in France's widespread network of *colonies de vacances* (summer camps). The experience was not considered traumatic. To the contrary, a consensus emerged that an extended stint away from home was essential to becoming a well-socialized citizen of the Republic. Although massive numbers of French children were evacuated from Paris during the Second World War, the experience barely left a trace on public memories of the war.[12]

A different ideal of family and childhood dominated in Britain, at least for working-class children. Married women who worked outside the home were exceptional in interwar Britain. Rather than targeting children directly with social assistance programs, the British state tended to see the family as a cohesive unit, and sought to reinforce family solidarity. British liberals feared that direct assistance to children—in the form of a hot lunch at school, for example, would encourage fathers to neglect their paternal obligations. Britain's upperclass boys may have left home at a young age for boarding schools, but within a culture that generally anchored working-class children in the home, evacuation was experienced as a major rupture for both children and their parents.[13]

When London's children entered the homes of their rural hosts, two Britains collided: The Britain of the urban poor, still in the throes of Depressionera misery, and that of the more well-off rural gentry, who typically hosted evacuated children (since these families were most likely to have spare rooms).

Middle-class citizens were shocked by the alleged ill manners and "savage" behavior of the young refugees, widely seen as bed-wetters with "dirty habits and lousy heads." The myth of British wartime solidarity seemed to evaporate the first time a "dirty evacuee" soiled the sheets or failed to display middle-class table manners.[14]

British responses to the evacuations thus reflected the very specific cultural, gender, and class norms of the United Kingdom in the 1940s. But the community of prominent psychoanalysts and child-welfare experts who wrote about evacuated children in the 1940s obscured the culturally specific sources of this evacuation shock. Anna Freud was particularly instrumental in transforming the evacuations from a singular British experience to a universal lesson in human development. Between 1941 and 1945, Freud and her longtime collaborator Dorothy Burlingham ran three residential homes for evacuated children, sponsored by the American Foster Parents' Plan for War Children.

Like her father, Anna Freud exploded sentimental myths of childhood innocence. To the extent that Europeans had worried about the impact of war on children during World War I and the Spanish Civil War, they had focused mostly on the threat to children's health and welfare. Freud, by contrast, worried about the psychological consequences of war. And rather than seeing war as a corrupting or brutalizing influence, she insisted that war actually fed children's natural appetite for violence. "It is a common misunderstanding of the child's nature which leads people to suppose that children will be saddened by the sight of destruction and aggression," Freud and Burlingham explained. "If we observe young children at play, we notice that they will destroy their toys, pull off the arms and legs of their dolls and or soldiers, puncture their balls, smash whatever is breakable, and will mind the result only because complete destruction of the toy blocks further play."[15]

The real menace to children was therefore not bombing, the black market, or milk shortages, but the loss of emotional security within the family. "The war acquires comparatively little significance for children so long as it only threatens their lives, disturbs their material comfort, or cuts their food rations ... It becomes enormously significant the moment it breaks up family life and uproots the first emotional attachments of the child within the family group. London children, therefore, were on the whole much less upset by bombing than by evacuation to the country as a protection against it," Freud concluded.[16]

The evacuation of children, envisioned as a humanitarian solution to the plight of children during wartime, was recast by Freud and her followers as a humanitarian crisis in its own right. Her theories relied on the assumption that mothers and fathers had distinctive roles to play within the family. There was no risk of trauma when Daddy left home to fight in the war, Freud claimed, as children took their fathers' absences in stride. "The children were always more or less used to their coming and going and not dependent on them for their primitive gratifications. Consequently, parting from them is no real shock," she reasoned. The separation of children from their mothers, by contrast, risked adding "thousands of artificial war orphans ... to the smaller number of children who are really orphaned by the war."[17]

John Bowlby, a fellow analyst, was also instrumental in disseminating theories of maternal attachment. In 1940, Bowlby warned that the evacuation of small children posed grave risks to children, and by extension, to all of Britain. "The prolonged separation of small children from their homes is one of the outstanding causes of the development of a criminal character," he insisted, raising the specter of the "chronic and persistent delinquent.... In a large number of these cases the child's bad character can be traced unequivocally to prolonged separation from his mother (or mother substitute) in early childhood."[18]

Bowlby's ideas garnered international recognition through his work with the United Nations. In a 1950 report for the United Nation's World Health Organization (WHO), entitled *Maternal Care and Mental Health,* he linked "maternal deprivation" in early childhood to a host of psychic maladies, ranging from delinquency and depression to retardation. In extreme cases, maternal deprivation transformed children into "affectionless characters" doomed to a lifetime of crippled emotional relationships.[19] Perversely, Bowlby insisted that his theories should relieve pressure on imperfect mothers, since what he required of moms was simply their near-constant presence. Bowlby famously maintained that removing a neglected child from a "bad" mother was typically misguided. "It must never be forgotten that even the bad parent who neglects her child is none the less providing much for him ... It is against this background that the reason why children thrive better in bad homes than in good institutions can be understood."[20] Bowlby's ideas, particularly the concepts of "separation anxiety" and "maternal deprivation," quickly became mainstream in postwar Britain and the United States. *Maternal Care and Mental Health* was abridged and published for the general public by Penguin in 1953. It sold more than 400,000 copies in English and was subsequently translated into fourteen other languages.[21]

In fact, there was no consensus in Europe, or even within Britain, that wartime separations would produce a generation of "affectionless characters" and criminals. British day-care centers closed shop after the war more because of the government's economic policies than because of Bowlby's childcare prescriptions.[22] Many British schoolteachers welcomed the evacuations as a chance to expand children's horizons beyond the confines of their urban neighborhoods. Teachers in Cambridge boasted that "pampered and nervous kiddies have gained in assurance, have learned to think and act for themselves, and in every way have become free to develop their own individuality."[23] Children's own memories reflected their mixed reactions to the experience. Some suffered bouts of homesickness, social exclusion and even neglect or abuse. But others recalled the evacuations as a gateway to social mobility, and valued the lifelong bonds they formed with their host families.[24]

Psychoanalysts nonetheless successfully defined the legacy of the evacuations in postwar Britain and America, in part because their international networks and professional status guaranteed them a wide audience and institutional support. "Evidence of the adverse effects of separation from their families on children of all ages was provided on a tragic scale during the Second World War," Bowlby maintained in his WHO report.[25] Psychologist Susan Isaacs concluded that the evacuations demonstrated the admirable tenacity of family solidarity among Britain's urban poor. "Among the simple and the poor, where there is no wealth, no pride of status or of possessions, love for the members of one's own family and joy in their bodily presence alone make life worth living. So deeply rooted is this need that it has defied even the law of self-preservation, as well as urgent public appeals and the wishes of authority."[26] In her view, family unity was a force of nature with which policymakers were ill advised to tamper.

*   *   *

British evacuees were among the first children to flee from the Nazis without parents in tow, but nowhere near the last. As racial persecution intensified in the Third Reich, humanitarian agencies mobilized to remove Jewish children from Hitler's grasp. Approximately 18,000 Jewish children and youth left Nazi Germany on their own before the onset of the war in 1939. The Youth-Aliyah brought some 12,000 children from Hitler's empire to safety in Palestine, including 3,200 unaccompanied children from Germany. The Kindertransports famously ushered close to 10,000 Jewish children from Central Europe (Germany, Austria, and Czechoslovakia) to the United Kingdom in 1938 and 1939.[27] Only a tiny minority of Jewish refugee children landed in the United States before 1945. While American agencies also mobilized on behalf of Jewish refugees, they were stymied by nativism and isolationism at home.

The German-Jewish Children's Aid (GJCA), founded in 1934 (renamed the European-Jewish Children's Aid (EJCA) in 1942), was the most ambitious

American rescue effort. In January 1941, the GJCA was integrated into the National Refugee Service and began to cooperate with the United States Committee for the Care of European Children. The U.S. Committee, an umbrella agency that sponsored refugee children, was founded in 1940 under the sponsorship of Eleanor Roosevelt. After the war, Jewish refugee children continued to arrive in the United States under the auspices of EJCA and the U.S. Committee.[28]

Children were chosen for British and American rescue schemes in Germany by social workers with the Reich Agency for Jews in Germany *(Reichsvertretung der Juden in Deutschland)*, the central governing body of the Jewish community in Germany. In Vienna children were selected by the child emigration office of the Jewish Community of Vienna *(Israelitische Kultusgemeinde Wien)*. In Germany, Norbert Wollheim recalled, "We had to deal with thousands and thousands of applications. We were not even able to read all the letters we received, from all over the country." The window of opportunity was brief. Conditions for Jewish children in Nazi Germany declined progressively in the 1930s. But many families did not consider sending their children abroad until after the shocking brutality of the November 1938 Kristallnacht pogroms. The Kindertransports ended only ten months later, with the onset of the war. In June 1939, two months before the doors to emigration closed, 8,000 children in Vienna were still waiting for a spot in a Kindertransport.[29]

Children chosen for the Kindertransports tended to attribute their escape to luck or fate, but other forces were often at play. Until March 1939, the workers of the IKG in Vienna tended to privilege children seen to be *most* at risk. These included teenage boys in danger of arrest, orphaned children, and children whose parents had been deported. This policy reflected the fact that until March 1939, refugee children destined for Britain traveled on the corporate affidavit of the Refugee Children's Movement, which meant that they did not have to have individual foster homes lined up in advance. After March 1939, however, children traveled on individual affidavits. Every child was required to have a foster parent willing to sponsor him or her. The selection process therefore became more sensitive to the preferences of host families. And British foster parents, for the most part, were not interested in hosting teenage boys, special-needs children, or social cases. After 1939, children were largely chosen based on their perceived adoptability.[30]

Pressure to select attractive and "assimilable" children came in part from humanitarian workers in the United Kingdom and the United States. In 1936, Lotte Marcuse, placement director of the German Jewish Children's

Aid, wrote a memo to the Reichsvertretung in Germany requesting fewer children over the age of 14. She warned parents in Germany that "false information with respect to psychic or physical special needs or existing behavior problems can result in the return of the children."[31] In Nazi-occupied France in 1942, a Quaker official compared the selection process to interviews for a prestigious academic fellowship; he observed, "like a Rhodes Scholarship examination, the interview often terrifies applicants." Selecting children for emigration required making choices between the children who were the most needy and those who would make the best impression, he maintained, since "children in better situations are often more brilliant and of better social and moral worth." The Quakers were optimistic, however, that "after morons, diseased, and amoral children have been sifted out, there is sure to remain an embarrassment of riches."[32]

Representatives of the Jewish community in Germany and Austria were thinking strategically. By selecting attractive ambassadors of European Jewry, they hoped to ease the way for more Jewish children and adults to escape in their footsteps. Refugee children were inculcated with a heavy responsibility to "make oneself loved" abroad. The *Judisches Nachtrichtenblatt* of May 9, 1939 lamented, "So many of the children serve as advertisements for those remaining behind, through their charm and attractiveness. But unfortunately not all display the flawless manners required for winning friends for Jewish children in England. It would therefore have been good if each child . . . had been told by their parents how enormously important it is to make oneself loved through flawless conduct, for the resulting good opinions . . . would serve . . . many thousands left behind, longing for the chance to go abroad."[33]

The first German refugee children arrived in New York in November of 1934. Between 1934 and 1945, a total of 1,035 children were sponsored by the GJCA and the U.S. Committee. After the Second World War the EJCA continued to sponsor Jewish orphans who survived the war. In 1949, the EJCA reported that it had sponsored 1,971 young refugees since 1946.[34] Humanitarian agencies in the United States could sponsor children from Europe on a corporate affidavit, which replaced the individual affidavit typically required from a relative or employer in the United States. The affidavit guaranteed that the refugees would not become a public charge, that they would attend school to age 16, and would not work for pay (a stipulation demanded by labor unions).

During the first wave of transports, there were wretched scenes at the train stations, until Nazi authorities banned parents from accompanying their children to the platform. The day her son departed, Hertha Nathorff, a physician in Berlin, wrote in her diary, "My child is gone! . . . The children feel so very important . . . whereas our hearts are breaking."[35] Like Ruth Kluger, many Jewish youth were eager to leave Germany, which sometimes caused tensions between children and their parents.[36] Other parents felt compelled to justify their decision to separate from their children. In a letter to his child's foster parents, Joseph Julius confessed, "The sunshine is leaving my life along with this boy . . . On that note I want to simply say that only the most extreme economic distress forces me to act in his interests . . . He is traveling happily, because he is not yet aware of the weight of this journey."[37]

Of course, not all young refugees left their parents willingly. Some experienced the separation—and their parents' subsequent disappearance—as a rejection. Vera Schaufeld was nine years old when she left Prague on a Kindertransport. She received her last letter from her parents in November of 1940. After that, "I imagined that my parents must have forgotten me or that I must have done something really terrible to deserve to be in England. . . . I used to go through all the things that I'd ever done wrong as a child, and said that it was because I'd done these things that I didn't deserve to be with my parents," she recalled.[38]

American authorities feared that the arrival of refugee children from Europe would provoke an anti-Semitic backlash. The children therefore traveled to the United States under a veil of secrecy.[39] The number of children saved was meager by any standard. In 1939, as the Nazi menace spread beyond German borders, a mere 32 children arrived in the United States under GJCA auspices. Many quotas went unfilled.[40] In that year, Senator Robert F. Wagner of New York and Representative Edith N. Rogers of Massachusetts introduced a bill to Congress that would have provided an additional 20,000 nonquota visas to Jewish children under the age of 14. In hearings on the bill in April 1939, American nativists depicted Jewish refugee children as future Communists and anarchists who threatened American values. They also alleged that children immigrating to the United States without their mothers would become sociopaths due to a lack of maternal care. Anti-immigration activist Alice Waters testified:

> Let us not be maudlin in our sympathies, as charity begins at home. . . . No society, no state, can successfully assume the tremendous responsibility of fostering thousands of motherless, embittered, persecuted children of undesirable foreigners and expect to convert these embattled souls into loyal, loving

American citizens. . . . If these so-called innocent, helpless children are admitted as refugees into America, I am sure they will become the leaders of revolt and deprive my children of their right to worship God, of free speech, and of life, liberty and the pursuit of happiness.[41]

A full two-thirds of American citizens agreed with Waters, according to a 1939 Gallup Poll, enough to ensure that the bill did not even reach the House floor for debate.[42] Ironically, even as Waters depicted motherless children as a threat to American society, American and British immigration policies forced refugee children to separate from their parents. Had the United States or Britain opened their gates to adult refugees, children would certainly have emigrated with their mothers and fathers.

Only a trickle of children found shelter in the United States, but they left a rich paper trail. The GJCA and local social work agencies assiduously tracked the progress of Jewish refugee children in the United States. Drawing largely on psychoanalytic theories, American social workers typically interpreted children's reactions to displacement and persecution in psychological terms. They looked within the child's individual psyche and family of origins, promoting self-reliance and "independence" as core American values and the mark of successful psychological "adjustment" to American life.

*   *   *

In the mid-1930s, many young refugees still imagined their stay in the United States as an interlude. "They held the conviction, prevalent in Germany at the time, that Hitler's reign of terror would soon be over, and that they would return to the Fatherland," recalled Elsa Castendyck of the U.S. Children's Bureau in 1943.[43] But during and after the Second World War, refugees increasingly came to the United States with the intention to stay. Throughout its existence, GJCA social workers felt that their mission was to transform refugee children into integrated Jewish-Americans. "We are glad to have children come in as our guests, but they are expected to make this their home and therefore they have to be brought up like American children," maintained Lotte Marcuse in a 1941 memo to colleagues in Europe.[44] Marcuse, the GJCA/EJCA's Director of Placement, was herself a recent transplant from Germany. But her approach to child welfare reflected the broader assumptions underpinning American social work at mid-century more than her German training, particularly the influence of psychoanalysis.

why psychoanalysis became popular

Several factors explain the ascendency of psychoanalysis in mid-twentieth-century America. The First World War had stimulated the appropriation of psychology for military and political ends in both Europe and the United States. As early as the 1920s, American social workers began to embrace psychoanalytic theories. Between the two World Wars, social workers began to organize as a profession, divorcing themselves from their philanthropic origins. Psychoanalysis was attractive at this moment because it offered a set of scientific methods and theories that justified social workers' claims to possess professional, scientific expertise. The mental hygiene movement was also taking off in the United States, thanks to the institutional support of the U.S. Children's Bureau, interwar veterans' bureaus and child guidance clinics, and foundations such as the Commonwealth Fund Program for the Prevention of Delinquency and the Laura Spelman Rockefeller Memorial Parent Education Program.

World War II was an even greater boon for the development of psychiatry and psychoanalysis in the United States. When Pearl Harbor was bombed, the U.S. Army employed only 35 psychiatrists. By 1945, over a thousand psychiatrists had been trained by the army and most of these psychiatrists were enthusiastic advocates of psychoanalytic theories and methods. After the war, America's expanding research universities provided further institutional support for the development of the psychological profession.

Underpinning these developments was a cultural and intellectual climate favorable to psychoanalysis. After the Second World War, in particular, American child psychologists widely embraced Anna Freud's ego psychology. With its emphasis on the importance of the individual in managing destructive impulses and drives, her theories aligned well with Cold War individualism and conservatism. Psychoanalysis also met an American demand for more scientific, rational, and "modern" approaches to social work, criminology, and child-rearing. Psychoanalytic child-rearing techniques were especially popular, and widely disseminated to American parents through publications like *Parent Magazine* and Dr. Benjamin Spock's *Baby and Child Care*.[45]

Psychoanalysis was also cost effective. The rise of psychiatry and psychoanalytic social work coincided with a general movement away from social and economic reform among social workers. Even as psychoanalysts sought the source of personality disorders in the environment, they defined that environment narrowly. It was not the environment of the city, the workplace, the street, or the market that mattered, but the emotional environment within the family. American social workers increasingly located the source of social ills in the individual's relationships with his or her parents in childhood. And they encouraged troubled individuals to "adjust" to social reality, rather than working to transform that reality.[46]

"Dependence" on welfare support had long been a concern of philanthropic and religious charities. But within a psychoanalytic framework, dependence was no longer understood as evidence of moral weakness. It was instead recast as an expression of unfulfilled childhood needs. In 1940, Gordon Hamilton, whose 1938 *Theory and Practice of Social Casework* became the standard text for psychiatric social workers in the United States, lamented the reluctance of some social workers "to see poverty as anything except a purely economic event, without acknowledging the possible existence of childhood dependency wishes which, if they do not actually cause, may prolong dependency."[47]

American social workers rigorously applied psychoanalytic theories in their work with European refugees, emphasizing individual and family responsibility, and attributing "adjustment problems" to early childhood relationships in the family. They also strongly favored the placement of refugee children in foster homes rather than orphanages or boarding schools. Out of the 870 unaccompanied children sponsored by the United States Commission for the Care of European Children in 1941, 801 were placed in foster homes and only 69 in group care.[48] Social workers in the United States linked foster care and family placement not only to children's psychological "best interests" but to what they represented as distinctly American values of individualism, self-reliance, and family solidarity.[49]

In fact, even when refugee children arrived in the United States with their families intact, many refugee parents actually sought to place their offspring in collective homes while they got on their feet. This was a common and widely accepted strategy in Europe, where "orphanages" often sheltered children whose parents were struggling with unemployment, illness, or homelessness.[50] American social workers denounced this practice as a vestige of the old world. Marcuse explained: "Our philosophy and our principles make us expect refugee families to struggle through their adjustment as a family unit, even though that may be hard."[51] Social workers construed this policy as a lesson in the American values of "individual responsibility" and "self-sufficiency." "The emphasis on the importance of the individual rather than the state and the individual's responsibility as a member of a democratic country should be emphasized," advised one pamphlet for refugees immigrating to the United States.[52]

Beneath a stark rhetorical opposition between American individualism and European collectivism, however, American social workers were actually deeply concerned about the integration of refugees into a particular vision of the American national community. Concern about the assimilation of immigrants was nothing new in the United States, but since the 1920s American social workers had increasingly participated in the project of "Americanization."[53] Here too, within the framework of psychoanalysis, social workers blamed the failure of immigrants to adapt to American norms on a deficit of individual will and early childhood experiences. GJCA workers specifically touted family placement as the quickest way to integrate refugees into Jewish-American society. Lotte Marcuse explained in a 1941 memo: "Our immigration law does not permit us to bring in large groups of children and care for them in camps ... We are convinced that placements in the homes of stable and understanding families provides the best substitution for a child's own home ... Children go to the same kind of schools as American children. They go to the public libraries, Community Centers, and have every opportunity to identify themselves with their new country which is theirs to stay."[54]

In letters to their parents in Europe, refugee children often bragged about their quick adjustment in America—if only to relieve them of worry. After his first month in the United States, Hans Jürgenson wrote to his father, "You asked, when do you get the first English letter—now you have it! I like the school very much, and the teachers and boys are very nice to me; my English will be better every day."[55] But GJCA social workers reported widespread resistance to their "American" values and "individualist" methods. Deborah Portnoy, a field representative with EJCA, reported after the war that local agencies were deeply concerned "about the inability of these young people to mix readily in the American community." Refugee youth, she lamented, "associate mostly with other European immigrants ... There is an unwholesome quality in their association with each other."[56] When children failed to assimilate American customs or values quickly enough, social workers typically blamed psychological "resistance." "There have been a few children who showed a definite resistance to learning English. This seems to have occurred in cases where there were certain psychological and emotional problems in relation to the separation from the parents," explained a 1938 report.[57]

The children, not surprisingly, craved the company of other refugee children, who provided a familiar community and a source of support. But social workers saw these bonds as pathological. In 1948, Portnoy complained, "The case worker tries to individualize but the European adolescents react as a group. They still retain their 'herd' psychology."[58] Her frustration conveys an anti-Semitic stereotype about Jewish "clannishness," as well as her assimilationist vision. These concerns did not change significantly between the 1930s, when Jewish refugees first began to arrive in the United States, and the 1950s, when many of the new arrivals were Holocaust survivors.

The EJCA attempted to combat this "herd" mentality by placing refugee children in families (rather than institutions) outside of New York. Marcuse explained, "We do not place the children in groups because we pledged to the United States Government that we would NOT have these children singled out from the life of the American community, and institutional placement . . . means a singling out of children from the life of the general community."[59] These policies were deeply unpopular among refugee youth. In spite of concerted efforts to disperse refugees across the American heartland, by 1941 17 percent of GJCA clients remained in New York City, not least because of the children's own resistance to leaving the city.[60]

The familialist policies of the GJCA also faltered in practice. Initially, the agency often placed refugee children with relatives in the United States in the name of family unity. But it turned out that blood was not thicker than water. Relatives often took in refugees out of a sense of guilt or obligation toward distant kin. Sometimes they made it clear that the burden was too onerous. Jack Feller in Lakewood, Ohio thus responded negatively when the International Refugee Organization asked him to adopt his orphaned great nephew and niece, Holocaust survivors, after the war. Feller replied bluntly that he was "in no position to assume any more responsibilities, moral, physical, or financial" for his destitute relatives. "I don't know whether you are aware of the present economic conditions in this country, how much it would cost to clothe, house, and feed all these people and pay for medical care," he replied, complaining that "a lot of European people believe we Americans are all rich."[61]

Dora (Doris) Cybulski, age 16, was unhappily reunited with her uncle and aunt in Utica, New York after her parents were killed by the Nazis. "Everything was all right for about a year, but after that my aunt, Mrs. Cybulski, started quarrels; these always ended with her saying 'I had to go to work when I was a child, and what's wrong with her that she has to go to school?' or 'Is she going to be a doctor, the Miss from Paris?' . . . As much as I'd like to finish school, I started to look for a job, just to make everything quiet at home. Unluckily it seemed that everything was against me . . . the people prefer to give the job to American kids, and most of the time they require a high school diploma. I would appreciate very much if you could help me in any way," she appealed to her social worker.[62]

The EJCA itself gradually concluded that Jewish children housed with their relatives fared poorly compared to those placed in collective homes or with foster parents. "We know from all of these experiences that the mere fact of relationship alone does not insure a happy placement," conceded an American

social worker in 1943. By 1948, EJCA reported that up to one-half of placements with relatives in the United States typically failed, and increasingly
resorted to placing refugee youth in boarding homes. In a study of foster placements in Detroit, social workers found that two-thirds of placements with
relatives failed, compared to half of placements with nonrelatives.[63] Gertrude
Dubinsky in Philadelphia noted several cases of youth who were unhappy in
foster homes but thrived in collective settings. Ruth Wellhoefer, for example,
reportedly floundered in her cousin's home, thanks to her "unusual arrogance,
stubbornness and great readiness to condemn everybody and everything about
her without any consideration." She fared better in a children's home. "I believe we could have done a much better job if we had conceived it as a boarding home job from the beginning," Dubinsky conceded.[64]

Foster parents and young refugees often clashed around issues of money and
entitlement. "In return for their generosity, foster parents naturally expected
some degree of emotional response from the child—affection, gratitude, love.
When in certain instances it was not forthcoming, the foster parents felt
cheated," noted Elsa Castendyck of the U.S. Children's Bureau.[65] Rosalie
Blau's foster mother was so frustrated by the child's alleged "ingratitude" that
she "periodically brought her to an institution for a talking to and to show her
how much better off she is than the children there."[66]

The problem of children's entitlement was considered serious enough to endanger the entire rescue scheme. Castendyck speculated that rumors of American riches were the greatest obstacle to the rescue program: "America, they
thought, was a land of luxury. They would live with rich relatives or other
wealthy people. The children came during the Depression. The reputed 'rich
relatives' more frequently turned out to be modest shopkeepers who could
give them few luxuries . . . Small wonder then, if dissatisfactions and malad-
justments were frequent."[67]

And yet many of these conflicts were based on misunderstandings. Early
arrivals, in particular, often hoped to be placed with wealthy foster parents
who would provide affidavits for their relatives or send money to their parents
and siblings back in Europe.[68] And foster parents' own motives were sometimes
questionable. In one town, a rumor circulated that GJCA was looking for families in need of servant girls. Word spread that by taking in a refugee child, "Not
only would one be doing a good deed but solving his servant problem."[69]

In a similar vein, social workers and foster parents were often at odds with
young refugees over plans for education and employment. These conflicts reflected different expectations about education and class among middle-class

Jews in Europe and the United States. In both the United States and England, refugees who aspired to higher education were discouraged, particularly girls.[70] In Germany and Austria, however, middle-class status had long been linked to higher education. More Jewish women also attended universities in Germany than in the United States. Middle-class Jewish youth from Europe expected to pursue the same professional track that would have awaited them at home.

Representatives of the GJCA sought to lower these expectations, warning parents in Germany that a "college education cannot be guaranteed for every child."[71] A training guide for social workers lectured, "The fact that all honest work is respected in America and there is no stigma attached to either manual labor, farm work, or domestic service should be emphasized at every opportunity." Social workers claimed that they were doing a disservice to refugees if they catered to their career ambitions. "If we assume that the man is physically able to work and is not 'mentally ill' . . . but the newcomer refuses it—and yet we continue assistance—we are supporting him in an 'unreal' situation—and continuing a pattern of dependency," argued Beatrice Behrman, a social worker affiliated with the United Service for New Americans in Baltimore.

Having been deprived of the opportunity to attend school during the war, many refugee youth were hungry for education and eager to make up for lost time. Tusia Kaufer in Philadelphia was reportedly "most determined in her desire for an education, and when the agency was not immediately ready to help her in her planning, she herself went to Temple University and registered there for extension courses in chemistry." Her social worker was "much concerned about this young woman's independence." The agency pressured her to abandon her studies in chemistry to become a secretary. Tusia finally relented and began secretarial school in March 1948. The worker concluded that the girl's rehabilitation had been successful: her initial refusal to become a secretary reflected her "fears of abandonment" by the agency and her unconscious wish to remain a "dependent child."[72]

There were a few success stories. Marion Eijger was considered a model of resourcefulness. She had "not had supervision for some time," Lotte Marcuse reported proudly. "She is surprisingly Americanized in so short a time, and as she herself says, she has been able to accept American cultural patterns."[73] But such success stories often only encouraged American social workers to look within the child when adjustment proved more challenging. In this view, all refugees suffered terribly during the war. But some proved resilient, while others failed to recover. Within a psychoanalytic framework, the "failures" could be blamed upon "unsatisfactory inter-family relationships . . . in the children's own homes" rather than experiences of persecution.[74]

In one revealing case, Marcel Kovarsky, Executive Director of the Jewish Child Welfare Association in St. Louis, reported his frustrating experiences with Anna, a 17-year-old Czech-Jewish Auschwitz survivor. "Her adjustment, compared with other children who had experienced similar deprivations, was notably poor," he reported. Anna's inability to adapt, Kovarsky maintained, was the product of her pampered early childhood:

> As a child Anna was indulged by her parents, who, according to her own account, granted her every whim . . . She always had a special interest in food and after her liberation ate so heavily that her weight rose to 160 pounds. We were inclined to accept this as the normal reaction to a concentration camp until we observed her gleeful expression as she described the wonderful fruits and vegetables that she ate right off the farm as a child . . . In essence she is an emotionally immature and intellectually inadequate girl who continues to look for someone who will treat her like a young child as her parents did. The resemblance is much closer to the maladjusted youngster whom agencies see in their daily practice than it is to our mental picture of the strong, self-reliant survivor of Nazi barbarism.[75]

Anna, in short, was more a victim of bad parenting than of Auschwitz.

The Kindertransport and American emigration schemes ultimately reflected both the fulfillment of humanitarian ideals and their limitations. American efforts to rescue Jews from Nazi Europe were stymied from the outset by Nazi regulations as well as a nativist Congress and American public. But other limitations were internal to the logic of mid-century humanitarianism and social work itself. Refugee children were inculcated with the importance of adopting "American" values, which meant gratitude, hard work without complaint, "self-help," and "independence." But even as social workers defined these qualities as distinctly "American," they blamed children's failure to assimilate them on individual pathologies and family dynamics, rather than on cultural difference, social conditions, or experiences of persecution.

The entire rescue scheme was moreover premised on a profound hierarchy between adults and children. Children were generally seen as both more innocent and more assimilable than their parents, and therefore more attractive immigrants. Whereas the specter of supposedly inassimilable Jewish "aliens" flooding the American and British labor markets provoked nativism, anti-Semitism, and the closing of borders, the admission of children without their parents was more palatable. American social workers claimed to uphold the value of family solidarity. But in the final analysis, nativism trumped psycho-analytic theory. American immigration policies themselves encouraged parents and children to separate. Efforts to transport unaccompanied children to safety reflected the notion that children, as society's most "innocent" and vulnerable population (as well as the most malleable), should be first in line for protection. But it also represented a concession to the anti-Semitic and anti-immigration sentiments of the day, and profound suspicion of the children's grown-up parents, who were consigned to their fate in Europe.[76]

*   *   *

The vast majority of Europe's Jewish children did not escape to London, New York, or St. Louis. Helga Pollak was one of the children who never made it onto a Kindertransport. Helga was born in Vienna in 1930, where her father ran a well-known coffee and concert house on the Mariahilferstrasse. Her parents divorced when she was young, and when the Nazis annexed Austria in 1938, her mother fled to the United Kingdom. Soon afterward Helga was sent to the safety of family in her father's hometown of Kyjov in Southern Moravia. Her father, a decorated and disabled World War I veteran, remained in Vienna until the summer of 1941, when he joined the rest of his family in Kyjov. In January of 1943, the entire family was deported to the ghetto/concentration camp of Terezín/Theresienstadt in Bohemia.

When Helga and her father arrived in Terezín, she was separated from him and assigned a place in room 28 of Girl's Home L410. Her first night she wrote in her diary, "The girls here haven't made a good impression. When I came in, they told the house-mother that she should make sure I am not allowed to move in . . . It all depresses me."[77] Helga, along with Ruth Kluger, were among approximately 12,000 children who passed through the Terezín camp between 1942 and 1945.

Terezín was the site of one of the most ambitious child-welfare schemes behind ghetto walls in Nazi-occupied Europe. While they could not prevent their children's deportation to the East, the Jewish community in the ghetto mobilized to improve children's welfare even under the most catastrophic conditions. These educators grappled with many of the questions faced by social workers in the United States and Britain. In their diaries, letters, meetings, and pedagogical tracts, they passionately debated how best to protect children from the upheavals of racial persecution, war, and displacement, and how to prepare them for an imagined future after the war. The answers that emerged from Terezín were quite different than those proposed by American social workers. But they would also endure well beyond 1945, shaping the convictions of those who mobilized to rehabilitate the few children who survived.

Reinhard Heydrich, head of the Nazi Sicherheitsdienst (SD) Security Service, established the Terezín ghetto-camp was shortly after his appointment as Reichsprotektor of Bohemia and Moravia in 1941. Under Heydrich's direction, the persecution of Jews in the Bohemian Lands intensified. Terezín, created in a garrison town north of Prague, had qualities of both a ghetto—a quarter of a city where the Nazis attempted to enclose Jews before deporting them—and a concentration camp. It was initially intended to be a transit camp for Jews and political prisoners on their way to the death camps in the East. The first Czechoslovak Jews arrived there in November 1941. Beginning in June of 1942, they were joined by Jews from Germany, Austria, Danzig, and Luxembourg. In January of 1942, transports to the East began. A total of 141,184 Jews ultimately passed through Terezín, 88,202 of whom were deported further, mostly to their deaths in Auschwitz. Another 33,456 people died of illness or starvation in the camp, 1,654 were released prior to liberation, and 16,832 were liberated in 1945.[78]

Terezín was, in Ruth Kluger's words, "a stable that supplied the slaughterhouse," but it developed a second function as an alibi for the Final Solution.[79] As elderly German and Austrian Jews and decorated World War I veterans (such as Helga's father) were forced from their homes in 1941 and 1942, some prominent Nazis intervened on their behalf. Heydrich realized that he could use Terezín to deflect internal criticism about Nazi racial policies. At the Wannsee Conference on January 20, 1942, he specified that German and Austrian Jews over the age of 65, along with decorated and disabled war veterans, would not be deported to the death camps (at least not immediately), but rather "relocated" to Terezín, where they would (supposedly) live out their retirement in peace. This "practical solution," he explained, would "eliminate the many interventions [on behalf of these Jews] with one stroke." Prominent Jews whose disappearance might generate unwanted publicity were also deported to the camp.[80]

In the spring of 1943, the propaganda stunt became more ambitious. On December 18, 1942, twelve allied governments protested the Nazi treatment of the Jews. Following the deportation of Danish Jews to Terezín, the Danish government pressured Nazi authorities to inspect conditions in the ghetto. That spring, the Nazis launched a cynical campaign to "beautify" the camp for international consumption. They painted park benches, planted flowers, and renovated barracks. Beautification culminated in the carefully staged visits of Red Cross delegates on June 23, 1944. The dignitaries were treated to a well-orchestrated program of soccer games and theatrical events, including a production of the children's opera, *Brundibar*. But while the scenery was meticulously designed, the Nazis paid little attention to the welfare of the "actors." Pajík, a 12-year-old resident of the Terezín boys home L417, noted in his diary on June 17, 1944, "There are benches everywhere, the houses are neat etc. On the other hand, when I see through the windows of the old-people's home, the people—old people, all crowded together—the correct impression of Terezín comes back to me. For the Nazis, this is a mere detail." The day of the Commission's visit the children enjoyed an extravagant lunch of tongue, mashed potatoes, onions, and cucumber salad. The leader of the Jewish Council of Elders was provided with a car, and the bakery delivery men wore white gloves.[81]

Having constructed the set, Nazi officials decided to produce a propaganda film detailing the conditions in the "spa town" of Terezín for international consumption.[82] Children were assigned special roles. Marta Fröhlich and her sister were brought to a swimming pool, dressed in swimsuits, and filmed singing songs and splashing in the water.[83] In a satirical essay in *Vedem*, the ghetto-camp's literary magazine, Herbert Fischl reported, "Orthodox Jews and rabbis were sent to the Stadtkapelle and had to jump up and down to the rhythm of a jazz band. Oh and the food! The Jews lick their chops after devouring the excellent cakes and sweet buns (naturally, only when the camera is pointing at them) and afterwards they practically pumped their stomachs out."[84]

In these conditions, Jewish leaders created children's homes. Due to near constant transports in and out of the camp, the number of youth involved fluctuated, but between 2,000 and 3,875 children at a time typically lived in Terezín, approximately half in children's homes run by the Department of Youth Welfare. In September of 1943 the Central Statistical Department of the ghetto reported that there were 2,083 children between the ages of 7 and 14 in the camp, 1,088 boys and 995 girls.[85] Children under the age of four typically remained with their parents in adult quarters. For the older children, residence in a children's home was considered a privilege. The conditions were less crowded, the food was better, and the children were somewhat insulated from the misery of camp life. Jana Renée Friesová, deported to Terezín at age 15, was assigned a place in Room 15 of the girl's home. Although she was anxious about fitting in, she recalled, "Joy conquered anxiety, for now I was where only few could be. There were thousands of girls in Terezín and just a few hundred places in the girl's home. Bunks became vacant only when their occupants received notice to join a transport to the east."[86]

The children's "homes" actually consisted of rooms, each housing up to 40 children grouped according to gender, age, and language. There were separate Czech and German homes. These rooms were plagued by constant infestations of fleas and bedbugs. Helga wrote in November 1943, "We are lying on three-tiered beds pressed against each other like herrings . . . We live and eat like monkeys on a tree or chickens in a chicken coop."[87] Residents secretly received formal schooling and cultural instruction. Many teachers in the camp were well-known artists and intellectuals, though the quality of instruction suffered from the lack of textbooks and teaching materials. Several homes published their own literary journals. Famously, the children of Terezín produced over 4,000 works of art under the instruction of Viennese artist and former Bauhaus member Friedl Dicker-Brandeis.[88]

The youth welfare program reflected a conscious decision by the Jewish administration of the ghetto to sacrifice the elderly for the sake of youth. The elderly were systematically starved in order to provide more food to the children and to privileged adult workers. The Jewish Council of Elders invested in the young because they hoped that healthy children would one day repopulate the Jewish community, and because they believed that a more productive workforce would insulate the population from further deportations. Mortality among the elderly was appalling as a result: 10,366 out of 12,701 people who died in the camp in 1943 were over the age of 65.[89] But even with additional rations, the children were often hungry. Breakfast was ersatz coffee and bread. Other meals typically consisted of a barley soup and (sometimes) potatoes, occasionally supplemented by a piece of sausage. The children's artwork reflected their obsession with food, featuring pictures of chickens, eggs, cakes, cocoa, apples, and sardines.[90]

The routine in most rooms included a collective breakfast, assembly and roll call, chores and morning exercise, schooling, and evening activities. Older children participated in these activities on top of an exhausting regimen of forced labor. Some of the rooms had their own house song, uniforms, insignia, and even a parliament. "A mixture of school and a youth movement's summer camp . . . that was the first impression that you got from the Youth Home L417," wrote Maximilien Adler on the first anniversary of the boy's home.

Youth Home L417 was founded on July 8, 1942, and the girls' home L410 was created a few months later on September 1, 1942. Other homes for small children, older youth, and apprentices quickly followed. One year after L417 opened its doors, educators in the Department of Youth Welfare published a commemorative volume reflecting on their ideals and hopes. There was little discussion of children's psychological responses to deportation in the volume. The children's teachers were deeply reflective about pedagogy and concerned about the negative effects of ghetto life, but they understood those influences primarily in hygienic, moral, and cultural terms, and not in terms of individual psychology or family dynamics.

The pedagogy of the Terezín children's homes was self-consciously collectivist. Almost all members of the Department of Youth Welfare were committed Zionists or Socialists. They adapted the educational methods of interwar Zionist and Socialist youth movements to camp conditions, creating a kind of ghetto scout movement. Interwar Zionist movements in Czechoslovakia had been strongly oriented toward the cultivation of a self-consciously Jewish national community, but not toward emigration to Palestine.[91] Many educators involved in Terezín's Department of Youth Welfare had come of age in these interwar youth movements, either as participants or youth leaders. Gonda Redlich, the head of the Department of Youth Welfare, Franta (Francis Meier), the charismatic *madrich* (guide) of room 7, and their colleague Fredy Hirsch had all been active in the Maccabi Hatzair Zionist youth movement in interwar Czechoslovakia, attended their summer camps, and were committed leftwing Zionists before the war. Redlich had taught Jewish history, coached soccer, and led a group of boy scouts at a Jewish school in Prague. Rosa Engländer, who led the girls' home, was a Communist who had studied psychology and intended to devote her life to youth education.[92]

These educators generally promoted progressive pedagogical methods. They emphasized self-government, the development of children's agency, creativity and freedom. Maximilien Adler wrote that L417 had become, by necessity, a model for the progressive schools of the future—in part because teachers lacked books, teaching materials, and desks. "In more peaceful times one would consider such a youth home impossible. And still. In this war the children are being inspired in a home without drills and lessons in the traditional style. The new methods of education of children through work and self-affirmation represent the core of the school of the future."[93]

In the Warsaw ghetto in Poland, similar ideals animated the pedagogical activism of Janusz Korczak, whose home for Jewish orphans had already been a laboratory of progressive pedagogy before the war. After Korczak's Orphan's Home was relocated within ghetto walls in 1940, he continued to promote child-centered pedagogy, self-government, and art education while waging a losing battle against starvation and disease. The Central Organization for Orphan Care (CENTOS), founded in 1924, was the main child welfare organization in the Warsaw ghetto, and provided assistance to 45,000 children in July of 1942, including 4,000 orphans in 30 homes. But in contrast to Terezín, there was no unified pedagogical program in the Warsaw ghetto. Material conditions varied dramatically from institution to institution. Korczak denounced the Central Shelter Home, which housed one-third of the orphans in the Warsaw ghetto, as "a macabre building of tortures," "a murder shop," and "a slaughterhouse for children." He briefly served as director of the Central Shelter Home in February 1942 and attempted to improve conditions there. But child welfare efforts in the Warsaw ghetto were circumscribed by the harsher material conditions (with a higher mortality rate for children in particular) in Warsaw.[94]

In the context of ghetto life an emphasis on cultivating children's individuality could only go so far, in any event. By necessity and conviction, educators in Terezín also stressed the importance of collective discipline, cleanliness (a matter of preventing outbreaks of typhus and other diseases), order, and self-sacrifice. They embraced progressive pedagogical methods at the same time that they rejected the individualist ethic often associated with these methods. This was not unusual in Central Europe. Interwar socialist, Zionist, and nationalist movements in the Bohemian Lands had married progressive pedagogical methods to collectivist politics. But it seemed even more urgent in the context of ghetto life, where the struggle for survival seemed to encourage an "every man for himself" attitude. Rosa Engländer denounced ghetto society as a Hobbesian world "filled with corruption, boundless drive for self-preservation, uninhibited egoism, hunger for power."[95]

The youth activists in the Department of Youth Welfare hoped to save ghetto children from this corrosive egoism. Franta, the leader of Room 7 in L417 (for Czech-speaking adolescents), even suggested that the camp experience had some unexpected educational benefits. "Watching the boys, we realize that . . . certain changes for the better also resulted from Terezín." In Terezín the children learned to put the collectivity first. "Today, 40 boys are forged into one unit, against which all else pales . . . A group came together, differing in age and social strata: sports-minded children and children of solely intellectual inclinations, strong and weak, from cities and farms—a colorful mixture."[96] Franta was not alone in his convictions. Dr. G. Bäuml maintained that "the group, the social organism, is the foundation of all of our educational efforts . . . Only within the collective can a child or a young person be educated for the community. And many, who came here as asocials, are learning to fit in without even being aware of it."[97] In short, educators

envisioned the boys' home as a means for encouraging cross-class Jewish nationalist solidarity.

But what *kind* of community did educators aim to construct? Even as Terezín's educators agreed on the need for collective education, they remained divided about the nature of the desired collectivity, and by extension, about the
future of the Jewish community. Dr. Franz Kahn posed the question directly.
Education, as he understood it, served to prepare a society for the future. But
what kind of future did they imagine for the youth of Terezín? "The Terezín
ghetto society can only be provisory, a passageway. But a passageway—to where?
Who dares to finally answer this question?"

Although signs were clear by 1944 that deportation meant death, few were
inclined to confront the possibility that Terezín's children had no future at all.
Rather, they focused on preparing for the postwar regeneration of the Jewish
community. The central question was the extent to which education in the
ghetto should be self-consciously Zionist. For Kahn, Redlich and many other
educators in Terezín, the answer to the question "where to?" was unambigu-
ous. The only way forward was "education for collective responsibility and
Judaism. They are one and the same."[98] Israel Kestenbaum agreed that "for us
nationally-conscious Jews, education can only be Jewish," while Leo Janowitz
maintained that youth in the camp should be encouraged to embrace their
"belonging to the Jewish fate."[99]

But some educators, parents, and youth objected to the heavy handedness
of the Zionist approach. Gideon Klein, the Czech-Jewish musician and com-
poser, reported sharp conflicts over the content of "political education" in the
camp. The relationship between parents and the Department of Youth Welfare, Klein reported, was often "more than unfriendly." While the educators
were mostly Zionists and Socialists, the majority of the interned families
were assimilated Jews from middle-class backgrounds. "These circumstances
led to misunderstandings, which often developed into bitter conflicts of an
ideological nature." Most residents of L417 were Czech-speaking boys from
the Protectorate, and a good 50 percent had been raised in secular or non-
Jewish milieus before the war. These boys reacted negatively to the sudden
shift to a Jewish education.[100] Tensions between Zionists and assimilationists
were ongoing. In October 1942, the Department attempted to introduce morning prayers for the small children. The issue was deeply contentious. "Many
indifferent or assimilationist counselors are opposed to Hebrew education,"
Redlich noted in his diary. During an inspection of a children's home, Redlich
once overheard a child refer to "Zionist pigs."[101]

In the summer of 1943, Valtr Eisinger, the leader of the room for Czech boys aged 12 through 15, reached an agreement with Redlich to establish "the principle of non-political education." According to Klein, however, "This agreement was actually put into practice only on the surface. In the realm of L417 different groups of youth developed, each of which had its own character, including a political character." The boys in room 1 established self-government, began to publish the literary magazine *Vedem,* and anointed themselves the Republic of Shkid, after Makarenko's post-Revolutionary home for orphans in Russia. "The Jewish problem is considered from a social perspective. This political education is founded on a much wider ideological basis and does not necessarily lead to assimilation, but rather can give Jewish consciousness a modern and truly progressive form," Klein explained.[102] But in June 1943, after reading an issue of *Vedem,* Redlich lamented in his diary, "The literary value is really very great. But anyone who looks for a jot of Jewish spirit in the paper will look in vain."[103]

To read the words of the children themselves, the homes in Terezín succeeded in cultivating collective loyalties, and in creating an island of precarious stability. In the first issue of *Bonaco,* the girl's literary magazine, editor Jarka affirmed, "Although we are in Terezín, we are not losing our optimism and we still have zest for life and for work . . . We want to convince ourselves that we are the equals of those who have not had the pleasure of becoming residents of a ghetto."[104] Pepík Stiassný affirmed that in spite of terrible deprivation, the children maintained a positive attitude. "The collective mantra of the children of Terezín is 'no matter what, we are still alive.'" Sojka reflected that ghetto life had even improved her character. "When I arrived, I was an inexpressive, shapeless substance," she recalled. "I learned to be independent and patient here, not to throw up my hands at the first sign of trouble."[105]

In some respects, Ruth Kluger believed that she was happier in Terezín than in Vienna, thanks to the company of other children. "In a way, I loved Theresienstadt, for the nineteen or twenty months which I spent there made me into a social animal . . . Most of what I know about living with others I learned from the young Socialists and Zionists who took care of the children in Theresienstadt." This determination to view Terezín as a positive pedagogical experience did not render the children immune to suffering, however. In spite of some positive memories, Kluger did not romanticize Terezín: "It was a mudhole, a cesspool, a sty where you couldn't stretch without touching someone. An ant heap under destructive feet."[106]

The children were particularly anguished by the constant waves of deportations. Deportation to the death camps was a family affair, and the fate of women and children depended on the status of their husbands and fathers. Men who enjoyed the protection of members of the Jewish Council, or who were labeled "indispensible" workers, protected their wives and children from deportation by extension. But a woman or adolescent who did "indispensible" labor could not protect her husband, parents, children, or even herself from the extermination camps. In a 1944 lecture, Edith Ornstein, who led the department of women's labor, demanded that women in the ghetto be accorded the right "to be granted protection from transports . . . on the basis of their own efforts, a right that was self-evidently granted to men from the beginning . . . Women have now proven through their own accomplishments . . . that their labor is just as indispensible to the ghetto as that of their husbands, and that their contributions should therefore be judged just as independently."[107]

Children were just as vulnerable to the principle of family unity. In late August 1943, before a wave of deportations in early September, Ruth Gutmann from Room 28 described her devastation upon learning that her best friend would be included in the next transport. "My first thought was that I can't live without her." She watched the father of another friend cry as he helped his daughter pack. Helga Pollak wrote in her diary on September 5, 1943: "The goodbyes were very difficult, we were all very brave . . . Although I slept that night, I had terrible dreams, and when I woke up I had black circles around my eyes."[108]

Helga was deported to Auschwitz on the transport of October 23, 1944. The night before her departure, she wrote a note in the journal of her friend Flaška: "I hope that we will meet each other again in the beautiful outdoors . . . where we can breathe freely and develop our ideas and not live like we do here in prison chains."[109] Miraculously, both Helga and her father survived and were reunited in April of 1945. Eventually she rejoined her mother in England. Helga and Ruth Kluger were two of only 142 children under the age of 15 to survive deportation from Terezín.[110]

Immediately after the war, Zeev Shek reflected on the futility of the effort to save the children of Terezín. Jacob Edelstein, the first leader of the Jewish Council of Elders, had boldly shifted resources toward the young in the camp. "This was perhaps somewhat unusual and cruel towards the older inmates, but given the times it was the only just solution . . . if it was possible at all to see a joyful sight in Terezín, it was children at play, children who looked relatively healthy and apparently carefree." But while the Jewish Council could provide the children with extra rations and a feeling of community, they could not save their lives. "None of the effort . . . bore fruit. It made the children's stay in the ghetto a little easier. It could not prevent their terrible fate."[111]

The Department of Children's Welfare could not save the lives of the children of Terezín, but the ideals of Terezín's educators echoed beyond the ghetto walls and went on to shape the politics and pedagogy of relief in liberated Europe. In contrast to the American and British emphasis on family values, self-reliance, and independence, educators in the ghetto self-consciously aimed to teach their wards that they could not survive in isolation. Rather than focusing on children's individual psychological responses to persecution and displacement, they saw the ghetto environment as the source of moral corruption, and aimed to reform that environment.

These two approaches did not reflect a simple clash between Anglo-American "individualism" and continental "collectivism," however. In both New York and in Terezín, educators saw their child-saving efforts as a form of socialization for particular national and familial collectives. Their differences ultimately reflected an emerging debate about which community—American, European, or Zionist—promised a better future for Jewish youth. These debates would dominate discussions of how to reconstruct European societies and families after 1945. The nationalist approach, advocated by the Department of Youth Welfare in Terezín, was taken up with passion by many European Jews who survived the war, along with many Displaced Persons and policymakers from occupied Eastern and Western Europe. British and American humanitarian workers would meanwhile bring their psychoanalytic theories and familialist principles to Europe along with care packages and chocolate bars after 1945. The pioneering, if ultimately inadequate, efforts to save Europe's children that developed during World War II were, from the beginning, inseparable from the question of who would control Europe's children and future after the war ended.

A "Psychological Marshall Plan"

In 1940, Howard Kershner, Director of European Relief for the American Friends Service Committee, was stationed in Vichy France, where Quakers were organizing relief for Jewish and Spanish refugees. He had seen any number of wartime atrocities in his years of service, including violence directed at civilians, bombings, starvation, and disease. Now he added a new item to the litany of civilian suffering: "One of the greatest tragedies of all times is the separation of families in Europe today: wives in one country, husbands in another . . . babies who have never seen their fathers; scattered fragments of families not knowing if their loved ones are living or dead, and often without hope of ever seeing them again. There are multitudes of wretched souls for whom it seems the sun of hope has set."[1]

The "discovery" of familial separation as the quintessential wartime tragedy was a major legacy of the Second World War. In the years that followed the war, the conviction that the separation of parents and children represents an irreparable form of psychological upheaval attained the aura of self-evident truth. In the short term, this conviction profoundly shaped the mission of the relief workers who descended on Europe to rehabilitate war-torn families. It was not coincidental that Article 16 of the 1948 Universal Declaration of Human Rights declared, "The family is the natural and fundamental group unit of society and is entitled to protection by society and the State," while Article 12 protected families from "arbitrary interference." Based on an understanding of the Nazi regime as an assault on family unity and parental rights, postwar humanitarian workers and child welfare experts sought to reestablish the unity of broken families as much as the sovereignty of occupied nations.

The reconstruction of families after the Second World War did not simply involve a "return" to prewar normality, however. It instead stimulated the invention of new visions of healthy families and childhoods. The focus on family reconstitution after World War II was specifically buttressed by new psychological and psychoanalytic theories, particularly a view of family separation as a form of psychic trauma.

The concept of trauma had first been defined as a neurological condition in Great Britain in the 1860s and 1870s, when it was used to describe the disturbing symptoms afflicting early railroad travelers, including headaches, vertigo, sleep disorders, ill temper, paralysis, and impotence. From its origins, trauma was thus associated with displacement. Initially considered a result of injuries to the nervous system, in the 1880s continental psychiatrists, such as Jean-Martin Charcot in France and Hermann Oppenheim in Germany, developed a view of trauma as a psychological or emotional condition akin to hysteria or neurosis. During the First World War, the concept of trauma entered military, medical, and government circles, and became known to a wider public as a psychiatric condition afflicting soldiers in the trenches.[2]

The Second World War was far more deadly to civilians than the Great War, and the diagnosis of trauma spread from military hospitals to nursery schools. Drawing on Freudian theories, many psychoanalysts and social workers in Europe and America located the source of psychological disarray in the family as well as the battlefield or concentration camp. Taking this logic to the extreme, experts such as Anna Freud and John Bowlby concluded that the separation of children from their mothers was more threatening to young children than the violence of war itself.

New international humanitarian organizations were at the forefront of the postwar campaign to reconstitute shattered families. As of September 1945, the United Nations Relief and Rehabilitation Administration (UNRRA, 1943–1947) was charged with housing, feeding, clothing, and repatriating over six million DPs in Europe, including more than 20,000 unaccompanied children.[3] UNRRA workers did not simply understand their mission in terms of providing shelter and preventing starvation and disease, though these were formidable tasks. In a shift from earlier relief efforts, post-WWII humanitarian workers anointed themselves agents of psychological reconstruction. "It is time to do something beyond giving food. The girls who come here weighing 62 lbs must be fattened up, but they must also see something which is worth fattening up for," urged Austrian psychologist and émigré Ernst Papanek in 1946.[4] In June 1945, UNRRA issued a report on the "Psychological Problems of Displaced Persons," stressing the importance of psychological rehabilitation to postwar reconstruction. The report proclaimed, "The United Nations Administration is concerned not only with relief—that is with the provision of material needs—but also with rehabilitation—that is with the amelioration of psychological suffering and dislocation. For men do not live by bread alone."[5]

Refugee camps and children's homes in Europe became self-declared laboratories, where humanitarian workers debated new ideas about child development and human nature through their observation of individuals displaced by war and racial persecution. French child psychiatrist Georges Heuyer declared in 1948 that the war had "experimentally created conditions that have nourished . . . the development of a large number of intellectual and affective symptoms that we encountered only sporadically before the war."[6] In these "controlled experiments," many British and American child welfare experts sought and found confirmation of a set of universalist psychoanalytic principles.[7] But familialist and psychoanalytic visions for the reconstruction of European youth did not go not uncontested. Continental pedagogues and child-welfare experts simultaneously articulated more collectivist methods and visions for the reconstruction of Europe's lost children, through which they hoped to rehabilitate European youth in their own image.

*   *   *

The United Nations Relief and Rehabilitation Administration was established in 1943 in anticipation of the overwhelming task of reconstructing liberated Europe. The agency was called (and soon became) a "United Nations" agency, but it preceded the founding of the actual United Nations in 1945. With memories of the First World War looming large, the Allies hoped that rational planning could prevent a peace darkened by epidemics, starvation, and chaos. UNRRA specifically reflected Franklin Delano Roosevelt's goal of exporting a "New Deal for the World," as the ideals and values of New Deal Liberalism were shipped to Europe along with tins of coffee, chocolate bars, vitamins, and cigarettes. Social workers schooled in America's expanding federal welfare agencies brought a firm belief in the principles of casework to Europe, along with a penchant for acronyms. This entailed focusing on the individual needs of each refugee "client." The professionalization of relief work after World War II also demanded a distinctly apolitical ethos. UNNRA workers adhered to what humanitarian worker and writer Francesca Wilson identified as a "non-proselytizing impulse." This ethic was to distinguish UNRRA from earlier humanitarian efforts, such as the politicized relief campaigns of the First World War and the Spanish Civil War.[8]

The architects of UNRRA and its successor, the International Refugee Organization (IRO, 1947–1951), carefully studied the perceived missteps of interwar relief efforts, particularly those of Herbert Hoover's American Relief Administration, the League of Nations, and the International Red Cross. From the vantage point of 1943, the ARA in particular was blemished by its unilateral pursuit of American political interests in Central Europe.[9] The humanitarian campaigns that followed the First World War also appeared hopelessly disorganized to the efficiency-minded technocrats of the 1940s.[10] During the First World War and the Spanish Civil War, governments and a multitude of private, religious, and political organizations had competed in the field to save civilian victims of war and to secure their political loyalties. James T. Shotwell, who drafted the Charter of the United Nations, compared this disorganized approach to UNRRA's more universalist ambitions. "There was no such organization as UNRRA at the end of the First World War, for the American organizations for relief, the greatest of which was under Mr. Hoover's direction, were never officially coordinated . . . This was inevitable so long as the governments, as well as private organizations, still thought in terms of charity."[11] This time around, relief organizations would do better, Wilson insisted. "In the interim of the two wars the idea that it is better to plan beforehand than to muddle through has gained ground, and we have this time an official super-state body in charge of relief, the UNRRA. . . . This is an advance of incalculable importance on last time when no prior survey of needs was made and nation was allowed to compete with nation for food and necessities."[12] On the ground, this meant that private relief organizations were placed under UNRRA's direct supervision. With the significant exception of Jewish agencies, humanitarian organizations were not permitted to target specific religious or national groups.[13]

While UNRRA was designed as an exercise in international cooperation, its structure reflected international inequalities. Delegates of forty-four nations participated in the first meeting of the UNRRA council in Atlantic City in 1943. Each pledged to contribute one percent of their country's national income to its budget. But the majority of the funds flowed from the American and British treasuries. Altogether, UNRRA spent some four billion dollars between 1945 and 1947. The United States footed 73 percent of the bill, while the United Kingdom paid about 16 percent of UNRRA's costs.[14] UNRRA was active primarily in the American and British zones of Germany (and throughout Southeastern and Eastern Europe and Italy). Although the Soviet Union belonged to UNRRA's Central Committee, Soviet authorities barred the organization from operating in the Soviet Zone of

Germany, and the USSR did not belong to the IRO. French military authorities also assumed direct responsibility for displaced children in the French zones of occupation. UNRRA personnel were also largely Anglophone. Out of 12,889 UNRRA workers in December 1946, 37 percent were American and 34 percent were British. A full 44 percent of UNRRA's employees were women.[15]

Although women rarely rose to commanding positions in the organization, relief work did open up new opportunities for women's activism internationally. Wilson herself was convinced that women were particularly well suited to humanitarian work. "Woman's whole experience throughout the ages had made her more adaptable than men," she insisted. They were "more ready for the thousand and one interruptions, make-do-and-mends and improvisations that emergency work involves but which exasperates a capable man."[16]

Aleta Brownlee served as the director of the UNRRA child welfare team in Vienna from 1945–1951. In her 1951 unpublished memoir, she recalls the mixture of idealism and thirst for adventure that drew her to Europe. She had received her M.S.W. from the University of Chicago's Social Work school and was working as a consultant for the U.S. Children's Bureau when she received a phone call asking if she would be interested in a job overseas. Brownlee hesitated at first, as she was a committed pacifist. But UNRRA's mission spoke to her idealism. "The first great international relief organization supported by all the United Nations, engaged in constructive, or at least reconstructive work, seemed to be something new and hopeful . . . I was to find it so in spite of all the frustration and difficulty encountered in my work," she recalled.[17]

Susan Pettiss was animated by similar idealism, along with a desire to escape a troubled home life. Pettiss, a native of Alabama, also had experience working in New Deal welfare agencies. She fled to the ruins of Europe to escape the ruins of her marriage. "The dramatic events on a hot summer's night in Mobile made me realize that there was no safety or future in my marriage to an alcoholic, abusive husband," she recalled. Her first encounters at the UNRRA training school at the University of Maryland were transformative. "I suddenly found myself part of a group of interesting, exciting companions who laughed a lot, had fun as well as serious 'bull sessions' solving the problems of the world . . . I realized at College Park that I had been bored most of my life." For Pettiss, joining UNRRA represented an opportunity to restart her life under the cover of humanitarianism.[18] She was probably not alone in seeing relief work as an opportunity to escape a troubled home life. Wilson warned in 1945, "People who have made a mess of their lives in their

own country are eager to leave it ... Drug addicts, alcoholics, criminals fleeing the law, work their way into relief work. ... Many adventurous people ...
are trying to climb on the bandwagon of relief." Put in a more positive light,
relief work offered women an opportunity for travel, adventure, and professional responsibility and authority. Wilson even worried that women's unac-
customed authority in the field could go to their heads. "Obscure women in
their hometowns, they exact obedience from their subjects, once they are the
Queens of Distressed Ruritanians," she warned.[19]

At the UNRRA training school at the University of Maryland, new recruits
took courses on European history and politics as well as language classes. Their
studies were interrupted by long hikes, trips to the pub, and earnest late-night
discussions. "A pervasive idealism infected both faculty and trainees," all of
whom "hoped to see established a true world community," Pettiss recalled."[20]
"After eight weeks, we were dramatically told to get ready for the trip. Mad
dashing into Washington to Headquarters to sign all sorts of documents, check
health examinations, shots, buy last minute purchases, etc," Pettiss wrote in
her diary on March 17, 1945. Brownlee finally boarded a military ship for
Europe in August 1944 in the middle of the night, wearing a pink seersucker
suit and carrying a gas mask, a helmet, and a musette bag. "I was off on the big
adventure which proved to be more military than I expected."[21] After weeks
of travel, she landed in Vienna, where she expected to complete her mission
in six months. Instead she stayed almost five years, serving as a child welfare
consultant with both UNRRA and the IRO. Pettiss remained in Germany
for three years and eventually supervised the care of Jewish children who fled
into the American zone from Eastern Europe after World War II.

*   *   *

UNRRA workers such as Pettiss and Brownlee linked the psychological rehabilitation of individual children to a broader campaign to cultivate democratic values in postwar Europe. Their focus on reconstituting families was
buttressed by emerging theories of totalitarianism, which located the evil of
both Nazism and Communism in the destruction of the private sphere.[22] In
the aftermath of Nazi rule, American and British relief workers typically
believed that the reconstruction of democracy in Europe required the advancement of liberal individualism. This goal was based on the questionable
assumption that Nazism was hostile to all forms of individualism.[23] The Unitarian Service Committee (USC), a human rights organization affiliated with
the American Unitarian Association, even launched a Mental Health Program

in postwar Germany aimed explicitly at cultivating individualism among children. Helen Fogg, the program director, explained, "Children and young people growing to adulthood in Germany . . . are, for the most part . . . growing up in the grip of the very attitudes and patterns, the human and psychological climate, which was a factor as powerful as the economic and political factors in the rise of a totalitarian leader. This climate currently discourages faith in the individual which is the strength of self-government."[24]

But the "individualism" promoted by relief workers and occupation authorities was a vague aspiration at best. The question of where and how healthy individuals and democratic citizens should be formed remained open to debate. While some agents of reconstruction stressed free markets or civil rights, and others looked to constitutional and legal reforms, psychologists, social workers, and child welfare experts turned specifically to the family. They located the formation of healthy individuals in emotional relationships between parents and children.

The Jewish emigré community in the United States was particularly important in theorizing relationships between the family, the psyche, and totalitarianism. Beginning in the 1930s, Eric Fromm and other Frankfurt School researchers had traced the origins of fascism to the dynamics within what they called the "authoritarian family." In a 1936 essay, Fromm used psychoanalysis to explain Nazism's appeal to Germans. The structures of absolute paternal authority in German families, he argued, prepared lower middle-class and working-class children to submit to the absolute authority of Hitler and the Nazi Party.[25] But in contrast to postwar theorists, Fromm and his colleagues did not construe the family as a private sanctuary from mass politics. Instead, they saw family dynamics as the very source of political attitudes. In the wake of the Second World War, by contrast, émigré psychoanalysts generally depicted parental authority as a bulwark against totalitarianism, rather than its source. They warned against state intrusion into family life, with explicit reference to Nazism and Communism. Anna Freud, for example, opposed state intervention into the family except in cases of extreme physical abuse or neglect. Charges of emotional abuse by government social workers, argued Freud and her colleagues, could be too easily abused by a totalitarian state.[26]

A particular understanding of Nazism (and Soviet Communism) as an assault on family sovereignty was at the heart of West European reconstruction. The notion that the Nazi regime spelled the demise of the family and the private sphere had become a trope of antifascists soon after the Nazi seizure of power. In 1938, Erika Mann, Thomas Mann's daughter, published an exposé of educational methods in Nazi Germany entitled *School for Barbarians*, in which she defined the evil of Nazism in terms of an attack on the family. "The break-up of the family is no by-product of the Nazi dictatorship, but part of the job which the regime had to do if it meant to reach its aim—the conquest of the world. If the world is to go to the Nazis, the German people must first belong to them. And for that to be true, they can't belong to anyone else—neither God, nor their families, nor themselves," she wrote.[27]

The Nazi attack on family unity was personified in the figure of the child informant. Children who informed on their parents, placing the state above loved ones, dramatically represented the alleged Nazi assault on the domestic sphere and the totalitarian quality of Nazi pedagogy. The image of the child informant was even dramatized in a scene in Bertolt Brecht's *Furcht und Elend des dritten Reiches (Fear and Misery of the Third Reich)*. Set in Cologne in 1936, the scene depicts a middle-class husband and wife who worry that their little boy has gone to denounce them to the Gestapo when he goes out to buy some candy.[28] French researcher Alfred Brauner claimed in 1946 that German children "denounced, if required, their father, who remained loyal to his old political party, and their mother, who preferred to believe the priest rather than the Führer. They are the youth who blindly executed all orders, and were prepared for this voluntary submission since their earliest childhood."[29] While the number of children who actually informed on their parents was certainly small, the trope of the child informant bolstered the consensus that restoring parental rights was essential to the reestablishment of liberal democracy.

British and American humanitarian activists also drew on a deeper liberal tradition, which positioned the family, in opposition to the state, as the bedrock of civil society—a private realm in which rational male citizens should be free to exercise their authority over their female and minor dependents.[30] The reassertion of male authority on the domestic front was, in this framework, central to the rebirth of civil society in postwar Europe. If the Nazis had destroyed the sovereignty of the family, reconstructing private family life represented both denazification and democratization. The family thus came to be seen as an apolitical sanctuary that represented a post-war "return to normality."[31]

This search for "normality" was not only high on the agendas of politicians, social scientists, and humanitarian workers in liberated Europe. DPs themselves often looked to marriage, the family, and childrearing as the means to reconstruct their lives. Reporting on displaced youth at the International Children's Center in Prien, Germany, Jean Henshaw of UNNRA observed,

"In many instances the insecurity of youth and their compelling need for family and the security of human relationships finds expression in the wholesome relationships of early marriage."[32] French social worker Charlotte Helman recalled an "explosion of life" among liberated Jews in Bergen-Belsen in the summer of 1945, where "many young girls of fourteen or sixteen years became pregnant."[33] In the DP camp at Wildflecken in Germany, UNRRA worker Kathryn Hulme was exasperated by the fertility of Polish refugees. "Like our DPs, we lived on hope, but unlike them, we had something more to do than sit around and produce babies at such a fruitful pace that soon the per capita birth rate of DP-land would exceed that of any other country except perhaps China," she quipped.[34] Jewish DPs had a birthrate of 50 births per thousand people in late 1947, one of the highest in the world. Atina Grossmann argues that this Jewish baby boom represented a form of personal agency and the affirmation of life in the aftermath of the Holocaust.[35]

In an expression of their self-declared "individualist" values, United Nations' social workers pledged to uphold the "best interests of the [individual] child" as the guiding principle of child welfare. They determined these interests according to criteria including "the existence or absence of wholesome relationship between the child and its parents, foster-parents or other persons"; educational opportunities; the availability of food, clothing, and medical care; access to citizenship rights; the likelihood of discrimination; the wishes of the child, and finally, "the desires of a natural parent, foster-parent, or other near relative by consanguinity." But there were no guidelines for weighing these measures against one another if and when they conflicted. And it was clear from their magnitude that they would conflict.[36]

The "best interests" paradigm, along with the commitment to individual casework, was itself intended to repudiate Nazi racism. Focusing on the psychological, economic and social interests of individual children through casework implied the rejection of other possible criteria for making social welfare decisions, such as the interests of the nation, the ambition to mold model comrades for a socialist society, or the goal of creating a master race. It also reflected a commitment to environmental, rather than biological theories of child development. The Unitarian Service Committee explicitly promoted its "mental health approach" to social work as an antidote to Nazi eugenics. Gunnar Dybwad elaborated in a USC pamphlet, "In reading German case records . . . one invariably encounters the term *Anlage,* an inherited trait or quality. Laziness, lying, stealing, and sex misconduct are all readily explained as due to the child's *Anlage.* With such overemphasis on biological factors there is a corresponding underemphasis on emotional values and interpersonal relationships. Criminality on the part of an uncle seems to be to the German social worker of greater significance than the quality of the emotional ties between child and parents."[37]

In 1949, Dr. Clemens Benda, a German émigré and Harvard psychiatrist working with the USC, called for nothing less than a "Psychological Marshall Plan" in Germany.[38] Helen Fogg, who led the USC's Child & Youth Programs division, explained in a 1951 memo that in postwar Germany, "authoritarian attitudes and procedures . . . still dominate much of family life, education at all levels . . . social work agencies, and society as a whole, despite the frequent sincere assertions of many Germans that 'democracy' is something they want."[39] "Modern" psychotherapy promised to eradicate both the children's psychological scars and the lingering racist and anti-democratic attitudes in German society. The USC promoted these methods through a series of summer workshops for German social welfare professionals, held outside of Berlin between 1949 and 1953.

Psychoanalysis and Unitarianism may seem like strange bedfellows, but Unitarian relief workers, like UNRRA workers, explicitly stressed the universalist assumptions at the heart of psychoanalytic principles. Fogg reported that Germans who attended the USC workshops initially greeted their American colleagues with skepticism. How could rich Americans possibly understand the challenges faced by German families after the war? Soon enough, however, "Doubt and rejection lost out through discussion . . . of basic human needs and of the psychological development of personality, through which it became clear that the problems being discussed were neither exclusively German nor exclusively American problems. They . . . are rather fundamental problems all over the world."[40] UNRRA workers echoed these themes. While Nazi ideology had insisted that immutable biological differences divided races and nations, psychoanalysis stressed the universal building blocks of the human psyche. "National groups differ in the stress they lay on various strivings or failings," explained a 1945 UNRRA report. "Nevertheless, the main attributes of human personality—conscience and guilt, love and hate, rivalry and friendship, self-esteem and inferiority, are found to be surprisingly constant. Those attributes are hammered out in the experimental workshop of the family."[41]

Within this psychoanalytic framework, UNRRA and IRO social workers typically defined children's "best interests" in terms of the reunification of biological families, and especially mothers and their children. Following Anna Freud and Dorothy Burlingham, Thérèse Brosse argued in 1946 that the "trauma" of war for children was not the consequence of violence and hunger. Rather, children were traumatized by separation from their mothers. "It is not the actual events of war, such as bombardment and military operations, which have affected these children emotionally," she argued. "What does affect a child is the influence of events on emotional ties in the family . . . and above all, the sudden loss of mother."[42] UNRRA and IRO workers implemented these principles not only through their efforts to reunite families, but also by privileging foster-care or family placement over collective placement in orphanages for refugee children. Journalist Dorothy Macardle reported from liberated Europe, "Educational psychologists are very generally in accord with Dr. Anna Freud in the conclusion she has expressed repeatedly: that for little children even a mediocre family home is better than the best of communal nurseries."[43]

While many UNRRA workers jumped on the Freudian bandwagon, not everyone in postwar Europe was convinced that the psychological scars of displaced children could be healed with family values. On the ground, the familialist visions of UNRRA workers and of American and British psychoanalysts conflicted with the more collectivist ideals of continental European politicians and pedagogues. Familialist solutions posed particular problems for many Jewish children in postwar Europe who had neither families nor physical homes to which they could return. In postwar France and Poland, for example, Jewish relief organizations pioneered child welfare schemes that focused intensively on restoring the psychological health of Jewish youth after the Holocaust. But out of both necessity and conviction, these organizations tended to promote collective living as a route to individual psychological rehabilitation and to the regeneration of the decimated Jewish community.[44]

In France, the Oeuvre de Secours aux Enfants (OSE) was the largest and most important Jewish child welfare organization. Founded in 1912 in St. Petersburg to promote public health, the French branch of the OSE was established in 1933. During the Second World War, it undertook one of the most widespread underground campaigns to save Jewish refugee children in Europe by hiding them in foster homes and in Catholic institutions. After the war, animated by a devoted group of pedagogical reformers, psychologists, and former resistance activists, the OSE maintained 25 children's homes for close to 2,000 Jewish children, largely funded by the American Joint Distribution Committee (JDC). The JDC, widely known simply as "The Joint," was the major Jewish relief organization in postwar Europe. OSE educators promoted collective living as a therapeutic antidote to wartime displacement,

and attempted to restore a Jewish identity to hidden children who had survived the war in Catholic foster families and institutions.[45]

In Poland, meanwhile, the Central Committee of Jews in Poland (*Centralny
Komitet Żydow w Polsce*, CKŻP), founded in Lublin in 1944, took on the task
of providing relief to Polish-Jewish youth, including survivors of German
concentration camps, former hidden children, and some 30,000 Jewish children who had survived the war in the USSR and returned to Poland after the
Nazi defeat. Between 1944 and 1950 the Central Committee served as an
umbrella organization that represented Jewish interests to the Polish government and provided social and legal assistance to Polish Jews. The leadership
of the Committee included representatives of several Jewish political parties
and movements that had reestablished themselves after liberation, continuing prewar political traditions that had been preserved in ghettos and among
partisans. These included Communists, the Bund (secular Socialists who sought
to cultivate a self-consciously Jewish identity but did not encourage immigration to Palestine), as well as Zionist movements such as Ichud, Poale-Syon
Left, Poale-Syon Right, and Hashomer Hatzair.[46] The CKŻP's Education Department, also heavily supported by the JDC, operated 11 children's homes
for 1,224 children in July 1946, as well as 45 half-boarding homes with 4,067
residents, a psychological clinic, and a Child-Tracing branch charged with re-
claiming Jewish children from Christian families and institutions. The Central Committee's School Department operated 28 Jewish schools for 2,236
children in 1946, all but four offering instruction in Yiddish.[47]

The conflict between familialist and collectivist visions for the rehabilitation of Europe's Jewish children was most directly expressed in the work and
writings of Ernst Papanek, a prominent Austrian socialist and follower of the
Austrian psychologist Alfred Adler. Papanek directed homes for Jewish refugee children run by the OSE in France during World War II, and returned to
Europe after the war as the head of the Unitarian Service Committee's efforts on behalf of displaced children. He was born in Vienna, were he studied
philosophy, psychology, and pedagogy. During the 1930s, Papanek became
an educator with the Socialist youth movement and was an elected member
of the city council in Vienna in 1932. In February of 1934, the Social Democratic party was banned and Papanek and his family fled to Prague. He continued to write and publish on child psychology in exile, editing a pedagogical
journal for the League of Nations. In 1936, Papanek began to work with
child refugees, assisting efforts to evacuate Republican youth from Spain during the Spanish Civil War.

Soon after the Nazi annexation of Austria, Papanek and his family fled to France, where he began his work with the OSE. Together with his wife, Helene Papanek, a doctor, Papanek directed four homes for Jewish refugee children in the Montmorency region. Just before the German occupation of Paris in June 1940, his colony of refugee children fled from Montmorency to a chateau in Montintin (Haute-Vienne) in the South, and soon afterwards, the Prefect of Limoges warned Papanek of his imminent arrest. His family made a hasty escape to New York, where he obtained a Social Work degree from Columbia University. The OSE subsequently hid many of the children in Papanek's care in Catholic families, though some were caught and deported. A handful managed to escape to the United States.

Papanek was adamant in his faith in the restorative value of collective education for victims of racial persecution. While Anna Freud portrayed the separation of children from their mothers as a universal recipe for dysfunction, Papanek countered that particularly for Jewish refugees, the collective setting of a children's home offered an oasis of security. "The children described by Anna Freud had . . . never experienced dangerous situations in which they could not rely on their parents and find help and shelter with them . . . The refugee children in our homes in France . . . had left behind them families that in hours of danger had been unable to offer them any protection or security. Certainly the separation of these children from parents in such a tragic situation could not leave them with a sense of lost security . . . These children felt rather that they had now come to an environment less terrifying, more capable of managing its problems—and consequently more protecting," he insisted.[48]

Papanek was convinced that because Jewish children had been persecuted as members of a group, they required a community of peers in order to recover from their experiences. He thereby challenged the universalist underpinning of psychoanalytic theories, insisting on the distinctive needs of Jewish refugees. "Group treatment is always indicated where mass neurosis has been created by a trauma suffered by many in common with many," he maintained. "It will not be sufficient to place the refugee child in a nice, decent, family home. More than any other child, he must gain anew the feeling that he is accepted, that he is a member of a group."[49]

At a deeper level, these views reflected Papanek's training as an Adlerian psychologist, as well as the influence of the Austrian education reform movement in which he came of age. Papanek was a member of the second generation of the Austro-Marxist pedagogical reform movement, which had begun with Karl Seitz's *Freie Schule* movement in turn-of-the-century Vienna. Seitz and his followers led a tenacious struggle against clerical and Christian Social influences in the Austrian public school system. The movement continued in interwar Austria, animated by Socialist reform pedagogue Otto Glöckel. Individualist and collectivist ideals were entangled in the pedagogical and psychological theories of reformers such as Seitz and Glöckel. They aimed to equip working-class children to persevere in the class struggle and to stand up to the traditional enemies of Austrian Social Democrats, including the Catholic Church and Christian Socialists.[50]

Alfred Adler's "individual psychology" was highly influential among these reformers, particularly within the school reform movement and in new city-sponsored child guidance clinics in interwar Vienna. Adler, an Austrian psychologist, rejected the biological underpinning of Freud's theory of the self, with its insistence on biological (hence, universal) instincts and drives. Instead, he stressed the role of the environment and community in shaping human personality. In contrast to the Freudian view of society as an authority "we fear and for which we have undertaken so many repressions," Papanek explained, the Adlerian school held that "only the community can make a human being out of an organism . . . What kind of human being one becomes is not biologically predestined."[51] Adlerian psychology was highly influential among child welfare experts in both the OSE and in the Polish CKŻP, which even sponsored lectures on Adler's theories for Central Committee educators.

When Papanek fled to the United States in 1940, he discovered that his collectivist orientation clashed with the psychoanalytic approaches favored by American social workers, who flatly rejected his proposal to establish OSE-style children's homes in the United States. At a 1942 lecture at the New York School of Social Work he was savagely attacked. "I wasn't aware that the word *institution* had such an unfortunate connotation in this country. 'This is not the American way!' they shouted at me. In America, children were sent to institutions only as a punishment or because of a conspicuous inability to cope with life on the outside . . . The home is the only sacred institution in America. I should have understood that."[52]

Upon arrival in the United States, Papanek conducted research with child refugees from Europe, surveying their attitudes toward their fresh experiences of displacement and collective living. Most expressed profound sadness, homesickness, and anxiety about their families' safety. But a surprising number of Papanek's interlocutors also reported positive experiences. In response to the question "how did you feel when you left your home country?" one 16-year-old Austrian boy wrote, "I felt curious as to what the rest of the world was like. I was rather glad that we had to leave, because I thought were it not for Hitler's invasion, I would never have been able to see the world." A 15-year-old recalled, "My first taste of freedom intoxicated me." Many young refugees praised the solidarity they had experienced in children's homes. "What I like is that no differences are made . . . whether one is rich or poor, that is the same. And I love to be among other children," explained an 11-year-old Austrian girl. An 18-year-old German simply insisted, "Every child should be in an institution for some period!"[53]

Many of Papanek's informants were predisposed to a positive view of collective education by their experiences with the OSE. It is therefore worth exploring the OSE's methods in further detail. In 1946, the OSE housed approximately 1,130 Jewish children in twenty-five homes in France. Of this number 746 were boys and only 389 were girls—a reflection of the imbalanced survival rates among Jewish youth. French Jews accounted for 613 of the young survivors, while the others were Polish, Hungarian, or German citizens (though many had grown up in France as children of refugees). The OSE provided material assistance to an additional 12,000 Jewish children who lived with family members or in foster care.[54] The organization was also responsible for the rehabilitation of 430 young survivors of the Buchenwald concentration camp who were invited by the French government to convalesce in France in 1945. Elie Wiesel eventually became the most famous of the so-called "Buchenwald Boys," who were, in fact, mostly adolescents between the ages of 12 and 21.[55]

The children's homes organized by the OSE and by the Central Committee in Poland became sites of lively and reflective debate about the psychological consequences of persecution, the future of the Jewish community, and the merits of familial versus collective education. One surprising reality of postwar Europe was that many of the children in OSE care in France, as in the Central Committee's orphanages in Poland, German DP camps, and kibbutzim headed toward Palestine, had at least one surviving parent. As of September 1946, out of the 1,207 wards of OSE homes, 34 percent had two surviving parents and only 26 percent were full orphans.[56] In the general population of Jewish children in France at the time of liberation, an OSE study of 9,743 children found that 47 percent had two parents, thanks to the relatively high survival rate of naturalized French Jews.[57] Among the 866 youth living in the CKŻP's orphanages in Poland in December 1946, only 228 were full orphans, since many of these youth had survived the war in the USSR along with their parents.[58]

The leaders of the OSE and CKŻP did not generally challenge the conventional wisdom that the family represented an irreplaceable source of security, particularly for young children. Educators within the CKŻP for example, insisted that their children's homes "should resemble a familial home, the natural environment for children, as much as possible."[59] But these educators also recognized that Jews in postwar Europe faced catastrophic social conditions. Their apartments and property had been confiscated by Germans or by opportunistic neighbors.[60] Widowed men were generally considered unfit parents. And a severe housing crisis in both France and Poland made it almost impossible to find suitable lodging for a family. Madame Esther P., Polish, age 54, was a widow and the mother of four children living in Paris. Her children were hidden in the French countryside during the war. The Germans had seized her apartment and she was unable to reclaim it. "Exhausted by these experiences" she lived in a "single, unsanitary room," unable to pay her debts. She entrusted her youngest daughter to the care of the OSE. Mr. L. Bernard, aged 35, and his wife, aged 32, had two small children, aged 4 and 3, and had adopted their orphaned nephew. Mrs. Bernard returned to Paris from hiding in April 1945 to find her apartment pillaged. The family sought shelter with extended kin. Eight people were crammed into a two-room apartment, and four of them slept on the floor. The Bernards also sought to place their children in an OSE home.[61]

Returning Jews faced similar or worse conditions in Poland. Eleonora Heit wrote a letter to the CKŻP leadership begging the committee to admit her eight-year-old daughter into its children's home in Krakow. Heit was a widow who had survived Auschwitz. She had lost her entire family and all of her in-laws during the war. She returned from the camps "physically and psychologically broken," she reported, and suffered from a heart ailment. "In general I am at the end of my strength . . . I am unable to work and care for the child . . . in addition I believe that my illnesses (frequent attacks) are scaring the child and that the miserable conditions in which we live are negatively affecting the child's psyche."[62]

The creation of children's homes for Jewish children was not merely a pragmatic gesture, however. While the CKŻP represented a variety of political movements (until 1948, when Communists began to dominate the organization), its educational programs bore a strong Socialist and nationalist imprint. The committee's ideological and pedagogical goals, ratified on July 10, 1945, included the cultivation of "understanding for the universal ideals of democracy, progress, and fraternity," "devotion to the rebirth of Polish democracy," a "positive and warm attitude toward the Soviet Union," and an emphasis on the principles of "social solidarity and altruism." In addition, children were to acquire a "love for the Jewish language, literature, and history, feelings of connection with the Jewish nation around the world, and particularly with its democratic and progressive forces" in CKŻP homes.[63]

Central Committee pedagogues, like their colleagues across Europe, were severely distressed about the mental health of surviving Jews in Poland. "It is no exaggeration to say that there is not a single Jew today who survived the occupation and is now completely psychologically normal," reported the directors of the Committee's psychological clinic at the end of 1946.[64] They embraced the lesson that "happy, strong, harmonious, humans have had a happy childhood." But psychoanalytic methods barely filtered into the Committee's day-to-day practice. Rather than probing children's pre-war family dynamics to explain their postwar maladies, researchers in the CKŻP psychological clinic focused on the immediate past and future. They conducted intelligence tests, personality tests, and career-aptitude surveys, and encouraged children to write about their wartime experiences as both a therapeutic and a commemorative practice.[65]

The 1948 Yiddish film *Undzere Kinder* documented and dramatized contemporary debates within the Polish-Jewish community about how to rehabilitate Jewish children (and adults) in the aftermath of genocide. The film reflected the educational priorities and practices of the CKŻP. *Undzere Kinder* was the last Yiddish film made in Poland, but was banned by Polish authorities and never screened there. Partially documentary, it was filmed in an actual Central Committee orphanage in Helenówek, near Łódź. The film features the celebrated comedic duo Shimon Dzigan and Israel Shumacher, recently returned from the Soviet Union, where they had survived the war. In the opening scenes, the entertainers, playing themselves, perform "songs from the ghetto" in a variety show in Łódź. Their performance is rudely interrupted by whistles and catcalls from a child in the audience—a ward of the nearby orphanage. After the performance, the orphans confront the comedians backstage. They explain that their musical rendition of ghetto life is far too sentimental and romantic. In the ghetto, they object, "no one had the strength to dance."

Dzigan and Shumacher soon pay a visit to the children's home, where they encourage the children to act out their wartime experiences through song, dance, and theater. Shocked by the horror stories elicited, they wonder if they are doing more harm than good by stirring up memories of the recent past.

But the orphanage director, who has herself lost a child in the Holocaust, reassures Dzigan and Shumacher that creative expression is the best way for the children to heal from wartime trauma. "If we don't deal with these memories during the day, they will haunt the children at night," she insists. Even as *Undzere Kinder* documents the children's tragic experiences, the film ends on a hopeful note. The miraculous survivors appear healthy and happy as they play sports, feast on fruit, and sing *"mir zaynen do!"* (We are here!). The film ultimately affirms the promise of a brighter future for Poland's Jewish children, while rejecting the solution of silence about the past.

Significantly, however, the debate over collective versus familial education is not raised in *Undzere Kinder*, nor was it an extensive topic of debate among Central Committee officials. This reflected the political orientation of the CKŻP but also the social reality of Jewish children's lives in postwar Poland. In the French OSE, by contrast, educators and children engaged in a more explicit philosophical debate about the advantages and pitfalls of collective and familial life. In 1947, a young ward of the OSE outlined the stakes: "Is communal living inferior in relation to family life, or, to the contrary, does it offer certain advantages from a human, social, or psychological perspective? Can it forge human beings who in the future will be able to meet life's challenges, or should it always and everywhere cede the way to familial education?"[66]

Jacques Cohn, Director of the OSE's Pedagogy Department, believed that the tragic dissolution of Jewish families had in fact created an opportunity to craft a better future for European Jews. Collective education could serve the greater good of regenerating the Jewish community. "As a result of the material difficulties caused by the war, and of the moral disequilibrium resulting from persecution, collectivities have become more and more of a necessity . . . this situation should be exploited," he advised. But he was aware that the opportunity to educate Jewish youth in collective settings raised ethical tensions. "Do we have the right to sacrifice the individual development of a generation in the name of reforming society? . . . Only the future will tell," he speculated.[67]

The leaders of the OSE in France discovered that collective life was particularly challenging for the young survivors of Buchenwald. The Buchenwald boys were housed in Écouis, a large chateau about 70km from Paris. They violently rejected any routine that reminded them of camp life, reported Ernst Jablonski (a.k.a. Jouhy), a counselor who lived with the boys. Like Papanek, Jouhy was also a trained Adlerian psychologist from Central Europe. After moving to Paris, he studied psycho-pedagogy with the famous child psychiatrist Henri

Wallon and received a doctorate at the Sorbonne. Jablonski also had Communist sympathies. But he ultimately concluded that the Buchenwald boys were poorly served by a large institution. "The youth from the camps have only known collective living in its most abject form. . . . Much more than classes, sports, or discussions, our youth are in need of an intimate milieu such as the family."[68]

Another persistent concern of OSE educators was that children raised in institutions would grow up lacking essential skills, unprepared for the harsh realities of life in the real world. "A window is broken, a shoe needs repair, the child doesn't worry about it. Isn't everything provided for him, as they say, 'on a golden platter?'" worried Robert Job, director of the OSE Children's Department. In a family, by contrast, "Mom exposes the hardships of meeting life's expenses, Dad often returns home somber, full of worries: the child thereby participates in the situation and finds himself in direct contact with reality."[69]

In spite of these drawbacks, and perhaps for lack of alternatives, OSE leaders remained convinced that collectivities had much to offer Jewish youth. Like educators in Terezín, they believed that their children's homes could contribute to the cultivation of social responsibility. "The child raised alone in the family receives an egocentric education: he believes that everything is his due . . . But in the collectivity where the interest of the group is superior to individual interests, he acquires a social comportment and character," Job maintained. OSE educators did not hope to replace the child's parents, or even to mimic the family. Instead, they sought to capitalize on what they believed to be the distinctive benefits of collective life. "Children's homes have their own unique pedagogical advantages that no family can offer. The child is judged according to his conduct, his behavior, and also forced to constantly judge himself, his peers, to submit to discipline, to respect the work and the aspirations of his classmates," Jouhy explained.[70]

The key was to fashion the right kind of collectivity. OSE and Central Committee leaders alike drew inspiration from the pedagogical methods of the progressive reform movement of the early twentieth century. These principles, developed by pedagogical figures such as Maria Montessori, Anton Makarenko, Johann Pestalozzi, John Dewey, and Celestin Freinet, included a non-authoritarian approach to education, active, child-centered lessons, and an emphasis on cultivating each child's individual personality. OSE and CKŻP activists hoped that enlightened pedagogical methods would distinguish their children's homes from the orphanages of the past. The word "orphanage" itself, Job declared, "was prohibited . . . An orphanage is considered a work of charity; the children are dressed in the same uniform: on Sundays, at Mass, Saturdays, at the synagogue, the places of honor are reserved for them. We don't want our children to feel different from others at any cost. No orphanage complex!"[71] Jouhy was confident that "the majority of disadvantages of life in an orphanage can be avoided through the application of the methods of progressive education."[72]

Child-welfare leaders in the CKŻP also stressed the differences between their enlightened children's homes and the drab orphanages of interwar Poland. At a conference in Krakow in 1947, one educator elaborated that "before the war there existed 'institutions,' 'orphanages,' . . . and other so-called charitable institutions, where children were assembled—orphans, abandoned children, children who were raised in sad barracks, creating a group of malcontents who were unprepared for life . . . In this type of institution, citizens of the lowest social category were educated." The catastrophe of the Second World War had changed all that, brutally leveling social distinctions among Poland's Jews. "The element which we are assembling in our children's homes is not recruited only from the so-called lowest social sphere. The war spared no one. Along with the orphaned children of illiterates we have the children of doctors, professors, merchants, and artisans." The goal of CKŻP homes was therefore not to dispense charity to social outcasts, but to awaken the children's sense of self-worth and dignity, to educate "creators of a new world" who would regenerate the Polish-Jewish community.[73]

The elevated status of the orphan (and the orphanage) among postwar Jewish communities clearly reflected the specific concerns of the Jewish community in the aftermath of genocide. But it also paralleled a broader development in postwar Europe, as private charities were replaced or deputized by state welfare programs with more universalist (and often explicitly nationalist) agendas. The 1940s were the heyday of state planning and intervention in Europe's dictatorships and democracies alike. The orphanage or children's home was only one of many sites in which European policymakers and social workers sought to remold and improve populations after World War II.[74]

Thomas Buergenthal, liberated from Auschwitz at the age of 11, found himself in a Central Committee orphanage in Otwock, Poland, after the war. He recalled the home as a "halfway house between one life and another . . . It was here that I underwent a transition from a perennially frightened and hungry camp inmate, struggling to survive, to a relatively normal 11-year-old child . . . I enjoyed almost every minute of my stay." As a resident of the children's home, Buergenthal attended the local Polish school, played soccer and ping-pong, participated in a Scout troop, staged musical recitals, and worked in the garden. His only unpleasant memory was of retrieving the mail at the post office in Otwock each day. This chore entailed a hike past the local Catholic orphanage. Buergenthal was assigned this job because he could supposedly "pass" as a Pole. But the Catholic orphans quickly deduced where he came from and pelted him with stones and slurs. "Being fast on my feet, I usually managed to outrun them, although I could not escape their anti-Semitic catcalls. The worst part of my job as a mailman, though, was that there was never any mail for me."[75]

The pedagogical workers of the Oeuvre de Secours aux Enfants and CKŻP shared many of the ideals and methods of secular child welfare experts in postwar Europe. In Sèvres outside of Paris, for example, another pedagogical experiment with refugee children was under way, animated by similar principles. Yvonne and Roger Hagenauer's Maison d'Enfants, founded in 1941 and supported financially by Vichy's Secours National welfare organization, covertly sheltered more than 60 Jewish children during the war, along with other displaced and neglected children.[76] After the war the "Petite République," as the home was known, continued to shelter over a hundred orphans, refugees, and other endangered children. Like OSE and Central Committee leaders, the Hagenauers were committed to progressive pedagogy, and especially to the ideals of active learning and self-government.[77] Similar "children's republics" flourished across postwar Europe, most housing young victims of the war. These pedagogical experiments all aimed to rehabilitate children psychologically and to instill democratic values in their wards. But in contrast to the American and British humanitarian workers who arrived on the Continent with UNRRA and the IRO, their leaders did not see those goals as incompatible with collective living.

The methods of the OSE and the CKŻP reflected the particular social circumstances of postwar Jewish families in Europe, as well as long-standing pedagogical traditions. In Eastern Europe, competing nationalist, religious, and Zionist movements had begun to construct networks of institutions for collective education and child welfare in the late nineteenth century. Educators developed these institutions to both improve children's welfare and to secure their national loyalties in multilingual regions. In France, children of the popular classes had long experienced collective education in municipal nurseries and in *colonies de vacances* as well as in interwar youth movements. These camps, youth movements, and child-welfare institutions provided the infrastructure for postwar children's homes along with educators seasoned in the methods of progressive pedagogy.[78] The methods of the OSE and the CKŻP thus represented the cross-fertilization of several European traditions: the collectivist practices of Zionist movements in Eastern Europe, the Socialist and nationalist heritage in Central and Eastern Europe, the ideals of turn-of-the-century progressive pedagogy, and the legacy of republican pedagogical and social institutions in interwar and postwar France.[79]

The youth of the OSE did not leave the final word to the adults. *Lendemains,* the literary journal of the OSE, published several essays in which OSE children weighed in on the debate over collective versus family life. Those lucky enough to return to their parents were typically overjoyed. But even children happily reunited with their families often praised their experiences in OSE homes. In 1947, shortly after being reunited with her mother and father in Metz, Myra Kaplan asserted that the pedagogical theories of her educators held no weight for her. "I don't like theory. It seems to me that I have sufficient experience of familial life and collective living. I believe I know them because I have experienced them, the advantages and disadvantages of these two ways of life." Kaplan was decidedly homesick for her OSE days. "One day, I found myself in a children's home," she recalled. "In spite of the tragedy that these words represent, my first impression was one of wonder . . . in spite of the crumbling ceilings, in spite of the shortage of toilets . . . my final impression remained one of wonder." Reunited with her family, she was surprised to discover that she felt lonely. "I found myself alone, all alone. Alone on the way to school, alone in the school . . . The collectivist way, so new for me, had completely overcome me. I could proudly say to someone who asked my preferences that I am happy everywhere . . . But my preferences tend more toward communal living."[80]

*   *   *

In Germany's DP camps, East European refugees and Jewish activists also questioned the restorative value of the family for displaced youth. While they were often motivated by politics, they too spoke in the language of psychological rehabilitation and children's "best interests." In a typical appeal, Yugoslav leaders in Munich demanded that 1,000 displaced Yugoslav children in the American Zone of Germany be removed from their parents in DP camps and placed in separate children's camps in 1945. "These children have to live in big common rooms . . . in promiscuous company where couples are living in concubinage, where drinking and playing cards are the order of the day . . . The only means of protecting our youth against such a future consists in creating a camp, reserved for them, where they could be educated physically, morally, and intellectually." In response, UNRRA child welfare officer Eileen Davidson merely called for more parental responsibility. "Yugoslav parents within the Assembly Centers should themselves accept the responsibility of bringing about a better atmosphere for their children . . . a spirit of self help must exist within the community," she replied.[81]

An alleged lack of parental responsibility among DPs was in fact a nagging concern among UNRRA and IRO humanitarian workers. At the same time that they celebrated the restorative value of the family in the abstract, UN workers were deeply ambivalent about the ability of real refugee mothers to care for their children properly. Caseworkers reported with dismay that many mothers in DP camps actually abandoned or neglected their children after the war. "In the life of distress they [female DPs] have led in the past few years, maternal instinct has suffered a serious decline," lamented IRO Child Care Officer Yvonne de Jong in June of 1948.[82] "Isolated cases are met with in which the infant has been put to death; more in which gross neglect, e.g. by starvation has taken place and considerably more in which the child has been abandoned," another UNRRA worker noted in 1946.[83] Unlike OSE activists or East European DPs, however, UN workers did not generally turn to collective education to support or replace fragile families. Instead, their concerns inspired programs that aimed to cultivate homemaking skills among refugee girls and women.

These programs reflected a conviction that women's wartime experiences in camps, ghettos, and barracks were not simply dehumanizing—they were profoundly defeminizing.[84] The rehabilitation of displaced women often focused on the body. Social workers cited the lamentable hygienic conditions and absence of privacy in wartime ghettos, camps, and labor barracks as particularly degrading to women and girls. Concerned officials suggested that when women were forced to surrender the privacy and cleanliness of their bodies during the war, they "let themselves go" down a slippery slope that culminated in the surrender of sexual virtue.

Jewish and non-Jewish social workers shared these concerns about the demoralization of refugee women, but the politics of rehabilitation differed. While Jewish DPs tended to celebrate the fertility of surviving Jews, Catholic authorities were particularly concerned about the alleged promiscuity of displaced women and girls. On Christmas Day, 1946, 90 Polish children were repatriated from the British Zone. Scandalized Polish repatriation officials reported that "among these children not a single one was still a virgin." They did not seem to consider the possibility that the girls might have been rape victims.[85] French and Belgian Catholic relief organizations were also alarmed about the reported sexual ruin of women laboring in Germany. Some 50,000 French women toiled in German war factories during the war. A 1943 report described one barrack for female foreign laborers in Germany as "a true 'hell' of immorality and misery: one finds corpses of newborn babies thrown in toilets and garbage cans."[86] Another French social worker in postwar Berlin warned of a sensational decline in maternal instinct. "The sale of children to the Germans is a frequent practice, and according to the latest information, a child is worth 700 marks."[87]

If displacement resulted in defeminization, the imagined remedy was to restore traditional gender roles after the war. Edith Ornstein, a German-Jewish woman charged with the conscription of female labor in Terezín, scrutinized the effects of deportation on gender roles in a lecture that she delivered in the ghetto in 1944. In Terezín, she reported, women separated from their husbands initially responded with catatonic depression, apathy, and "hysterical outbursts." Many "let themselves go" physically and emotionally. But those who preserved some semblance of a "normal" family life and a feminine appearance fared better than others, she claimed. "It seemed as if the majority of women lost all interest in life . . . These conditions were unbearable for all of us. It was necessary to shake women out of their lethargy. . . . we attempted, as much as possible, to take care of our appearances, and through our example to show that even under these living conditions, one should not lose their bearings."

While urging women to maintain a feminine appearance in order to preserve their dignity, Ornstein viewed the conscription of female labor as a more positive challenge to traditional gender roles. Forced labor was a harsh shock to many middle-class women, who had been accustomed to living as "small queens" in their own households, Ornstein reported. Most, however, successfully adapted to the discipline of camp labor, and performed their jobs well. Working outside the home, she argued, had even rendered women in Terezín "more self-conscious, more secure, and more independent." Had the femininity of Jewish women been irreparably "damaged" by these experiences? "That will be for future social orders to decide," she speculated.[88]

As early as 1944, humanitarian workers began to worry that the femininity of displaced women had in fact been severely compromised. That year UNRRA formed a special task force to address the anticipated needs of repatriated women and girls. The group connected the refeminization of returning female laborers and camp inmates to a broader struggle for democratization, insisting, "In some important respects it will provide an opportunity to demonstrate the contrast with Nazi philosophy which has not held women in high esteem." Gender-specific rehabilitation programs explicitly sought to cultivate women's domestic skills. "In arrangements for housing, for the preparation and serving of food, and for occupational activities it may be possible to find many useful outlets for women's domestic interests which will have an important rehabilitative effect." Women were to be rehabilitated from wartime trauma through liberal portions of butter and fat, the distribution of sewing equipment, the application of makeup, and private sleeping quarters and toilets. "The women's quarters in assembly centers should provide as much individual and group privacy as facilities permit, with every incentive to stimulate personal cleanliness and interest in personal appearance ... A simple workroom with facilities for sewing, mending, and pressing, and even primitive facilities for hairdressing would be greatly appreciated by the women and girls and would be of distinct value to those who are depressed or worried about the future."[89]

These gendered rehabilitation schemes targeted young girls as well as women. In June 1946, officials working with the Unitarian Service Committee toured UNRRA child welfare centers and recommended mandatory home economics courses. In these classes, social workers were to "re-educate the often repressed and perverted instincts of motherhood and family life" among refugee girls.[90] Vinita Lewis, an IRO Child Care Officer, agreed that girls in the Aglasterhausen Children's Camp in Germany lacked normal feminine instincts, not to mention basic housekeeping skills. "They have no opportunity to learn to give any attention to anyone but themselves. They compensate for this by developing friendships with other girls of their age. That is very good if it can be redirected to develop between two persons of the opposite sex, because later it forms a good basis for a compatible marriage relationship," she maintained. "Few of the girls have had opportunity for education in homemaking ... The girls do not know how to scrub floors and wash pounds and pounds of clothing ... When the girls go out from Aglasterhausen they will be thrown together with people in communities who expect them to have accomplishments similar to those of other girls and young women. They will not be excused for having lived in DP camps ... during the war years."[91]

These rehabilitation programs reflected the gendered dimensions of relief work after the Second World War, as well as the limits of postwar individualism and familialism. At the same time that child welfare activists invested the family with utopian potential to renew and rehabilitate European societies, they condemned actual DP families as sites of dysfunction. And at the same time that they upheld the virtues of individualism, they insisted that restoring psychological stability to individual girls—and political stability to war-torn Europe—required re-anchoring women in the home. The role of women and girls in the reconstruction of Europe was not to become emancipated individuals, equipped with universal "human rights," but rather to ably perform their assigned roles as mothers and wives, so as to guarantee the healthy development of male individuals.

Anxieties about the stunted maternal capabilities of displaced girls reflected a more pervasive panic about the moral effects of war and displacement on children and youth, and implicitly, on European civilization. Humanitarian workers and psychologists frequently deployed the psychoanalytic concept of regression to describe individual responses to displacement. "The most characteristic personality change of people under circumstances of severe emotional strain is *regression*," instructed a June 1945 UNRRA manual. "By regression we understand falling back to earlier, more primitive and for example infantile habits. The acquired forms of civilization easily vanish, and the loss of cultural decorum is one of the first symptoms one can observe in displaced persons . . . The means of cleanliness decline; people do not take any interest in hygiene . . . Finally, their behavior becomes rougher and more childish." Disturbed refugees, in this view, exhibited traits that human civilization itself had repressed over the centuries. "Living for many years far from the family home, they have become savages like the domestic animals in destroyed and abandoned villages," claimed Joseph Weill, director of the OSE, shortly after the liberation of France.[92] These links between wartime displacement and regression were grounded in the Freudian notion that the psychological development of the individual retraces the developmental path of humanity, from its primitive origins to civilized society (ontogeny recapitulates phylogeny). Brutalized refugees supposedly exhibited traits that were both infantile and "natural" to human beings in their primordial state.[93]

The developmental logic underpinning these theories reflected contemporary racial, gender, and social hierarchies. Swiss psychoanalyst J. Wolf Machoel theorized that when confronted with danger, the refugee "becomes an individual without reason, moved only by the instinct of self-conservation, the desire for security, no matter where or how." But this "collective psychosis" did not afflict all populations uniformly. Groups that were inherently less developed were most likely to succumb to irrationality, according to Machoel. "This paralysis of reason changes men into beings without precise thought and transforms a collectivity into an amorphous mass. It especially attacks certain categories of the middle class and of the population with a less elevated level of culture, as well as women and elderly people," he claimed.[94]

Many European educators attributed the civilizational decline afflicting postwar youth to a broader crisis of authority. In this view, youth who had survived wartime displacement, occupation, and persecution had lost all respect for their parents, teachers, and religious and political leaders. In France, child welfare authorities placed the blame for this crisis firmly on absent fathers.[95] Psychologist Simone Marcus-Jeisler reported that during the war 1,600,000 French POWS were away from home for more than five years. The absence of fathers had several negative consequences on French youth, according to Jeisler. "The most important has been the diminution, and even the disappearance, of authority, which has caused behavioral problems, vagabondage, delinquency ... many children of POWs suffer from delayed maturity as a result of the absence of masculine influence."[96] Nor did the dangers subside when fathers returned home. Wartime conditions allegedly produced a literal reenactment of the Oedipal drama in French bedrooms, Jeisler reported. "Frequently, the son took the place of the father little by little, protected the mother, became her 'little man,' and often, in order to economize on heat, shared the bed with her. This situation ... has created veritable domestic tyrants, who even go so far as to make sexual demands on their mothers. One can imagine the conflict that will almost inevitably erupt when the father returns, as he will have to dethrone a veritable rival."[97]

Educators of Jewish children also diagnosed a severe crisis of authority among refugee youth after the war. But in contrast to French psychologists, they were not typically worried about the absence of paternal discipline. They instead lamented the inability of Jewish youth to trust any authority figure at all. Gwendolen Chesters of UNRRA and the British Home Office reported that "in consequence of the harshness of much of their experience, their attitude to authority of any kind was ... one of great intolerance. For years their experience of it had been of some bad force seeking by every means to exploit them." Authority, to young camp survivors, was therefore "something to be circumvented by every sort of ingenuity or challenged with unyielding defiance."[98]

The young survivors of Buchenwald were in decent physical condition after months of lavish feeding by American troops, OSE educators reported. But in spite of a quick physical recovery, deep scars marked their souls. Robert Job found that "they had lost all confidence in themselves and the world around them."[99] Jean Henshaw of UNNRA was less sympathetic. She diagnosed "poor work attitudes, cheating, lack of respect for personal property of others, acquisitiveness, occasional forgery and deceit, extremes of aggressiveness and shyness, and abnormal sex behavior" during a visit to the International Children's Center at Prien in 1947.[100] The director of the OSE's Ambloy home (for Orthodox boys) bluntly concluded that the Buchenwald boys "were true psychopaths, cold and indifferent by nature, and that this was the reason they were able to survive camp life."[101]

In one frequently cited incident, the Buchenwald Boys in Écouis were served a special French treat for dessert one evening: hunks of ripe Camembert. The runny cheese was soon catapulted across the dining hall. The boys, turned off by the pungent smell, were convinced that they were being poisoned, or that the Camembert was actually "spoiled merchandise that wasn't good enough for the others," Ernst Jablonski recounted. "We explained to them in vain that it was the natural odor of the cheese, etc. And there you have an important trait that we have to contend with daily: mistrust."[102]

Camembert was not the only source of distrust between refugee children and their guardians, but food was a subject of frequent conflict. While humanitarian efforts following World War I had focused mainly on the efficient delivery of calories, postwar relief workers emphasized the emotional significance of feeding, effacing the mind-body distinction. UNRRA's 1945 report elaborated, "Food is the primal token of security. In childhood, the most potent source of reassurance that we are loved, lovable, and worthwhile, is regular and friendly satisfaction of our hunger by familiar food and drink . . . the psychological consequences of starvation usually heal more slowly than the physical." The distribution of food was considered essential to the larger project of restoring refugees' shattered faith in authority. UNNRA experts advised that above all, "supplies must be *felt to be* distributed generously. It may not be possible to issue unending quantities, but fair distribution of available stocks, issued promptly and ungrudgingly, will convey the implication so badly needed by displaced persons of a generous protective authority."[103] But long after they had left the concentration camps, Robert Job lamented, the Buchenwald boys could not abandon the survival strategies that they had acquired in the camps, or overcome their distrust for adults. "There was no limit to their gluttony," he reported. "They pocketed remains of food, in such quantities they could not possibly eat. This food was later discovered among their belongings, under their mattresses, between their blankets, and it testified to their unbalance and their disarray."[104]

As social workers and psychologists sought to reestablish refugees' shattered trust in authority, they infantilized DPs, regardless of age. A 1945 UNRRA guide advised relief workers to lead dependent and mistrustful refugees to self-sufficiency by fulfilling their perceived "need for a strong parental authority," elaborating, "The rehabilitation process by which they regain their adult independence must . . . be based to a very large extent, as it originally was in childhood, on the existence of respect and affection for the authority which controls their lives. Where authority is accepted, the necessary process of weaning and the imposition of tasks and responsibility are accepted . . . Where there is no respect for authority . . . then there is at best a transient and unwilling acceptance of discipline."[105]

When refugees failed to recover their faith in authority, humanitarian workers were quick to blame the victims (or their mothers). Like their colleagues in the United States, social workers in liberated Europe invoked such cases to affirm the validity of universal psychoanalytic principles. All refugees had suffered under Nazi rule, but only some did not regain their balance. Early childhood experiences supposedly explained cases of failed rehabilitation. Robert Collis, an Irish pediatrician who cared for 500 children liberated from the Belsen concentration camp, observed "the most unexpected difference in reaction between individual children who had undergone . . . the same mental trauma," and looked to children's infancy to explain these differences: "A child who has experienced an unsatisfactory sucking at the breast, perhaps associated with an unhappy weaning, may show in later life symptoms usually associated with loss of security and rejection, while a child satisfactorily breastfed and happily weaned will show characteristics of self-reliance and poise . . . I got the impression from the study of many of these children that the factor of their early home life had a very important influence upon their reactions later, when their parents were killed, their homes destroyed, and they themselves exposed to horror in its most extreme form."[106] Collis's views reinforced a broader maternalist ethic in postwar Europe. In the case of a seemingly well-adjusted DP child, he concluded, "had the mother failed the child at any time, then the internal wound might have been too much for the child's powers of mental recovery, and she might have become one of those unfortunates who are beyond help."[107]

The postwar campaign to rehabilitate displaced children was far from unified. It openly pitted the collectivist visions of nationalist, Zionist, and socialist child welfare experts against the psychoanalytic and familialist theories of British and American psychoanalysts and humanitarian workers. But in spite of serious fault lines, all of these efforts reflected the triumph of a new paradigm of relief focused on the psyche. Activism around displaced and refugee children ultimately became a forum for more fundamental debates about human psychology and development: the nature of trauma, the emotional consequences of separating children from parents, and the value of familial versus collective education. Even as British and American social workers claimed to promote individualist and universalist values through their psychoanalytic methods, they could not imagine healthy psychological development outside the social context of the family. They construed the private sphere of the family as a bulwark against the threat of totalitarianism. Humanitarian workers aimed to anchor both children and women in the family after the Second World War in the name of democratization and psychological rehabilitation. In the process, they institutionalized a gender-specific vision of humanitarianism and human rights: one in which the family, as much as the individual, was the privileged subject and object of human rights activism.

Renationalizing Displaced Children

In 1948 the United Nations' *Convention on the Prevention and Punishment of Genocide* equated the denationalization of children with genocide. The Convention officially condemned "forcibly transferring children of one group to another group" enacted "with intent to destroy, in whole or in part, a national, ethnical, racial or religious group, as such." That same year, the "right to a nationality" was enshrined in Article 15 of the 1948 Universal Declaration of Human Rights, along with the principle that "no one shall be arbitrarily deprived of his nationality nor denied the right to change his nationality."[1]

By the end of the twentieth century, the notion that denationalization constitutes an abuse of human rights would be invoked in debates about international and interracial adoption, bilingual education, and the kidnapping of aboriginal children in Australia and South America.[2] But the origins of this moral prohibition can be traced back to the very specific context of Eastern Europe in the early and mid-twentieth century. Only a year after the convention was signed, Vinita Lewis, a social worker with the IRO in Germany insisted, "Even if his future destiny lies in a country other than that of his origin, he [the displaced child] is entitled to the basic Human Right of full knowledge of his background and origin."[3] In postwar Europe, children enjoyed (or endured) a "human right" to an ethnicity, even if they ultimately settled outside their country of origins.

The 1948 Genocide Convention and the Declaration on Human Rights reflected the profound tensions between national sovereignty, individual rights, and internationalism that shaped the postwar reconstruction of Europe. Even as the defeat of the Third Reich generated a wave of utopian internationalism,

1945 was simultaneously one of the most violently nationalist moments in European history. Government officials and policymakers across Europe viewed postwar reconstruction as an explicitly nationalizing project, an effort to recover the national sovereignty and restore the national "honor" compromised by the Nazi occupation. They linked national sovereignty not only to control over territory and resources, but also to control over women and children, symbols of the nation's biological future. Just as postwar governments and individuals pursued the return of homes, furnishings, bank accounts, and artwork that had been plundered by the Nazi regime, they also insisted on compensation for lost human patrimony.

Humanitarian workers in postwar Europe were forced to navigate between the international ideals that had inspired many of them to undertake relief work, and a vision of reconstruction centered on the reassertion of national sovereignty. Through their efforts to rehabilitate displaced families, international organizations and postwar governments alike ultimately strengthened the principle of national sovereignty in postwar Europe. But they came to promote nationalist goals in more universalist terms, as they linked the renationalization of refugee children to their psychological "best interests," democratization, and the advancement of human rights.

*　　*　　*

The 1948 Genocide Convention was drafted by Polish-Jewish activist and lawyer Raphael Lemkin. Lemkin was a veteran of the bitter conflicts over minority rights in interwar East Central Europe. The Nazi invasion of Poland in 1939 left his home burned to the ground and his mother dead. He immigrated to the United States in 1941 and began a lifelong crusade to strengthen international legal protections for minorities. Lemkin denounced the forcible Germanization of East European children, in particular, as one of the Nazi regime's greatest crimes.[4] From the outset, he promoted an expansive understanding of genocide. "Cultural genocide," in his view, represented a first step down a slippery slope toward biological annihilation. In his seminal 1944 work *Axis Rule in Occupied Europe,* he elaborated, "Genocide has two phases: one, destruction of the national pattern of the oppressed group; the other, the imposition of the national pattern of the oppressor. This imposition, in turn, may be made upon the oppressed population which is allowed to remain, or upon the territory alone, after removal of the population and the colonization of the area by the oppressor's own nationals."[5] By linking denationalization and forced population transfers to genocide, Lemkin equated East European victims of

Germanization with Holocaust victims. He also anchored a longstanding Central and East European conception of children as a form of "national property" into still inchoate norms of human rights and international law.

In some respects, as Mark Mazower has argued, Lemkin's vision reflected the last gasp of an old order. His goal was to resuscitate the interwar League of Nations, but with stronger legal enforcement of minority rights. The Great Powers saw the interwar regime of minority protection as a destabilizing force, and opposed any attempt to transpose minority rights into the new international order. The Genocide Convention itself was only ratified once the criminalization of "cultural genocide" was struck from the text.[6]

Significantly, however, many East European delegates supported the concept of cultural genocide. A Czech representative to the UN specifically invoked Hitler's "gigantic plan for the complete Germanification of the Czech nation" in defense of the clause.[7] And if we examine the practices of UN social workers in the field, as well as the rhetoric of Jewish and East European policymakers and humanitarian workers, it is clear that some aspects of Lemkin's vision—which reflected a broader East European culture of collective rights—*did* survive in postwar Europe. These collectivist and nationalist ideals were integrated into postwar understandings of human rights and humanitarianism and had real consequences for European refugees.

The rejection of minority rights, moreover, did not reflect the advancement of liberal individualism. It rather reflected a growing international commitment to strengthening national sovereignty after World War II. Within this framework, the United Nations rejected the "interventionist" approach of the League of Nations, leaving the Genocide Convention and the 1948 Declaration on Human Rights legally toothless. We cannot project contemporary understandings of human rights onto the immediate postwar era. Even as the United Nations rhetorically celebrated the concept of individual "human rights," for example, the General Assembly had no problem with forcible assimilation or population transfers, since ethnic homogeneity was seen as the best guarantee of international stability. Nor did UN founders perceive a tension between the rhetoric of human rights and the defense of racial hierarchy. Within a framework that justified empire as a humanitarian force in the world, Allied leaders believed that the rhetoric of internationalism and human rights were entirely compatible with the persistence of imperial rule.[8]

And yet, even if the universalist and individualist ideals expressed in the founding documents of the United Nations were purely aspirational, they were not inconsequential. Anti-colonial leaders were not blind to the contradictions between rhetoric and reality in the new global order, and they used the United Nations to make their own demands for national sovereignty. By 1946, the United Nations General Assembly had become a prominent forum for anti-colonial agitation.[9]

Many of the foot soldiers of postwar relief efforts in Europe also took the rhetoric of internationalism at face value. Susan Pettiss recalled joining UNRRA firm in the conviction that "the chaos immediately following the end of World War I with clogged roads, epidemics, and widespread hunger could not be repeated. We would, this time, achieve a permanent peace and help establish a unified world."[10] Joseph Weill of the French OSE was optimistic that wartime suffering had laid a foundation for uplifting internationalism. "The misery and suffering that are ransacking Europe are contributing to the progressive unification of the continent's civilian population . . . The war was intended to destroy homes and instead it created a great family united in outrage," he declared shortly after the liberation.[11]

These sentiments inspired utopian projects for the rehabilitation of European children after the war. Philanthropist Vera Stuart Alexander even raised funds for a "Stateless Children's Sanctuary" in the West Indies shortly after the liberation. "The children have been the victims of a narrow nationalism and we would have the United Nations grant them a passport subscribed to and endorsed by all 55 nations so that they may work, travel freely, and settle anywhere in the world. Having lost their birthright, the children would at least inherit the earth," the project's brochure proclaimed.[12] Alexander's vision was far-fetched even in the haze of liberation, but Europe's children were attractive targets for internationalist pedagogical projects. In 1950, Thérèse Brosse, writing for UNESCO, spoke of a precious opportunity to raise a new generation steeped in internationalist values: "We must act quickly if we are to take advantage of the special opportunities of the post-war period, for if the international aspirations of young people . . . do not find satisfaction in a healthy and unrestricted universality, they may once more seek fulfillment in the limited field of restrictive groups and yet again endanger the world's equilibrium," she warned.[13]

Postwar internationalism was substantiated in an explosion of new intergovernmental and nongovernmental organizations. A United Nations survey conducted in January 1951 counted 188 officially recognized international organizations, one-third of which had been founded after 1945. Humanitarian ventures were among the most ambitious new efforts. The Church World Service, founded in 1946, unified the relief efforts of 17 different Protestant denominations in the United States. Within a year the organization provided 80 percent of the relief goods sent from the United States to Europe and Asia. The Lutheran World Relief (est. 1945), Catholic Relief Services (est. 1943), Unitarian Service Committee (est. 1940), American Friends Service Committee (est. 1917), and the American Joint Distribution Committee (JDC, est. 1914) were not far behind. The largest non-denominational relief organization, the Cooperative for American Remittances to Europe (est. 1945), quickly joined forces with UNRRA to distribute its famous "CARE packages" to needy Europeans.[14] But the most far-reaching new organization was the United Nations and its affiliated agencies, including UNESCO (the United Nations Educational, Scientific, and Cultural Organization, est. 1946), the World Health Organization (est. 1946), UNICEF (est. 1946) and UNRRA (est. 1943). None of these new international institutions were premised on the death of the nation-state. They did, however, rhetorically promise to usher in a new era of international cooperation and to uphold values that transcended state borders.

And yet nationalism was never far from the surface of postwar reconstruction efforts. In Eastern Europe, policymakers emerged from the cataclysm convinced that only ethnic cleansing could guarantee their borders. Some eighteen million people, including twelve million Germans, were unsettled in postwar population transfers, officially sanctioned by the Allies.[15] The campaign to recover national sovereignty in liberated Europe was brutally gendered. Across Europe, reconstructing national "honor" entailed purging and punishing collaborators of all kinds, but especially women who had (allegedly) enabled the national enemy to penetrate their bodies. In France, Germany, Italy, and Czechoslovakia, women suspected of consorting with occupying soldiers were publicly humiliated in savage spectacles of retribution.[16]

The experience of displacement itself strengthened nationalist sentiment among many refugees.[17] As Hannah Arendt observed in *The Origins of Totalitarianism*, "Not a single group of refugees or Displaced Persons has failed to develop a fierce, violent, group consciousness and to clamor for rights as—and only as—Poles or Jews or Germans, etc."[18] In fact, some refugees responded to their experiences of wartime displacement by shifting their national loyalties, embracing internationalist or socialist ideals, or rejecting nationalism altogether.[19] But DP camps did become hotbeds of exile nationalism and political agitation, as East European anti-Communists mobilized in the name of protecting national sovereignty from the Soviet Union, and many Jewish refugees oriented themselves toward a future nation-state in Palestine.

UN workers themselves participated in the nationalization of refugees. An individual's eligibility for UNRRA and IRO services depended on nationality, which meant that UNRRA authorities classified many refugees whose nationalities were ambiguous or contested. UNRRA and the IRO also organized DP camps along national lines in order to facilitate repatriation and avoid national conflicts. Initially, Jews were assigned to refugee camps based on their national citizenship. But serious tensions erupted when Jews were accorded what some non-Jewish refugees considered to be unmerited "special treatment." In Graz in 1945, military personnel had to be stationed in a DP camp to prevent Christian Poles from attacking Jews, after the JDC provided them with extra rations for the High Holidays. On another occasion, Poles in the Hohne-Belsen camp initiated a pogrom, destroying Torah scrolls, vandalizing the Jewish prayer house, and shooting the rabbi.[20] Clearly rabid anti-Semitism did not disappear at war's end.

American authorities created separate camps for Jews after Earl Harrison's August 1945 report decried the treatment of Jews in the American zone, provocatively alleging that "as matters stand now, we appear to be treating the Jews as the Nazis treated them except that we do not exterminate them." Harrison was particularly insistent that Jews required separate camp facilities and contested the notion, popular among Allied military officials, that segregating Jews perpetuated Nazi racism. "While admittedly it is not normally desirable to set aside particular racial or religious groups from their nationality categories, the plain truth is that this was done for so long by the Nazis that a group has been created which has special needs," he countered. "Refusal to recognize the Jews as such has the effect, in this situation, of closing one's eyes to their former and more barbaric persecution."[21]

At first, the national segregation of refugees rubbed against the internationalist ethic of UNRRA workers, but many gradually came to see it as a necessity. "At first I couldn't understand why the Army and UNRRA almost immediately set up different camps for Poles, Ukrainians, Jews, Western Europeans, etc.," recalled Susan Pettiss. "Imbued with the idealistic sense of 'one world' I felt disillusioned when that unity didn't materialize right away. I soon realized, however, that for both psychological and practical reasons, national grouping was best during the insecure and traumatic times in the lives of the displaced."[22]

Pettiss's remarks suggest that support for the nationalization of DPs was not merely a pragmatic concession. Humanitarian workers gradually resolved tensions between their universalist ideals and the primacy of national sovereignty in postwar Europe by reframing nationalist goals in more individualist terms. UNRRA and IRO social workers, in particular, promoted the renationalization of displaced persons as a form of individual psychological rehabilitation. Nationalist claims on children rooted in existing Zionist, nationalist, and Socialist traditions in Central and Eastern Europe thereby gained new legitimacy after the war as they were incorporated into new international norms and laws.[23] Emerging ideals of human rights, family, and democracy in postwar Europe were therefore not simply imposed from above by Allied occupation authorities and humanitarian organizations, but were also informed by long-standing local practices in Central and Eastern Europe.

In multilingual regions of Habsburg Central Europe, nationalist activists had begun to tout the value of children as "national assets" in the late nineteenth century. In the Bohemian Lands, German and Czech nationalists competed to build an extensive network of nationally segregated schools, orphanages, nurseries, kindergartens, and summer camps in order to prevent children from being "Germanized" or "Czechified" in the schools and welfare institutions of the national enemy. These nationalists claimed that each child had a single, authentic national identity. They insisted that they were mobilizing against the denationalization of children as a defensive strategy for demographic survival. But these were highly polemical claims. Well into the twentieth century, many parents and children in multilingual regions of Eastern Europe were bilingual, indifferent to nationalism, or flexible about their national loyalties. Nationalist campaigns to prevent alleged denationalization represented nothing less than an aggressive strategy through which middle-class activists sought to first create and consolidate national communities in East Central Europe.[24]

The campaign to eradicate national indifference radicalized after 1918. At the end of the First World War, the supranational Austrian Empire was replaced by aggressively nationalizing successor states. In the bilingual regions of Habsburg Austria, nationality had typically been a matter of individual choice. In interwar Poland, Czechoslovakia, and Yugoslavia, by contrast, government officials and local nationalist activists increasingly resorted to forcible classification in order to stamp out national indifference and side switching. Thousands of self-declared Germans were reclassified as Czechs during the 1921 Czechoslovak census, and even fined or imprisoned for declaring a "false" nationality. In Polish Silesia and Yugoslavia, parents who professed to be German were reclassified as Poles or Slovenes by the state and required to send their children to Polish or Slovene-language schools.

When the Nazis overran Eastern Europe, they sought to enrich their demographic power and to avenge interwar policies of "Polonization," "Czechification" and "Slovenization" through the Germanization of children deemed to possess German "blood." The Nazi state appropriated practices of forcible national classification that had been fine-tuned for decades in Eastern Europe, and turned them to the purposes of their own racial order. While the seizure of children during the Armenian Genocide had been carried out in an ad hoc manner along routes of deportation, the Germanization of East European children under Nazi occupation was centrally-planned, and justified by an elaborate racial ideology.

Nazi Germanization policies and criteria for assessing "Germanness" nonetheless varied widely across occupied Eastern Europe. In parts of the Bohemian Lands, local Nazi officials accepted almost any willing candidate into the Nazi Volksgemeinschaft, enrolling children in German schools and in the Hitler Youth based entirely on their parents' political sympathies. Some 50 percent of children in German schools and in the Hitler Youth in some regions of Bohemia could not speak a word of German. In the occupied city of Łódź, practices of Germanization were more violent, in keeping with the harsher Nazi occupation regimes in Poland and the Soviet Union. Children were selected for Germanization by racial scientist Dr. Herbert Grohmann, who focused exclusively on the children's geneaology and physical appearance. In a single week in January 1941, he examined 448 Polish foster children and orphans for Germanization, and declared 32 to be "racially valuable." Another 54 were deemed "racially usable" and the rest ruled unworthy of Germanization and returned to Polish foster parents or orphanages.[25]

While most Polish children selected for Germanization were removed from orphanages and foster homes, some were kidnapped from their parents. In December 1941, the District Court in Łódź ordered Janina Rutkiewicz, an unmarried Pole, to relinquish custody of her 11-month-old son, Henryk. Henryk's father was a German police officer. Shortly after his birth, Grohmann determined the child to be "racially valuable" and ordered that he be transferred to a German Lebensborn home, but his mother refused to relinquish him. Soon afterwards, Henryk was seized from his mother through a court order. "Although this measure is, in reality, fully in accordance with the child's own best interests, his mother has resisted it with all her energy. She thereby denies her child the possibility of a future education and professional training, and deprives the German nation and community of valuable German blood," the court ruled.[26]

The Nazi regime used the term "re-Germanization" to justify this scavenger hunt for German blood. The term was itself a product of the longstanding battle for the souls of children in multilingual regions of Eastern Europe. After the war, Nazi Lebensborn officials were tried at Nuremberg for kidnapping and Germanizing East European children. Nazi Lebensborn homes had not only provided prenatal and postnatal care to single Aryan mothers, but also served as centers for Germanizing East European children. Max Sollmann, chief of the Lebensborn program, asserted that the Nazis had only seized children who had themselves been "kidnapped" from the German nation between the wars. "There were various tests such as are usually given to children today, not in order to separate the lot according to wheat and chaff, but to make sure that this expensive process which had such important consequences for the well-being of the child would only be used in the cases of children who were actually ethnic Germans," he claimed.[27]

During the Second World War, Nazi efforts to Germanize children provoked widespread resistance in Eastern Europe. In the Bohemian Lands, the Nazis ultimately abandoned their goal of Germanizing Czech children, and settled for the less controversial policy of indoctrinating them with Nazi values as Czechs, a policy they called "Reich Loyal Czech Nationalism." In 1943, Robert Gies, advisor to Deputy Reichsprotektor Karl H. Frank, reported that planned Germanization measures in the Protectorate of Bohemia and Moravia "could not be carried out . . . The mere examination of the children would have caused some sensation and would have brought about a state of affairs unbearable with regard to the present situation in the Protectorate, and especially to the maintenance of labor peace necessary for the unlimited production of war material," ordering that "further measures are not to be undertaken."[28]

After the war, the Germanization of children was widely remembered as one of the Nazi regime's greatest offenses against humanity. Stories of children stolen for Germanization circulated widely in the Western press and among humanitarian and relief organizations, as well as within Eastern Europe. American journalist Dorothy Macardle reported in 1951 that during the Nazi occupation, "Children were taken from orphanages, from streets and parks, and even from their homes. It was the sturdy, fair-haired boys and girls who were lost, as a rule. Pairs of twins were found to be in special danger: numbers of these were seized. The German motives were obscure, and appalling rumors and conjectures added to the torment of parents whose children had disappeared."[29]

Meanwhile, East European officials heavily exaggerated the number of children reportedly kidnapped by the Nazis. The Polish government declared that at least 200,000 Polish children had fallen victim to Germanization during the Second World War. Based on a survey of postwar documentation, it has been more credibly estimated that around 20,000 children were probably kidnapped from Poland and up to 50,000 from all of Europe.[30] But precise numbers are difficult to come by, as they depend both on the definition of "kidnapping" and the definition of "Germanization" in a context in which national loyalties were ambiguous, and in which many East Europeans voluntarily joined the Nazi Volksgemeinschaft or abandoned their children to German families under material or ideological pressure. East European officials in the 1940s would have made little distinction between the forced removal of a child from his or her living parents, a Czech child placed in a German school by his or her parents, or a child abandoned by a Polish mother to German foster parents. According to the nationalist logic of the time, children could be "kidnapped" not only from their parents, but also from the national collective. This logic endured after the Second World War and was institutionalized in the United Nation's efforts to recover and renationalize Europe's lost children.

Lemkin's concept of cultural genocide assumed that the cultural assimilation of a minority group represented a stepping-stone to extermination. In reality, Nazi racial planners sought to Germanize only those children they believed could become Germans through assimilation. It was precisely those minority groups deemed incapable of assimilation (such as Jews and Roma) that were targeted for annihilation. Others, like non-Germanizable Poles and Czechs, were slotted to become manual laborers in the Nazi racial state. But a perceived link between denationalization and biological destruction resonated widely after the war. East European officials deliberately conflated Germanization and genocide as they sought to place themselves at the top of an imagined hierarchy of victims. A 1948 Polish memo to the IRO asserted typically, "Violating all human rights and trampling on the Rights of Nations, Germany organized the systematic robbery of children with the dual goal of strengthening their own nation's biological power and furthering the biological destruction of occupied nations. These were, according to their plans, sentenced to total annihilation."[31]

Conflicts specific to East Central Europe during the first half of the century thus shaped new international institutions and emerging notions of human rights after World War II. The architects of the United Nations intended to address the perceived weaknesses of the system of minority protections created by the interwar League of Nations through the more universal principle of human rights.[32] And yet, the promise of human rights remained dependent on national citizenship. And within a framework that saw national sovereignty and ethnic homogeneity as the basic recipe for European security, national claims on children largely triumphed over individual rights, and were anchored in the practices and ideals of new international institutions after the war.

*   *   *

A central task of UNRRA's Child Search Teams was to comb the German countryside in search of children who had either been kidnapped by the Nazis or left in the care of German foster homes and institutions by their parents. Once identified, unaccompanied children were subject to the authority of their respective national liaison officers, who were empowered to approve all decisions about adoption, resettlement, or repatriation. Orphaned or abandoned East European children could not legally be adopted by foster parents of a different nationality, in accordance with the domestic laws of Poland, Yugoslavia, the Soviet Union, and Czechoslovakia.[33] These national rights to children were anchored in the convictions of UN workers themselves. In a 1948 memo one IRO official warned, "Every child's future is too important to be decided by a representative of a foreign nation . . . There can be no doubt that in order for things to run smoothly, the guardian must be of the same nationality as the child. If such a line is followed, nobody will be able to reproach the IRO for its desire to assimilate, denationalize children or to develop cosmopolitans."[34] Jean Henshaw boasted of the UNRRA Children's Center in Prien, "One of our major tasks has been a program for renationalizing children. Where we have had adequate DP staff from the children's home country . . . we have had outstanding success in awakening the spirit of national pride and feeling."[35]

In many explicitly internationalist projects to rehabilitate displaced children, young refugees were organized in separate national homes. In the Pestalozzi Village in Trogen, Switzerland in 1950, 132 orphans were housed in eight distinctive national houses, each appropriately "decorated and furnished in national style."[36] Each house had its own school where children were taught in their mother tongue with textbooks from their native lands. A teacher in the village boasted in 1948, "It is really amazing to observe with what toughness and vitality even the smallest group preserves its national character if soundly organized. In each of these small colonies the very best elements of national culture come to the fore, the colorful variety of literary and musical talent, folklore, jest, and humor."[37] This was more than a matter of practicality. The cultivation of each child's national identity was vital to his or her individual psychological well-being, according to Thérèse Brosse: "In the course of our visits to the children's communities, we saw indeed how much the children need a country of their own if they are to be psychologically normal and to feel 'like other people.' . . . The all-important requirement for children who have been moved from one country to another: to settle the child and provide him with a country of his own and a language and culture which that implies."[38] UN social workers were convinced that a firm sense of national identity, like a stable family, was essential to the psychological rehabilitation of displaced persons.

UNRRA's Search Teams traveled door-to-door in their search for lost children. H. Weitz, an UNRRA child welfare officer in the French Zone of Austria, recalled how she personally navigated the bombed-out roads of rural Germany in her quest. At first she encountered resistance from local German officials, but she gradually won their cooperation. "A visit to the Bezirk usually lasted about twenty minutes. After a cigarette was lit and as soon as they realized I was not a member of the occupying forces, i.e., that I did not eat their butter, a new interest seemed to creep in and we set out to plan a course of action," she recalled.[39]

Simply identifying displaced children required intensive detective work. Many children came from regions where blurry lines between so-called Volksdeutsche and Poles, Czechs, and Slovenes had become blurrier during the war. But UNRRA workers operated on the assumption that every displaced child possessed a single "authentic" nationality of origin, which could be scientifically determined through an ethnographic and psychological investigation.[40] Only in exceptional cases did humanitarian workers acknowledge the potential ambiguity of national belonging, as in Italy, where IRO officials created the category of "Undetermined Venezia Giulians" to designate refugees in Italy from Venezia Giulia with indeterminate national loyalties.[41] One UNRRA worker elaborated in a 1946 report, "The question of nationality is most perplexing in the cases of children coming from Silesia because of the mixed German and Polish population in that area before the war. In the absence of identity papers less dependable factors must be relied upon . . . Our most skillful interviewers report the children's psychological reactions to questions about nationality are significant. The unquestionably German child usually replies freely and promptly. The response of the non-German child, though he says he is German, is often characterized by embarrassment, hesitation, confusion, or frantic appeal to a member of the staff for help in making reply."[42]

No one considered the possibility that a Silesian child, coming from a region with a long history of national indeterminacy, might have been genuinely confused about his or her national affiliation, or belong to a distinctly regional Silesian community.

Parents' identities were also contested. As Cold War tensions intensified, allied officials suspected that East European authorities were making fraudulent claims on refugee children, in order to force their repatriation. In one case, a Russian woman named E. M. Uschakova claimed to be the mother of Therese Strasinkaite, an orphaned Lithuanian girl in Germany. Uschakova maintained that the girl's real name was Tamara Sharkow. But Therese countered that she had personally witnessed the death of her mother at the age of four, and refused to return to Russia.[43] In 1952, U.S. occupation authorities even employed German forensic scientists in Germany to conduct what they called an "anthropological examination" of Mrs. Georgette Cadi in France and Josette Phellipeau, a displaced child in Germany. Genetic biologists K. Saller and H. Baitsch produced a lengthy report comparing the cranial structure and facial features of Cadi and Phellipeau, concluding that "the nose must be considered as a strong indication that the child Josette stems from Mrs. Cadi." They also found similarities in the "metric characteristics of the head and face" and the "finer morphology of the skin upper lip and the formation of the chin" of their two subjects.[44]

It was no coincidence that the verification of children's identities was challenging. German officials had systematically changed the names and destroyed the records of East European children designated for Germanization. Many displaced children had no memory at all of their parents or origins. In 1947, Jean Henshaw described Polish and Yugoslav children in the Children's Center in Prien who had "renounced their country, language, and culture and vehemently claimed they were Germans."[45] Once identified, UN Child Search Officers typically removed allied children from German foster parents as quickly as possible, but the separation could be brutal. "Very often the separation is extremely cruel; the child is very attached to his adoptive family and no longer remembers having had any other family," reported IRO child welfare consultant Yvonne de Jong in 1948.[46] Some children had to be removed from their foster parents by force. Child Care Consultant Eileen Davidson noted in her daily log for October 19, 1946: "Conference with Polish Repatriation Officer re: two adolescent Polish children who have been for two years with a superior German family and are asking permission to remain. They are orphans and have no family to return to. Permission refused. Children to be repatriated. Picked up both children at Ansbach much against their will."[47]

Custody battles over displaced children generated sharp political and emotional tensions between UNRRA, British and American military authorities, and local German populations. Citing the "best interests" of the children, British military officers typically preferred to leave the children with German foster families, insisting that they would be permanently scarred by separation from their foster parents. Of course, British authorities also objected to the repatriation of East European children for more prosaic reasons—in order to smooth relations between military authorities and local German populations, and increasingly, out of blatant anti-Communist sympathies.[48]

UNRRA and IRO officers, however, consistently favored removing children from German homes and returning them to their country of origins. In 1948, Eileen Davidson, then Deputy Chief of the IRO's Child Search Section, wrote a widely circulated memo arguing that this policy represented the "best interests of the child" from a psychological and political perspective. Her arguments rested on a conviction that German society had not been purged of Nazi racism and authoritarianism; the possibility of genuine integration for East European children in Germany was therefore slim.[49] "There was the case of two Polish children whose father had been in the SS and who were known as Volksdeutsche . . . The older girl worked long hours in the kitchen . . . She said that she always was told that she was a 'dumb Pole.'"[50] Aleta Brownlee in Austria was equally skeptical of the potential for genuine bonds between Austrian foster parents and non-German foster children. In the best case scenario, she concluded, "The small children were often loved as pets in the family—not as an own child toward whom the family felt responsibility, but as a small and charming animal might be loved." Many Austrian families wanted to keep East European foster children as a source of cheap farm labor, she alleged. After an article about UNRRA children's homes appeared in the *Das Steierblatt*, UNRRA offices were flooded with requests for foster children. "The undersigned is asking for a girl between 14 and 16 years old, if possible one good and healthy, a decent one who likes farm work," wrote one Austrian farmer.[51]

While many lost children adamantly refused to leave their German foster parents, UNRRA and IRO social workers were confident that the children would adjust quickly once restored to their native cultures. In the case of a group of Polish children, Davidson recalled, "They were gradually absorbed into the life of the center, and began to speak Polish . . . By the time that they had made the decision to go back to Poland, they were identified with the Polish group and had thus severed their relationship with their German friends."[52] In her 1951 memoir, Brownlee concluded, "It appears presumptuous in the extreme to conclude that any foreign nation can ever take more interest in the children of another nation than the country to which the children belong."[53] Eileen Davidson agreed. She speculated that East European children left in German foster families would suffer permanent psychological damage, even if they received love and good material care. "Far from securing the best interests of the child, one has to run the danger with the passage of years of contributing to the development of a warped and twisted personality, a misfit with roots neither here nor in his home country."[54]

These convictions were typical of UN workers and illuminate the broader assumptions underpinning postwar humanitarian work. Davidson's arguments reflect the extent to which discussions of children's individual psychological welfare dominated child welfare work after the Second World War, even as concepts such as "the best interests of the child" were fiercely contested. Her memo also reflects the self-representation of UN workers as agents of democratization and denazification in postwar Europe. UNRRA social workers saw their efforts to repatriate and renationalize displaced children as part of a broader mission to promote justice and restitution for Nazi war crimes. They defined democratization, justice, and the so-called psychological "best interests of the child" so as to privilege not only the reunification of families, but also the renationalization of displaced children. Children, in this view, required a stable familial and national identity in order to thrive as healthy individuals. Since it was not possible for many lost children to rejoin their families, national belonging seemed to be all the more vital to their well-being.

*   *   *

The golden formula of return to nation and family posed serious problems for surviving Jewish youth. Those who did return home in search of surviving relatives and possessions after World War II were often greeted with hostility and violence. Neighbors who had confiscated Jewish apartments and furniture were rarely inclined to return their wartime loot. Many survivors recalled being greeted with sentiments such as, "What, you're still alive?" Beginning in late 1945, ongoing anti-Semitism in Eastern Europe, culminating in the infamous pogrom at Kielce, Poland in July, 1946, provoked the flight of around 200,000 Jews (so-called "infiltrees") into the American zone. Most hoped to move on to Palestine. The majority of these Jewish refugees had survived the war in the Soviet Union, and not in German concentration camps, and so their families often remained intact. But many Jewish children and youth, even those with living parents, arrived in kibbutzim. These kibbutzim were typically formed in Poland, and then traveled together illegally to occupied Germany in the hopes of reaching Palestine.[55]

American and British social workers were initially skeptical about the separation of surviving Jewish youth from their families. In some cases, Jewish youth arriving in kibbutzim had actually been ferried off from Polish children's homes without their parents' consent. The children's homes run by the Central Committee for Jews in Poland (CKŻP) were typically led by Bundists or Communists who did not promote emigration. They instead encouraged Jewish youth to join in rebuilding a democratic and Socialist Poland after the war. But representatives of postwar Zionist movements saw little future for Jews in Poland, and viewed Jewish children's homes as fertile recruiting ground. In the Central Committee children's home at Otwock, Thomas Buergenthal recalled that a charismatic counselor named Lola from the left-wing Zionist youth movement Hashomer Hatzair infiltrated the staff in 1946, and became popular among the children. One day she invited Thomas, age 11 at the time, to go for a walk. She asked whether he had thought about immigrating to Palestine. Buergenthal's father had had Zionist sympathies, so he responded that he "would love to live in Palestine because then I would not have to worry about being called a dirty Jew or have Polish kids throw stones at me." Lola told him that she was drawing up a list of all the kids who wanted to emigrate, and explained the plan. "Starting soon, one kid at a time would sneak out of the orphanage and be picked up by some people from Hashomer Hatzair." They would then be smuggled on to Palestine. "It all sounded terribly exciting," Buergenthal recalled. "I immediately volunteered to be among the first to run away."[56]

Thomas's plan to run away with the kibbutz was disrupted by the miraculous reappearance of his mother, who had survived the war and finally located him in Otwock. But many other children covertly disappeared from Central Committee children's homes. Most Jewish youth in postwar Poland were not initially drawn to kibbutzim out of deep ideological or political conviction. They were more attracted by the opportunity to leave the "cursed soil" of Europe, and by the material benefits, educational opportunities, and companionship offered by Zionist youth groups.[57] The Education Department of the CKŻP reported with alarm that on November 8th and 12th 1946, nine children ran away from the Committee's children's home in Otwock with Hashomer Hatzair. Another three children vanished from the Committee's orphanage in Łódź between October 28 and November 1, 1946. The Committee also received reports from Przemysl and other provincial children's homes that "political groups are collecting children from children's homes with the goal of placing them in kibbutzim."[58]

Many of these children still had living parents. Out of the 866 Jewish youth living in the CKŻP's children's homes in December 1946, only 228 were full orphans.[59] Angry letters from parents in Poland soon flooded the offices of the CKŻP and the Polish Red Cross, demanding the return of children who had run away with kibbutzim. Kalman and Sili Wolnerman in Swidnica, who had survived the war in exile in the USSR, appealed to the CKŻP for the return of their 10-year-old daughter Gitla in June 1947. Gitla had been living in a children's home in Swidnica when she ran away with the Kibbutz Dror. "As a Polish citizen I certainly have the right to request the return of my daughter," Wolnerman protested. "But the individuals mentioned are foiling my efforts with the intention of sending my child overseas. . . . I don't have any intention of leaving Poland. I am a loyal citizen of the Polish Republic . . . There could be no more reprehensible injury to me than having my daughter torn away from me and not returned."[60] Pepi Neufeld was also furious about her son's alleged abduction. She complained to the Polish Red Cross that her 12-year-old son Zygmunt had been "artfully tricked out from me by the administration of the Kibbutz party Dror," which had promised her that her child would immigrate legally to Palestine and that she could follow a month later. "This was a lie," she fumed. Instead, her child endured the unsuccessful journey of the Exodus to Palestine and was now residing in a refugee camp in Germany. Neufeld demanded the immediate repatriation of her son to Poland, threatening the leaders of Dror that she intended to "look for justice in higher instances" if her demand was refused.[61] But both Neufeld's and Wolnerman's efforts were in vain—Gitla and Zygmunt left for Palestine before they could be repatriated.[62]

In the DP camps, debates over the merits of Zionist education were ongoing. In October 1945, DP leaders in the Central Committee of Liberated Jews in Bavaria even rejected a plan, sponsored by British Jewish agencies, to transport 1,000 young survivors to Britain for rest and rehabilitation after the war. The Central Committee resolved "to ensure that no one single child should, under any circumstances, be allowed to immigrate to any other country than the only possible haven for them—Palestine." Central Committee members obviously hoped to pressure the British government into opening Palestine to Jewish emigration. But they were also convinced that Jewish children would be emotionally better served in a community of survivors than in temporary homes in Britain, regardless of the material benefits on offer.[63]

Representatives of Jewish agencies and UN child welfare officials also initially clashed over the education of Jewish children. Although UNRRA and the IRO provided resources and support for the care of Jewish refugees, Jewish DP leaders and agencies such as the JDC and the Jewish Agency for Palestine (JAFP) retained significant authority over the education, welfare, and placement of Jewish children. At a 1947 meeting of UNRRA's Jewish Child Care Committee in Heidelberg, Ruth Cohen, representing JAFP, urged UNRRA officials to reconsider their policy of uniting Jewish children with their parents in DP camps. "Reuniting a child . . . with his parents or relatives . . . means sending that child into what we know at home as slum conditions," she maintained. Children placed in separate children's homes, camps, hachsharot (training farms), and kibbutzim, she argued, were better off from a moral perspective and more likely to get the food, clothing, and medical attention they needed. One representative of the JDC claimed that children's collectives bound for Palestine were actually preferable to family life, arguing, "The group leaders . . . are much better for the children than a disturbed mother and father in a DP camp."[64]

UN social workers were initially unsympathetic to this view. In one 1948 memo, an IRO Child Welfare Officer in Lower Saxony concluded in frustration, "In view of . . . the utter disparity between IRO's commitments towards unaccompanied children and their relatives, and the accepted Jewish principle, whereby an orphan belongs to the community, it is obvious that as regards unaccompanied children, our aims will always be completely at variance."[65] Marie Syrkin, a New York City high school teacher, shared her unease with Zionist pedagogy. Syrkin traveled to Germany's DP camps after the war as a representative of B'nai B'rith, and worked with educators in Jewish DP camps. At a 1947 meeting of teachers in the American zone of Berlin, she expressed concern that the "one-sided" education delivered to Jewish children in the DP camps amounted to sheer indoctrination. But Jewish teachers at the meeting defended their methods. "Maybe it's not good pedagogy to present only one side of a case," conceded one teacher. "But we can't afford such luxuries. The children have nothing, nothing. What should we talk about— the blessings of Poland? They know them. Or the visas for America? They can't get them. The map of Eretz is their salvation." Another teacher, an older man, simply countered, "I have been a teacher all my life, and I also know about modern methods. Indoctrination may not be good for normal children in normal surroundings. But what is normal here? . . . A crooked foot needs a crooked shoe."[66]

In spite of initial reservations, however, many UN workers and American authorities came to embrace the Zionist solution for Jewish refugee children. Social workers were persuaded by their encounters with Jewish youth who themselves passionately set their sights on Palestine. If Jewish youth initially joined kibbutzim in Poland for pragmatic reasons, the Zionist commitments of those who remained with their groups typically deepened in occupied Germany.[67] Louise Pinsky wrote of the 500 Jewish children in her care in Germany in 1946, "The children are all Zionists and all, without exception, wish and hope to get to Palestine ... Although not with parents, the children do get affection from the group ... It is not at all like an institution." Edith Feureisen, a 16-year-old Hungarian survivor, was a typical case. Her father had immigrated to the United States and obtained American visas for his three children. Edith was torn between her family and her Zionist loyalties. "I know that I will break my father's heart if I do not answer his call, but I also know that my duty is with my people," she wrote. "In America we may be comfortable for a year, for two, for ten, but the end will be the same—we will be driven out. I have learned a lot in Auschwitz ... unless we have a National Home, we will perish as a nation. I am young in years, but I am very old in experience. I am still strong and I want to work for my people." Edith gained the support of UNRRA workers, who attempted to persuade her father to accept her decision.[68]

UNRRA officials and American authorities also came to support the education of youth in kibbutzim and hakhsharot for pragmatic reasons. Relocating Jewish youth to training farms freed up space in overcrowded DP camps. And kibbutzim seemed to serve a valuable rehabilitative function. Jack Whiting, UNRRA zone director, expressed his enthusiasm for the creation of hakhsharot at the first meeting of the Jewish council in the U.S. zone in March 1946. Farm labor, he maintained, represented a valuable antidote to a perceived epidemic of "petty thieving, black marketeering, loose morals, etc." among DP youth.[69]

Sympathy with Zionist goals could also reflect a view of Jewish children as essentially different from their non-Jewish peers. This entailed recognition of the magnitude of Jewish losses during the war, on the one hand, and/or the persistence of anti-Semitism on the other. Robert Collis maintained that Jewish children were fundamentally different from other East Europeans liberated from Bergen-Belsen. He attributed these differences to deep-rooted ethnic traits, reporting, "Though they might call themselves Dutch or Italian, they seemed to us more Jew than anything else ... Indeed, when this thought struck me, I realized that it would never have entered my mind to regard a little Dublin Jewish child as Irish. Such an idea would be obviously absurd, so it would be equally absurd to think of the sixty-five Jewish children in the camp who spoke Dutch as in any way Dutch children."[70]

Of course, not all claims about the distinctive needs of Jewish children after the Holocaust relied on stereotypes. Contrary to the myth of postwar "silence" about the Holocaust, Jewish agencies and communities actively lobbied for the special needs and rights of Jewish children as victims of genocide.[71] Jewish agencies were particularly focused on the recovery of Jewish children who had been hidden with Catholic families and institutions during the war. These children represented both the future of the Jewish community and a living memorial to the millions murdered by the Nazis. Jewish philanthropists and religious authorities invoked children's psychological best interests as well as national interests as they fought for custody of hidden children. In a meeting with Pope Pius XII in September 1945, Leon Kubowitzki, Secretary General of the World Jewish Congress, appealed directly for the return of Jewish children in Catholic custody, insisting, "Those children are broken souls. We think we are the only ones who can give them the psychological climate they need to return to normal health, to a normal conception of life."[72]

The problem was that many guardians of Jewish hidden children were reluctant to relinquish their wards. In Poland, the education department of the Central Committee of Jews in Poland, in cooperation with the JDC, was determined to remove Jewish orphans from the custody of non-Jews as quickly as possible. But Central Committee officials reported bitterly that many Polish guardians would only relinquish hidden children for a "considerable price." Even worse, a bidding war had erupted among several different Jewish agencies and movements after the war. JDC officials estimated that 500–600 Jewish orphans remained in non-Jewish custody as of September 1947, and lamented that because of competition among Jewish agencies, "the ransoms requested by the persons holding possession of the children are frequently excessive."[73] The Central Committee's Education Department paid ransoms for 67 children between January 1946 and June 1947, spending a total of 600,000 Polish złoty, almost 10,000 złoty per child.[74]

The committee's list of Jewish children to be removed from Christian-Polish hands as of March 1946 included several difficult cases. Seven-year-old Mozes Liber reportedly lived with a "hysterical foster mother, who is probably a prostitute" and who refused to return the boy. The parents of 10-year-old Marietta Klaphola had survived the war and immigrated to Palestine, but her Polish foster mother would not even disclose the child's address until she was paid $1,000. Krysia Goldfeil was also living with a "hysterical" Polish foster mother and an alcoholic foster father, according to the Central Committee's investigations. "The child is extremely thin ... The conditions in which the child lives are extremely precarious and she is often ill. The price of the ransom for the child changes from day to day."[75]

Custody battles were also particularly numerous in France, where up to 10,000 Jewish children were saved from the Nazis in hiding. WIZO, the Union of French-Jewish Women for Palestine (founded in 1924), was deeply invested in the campaign to reclaim hidden children after the war. "We find ourselves before children who have been separated from their deported families for two or three years, who are now Jews in name alone ... First of all, to return them to Judaism, and then to prepare them if necessary for emigration to Palestine—these are the essential goals of our program today."[76] With time, it became evident that the actual number of surviving Jewish children was tragically small, but this only amplified the stakes. As of June 1945, the OSE in France reported that 1,200 Jewish children remained in non-Jewish families or institutions, but only 50 truly seemed in danger of conversion.[77] But this did not diminish their symbolic importance. In an appeal to the Vatican in March 1946, Rabbi Isaac Halevi Herzog, then chief Rabbi of Palestine, explained, "As of today every child signifies for us one thousand children."[78]

The most sensational postwar custody battle in postwar France was the 1953 Finaly Affair.[79] The case was a scorching episode in the history of French church–state relations. It was often compared to the nineteenth-century Mortara affair, in which a six-year old Jewish child from Bologna, Edgardo Mortara, was secretly baptized and then kidnapped from his parents to be raised as a Catholic. But the Finaly Affair also reflected a broader postwar preoccupation with the problem of confused identities. At the heart of the scandal was a heated debate over how the terms "nation" and "family" should be defined in the aftermath of Nazism.

Fritz and Annie Finaly, Austrian Jews, endured a typical odyssey of flight and persecution in Nazi-occupied Europe. They first fled the Nazis in 1938, shortly after the Third Reich's annexation of Austria, seeking refuge in Czechoslovakia and then Grenoble. In France, they gave birth to two sons, Robert in 1940 and Gérard in 1941. In 1941, the Finalys had their sons circumcised, a strong indication of their intention to raise them in the Jewish faith, given France's recent defeat and occupation. In 1942, shortly before they were arrested and deported, Fritz and Annie entrusted the boys to a neighbor. The neighbor subsequently asked the sisters of the Order of Notre-Dame-de-Sion to hide the children. Because they were too young to remain inconspicuous at the convent, the sisters placed them in the municipal crèche in Grenoble, where they were taken under the wing of Antoinette Brun, the crèche's headmistress.

Fritz and Annie were on one of the last transports that left Drancy for Auschwitz, and they did not return. As early as the spring of 1945, an aunt of the Finaly children, Grete Fischer, began to inquire after the fate of her brother and his children, and came into contact with Brun. In a letter in November of 1945, Brun cryptically assured Fischer that the Finaly children remained Jewish. "Your nephews are Jews, that is to say that they remain in their religion," she wrote. But Brun artfully dodged Fischer's attempts to reclaim the boys, insisting that their health was too fragile to travel. Ultimately she declared her intention to keep them, insisting that she had earned the right to raise the boys. "Out of good conscience, and because I am a Catholic, I took your two nephews into my care at my own expense and with all the attendant risks . . . I hoped to be able to return them to the hands of their parents, but if not to keep them and raise them until they are grown up . . . No one else had the courage to take them."[80]

Fischer, as well as her sister and brother-in-law Yehudit and Moshe Rossner, wanted to adopt her orphaned nephews. But Brun evaded the efforts of both aunts to reclaim the children, and in March of 1948, she had the boys secretly baptized. Finally, the Rossners took legal action. The case made its way to the French Supreme Court, which ordered Brun to return the children to their relatives in 1951. But Brun defied the court's orders, and the custody dispute soon took a sensational turn. Before their aunt could reclaim them, the boys disappeared under the cover of night, first to Switzerland, and then to Spain with the help of lower clergy.[81] In the middle of the night, Robert and Gérard, now aged 11 and 10, crossed the Pyrenees on foot in a snowstorm into Spain's Basque region, where they were hidden by an order of monks.

With the boys' disappearance, the conflict exploded onto the front pages of the French press. In the early months of 1953, the scandal deeply divided the French public. A rumor spread that Gérard had become ill and died.[82] One concerned citizen suggested that the Jewish community retaliate by kidnapping a Catholic child. "It is necessary to respond to kidnapping with another kidnapping (it's the only measure that remains to us) . . . One can find people who are ready to assume this responsibility," offered Alexandre Kogan in a letter to Jacob Kaplan, the Grand Rabbi of Paris.[83] The highest levels of the clergy (not to mention Franco's government) appeared to be implicated. Through negotiations between Kaplan and Catholic authorities, as well as diplomatic pressure on the Spanish government, the children were finally returned to the custody of the Rossner family on June 25, 1953, almost five months after their disappearance. Shortly thereafter, the family moved to Israel, where the Finaly brothers remain.

The Finaly affair inflamed longstanding tensions between Catholics and anti-clerical activists in France, who accused the church of attempting to defy the Republic and the rule of law. Some observers feared a second Dreyfus affair. French president Vincent Auriol suspected the Pope himself of ob-structing the children's return, and saw the affair as an audacious affront to Republican authority. "The state is falling apart (the Finaly Affair is another proof of this)," Auriol despaired in his diary that winter.[84] Jewish advocates accused the Catholic church of deliberately seeking to profit from the Holo-caust by converting the Jews they had saved. "If the church keeps the children indefinitely, it will be guilty of an atrocious form of 'illicit war profiteering' . . . making children pay with their souls for having saved their lives," opined journalist Maurice Carr in a private letter to Kaplan.[85]

As in other disputes over the custody of displaced children, both sides claimed to represent the sanctity of the "family" and invoked the "best inter-ests" of the children. But the Finaly Affair did not actually pit individual or familial rights against collective rights. Rather, the dispute revolved princi-pally around *which* collective—Jewish, French, or Catholic—had a rightful claim to these orphans. The affair not only inflamed longstanding domestic tensions between secular and Catholic camps in France, it went to the heart of ongoing international debates over which families and nations displaced children belonged to, and what those terms meant.

Commentators on the Finaly Affair were particularly divided about the nature of Brun's attachment to the Finaly boys, and attempted to define her maternal qualities (or lack thereof) accordingly. The children had been edu-cated mostly in boarding homes and religious institutions and saw Brun in-frequently. Those in favor of returning the children to their aunt and to the Jewish community depicted Brun as a fanatic spinster, devoid of maternal instinct, loyal only to the Catholic Church. Maurice Garçon, the lawyer for the Rossner family, described Brun as "an old maid whose celibacy has lasted a bit too long."[86] Other advocates for the children's return attacked what they called the "myth of Mademoiselle Brun's maternal attachment," insisting, "the children were not raised in a maternal home with Mlle Brun but were constantly and successively entrusted to religious institutions only to return during school holidays."[87] The editors of *Franc-Tireur* agreed that "her maternal instincts were not ever a factor. She was more obedient to her Catholic fanaticism than to something that one could call fondness for the Finaly children."[88]

Brun's defenders meanwhile insisted that it was a debased act of cruelty to separate the boys from the only mother they could remember. Brun's lawyer defended the sincerity of her attachment, maintaining, "It is not correct that Mlle Brun did not personally raise the Finaly children . . . Mlle Brun kept them with her in a continuous fashion during the six years from 1944 to 1950. During these six years, she surrounded them with the same maternal affection that she provided to the other nine children she adopted."[89] And in the Catholic journal *Aux écoutes* Paul Levy held that maternal affection was Brun's sole motivation. "Look no further, there is no fanaticism in the heart of Mlle Brun and there never was. Her fanaticism has been entirely invented. Or perhaps yes, she is today a fanatic. She . . . does not want to be stripped of her maternal love."[90]

The Jewish community meanwhile demanded the return of the children in the name of the sovereignty of both family and nation. In a speech on March 31, 1953, Rabbi Kaplan proclaimed, "Hitlerism attacked the Jewish family in particular. Entire families were wiped out. In many cases, the children were saved, thanks to the kindness of those who gave them asylum. It is self-evident that these children should have been returned to their relatives after the Liberation."[91] Anti-clerical activists also used the affair in an attempt to expose the Catholic Church's claims to represent family values as hypocrisy. In reality, argued J. Joet in a letter to Kaplan, "Only the Catholic family is sacred, and those who don't conform to canon law are nothing . . . It is high time. . . . that an immense clamor of indignation resounds in France, in Europe, and in the world to unmask the imposture of the Church that advertises the hypocritical claim to defend the family."[92] Writing in *Le Monde* in March 1953, Paul Benichou concurred, "The family is the family by law when it is Catholic; non-Catholic, it's a sort of miscellaneous band, provisory, without legitimacy . . . The Catholic family is sacred, the non-Catholic family is nothing; the sacrament of baptism pulverizes it simply by touching it."[93]

In a letter published in *La Semaine Juive,* a group of Jewish orphans sought to convince the Finaly boys (and the wider public) of the personal and emotional rewards that awaited them upon return to their "true" family and nation. "Dear Robert and Gérard," the letter began:

"We are writing to you because we are your brothers . . . Like you, we are descended from Jewish parents, and, like you, we have experienced the pain of losing them under the occupation . . . We would have very much liked to remain with our adoptive parents. When we had to leave them . . . we all experienced a painful dislocation . . . And what's more, we didn't know them, these uncles and aunts and cousins who had found us. They had become strangers to us. Some spoke a language that we don't understand. And they were Jews!"

Like the Finaly boys, they had adopted the Christian faith, new names, identities, and families. Some were baptized. Others ingested the anti-Semitism that surrounded them in hiding. At first, they admitted, they felt "revulsion" when introduced to their surviving family members. But eventually, the boys came to realize that "these 'foreigners' are of our blood, they knew and loved our parents . . . they searched the world for us . . . and finally they found us." The letter promised the Finaly boys that they would follow the same path back to their family and faith of origins. Indeed, as this letter illustrates, representatives of the Jewish community often effaced the distinction between nation and family after the war, insisting that they were one and the same. "Now you are on the eve of rejoining your family. Don't be afraid. Thousands of young Jews have followed the same path, and all, without exception, are today happy to have done so. . . . They have found tranquility in their small and large family, in the only milieu in which they are guaranteed to live sheltered from cruel hostility and onctious pity."[94]

From brief letters they wrote at the time, we get only a glimpse of the Finaly boys' own feelings about the conflict. Days after his final separation from Brun, on June 30, Robert wrote a letter (apparently never delivered) assuring her that he would "remain more faithful than ever to the religion that you taught us . . . Your son (and I am still your son), Robert."[95] A month later, Felix Goldschmidt reported to Rabbi Kaplan that the boys were struggling to adjust to their new Jewish identities. Language was a barrier, as Mrs. Rossner could not speak French and the boys could not yet speak German or Hebrew. But Goldschmidt also blamed the difficulties on the boys' experiences of maternal deprivation. The Finaly children had been "separated at a young age from any maternal presence, foreigners to any kind of symbol of affection," he reflected. "Gérard said to me after a few days: I have three mothers: Mama, my mother, and the Virgin mother!"[96] But only a year later, the boys seemed to be doing well. Robert wrote to friends in France to thank them for a Bar Mitzvah gift, and provided an upbeat report on his life in Israel. "Here . . . in

Israel, we are doing well because we are feeling well and have good friends . . . we know a good amount of Hebrew and speak it fluently with our friends."[97]

The Finaly affair was only the most widely publicized dispute over the fate of hidden Jewish children. Similar custody battles played out across occupied Europe. In France, these conflicts frequently pitted Jewish agencies against French government officials. François Rousseau of the French Interior Ministry was particularly incensed by what he denounced as the "kidnapping" of French-Jewish children. The case of Paulette Zujdman was especially contentious. Paulette, the child of Polish-Jewish refugees, was born in France in 1937. In 1943 her parents entrusted her and her sister to the care of Mr. and Mrs. Vigné in Monthléry. According to Rousseau, the Vignés had "assured the material care and education of the children, who they considered their own, under perfect conditions." But they also allowed her to be baptized. In 1948, Paulette, age 12, attended an OSE summer camp. At the end of the summer, the directors of the OSE center at Taverny learned that Paulette had converted and refused to send her home. Paulette, who was deeply attached to her foster parents, twice ran away from the OSE home and back to the Vigné family. Meanwhile, state officials conducted an investigation, and concluded that "no confessional pressure was exercised on this child who requested herself to follow the Catholic religion."[98]

In December of 1948 Mr. Vigné met with Jacques Cohn of the OSE to negotiate for Paulette's return, but Cohn refused to release the girl. In a letter to Mr. and Mrs. Vigné, dated January 4, 1949, he explained, "We insist that Paulette receive a Jewish education and lives in a Jewish milieu for a certain amount of time, such that later, when she is in a position to choose her path for herself, she can decide in good conscience the type of life she wishes to adopt."[99] The Vignés, outraged, continued to lobby for Paulette's return. But she was only released after the Interior Ministry intervened and threatened the OSE with the withdrawal of state support. The OSE and the Vignés finally agreed that Paulette would spend the Jewish holidays and vacations in an OSE home, and she returned to her foster parents on February 13, 1948. She wrote a letter thanking Rousseau a few days later, professing, "It is such a relief for me to have returned to my family . . . I thank you with all my heart."[100]

The dispute between Rousseau and the OSE reflected a broader conflict about memory of the Second World War in France. The Fourth Republic was founded on memories of universal resistance and shared suffering under Nazi occupation. In the eyes of Republican officials, segregating Jewish children or treating them differently from their non-Jewish peers perpetuated Nazi racism (and threatened to bring up unpleasant memories of French collaboration). French-Jewish agencies contested this blind universalism. They insisted that only a Jewish family (or institution) could serve the emotional needs of Jewish youth and the cause of postwar justice.[101] In July 1948, the director of the French Office National des Anciens Combattants wrote to the Central Consistory in Paris to request that Jewish orphans be left in the care of their Christian foster parents. "In many cases there are bonds between the children and the families that have taken them in . . . bonds so close that they cannot be ruptured without risking the onset of terrible disarray for the children," he maintained. But Leon Weiss, the President of the Consistory, countered that surviving Jewish children belonged first and foremost to the Jewish community. "A child does not belong to the family that saved him. . . . just as a deposit does not become the property of the depositary, whatever the risks taken during the time in which it was guarded."[102]

Painful emotional conflicts underpinned these custody battles. Sarah Kofman, who grew up to become a philosopher, was torn between her mother and the Christian woman, called Mémé by Sarah, who sheltered her and her mother in her Parisian apartment during the war. Although Kofman was never physically separated from her mother, her loyalties slowly shifted to the woman who saved her. "Knowingly or not, Mémé brought off a tour-de-force: right under my mother's nose, she'd managed to detach me from her. And also from Judaism."[103] While Sarah's mother was forced to remain hidden in the apartment day and night, anxious and depressed, Mémé took her out and passed her off as her own daughter, dressed her up in new clothes, and lavished her with bedtime kisses and rich foods. "I didn't think at all any more about my father, and I couldn't pronounce a word in Yiddish, despite the fact that I could still understand the language of my childhood perfectly. Now I even dreaded the end of the war!" she recalled.[104]

By the time Paris was liberated, Sarah's mother had grown to despise Mémé. Overnight, Sarah was forced to separate from "the woman I now loved more than my own mother." Her mother allowed her to visit Mémé only an hour a day and beat her if she came home late. Sarah ran away to Mémé but her mother filed a custody suit to get her back. In the hearing, Sarah's mother accused Mémé of "taking advantage" of her daughter. Sarah, in turn, accused her mother of abuse, "showing the court my thighs covered with bruises." The tribunal awarded custody to Mémé. But the decision did not bring Sarah the joy she had anticipated. "Without understanding why, I feel a very strange uneasiness: neither triumphant nor completely happy nor altogether secure." When Sarah returned to Mémé's apartment, her mother and two men were waiting at the door. They took her back to her mother's home, kicking and screaming, where she remained. "I struggled, cried, sobbed," she recalled. "Deep down, I was relieved."[105]

The struggle for the custody of Europe's surviving Jewish children was unique, not only because its intensity reflected the magnitude of Jewish losses. The favored postwar solutions to the problem of displacement—return to family and nation—were problematic for Jewish orphans who had been deprived of one or both. But the disputes that raged around the fate of Jewish children in postwar Europe also fit within a broader pattern.[106] Across Europe, displaced children became objects of fierce custody battles between competing families and nations, and between political movements that sought to mold them in their own image. Humanitarian workers and international child welfare experts in Europe after World War II insisted that the material and psychological "best interests" of individual children should guide their work. They sought to foster individualism and "human rights" in the name of a radical break from the fascist past. Simultaneously, however, UNRRA and IRO experts looked explicitly to both family and nation to achieve their individualist visions. Humanitarian workers ultimately sought to rehabilitate refugees as particular *kinds* of individuals, insisting that children had distinctive psychological needs that depended on their age, gender, religion, and nation. Equally important, within an international framework that accorded greater weight to national sovereignty, they concluded that nations had a collective right to reclaim their lost children, who were represented as a form of biological patrimony.

Hannah Arendt famously observed after World War II that the refugee camps of interwar Europe tragically exposed the limits of the universal ideal of "human rights." Ultimately, such rights were empty promises to displaced persons who lacked national citizenship. "The conception of human rights, based upon the assumed existence of human beings as such, broke down at the very moment when those who professed to believe in it were for the first time confronted with people who had indeed lost all other qualities and specific relationships—except that they were still human," she maintained.[107] After the war, humanitarian activists and international organizations constructed new internationalist and universalist regimes of human rights and child welfare. But Arendt's insight, it seems, applied to the postwar world of the DP camp and the orphanage as well as to the interwar refugee camp. In the name of children's rights and their psychological best interests, humanitarian workers and policymakers alike concluded that every child needed a nation to call home.

Children as Spoils of War in France

In 1946, Pierre Pfimlin, representing the French Ministry of Public Health and Population, declared that displaced children in Germany represented a valuable "blood transfusion" who promised to counter the "menace of extinction" threatening the French nation. "During the war years Germany was an immense prison, where humans belonging to all of the nations of Europe rubbed shoulders . . . This mixing of humans without historical precedent has left human traces—children were born. A lot of children. A good number of them have French blood in their veins . . . From a demographic point of view the child is the ideal immigrant because he constitutes a human asset whose value is all the more certain since his assimilation is guaranteed. It is impossible to say the same of any adult immigrant," he proclaimed.[1]

Pfimlin was not the only one to view Europe's refugee children as a potential demographic windfall after World War II. Across Europe, government officials saw displaced children as a rich treasure, and scrambled to claim them in the name of economic, social, and biological reconstruction. But Pfimlin's plan was remarkable in one respect: among the children he aimed to transform into French citizens were thousands of babies born to French fathers and German mothers. The children of France's former "blood enemies," Pfimlin hoped, would replenish the war-drained French population, and in the process, help guarantee the future peace and security of Europe.[2]

After the Second World War, the Allied powers were determined to prevent future outbreaks of German aggression in Europe. Forestalling imperialism required diagnosing its sources. Economic backwardness, Prussian bureaucracy, and an inherently authoritarian German psyche ranked high among the

146

explanations that shaped Allied reconstruction policies. But Pfimlin's solution to the "German problem" was based on another popular theory about the origins of Nazi expansion: the notion that overpopulation was its root cause. By strategically draining Germany of its "excess" population (and especially its children), French officials hoped to prevent Germany from rising again to seek *Lebensraum* (living space) in the East or West.

The French government hatched its plan to transform half-German children into French citizens after World War II based on the assumption that Nazi aggression had been a demographic assault on occupied Europe. Government officials, demographers, and diplomats depicted postwar migration policy as a strategy for redressing the consequences of Hitler's demographic warfare. As one French military official explained, "By initiating massive deportations and inflicting a long captivity on adults, one of the goals pursued by the Nazis was to reduce natality in the states that they planned to destroy . . . The Direction of Displaced Persons is now working to repair in part the damage inflicted on the Allies . . . by depriving Germany of the benefit of births that were due to the presence of millions of deportees on its territory."[3]

As European policymakers and humanitarian activists sought to reconstruct their war-battered societies, they looked to demography and population policy for solutions to a wide range of problems. For six years, Hitler had waged a bloody campaign to reengineer the racial demography of Europe.[4] Yet this campaign did little to discredit the science of demography itself, or to quell the ambitions of European policymakers to reshape populations at home and abroad. Government officials in Europe instead emerged from the war confident that population management was as much a necessary tool of national security, social policy, and economic development as it had been an instrument of war and racism. Population planning was a central focus of domestic reconstruction in Europe after World War II, a matter of international concern and of diplomatic negotiation and conflict. The family size, contraceptive methods, welfare benefits, and even childrearing practices of an ally, neighbor, or rival were as much topics for diplomacy and intervention as trade balances and military rearmament. Children became a precious spoil of war.

The Second World War brought foreign soldiers into the pubs of provincial cities, and into the kitchens and bedrooms of remote farmhouses. It brought colonial soldiers into metropolitan armies (already a major development during the First World War), unsettled refugees and displaced persons into unfamiliar lands, and transported millions of workers across the European continent to labor in German factories. And in spite of nationalist and racist laws that prohibited transnational or "transracial" sex, children resulted from these encounters. With these children came dilemmas that could not be solved within the framework of a single nation-state. Postwar officials struggled to determine which children to embrace and which to exclude from the privileges and duties of national citizenship. European (and non-European) governments meanwhile competed to attract migrants deemed valuable and to repel populations seen as inassimilable from a cultural, economic, or biological standpoint. Children, in particular, were central to the international politics of population and migration policy after World War II, as they represented future demographic strengths and weaknesses, shortages and surpluses.

The ambitious efforts undertaken to manage populations at home and abroad in postwar Europe were stimulated by necessity. Allied military authorities and NGOs agreed in 1945 that some twenty million prisoners of war, liberated concentration camp inmates, forced laborers, expellees, and refugees could not crowd Europe's roads and refugee camps for long without provoking a severe humanitarian crisis. UNRRA sought to repatriate millions of displaced persons as quickly as possible, and to a remarkable extent succeeded. In spite of seemingly insurmountable logistical challenges, including bombed-out roads and train tracks, shortages of fuel, and poor communication, 5.25 million Europeans were repatriated by Allied authorities in May and June of 1945 alone.[5]

The apparent success of the postwar repatriation campaign encouraged further experimentation with large-scale population management. But it was also clear that the problem of displacement could not be solved simply by sending people home. Many surviving Jews had no family or home to return to, and no desire to return to the sites of their persecution and deportation. Some East European DPs feared that they would be tried for collaboration with the Nazis, or persecuted by new Communist regimes. Borders had shifted, and parts of the Baltics, Poland, and Ukraine were now under Soviet rule. The Communist takeover in Eastern Europe stiffened the resolve of many anti-Communist DPs not to return home. Other DPs had formed new family attachments, or simply sought better opportunities and a fresh start abroad.

While massive wartime displacement was a serious humanitarian crisis, it also represented a limited opportunity to shift populations strategically in the pursuit of domestic reconstruction and international security. No government was more eager to transform this crisis into an opportunity than France. Francis Perrin, of France's new Institut National d'Études Démographiques (INED), declared in early 1946 that the millions of Displaced Persons crowding Europe's postwar refugee camps represented a rich resource for a country in need of labor. He was convinced that the French government had no time to lose in the race to pick the cream of the crop: "There are currently masses of available candidates for immigration in the world. Now is the moment to choose those who will be the most easily assimilable. In two years, it will be too late."[6]

Not surprisingly, however, postwar European governments did not simply seek human compensation in kind for the soldiers, Jews, civilians, and children they had lost. They instead evaluated the cultural and economic desirability of DPs in nationalist, gender, class, religious, racial, and age-specific terms. They saw wartime and postwar displacement as an opportunity to fill specific demographic needs, which they defined according to the imagined strengths and weaknesses of potential migrants. The resettlement of displaced persons ultimately became a forum for defining post-fascist migration policies, and for debating the possibilities and limits of assimilation.

* * *

In spite of France's longstanding pronatalist obsessions and its tradition of offering asylum, the idea of populating France with half-German children was not an obvious solution in 1945. During the First World War, the offspring of German fathers and French mothers were more likely to be considered "children of barbarians" than desirable immigrants. To some French observers, the solution to the problem of German/French children was abortion rather than adoption or assimilation. In one case, a French woman had even been acquitted for infanticide in 1915 based on the defense that her child was the product of a German rape. French Catholics and pronatalists countered that a woman's French blood and the power of French civilization could outweigh the influence of the German rapist, arguing for the assimilation of French-German children, but there was no clear consensus on the issue.[7] When Alsace and Lorraine were annexed to France in 1918, children of mixed Alsatian-German marriages (approximately 10 percent of the Alsatian population) were treated as second-class citizens. They were subject to lower rations as well as discrimination in employment and education. A 1918 government document elaborated that Alsatians would enjoy the privileges of French citizenship only insofar as "their quality as Alsatians and Lorrainers of French origin are incontestable, that is to say that their blood remains pure of any addition of German blood."[8]

These attitudes reflected the violent context in which the occupation children of the First World War were conceived, as well as the relations of power that they embodied. Children born to French women and German men during World War I were often conceived and born in the course of the invasion of Northern France and Belgium by German troops in August of 1914. Many were products of rape. Doctors theorized that children born under these violent circumstances would be permanently scarred by the traits of their "barbaric" German fathers. Telogeny, the theory of the contaminating seed, held that the traits of a woman's first sexual partner left an indelible imprint on all successive offspring, even if other men were the fathers. The sperm of German rapists thus threatened to disfigure an entire generation of French women and children. And even if they were not the product of actual rape, the children of French-German unions during the First World War constituted visible, living, traces of a brutal invasion and occupation.[9]

The children born to French soldiers and German women in the French-occupied zone after the Second World War were conceived under very different circumstances. They were generally products of fraternization between French men and German women, but rarely was the French party a victim of German aggression. Indeed, rape by French soldiers in the French occupation zone was widely reported. In the town of Freudenstadt, French soldiers reportedly chanted "we are the avengers, the SS of the French army" as they entered the city in April 1945, raping some 500 women in three days.[10] Children produced in this context were living symbols of Germany's defeat and occupation, and of the reconstruction of French virility in the aftermath of World War II. It was important to French authorities that this moment of victory be memorialized. The French Ministry of Population and local city authorities even sponsored summer camps for nearly 50,000 French children per year (including Jewish children) in the Black Forest region of Germany between 1946 and 1948. French children were sent to vacation in colonies de vacances in occupied Germany in order to experience "the horrors of the war and hopes for peace in a defeated Germany," take pride in the heroism of their "older brothers" in the French army, and leave with "a high ideal of the true face of France on foreign territory."[11]

French plans to solicit the immigration of German adults and children emerged gradually, and were selective. An immediate priority of the French Ministry of Foreign Affairs and the Ministry of the Interior after the liberation was to deport German-Jewish refugees who remained on French soil. A government memo written in early October 1945 specified, "It is desirable that the French government should, at the opportune moment, ask these refugees who are of no economic or demographic interest to leave our territory."[12]

An explicit hierarchy between assimilable children and non-assimilable adults underpinned government policies toward Jewish refugees. While rejecting adult Jewish refugees, French officials welcomed Jewish *children* who had survived the Holocaust on French territory, even if they were not French citizens. The arrival of these children served as a public means of reaffirming traditions of Republican solidarity and asylum that had been deeply compromised during the Vichy regime.[13]

Adult, German-Jewish refugees were not considered worthy additions to the French demographic profile in 1945. But non-Jewish, adult German laborers, particularly young men and women, were soon in high demand. French policymakers promoted German immigration in the context of an emerging consensus around France's labor and immigration needs. First, an underpopulated France, with its anemic birthrate, could not afford to reject immigration. Second, immigration had to be based on a policy of selecting "good migrants," which meant migrants who would assimilate quickly. Finally, time was of the essence. There was a short window of opportunity during which it would be possible to select and recruit these "good migrants" from the masses of DPs crowding Europe's refugee camps.[14]

The consensus ended there, as French officials in the Ministry of Population and the Institut National d'Études Demographiques (INED) disagreed about the precise basis on which the selection of postwar immigrants should proceed. At its core, the dispute was about the parameters of assimilation. Georges Mauco, France's most influential immigration expert, drew on his particular reading of psychoanalytic theories to argue that children's ethnic qualities were fixed at a young age. He insisted that immigrants should be chosen based primarily on their ethnic and geographic origins, which, in his view, determined their character, their propensity for productive labor, their criminality, and their assimilability. The demographer Alfred Sauvy and pediatrician and population expert Robert Debré, by contrast, were inclined to focus on individual qualities, and were more optimistic about the ability of foreigners to become French. But all agreed that immigrants should be chosen based on their capacity for assimilation, and all saw ethnicity as a major determinant of that capacity. Ethnic and racial stereotypes therefore profoundly shaped the logic of immigration policies in postwar France, even after an ordinance passed on November 2, 1945 officially banned the use of ethnic criteria in the selection of immigrants.[15]

French population experts were also united in their enthusiasm for German migration. In 1945, Mauco ranked Germans among the most desirable candidates for immigration to France, right up with Scandinavians, Finns, Danes, Irish, English, Belgians, and Swiss nationals. Indeed, Germans ranked well ahead of "northern Mediterraneans" and Slavs. Mauco was particularly opposed to migration from Italy and Southern Spain, based on the alleged low productivity and "superior criminality" of migrants from the Southern Mediterranean. He also excluded Jews, Armenians, Russians, and Assyriens, maintaining that "their adaptation and their assimilation has been particularly difficult" because of their tendency to congregate in "non-productive" economic sectors in cities rather than in the under-populated countryside. The very fact that Jewish refugees had been victims of genocide rendered them undesirable, according to Mauco, who saw Hitler's victims as "psychically and sometimes physically diminished by their despair or by persecution."[16] Mauco's racial hierarchy was highly influential in shaping postwar immigration policy, and was endorsed by de Gaulle himself.[17]

Sauvy and Debré shared Mauco's enthusiasm for German immigration, even as they enumerated the flaws they associated with German character. In a 1946 manifesto they elaborated, "The faults attributed to the Germans: collective cruelty, passivity and obedience . . . can disappear through contact with other populations . . . An addition of a reasonable quantity of German blood could be particularly precious, as the undeniable qualities of Germans should certainly contribute to the amelioration of certain disequilibriums and compensate for the excessive flow of Latins and Slavs."[18]

The French decision to recruit Germans to France after World War II was not only shaped by racism, however, but also by a conviction that German overpopulation posed an inherent security threat to Europe. Demographers incessantly compared relative population losses in Europe after World War II, noting with dismay that the Nazis seemed to have triumphed in their demographic assault on occupied Europe, thanks to the influx of some 12 million German expellees and refugees from Eastern Europe. A 1946 report by the Comité International pour l'Étude des Questions Européen concluded that while the Nazis had successfully devastated the populations of occupied countries, Germany's own population had actually grown by 7.5 percent since 1939, with menacing implications. "*The danger resulting from this state of affairs is extremely grave.* It is all the greater since while the German population has grown from 67 to 72 million, German territory has been reduced by about one-fourth since 1945, due to the loss of Eastern Prussia and Silesia."[19]

French diplomats and population experts alike depicted German overpopulation as a threat to Europe's security, as severe food shortages and overcrowded refugee camps encouraged a renaissance of Malthusian pessimism. In addition to the problem of overpopulation, German families had been shattered by the war, with seemingly disastrous consequences for morality and political stability. In 1948, among 30,000 schoolchildren in Dusseldorf, 32 percent lacked a father, the fathers of 6.9 percent were unemployed, and 2.6 percent were full orphans. Divorce rates had doubled during the war. "This disequilibrium makes Germany an unhealthy breeding ground full of risks for Europe and the world. Only extremist movement will benefit," warned a 1948 report from the French Ministry of Foreign Affairs.[20]

General Pierre Koenig, the military Governor of the French zone of occupation in Germany, shared these concerns. In March 1946, he warned, "While Germany will have difficulty feeding itself because its population will be too dense, Poland will not, at first, be able to cultivate its land because of a lack of manpower. To a lesser degree the situation in France will be the same." Only immediate action to depopulate Germany could counter the risk that Germany would once again seek out Lebensraum in the East and West. Fortunately, the defeat and occupation of Germany presented the French government with an opportunity to strategically raid the German population. "All of this part of Europe will find itself in an unstable situation, and a tendency toward expansion will naturally arise in Germany. Given that such an expansion is inevitable, it is necessary, beginning now, to plan it and direct it," Koenig advised.[21]

Promoting birth control and liberalizing abortion restrictions represented obvious strategies to contain German population growth. But French diplomats were skeptical about the efficacy and the desirability of encouraging antinatalist policies so close to home. The only solution, in the eyes of military authorities and population experts, was therefore to reduce the German population through selective emigration. Koenig was optimistic that young Germans would easily assimilate in postwar France. He suggested that France welcome "young German men in France who will marry French women, or young German girls who will marry French men . . . This will prevent the major risk of immigration, that is to say, the formation of inassimilable minorities." He was typical in his view of the French family as a central agent of assimilation. Not surprisingly, Koenig identified children as the most assimilable, and therefore the most desirable immigrants of all. "The ideal solution," he proclaimed, "would not be to introduce young people in France who are already formed—or rather deformed—but children, even babies, who are easily assimilable. For example, in Germany there are thousands of children of French origins, born during the years of war. This emigration should be organized in the very near future, while Germany is still under the effect of a moral crisis in consequence of the defeat."[22]

Officials in Paris received Koenig's suggestions with enthusiasm. At the Conference of Moscow in March 1946, Georges Bidault, Minister of Foreign Affairs, announced a plan to recruit up to a million German workers for immigration to France "in the interest of peace and to raise the standard of living of Germans themselves." In addition to recruiting German workers for French industry and agriculture, Bidault demanded the cessation of expulsions of ethnic Germans from Eastern Europe; strict limitations on the number of displaced persons allowed to settle on German soil; and the repatriation of refugees already congregated in Germany, all of whom threatened to exacerbate the perceived crisis of German overpopulation.[23]

German officials and representatives of the other allied powers responded to Bidault's proposals with a mixture of applause and skepticism. Some Germans feared a brain drain, and accused the French of attempting to poach the skilled labor most essential to German reconstruction. The German newspaper *Berlin am Mittag* suggested that Bidault's proposal represented nothing less than a belated validation of the Nazi quest for Lebensraum: "To admit that an overpopulated Germany will expand beyond its borders is to recognize that Hitler was right when he sought territorial enlargement," editors proclaimed.[24] Other German officials saw more promise in the proposal, however, welcoming it in the name of overcoming long-term French-German rivalry. German Undersecretary of State Fritz Eberhard praised the plan as "the first real chance to overcome the horrific blood-enemy mentality on both sides."[25]

In fact, French diplomats were not alone in their concerns about the strain of overpopulation in Germany. Many Germans, especially in Bavaria, where small towns swelled with DPs and refugees from the East, complained bitterly about the economic burdens imposed by the influx of newcomers. Not only did local Germans question the Germanness of so-called ethnic Germans from Eastern Europe, but they resented being forced to share their homes and limited food supplies with DPs (especially Jews) and German expellees, whom they depicted as lazy, uncivilized, criminal, black marketeers and freeloaders.[26] Some German and Allied population experts even suggested that the most surefire way to prevent future German expansionism in Europe would be to resettle excess Germans in "vacant" areas of Africa and South America. Colonialism abroad would prevent colonialism in Europe. German colonial fantasies were ironically rehabilitated as a solution rather than a cause of Total War. "The world's empty spaces are calling for human beings," argued the German Christian Democrat and economist Konrad Theiss in 1948. "Numerous interested parties, such as landowners, merchants, etc. are waiting in those continents for people to cultivate the virgin soil, to make it more valuable."[27]

German workers were themselves more skeptical about their prospects abroad, particularly in France. In February 1947, the Social-Psychological Institute in Baden-Baden conducted an opinion poll of 1,596 workers in the French occupation zone in order to measure their attitudes toward resettlement in France. The study found that German workers were rarely inclined to emigrate, since "Germany needs them and the French hate them."[28]

British and American diplomats, meanwhile, were typically more concerned about repatriating and resettling the DPs in their own occupation zones than shifting excess Germans to France. But some American voluntary organizations praised the French plan as a triumph of humanitarianism over nationalist hatred. The American Unitarian Association sent a glowing letter to the French Ambassador in the United States, commending Bidault's proposal. The Unitarians gushed that they felt "a holy joy upon learning that France, which has so cruelly suffered from German invasions, has raised itself to such a moral level as to invite such a large number of its former enemies into its own home in order to nurture them at its breast like its own children."[29]

French officials did not object to such flattering interpretations of their motives, but they privately discussed more self-interested reasons for raising the children of the enemy. In a memo to the Commisaire du Plan, which was responsible for economic planning in postwar France, diplomat Raymond Bousquet suggested that France required 1,400,000 to 1,500,000 immigrants in order to meet its future labor needs. The problem, as he saw it, was that introducing such a large number of foreigners into the French population threatened to leave it "invaded, peacefully or not, by a growing number of foreigners." In order to avoid the dilution of French character, Bousquet insisted on the need to carefully select immigrants who would easily assimilate. Germans ranked among the most attractive candidates, in his view. "Aside from our interest in compensating for the Latin contribution to our population . . . with a Nordic contribution, this immigration will have the advantage of absorbing, at least to a certain degree, the overpopulation of Germany which represents a perpetual menace to France." In order to facilitate assimilation, Bousquet held that the French government should target displaced German youth and children in particular.[30]

Unfortunately for French demographers, German religious and governmental officials did not perceive French plans to adopt German orphans as a selfless humanitarian gesture. In 1947 the French Ministry of Foreign Affairs announced proudly that France would welcome "several thousand German children without families, refugees in Denmark, in order to provide for their support and education and to make them into French citizens." On January 19, 1946, 200 German children from Denmark arrived in Baden-Baden. In order to guarantee the maximum chance of assimilation, only orphans between the ages of two and seven were considered candidates, "that is to say, having not yet received a German education." Approximately 80 young refugees were selected. But shortly after the children's arrival in the French zone, General Koenig was confronted by an angry delegation of German Catholic priests and Protestant ministers, who denounced the emigration scheme as nothing less than a devious "kidnapping of children" in the Nazi tradition. The program was soon suspended.[31]

While they refused to apologize for the scandal, French authorities ultimately shifted their efforts toward a less contentious goal. The fraternization of French POWs and occupation soldiers with German women had created a new kind of transnational family. Shortly after the collapse of Hitler's Germany, the French press began to circulate rumors about children of French-German unions, depicting the children as an unclaimed spoil of war. In May of 1946, one French newspaper wildly estimated that 300,000 occupation children had already been born in Germany to French fathers. While dismissing such projections as "pure fantasy," Henri Fesquet, writing in *Le Monde* in August 1946, agreed that these children were promising candidates for French citizenship. "From 1940 to 1945, Germany was ... an immense Babel where all races rubbed together ... From this promiscuous lifestyle ... children were born. And with them a painful problem that we cannot ignore." Admittedly, the problem was complex. It was no simple task to assimilate the children of the enemy. But Fesquet concluded that the demographic interests of France overruled any potential misgivings. The main challenge, in fact, was that Germans might be reluctant to abandon their children to the French state. "In spite of their racist theories, they don't ignore that the crossbreeding of French and Germans sometimes produces excellent results ... In this particular case, they make every effort to camouflage the children that we have the right to reclaim," Fesquet warned. In this context, Fesquet exhorted French occupation officials to act quickly to remove the children from German soil (and their German mothers). "In effect, it is advisable to remove these half-French children who we would like to form in our image from German influence as soon as possible," he urged.[32] There was no Bowlbyism here, no concern whatsoever about the effects of separating these occupation children from their mothers.

The French military government soon devised and implemented an elaborate and ambitious plan to repatriate children born to French fathers and German mothers in wartime and occupied Germany. This policy, French officials insisted, represented a just form of demographic restitution for Nazi war crimes, and a strategy for guaranteeing European security. In a 1946 memo, French Ambassador to Baden Jacques Tarbé de Saint-Hardouin justified the scheme to Georges Bidault, the Minister of Foreign Affairs. In strictly legal terms, he conceded, the children should be considered German nationals. But leaving the children in Germany, he reasoned, "would allow Germany to benefit from a demographic growth that it doesn't deserve and which would go against our principle ... of reducing the German population. These children of unknown parents represent a human treasure that a country with low population density cannot ignore."[33]

By August 1946, French occupation authorities had established infant's homes in the French zone in Tübingen, Bad Durkheim, and Unterhausen. German mothers who wished to abandon their children to these homes were required to provide proof of French paternity. They were also obliged to sign a document relinquishing all parental rights, although they were allowed two months to change their minds. The purpose of the homes was to prepare the infants for their future adoption in France. Since most of the mothers who abandoned their children were living in severe poverty, the first priority was to provide the infants with much-needed food and medical care. But French nurses and social workers also strove to rehabilitate the children morally and culturally. "Very often they are not more than 50 percent French, having only a French father or mother and another foreign parent. They therefore need serious basic education to compensate for their racial heritage and the immorality of their parents," concluded a social worker in the French military's Social Service branch.[34] After a stay of several months in the homes, the precious (albeit damaged) cargo was transferred to France, handed over to the French welfare authorities in the *Assistance Publique,* and registered as wards of the state. The children were issued new French "certificates of origins" to replace their German birth certificates, and given French names. These certificates erased all trace of the children's German origins and birthplaces. Then the children were placed in French adoptive families.[35]

In accordance with French law and the longstanding traditions of the French *Assistance Publique,* the adoptions were closed, the placement of the children was secret, and there was no possibility for future contact between birth mothers and their children. A French law dating back to June 27, 1904 stipulated that the placement of wards of the *Assistance Publique* was to be kept secret; officials thereby sought to sever all ties between abandoned children and their biological parents. This policy was intended to discourage parents from abandoning their children. Closed adoptions were also meant to protect the identity and honor of the birth mother and her family. By guaranteeing her anonymity, child welfare officials hoped to diminish the risk of infanticide and abortion. And child welfare workers at the time believed that a complete break with the past was in the best interests of abandoned children themselves, enabling them to get a fresh start in life.[36]

These laws were still vigorously enforced after the Second World War. Norbert Flad, born in June 1948 to a German-Catholic woman in Württemberg, was abandoned to a French infant's home six months later. In 1950, Norbert's birth mother contacted the Ambassador of France in the French occupation zone, seeking information about the whereabouts of her child; she had changed her mind. The Ambassador refused her request, replying that she had voluntarily relinquished her parental rights and "accepted a secret placement and the rupture of all connection with the child." He could only inform her that Norbert had been transported to France in October of 1949 and adopted by a French family soon afterward.[37]

Policymakers' focus on quick adoption was not merely a reflection of prevailing ideals of child welfare in France. It reflected the overriding goal of rapid assimilation. Conveniently, there was a growing demand for children to adopt, thanks in part to the liberalization of French adoption laws after the war. The adoption of children was still a new phenomenon in France, first legalized in 1923. French adoption laws passed in July 1939 and August 1941 allowed only couples over the age of 40 to adopt, unless the prospective parents had been married and childless for more than ten years. Adoptive parents could not have any legitimate children. Postwar reforms, however, allowed couples over the age of 30, widows and divorcees, and couples with legitimate (adult) children to adopt as well.[38] Pflimlin suggested that the quick adoption of French-German children would facilitate assimilation and meet the growing demand for children in France: "We know that in France there are currently many more people who wish to adopt a child than children available for adoption . . . the large majority of little immigrants will have a family without delay, a French family that will make them into true French citizens . . . That is doubtlessly the best way to resolve the problem of assimilation."[39]

French plans to enrich the population through international adoption brought social issues such as welfare rights, child abandonment, and child support to the attention of diplomats and military officials. Wartime relations between French men and German women also raised sticky issues of citizenship and national belonging, since basic laws about parental rights and citizenship in France and Germany conflicted. Children born to unmarried parents in Germany automatically received the nationality of their mothers, whether or not their fathers recognized them. In France, however, an ordinance of October 19, 1945 liberalized the 1927 nationality code, making it easier for children born abroad and out of wedlock to acquire French citizenship. Previously a child born to unmarried parents carried the nationality of the first parent to recognize him or her (typically the mother). Now, a child born abroad was considered French if recognized by a French mother or father, regardless of whether the parents were married. Children born outside of France had the option to decline the French nationality within six months of reaching the age of majority. Effectively, this law meant that the children of unmarried French occupation soldiers and German women were considered German according to German laws and French according to French laws.[40]

The French nationality code also stood in stark contrast to the policies applied to occupation children by UNNRA, the IRO, and British and American occupation authorities, who considered children born to unmarried German women and Allied soldiers to be German citizens and the sole responsibility of German welfare authorities.[41] An estimated 37,000 children were born to unmarried "Frauleins" and American GIs in postwar Germany and Austria. These children were not considered American citizens or entitled to any special welfare benefits. In a 1946 article entitled "Pregnant Frauleins are Warned!" *Stars and Stripes* outlined the American policy. Women expecting a child fathered by an American solider should expect no assistance by the American army. German women who became pregnant were advised to seek help from a German or Austrian welfare organization. "If the soldier is already in the United States, his address is not to be communicated to the woman in question . . . Claims for child support from unmarried German and Austrian mothers will not be recognized."[42]

The American military jealously protected the right of American men to sleep around. In the U.S. zone of occupation, there was no legal possibility for a German woman to file a paternity claim against an American man until 1955, when West Germany achieved full sovereignty. The U.S. military's disavowal of occupation children was accompanied by a relatively liberal policy regarding fraternization. After a brief period in which all fraternization was (unsuccessfully) forbidden, GIs were even permitted to board in private German homes. After 1948, it was possible for a GI to marry his German girlfriend.[43] This liberal approach to fraternization was never extended to African-American GIs, however. Several African-American GIs who dated German women were physically assaulted by white American servicemen. And they were systematically denied the opportunity to marry their German girlfriends by military officials and American immigration authorities who opposed interracial marriage.[44]

Baby-hungry French officials recognized an opportunity in America's rejection of its occupation children. In July 1946, one French official observed "the multitude of children born to American fathers who will be abandoned by their mothers in the American zones, for whom the Americans don't wish to take responsibility." He suggested that France should "collect all of these babies if no one wants them . . . They should be fine specimens."[45]

In the end, France never did attempt to claim the children of GIs, but the French government did provide well for its own occupation children. Any child recognized by a French father received full French rations if the father resided in the French zone. If the father returned to France, the child was still entitled to double the rations of a German child. Since rations for Germans in the French zone were the lowest of the four zones of occupation, this drastically improved the child's chances of survival.[46] In order to receive these benefits, however, German mothers were required to prove the French paternity of their offspring. In an age before DNA testing, this meant that state officials scrutinized the private correspondence and other evidence of intimate relations provided by German women who petitioned French military authorities for assistance.

These appeals conveyed the severe economic distress experienced by German women who had become pregnant by French soldiers. In 1946, German civilians in the French zone were officially allotted 900 calories a day.[47] German mothers of occupation children faced particularly severe challenges as they attempted to provide for their children. Not only did they carry the general stigma of single motherhood, but they were often ostracized for having had intimate relationships with a foreigner as well.[48] "I am 24 years old now and find myself in a situation of serious distress that is deteriorating by the day. In addition I am suffering emotionally a great deal from the bad treatment of my parents and the neighbors," wrote Mariane Döring, who had given birth to two children by French soldiers. In many cases, women who had become pregnant by French soldiers were denied welfare assistance by local

German authorities, even if the child was technically a German citizen. After she was turned down by the local German welfare office, Margot Steffens of Koblenz wrote to French authorities requesting that her child be temporarily admitted to a French children's home. She implored, "Through the bombings I lost everything . . . the efforts I have made to secure assistance from the German authorities have all been refused because . . . I have a French child."[49]

In their letters to French authorities, German mothers often denounced men who refused to take responsibility for or even acknowledge their children. Some still had genuine affection for their former lovers and lamented their disappearance. Others had few romantic illusions, and simply sought financial assistance. In several cases, German women appealed directly to French authorities in order to locate evasive fathers, with little apparent success. Hildegarde Steiner wrote to the mayor of Cruzy in France in search of her child's father, Augustin Crambade: "Although Mr. Crambade promised to marry me, I have had no news from him since his departure, although I have written to him several times. I kindly request you to inform me if Mr. Crambade has returned home, and if he still intends to marry me. For me it is a question of knowing . . . how to provide for myself and my child."[50] She received no reply. In Kaifenheim, Anna appealed directly to her children's father in an attempt to awaken a sense of paternal responsibility. "Your children are calling for you. One day you must hear it," she implored. "Hans-Josef will be five years old in July. Every day he says, 'When is my Papa coming, my Papa will bring me chocolate.' . . . Come just once and see them. You can go directly back to France. If you want to have one of the children you can pick one out if you don't want to take all three."[51]

Maria in Pomerania told a similar story of disappointed hopes. Like Mariane D., she suffered the scorn of her family and community during her pregnancy. "Two years have already passed since I have heard from you. You know well that our relationship was not without consequences," she wrote. "November 18, 1945 I gave birth to a little girl. But what I suffered during the nine months of pregnancy, I can't even tell you . . . Twice I went to the edge of the Moselle river to take my own life, but each time someone stopped me . . . Thank God I have a hard head and no one was able to shatter my strength." Fortunately, Maria's family had a change of heart once her daughter Inge was born. "After I had the child the whole world returned. Everyone spoils her and my mother is crazy with joy," she recounted. French authorities approached her and suggested that she give the child up for adoption in France, but Maria refused. "I have decided to keep her because I don't want to be separated from something so beautiful and sweet like our Inge, and if they take her from me I would be very unhappy."

Like Anna, Maria tried to foster the father's attachment to the child. "Everywhere I go people say to me 'what a beautiful child!' Not surprising with a father like you. She has the same pretty eyes as you, and her nose and face are also like yours, in sum she looks like you . . . And now, dear Roger, I come to you with a request . . . Help me a little by sending me something for your child from time to time, maybe some fabric or shoes, whatever you can send me."[52]

Most of these delinquent fathers refused to pay child support. Given the limitations of international law, German mothers had little recourse. One father responded to a request for support with outright hostility, depicting himself as a victim of scheming women. "How can you be sure I am the father after so many months? You really weren't with any other man? . . . I have had so much misfortune with women that I don't know what to believe."[53] Faced with the challenge of securing child support across national borders, many women saw abandoning their child to the French state as the only way to guarantee their child's welfare. The meager rations in the French zone and the precarious situation of unmarried women in transnational relationships aided and abetted the French campaign to recuperate occupation children.

French policymakers and social workers, however, justified their adoption scheme by depicting single German mothers as immoral or negligent. They contrasted the sad future faced by such children in postwar Germany to the happier prospects they would enjoy as French citizens. German mothers, argued French social workers, typically "abandon the child out of a lack of maternal sentiment or out of loyalty to their true family that would be compromised by the presence of a bastard child."[54] A 1946 French military report noted that the number of occupation children was increasing, due to "the promiscuity of German women." These women abandoned their children out of "disappointment in the refusal of the presumed father to marry her, desire to make a new life with a German man who is not inclined to welcome the child of a stranger," or "fear of the possible return of a German husband who is a prisoner or war or has been absent for a long time." French authorities rarely mentioned the economic strain faced by single mothers as a factor contributing to abandonment. They instead depicted the adoption scheme as a humanitarian gesture to rescue unwanted children.[55]

French authorities assessed the moral and maternal character of German women as they allocated welfare benefits to mothers in the occupied zone. In several instances, they removed children from their German mothers based on accusations of neglect or abuse. In a typical case, a French diplomat suggested that Marguerite Betram, who had given birth to two baby girls by a French-Algerian father, was unfit for motherhood. "The mother has not paid her rent for a long time, owes 336 Marks and is threatened with eviction. Somehow she manages to feed her daughters, claiming that it is with the assistance of her parents. In view of her bad conduct it is possible that her meager resources have another origin. The room is dirty but the children are in good health. Perhaps we could remove them from the mother."[56]

While speaking in the name of the children's best interests, French social workers in occupied Germany were clearly motivated by nationalist concerns. René Bourcier's German mother had left him in the care of the child's German grandmother in 1940. Mrs. Bentkowska, the social worker responsible for his case, suggested that the child be removed from his grandmother and sent to his father in France. While the child's grandmother flawlessly cared for her grandson, she threatened to Germanize him, the social worker warned. "She is raising him like a little German. . . . besides which this woman is very old and if she dies before the child is grown up . . . he will fall completely into the hands of the German community and become a German." The social worker suggested that "in spite of the issue of parental rights . . . wouldn't it be in the child's interest and at the same time the national interest to request French authorities to give the father custody so he can raise him in France like a French citizen?"[57]

Transnational families tested the limits of sovereignty and citizenship in occupied Germany, extending the regulatory authority of French social policy well beyond French borders. As families became entangled across state borders, so too did domestic and international politics. French occupation officials, diplomats, and policymakers pursued the best interests of the French nation, which demanded recuperating occupation children for France, but they spoke in terms of the best interests of individual children, blurring the lines between diplomacy, social work, and population policy.

While images of negligent German mothers justified the adoption scheme, letters written by these mothers reveal that many were reluctant to part with their children. Klara Herron in Hanover fell in love with a French POW, who promised to marry her. They had two children together. "After his return to France I repeatedly attempted to get in touch with him, but it was in vain. . . . Maybe he is married; I don't know anything . . . Of course I want to keep them, because I love them and I also loved this French man. But I currently find myself in an intolerable state of poverty."[58] In reality few German women were prepared to abandon their children. Most simply sought financial assistance from the French state. Gradually, enthusiasm for the adoption program subsided among French officials, largely because it produced meager demographic returns for France. As of 1946, there were 3,118 cases of mixed French-German children under investigation in the French occupation zone.[59] By 1949 the French military's Child Search division had identified 14,357 illegitimate children with French or allied fathers. Of this number, however, only 484 had actually been repatriated to France for adoption.[60]

The adoption program was also compromised by ongoing tensions between French claims to be agents of democratization in Germany, and its adoption policies, which were based on nationalist self-interest and racist and eugenic selection criteria. Local Germans were quick to point out the ways in which French adoption policies resembled Nazi schemes to Germanize children in Lebensborn homes. Rhetorically, French population experts took careful pains to differentiate their postwar immigration and nationality policies from the racist credos of the Nazis. Writing in 1945, Alfred Sauvy and Robert Debré insisted that "the idea of . . . 'the protection of the purity of the race' is nothing but a political polemic, with no foundation or value." The goal of French immigration policy was "not to conserve the purity of a race that doesn't exist," but rather, "to preserve the best qualities in the French type and character" by choosing the most assimilable immigrants possible.[61]

But from the beginning, French authorities walked a fine line as they parsed purported distinctions between racial, religious, eugenic, and cultural hierarchies. They were not willing to include any and all occupation children in the French national community. Occupation children were evaluated and selected according to rigorous hygienic, nationalist, and racial criteria. At a basic level, the entire adoption program was premised on the assumption that the German mothers of occupation children were undesirable immigrants. Since German women were reluctant to part with their children, French officials might have offered both German mothers and their children French citizenship. In 1947, Pierre Koenig, military commander of the French occupation zone, actually recommended this plan of action, but his proposal was rejected.[62]

Policies regarding the children of German women and North African soldiers most blatantly exposed the limits of the Republic's faith in assimilation. These children, occupation authorities concluded in 1946, did not represent a demographic windfall. They were instead to be "directed toward Northern Africa where they can be integrated into a community more suited to their descent."[63] The Governor of Algeria agreed, suggesting in 1947 that resettling the children in Algeria would "return all of these children to their community of origins."[64]

Parallel discussions emerged in postwar Germany with respect to children born to African-American soldiers and German women. Such children represented a small minority of occupation children—a mere 3,000 in 1950. But they were at the center of a broad public debate about the links between race and democratization in postwar Germany and the United States. Heide Fehrenbach has found that in the early 1950s, Germans promoted transnational adoption as the preferred solution to the perceived "problem" of black occupation children in Germany. Policymakers and child welfare officials in West Germany focused on the alleged financial burden that "foreign-looking" children posed to the German welfare system, and portrayed their mothers as immoral, materialistic, and greedy. Insisting that such children had no future in Germany, they depicted the adoption of biracial children in the land of their fathers as a humanitarian gesture.[65] Up to 7,000 black German children were ultimately adopted by African-American families between 1945 and 1968, no thanks to American immigration authorities, who were unenthusiastic about these adoptions. In 1951, for example, at a meeting with West German authorities, Lois McVey of the United States Displaced Persons' Commission suggested that black occupation children should instead be transported to Central or South America, "where issues of race hold less significance." McVey was much much more enthusiastic about the adoption of German orphans in the United States.[66]

German and French authorities were equally ambivalent toward children of French colonial soldiers and German women. Drawing on a tradition that had begun during the First World War, and intensified during the French occupation of the Rhineland in 1923, postwar Germans generally depicted French colonial soldiers as barbaric and violent. They considered their very presence in Germany a degrading affront to civilization. So-called "Rhineland bastards," born to German women and French colonial troops between the wars, had been subject to forcible sterilization under the Nazi regime. While relations between African-American soldiers and German women were largely attributed to German women's immorality or opportunism, relations between French colonial soldiers and German women after World War II were typically depicted as coercive, in spite of contrary evidence. German officials were eager to see the offspring of French colonial soldiers and German women leave German soil.[67]

French policies toward biracial occupation children reflected a broader set of concerns about North African immigration in postwar France, as officials transplanted French colonial hierarchies to the context of the German occupation. In the French empire, racial hierarchies were typically couched in a rhetoric of a civilizational hierarchy. The full privileges of French citizenship, in this logic, would be bestowed upon colonial subjects in the distant future, when they had internalized French ideals of culture and civilization. In the context of postwar France, assumptions about the alleged "cultural" inferiority of colonial subjects informed a migration policy that considered Germans to be more "desirable" migrants than French colonial subjects or citizens.[68]

The "obstacles" to North African immigration, Robert Debré and Alfred Sauvy specified, "stem far less from racial differences than from differences in civilization. . . . Islam is separated from [French civilization] by a massive gulf that renders the fusion of the two populations difficult, and without a doubt, undesirable. Currently one can observe that the results obtained are deplorable, both for public health and for morality in general." Algerians and other North Africans therefore ranked far below Germans on the list of desirable immigrants. Sauvy and Debré were particularly concerned that "the high birthrates of Algerian natives, relative to the depression of French natality" would create a "demographic current" of North Africans in France. "If that cannot be completely avoided, it should at least be channeled and limited," they advised in 1946.[69]

A year later, the Institut National d'Études Démographiques published a detailed study of North African immigration authored by Louis Chevalier. Chevalier shared his colleagues' skepticism about the potential for North African assimilation in France, even in the case of mixed marriages. Like Sauvy and Debré, he emphasized cultural barriers to assimilation. But he insisted that these barriers were so profound that assimilation was a hopeless cause. "Much more than a faith, much more than a religious practice, much more than a community pride, Islam is a manner of being, of feeling, of understanding, in sum, a temperament, a psychology that creates a profound refusal of all assimilation behind all the secondary appearances of Europeanization."[70]

French social agencies such as the Service Social d'Aide aux Émigrants, the French branch of the International Social Service, even launched a mission to "rescue" white women from what were described as ill-conceived marriages to North African soldiers after World War II. In a report on activities in Morocco in 1946, SSAE officials elaborated, "The Europeans took every indigenous man for an Arab prince, although further investigation often revealed that he was a nomad living in a tent with one or two wives; rich with a few sheep and a goat. . . . Some Arabs obliged their white wives to wear the veil. The degree of evolution of the Arabs living out in the countryside or in the villages unfortunately allows us to affirm that marriage with a white woman is a serious psychological mistake."[71]

In spite of experts' insistence that their prejudices against North African immigration were purely cultural, decisions made locally by French administrators exposed the blatantly racist underpinning of French adoption policies. Children of German women and North African fathers *were* actually transferred to France for adoption, for example, if they had light-colored skin. In a 1948 memo, French Ministry of Public Health and Population stipulated that "in the case of children with less visible North-African traits, it seems possible to place them in France for adoption."[72] In August 1947 two such children were selected for adoption in France on the basis of their skin color. "The children of North African fathers Agnès Valentini and Eugène Kientze were not particularly marked by their origins and their skin is white, and for this reason they were repatriated to Strasbourg. It seems that there is no reason why these children should not remain in the metropole, the available places in North Africa being reserved for children with colored skin," reported a French military official in the field.[73]

French social workers in occupied Germany also selected and rejected children for adoption based on their perceived biological or eugenic quality. In 1950, French Ambassador to Germany François Poncet reported that one-quarter to one-half of the children abandoned to French children's homes by their German mothers were actually rejected because of physical or developmental problems. "In general these abandoned children have very low intelligence quotients," he noted.[74] The rejected children were unceremoniously returned to their mothers or transferred to German orphanages. Tensions between the French mission to model democratic and humanitarian values in Germany, and the nationalist, eugenic, and racist concerns driving the adoption program plagued the scheme from the start. An early postwar report cautioned, "It is necessary that the greatest prudence presides over the recuperation of these children, that in no case it takes on the character of kidnappings which were so dear to the National Socialists." The same official, however, insisted on the need for vigorous biological selection, maintaining, "It is critical that we only accept children who are perfectly healthy and well-constituted into our children's homes and into France, and that we reject any child who could become a future burden to the state, even if French paternity is well-established."[75] The hypocrisy of French selection policies was not lost on local Germans. "The massive restitution of 50 percent of the children we have collected to their mothers cannot help but raise the feeling and spread the notion that the French government is as racist as the best of the Nazis," Poncet warned.[76]

By the late 1940s, French plans to rebalance European demography through transnational adoption were frustrated by numerous obstacles: the resistance of German authorities, the reluctance of German mothers to abandon their children, and accusations that French selection policies too closely resembled the Nazis' own racist Germanization policies. Above all, the French Lebensborn scheme was producing weak returns. And by 1949 to 1950, demographers were aware of growing evidence that a baby boom was underway in France. In fact, birthrates in France began to climb as early as 1939, and noticeably surged after the Second World War. But even as the press wildly celebrated the rising birthrate in 1946 and 1947, demographers speculated that this spurt was a temporary result of the war, as couples had delayed having children due to wartime separation. When birthrates continued to climb in 1948 and 1949, population experts were pleasantly surprised, but still thought they were seeing the effects of the war. But by late 1949 and early 1950, there was evidence that increasing natality reflected more than a postwar spurt. Adopting German occupation children no longer seemed so urgent.[77]

In light of these trends, Poncet urged that the adoptions be discontinued in August 1949, citing both the political cost and the "poor returns for the French community."[78] He concluded, "Experience has shown that the number of children susceptible of being received in France is very small and continues to diminish; on the other hand, the barriers of a political nature from the German side are increasing and, in my opinion, there is no ground for continuing this operation."[79] The last infant's home in the French zone was finally closed November 15, 1949. By the end of that year, 562 children had been repatriated to France for adoption—far short of the 300,000 once imagined by French policymakers and journalists.[80] The program ultimately fell victim to tensions that plagued the allied occupation more broadly: between France's self-image as a model of democratic values, and the nationalist and racist hierarchies that drove the market for displaced children.

While the adoption scheme failed to produce many new French citizens, it did represent a significant departure in French relations with Germany and in the development of postwar social and migration policies in Europe. Germans, once considered the blood-enemies of the French, gradually came to be seen as valuable and assimilable additions to the French population. It was the beginning of a new era of French-German economic and political cooperation in postwar Europe, as the exchange of babies presaged further political and economic exchange. The adoption program also precipitated the gradual transformation of French immigration and labor policies. The French government's failure to recruit sufficient migrant labor from its northern European neighbors set the stage for the massive recruitment of foreign laborers from Southern Europe and Northern Africa in the 1950s and 1960s.

The failed French adoption scheme also reflected the growing internationalization of social and family policies in postwar Europe. Under the specific conditions of occupation, French officials appropriated the authority (and incurred obligations) to support and regulate the families of German citizens. Diplomats and military officials made judgments more typically reserved for social workers, weighing in on issues such as child support, child abuse, custody, paternity disputes, and child welfare. Social workers became important actors in diplomatic disputes. The formation of unprecedented numbers of transnational families during and after the Second World War stimulated the creation of new bilateral and international policies regulating citizenship and social welfare. It provoked debates about the meaning of democratization and humanitarianism in postwar Europe, and how the constitution of families was linked to these terms.

While the French adoption program reflected a trend toward the internationalization of family policies, it also underscored the ongoing centrality of nationalism to the reconstruction of postwar Europe. Across Nazi-occupied Europe, the recovery of national sovereignty was linked to the recovery of children. French authorities, like East European governments, competed for displaced children in order to make up for their losses in a perceived demographic war with Germany, and to prevent future outbreaks of German imperialism. Wartime and postwar occupations are often linked in popular and official memory to economic expropriation, but it appears that children were also an important form of wartime plunder.

Postwar displacement and migration forced policymakers and citizens across Europe to confront questions about the limits of assimilation. The migration and social policies that emerged from these debates reflected differences between Eastern and Western Europe. In France, colonial racial hierarchies shaped postwar assumptions about which lost children should be considered assets to the French population, and which should be excluded. In Eastern Europe, the debate about the potential for assimilation reflected the recent history of conflicts between German and Slavic nationalist movements. But in East and West alike, Europeans generally emerged from the Second World War convinced that only national homogeneity could prevent the outbreak of a Third World War. The French case, despite its peculiarities, was typical of a broader trend. Across Europe, policymakers attempted to distance themselves from the Nazi past after World War II. But the doors to citizenship remained far from open, as racial and ethnic hierarchies did not disappear overnight.[81] Outright racial discrimination and anti-Semitism continued in postwar Europe, along with more coded forms of exclusion. Racial and cultural hierarchies had always been intertwined in Europe, even under Nazi rule, where cultural and political qualifications sometimes determined whether a person was seen as "racially fit" for Germanization.[82] After World War II, explicit references to race did not vanish from public discourse, but racial hierarchies were increasingly translated into the more malleable (and ultimately more effective) language of economic productivity, psychological stability, and cultural assimilability.[83]

Kathryn Hulme of UNNRA described the process by which DP camps began to empty out through emigration schemes in the late 1940s. Each scheme had its own set of openly discriminatory criteria. "Australia would take family units consisting of husband, wife, and unmarried children . . . Brazil wanted mainly agricultural workers eighteen to forty years of age, all nationalities and religious groups accepted, with the exception of Jews and persons of Asiatic origin . . . New Zealand sought two hundred orphans for adoption . . . and three hundred single women under forty to work in mental hospitals."[84] The majority of these emigration programs had explicit or implicit racial requirements. Australian authorities, for example, dreamt of populating their country with unaccompanied children after the war, mostly British orphans and "war babies." At least 3,000 unaccompanied children from Europe made Australia their new home. But non-white children, along with children with physical or mental handicaps, were excluded.

In postwar Austria, Slavic and Jewish DPs were deemed undesirable immigrants and citizens, in spite of a pressing need for industrial and agricultural labor. In a 1950 memo to the International Red Cross, Austrian Ministry of Interior officials bluntly announced that they were eager to find a "final solution to the DP question . . . From the Austrian perspective this goal can only be realized through the evacuation of the difficult-to-assimilate non-German-speaking DPs."[85] At the same time, however, the Austrian government gradually embraced ethnic German (Volksdeutsche) refugees from Eastern Europe, who made successful claims on the Austrian state based on their alleged regional and cultural ties to Austria, as well as their status as *Altösterreicher—*

former citizens (or children of citizens) of the Habsburg Monarchy. Of course, many East European DPs and Jewish refugees had also been citizens or former citizens of the old Habsburg Empire, but they were excluded nonetheless.[86]

In the United States, the 1948 and 1950 American DP Acts enabled over 400,000 European refugees to enter the United States. The legislation specified that 30 percent of the new Americans had to be agricultural workers and 40 percent had to come from territories annexed by the USSR. Baltic refugees (Latvians, Estonians, Lithuanians) informally enjoyed most-favored-refugee status, since they were primarily farmers and Protestants. While visiting Germany, Congressman Frank Chelf of Kentucky praised the Balts as "unmistakably intelligent, industrious, energetic, and showed every sign of having come from good stock and good breeding." Unfortunately, many Baltic refugees had also been Nazi collaborators. They looked clean-cut in part because, unlike forced laborers and Jews, many had voluntarily resettled in Germany during the war, accompanied by their money and possessions.[87]

The 1948 DP Act also defined a DP as an Allied national who had been in the western zones of Germany, Austria, or Italy as of December 22, 1945, intentionally excluding all of the so-called Jewish "infiltrees" who fled from Eastern Europe after the war ended (though the amended 1950 DP Act extended the deadline to January 1, 1950). Truman signed the bill, but called it "flagrantly discriminatory," "anti-Semitic," and "anti-Catholic." The DP Acts of 1948 and 1950 did ultimately permit around 100,000 Jewish DPs to enter the United States, in spite of the restrictions—in part because aid workers on the ground in Europe interpreted the requirements liberally. But the United States clearly joined other countries of emigration with its policies of selective humanitarianism.[88]

This broad preoccupation with recruiting "assimilable" migrants in postwar Europe and the United States not only perpetuated and reimagined racial hierarchies. It also privileged children over adults, as the young were consistently seen as the most malleable immigrants and therefore the most desirable future citizens of all. Transnational adoption after World War II was more than a solution to a humanitarian crisis. It provided a supply of assimilable children to population-starved nations and baby-hungry families, while conveniently excluding their "unassimilable" parents. The nationalist and racial hierarchies that underpinned postwar migration policies thus undercut a rhetorical preoccupation with reuniting families.

In both Eastern and Western Europe, postwar migration policies were crafted with an eye toward rebalancing European demography and constructing homogenous nation-states. And across Europe, policymakers pursued these goals in the name of compensation for Nazi crimes, economic reconstruction, and the protection of national sovereignty. In France, authorities hoped to resolve the "German problem" and a perceived population problem at the same time by transforming children of the former enemy into French citizens. East European policymakers faced similar dilemmas as they weighed the conflicting goals of increasing population and creating nationally homogenous states after World War II. But East European officials ultimately settled on different solutions, defining the limits to assimilation far more narrowly. Rather than attempting to enrich their populations with German workers and children, Czechoslovakia, Poland, and Yugoslavia shipped millions of Germans "home to the Reich" between 1945 and 1948. Here too, however, nationally entangled families complicated the goal of unmixing populations. In East Central Europe, the project of postwar reconstruction would ultimately demand the ethnic cleansing of families as well as territory.

Ethnic Cleansing and the Family in Czechoslovakia

On the morning of May 21, 1942, Reichsprotektor and Chief of the Reich Security Office Reinhard Heydrich was attacked in Prague by Czech partisans. He died from his wounds a few days later. In retaliation, on June 10, 1942, German soldiers rounded up all of the men in the small Bohemian village of Lidice and shot them into a mass grave. They burned and razed the village to the ground, intending to erase all traces of its existence. German soldiers meanwhile gathered the town's women and children and drove them to a high school in Kladno. They immediately selected two children for Germanization, and sent the rest on to Poland. Seven more children were deemed Germanizable in Poland, while the remaining women and children were deported to concentration camps. Nazi officials transferred these nine children to a Lebensborn home in Puschkau, near Poznan. Maria Hanfová, who was 12 at the time, later testified at Nuremberg that in Puschkau the children were taught to speak German and beaten or denied food if they spoke Czech. Her name was changed twice, first to Maria Hanff and then to Marga Richter.

Hana Spotová, age two, was also among the children chosen to be Germanized. German racial experts assigned her a new name and identity as Hanna Spott. After a brief stay in Puschkau, a German woman named Klara Warner adopted Hana. Lebensborn officials told Warner that Hanna was a German orphan whose parents had been killed by allied bombs. But she soon heard conflicting rumors about the child's origins. "When I picked up the child, a kindergarten teacher said, 'What a pity that the child is leaving, she was the prettiest here and learned to speak such nice German.' I was naturally surprised and asked, what do you mean, where is the child from? 'Don't you know?' These are Czech children whose parents were killed,' answered the kindergarten teacher. At the urging of my husband I later wrote to the regional home for Posen and asked for information about the origins of the child. But the only response I received is that the child is racially flawless . . . I had Hanna Spott in my care until March 1944. One day an NSV (*Nationalsozialistische Volkswohlfahrt,* the Nazi welfare organization) nurse came and took her away without any explanation."[1]

Hanfová and Spotová were among the lucky few, as they lived to return home. Only 17 out of 105 children from Lidice ultimately survived the tragedy—82 were gassed in Chelmno shortly after the 1942 massacre.[2] But immediately after the war, the fate of Lidice's 105 missing children remained a mystery. Czech government officials and a broader public still hoped that the children remained hidden, unaware of their origins, and that they would be recovered alive for the Czech nation.

The search for the lost children of Lidice after World War II seemed to represent a simple quest for the reunification of families divided by Nazi brutality. The Czechoslovak government, like governments across Europe, scrambled to claim children who had been displaced by deportation, kidnappings, and forced labor during World War II. Just as French officials sought to replenish the nation with children born to French soldiers and German women, the Czech government pursued the children of Lidice in the name of justice and the biological reconstruction of the Czech nation. But in postwar Eastern Europe, the goal of reuniting families conflicted with an ambition to create homogenous nation-states. At the same time that Czech officials trumpeted their campaign to recover and return "Germanized" children to their Czech families, they began a massive project of what contemporaries called "national cleansing" (*národní očista),* stripping three million Czechoslovak Germans of their citizenship and property and shipping them to Germany in cattle cars. Children, who represented the biological future of the Czech and German nations, were central to the postwar project of ethnic cleansing in Eastern Europe.[3]

The expulsions began immediately after the liberation of Czechoslovakia, with broad support from the population, Soviet military authorities, and Czech political leaders. The so-called "transfer" coincided with efforts to repatriate over 650,000 displaced Czechoslovak citizens from Germany (including the children of Lidice), while ensuring that undesirable displaced Germans did not return to their homes in Czechoslovakia. Ethnic cleansing also entailed a campaign to resettle at least two million Czechs in the homes and businesses that Germans had once occupied. All of these population transfers were complicated by nationally mixed or ambiguous families. Homogenous nation-states required nationally homogenous family units, and Czechoslovakia was home to as many as 90,000 Czech-German married couples with at least 150,000 children in 1945.[4]

Similar demographic reshuffling took place across liberated Eastern Europe. The removal of Germans from Eastern Europe began in the final year of the war. Some seven million Germans fled or were evacuated west to escape the advancing Red Army. At the Yalta Conference in February 1945, the Allies laid the foundation for further mass population transfers. Roosevelt and Churchill agreed that Eastern Europe would fall under the Soviet sphere of influence. The Red Army was already in Poland and Romania, and was poised only 40 miles outside of Berlin, so this was effectively a fait accompli. Allied leaders also agreed to Soviet demands to annex Polish territory East of the Curzon line, compensating Poland for the loss with territory taken from eastern Germany. With the stroke of a pen, millions of people were sentenced to lose their homes through forced displacement. Beginning in 1944, over 1,500,000 Poles who lived on the Soviet side of the Polish-Soviet border were deported west. At the same time, 482,000 Ukrainians were "repatriated" to the Soviet Union. Another 140,000 Ukrainians were forcibly resettled in Poland's western territories in a violent wave of deportations between April and June 1947. And 89,000 Slovaks crossed paths with at least 70,000 Hungarians as they were swapped across the Hungarian-Czechoslovak border.[5]

As postwar officials sought to unmix populations, they were forced to make decisions about the boundaries of families as well as the boundaries of the nation—a difficult task since both were highly permeable. Government officials and humanitarian workers professed that family reunification was central to the broader project of postwar reconstruction. But the wartime disintegration of families also created enticing opportunities to pursue nationalist population policies on a new scale. Czechoslovak officials deemed some families worthy of reunification, while encouraging others to dissolve or cleanse themselves of national ambiguity. Postwar Czechoslovak officials were not simply intent on removing Germans in order to conquer cities, towns, homes, farms, and factories for the nation-state. Cleansing was directed toward families as well as territory, toward individuals who stayed behind in Czechoslovakia as well as those stripped of their citizenship in the reckoning that followed World War II.

*   *   *

The hunt for the children of Lidice was a featured drama in the story of national "cleansing" and reconstruction in postwar Czechoslovakia. The search for Czechoslovakia's lost children affirmed images of a Czech nation unified in victimhood, sustained memories of German wrongdoing, and dramatized the ongoing campaign for postwar restitution.[6] Like the effort to reclaim Armenian children from Turkish homes in the aftermath of the Genocide, it was symbolically linked to the postwar regeneration of the Czech nation in the aftermath of Nazi occupation.

A radio address on January 8, 1946 rallied all Czech citizens for the search, asking that they immediately report any sighting of the 105 missing children to their local national council.[7] In liberated Berlin, German anti-fascists circulated flyers and posters featuring names and pictures of the missing Lidice victims, exhorting, "There can be no town hall in Germany, no police officer, no office, no church, no newspaper, no radio station, no political party, no union . . . no family, which does not cry out, 'What happened to the children from Lidice?'"[8] The Czechoslovak Interior Ministry published a booklet entitled *Kidnapped Czech Children* the same year, listing over 890 missing Czech children. Most were in fact Jewish children who had been deported with the assistance of Czechoslovak authorities. Number 52, Edmund Blum, "was deported to Terezín in 1944 as a half-breed. Transported to Auschwitz 24–28 October. No news since that time."[9]

A widespread press campaign broadcast details of the search efforts and celebrated successful repatriations. A 1947 article in *Národní osvobození* announced that 4,300 missing Czechoslovak children had been registered with the children's bureau in Prague (including deported Jewish children). Only 289 had been located and repatriated to their families. Since the work of UNRRA would end in July 1947, the newspaper demanded greater effort, urging, "It is necessary that the greatest possible number of kidnapped Czechoslovak children are located before July, so that this unfathomable Nazi crime inflicted on the smallest citizens of the Republic is atoned."[10] But by the time that the Ministry of Social Welfare ended its search for deported children in January 1949, only 740 children had been located and 629 repatriated.[11]

This reflected a common pattern. Representatives of Czech, Polish, French, Yugoslav, and Jewish agencies and governments all exaggerated the number of missing children after World War II. Rumors of untold numbers of lost children functioned as a kind of moral currency with which representatives of postwar governments made claims on allied officials, the German and Austrian governments, and international organizations. The Czechoslovak press continuously denounced the ongoing villainy of German civilians and allied authorities, who allegedly obstructed the return of Czechoslovak children to their homeland. "Kidnapped children are enslaved by Germans," declared *Svobodné noviny* in March 1947. Two years after the defeat of Nazi Germany, the newspaper alleged, many deported Czech youth continued to toil on German farms, unaware of the possibility to return home. Miša Kesselnauer, age 14, reportedly worked for a Bavarian peasant until the end of 1946 because her employers withheld news of the possibility of repatriation. According to *Svobodné noviny*, forced laborers "receive only small amounts of food and have no possibility of contact with the outside world. The majority were deported to Germany in their tender youth."[12]

As the Communist party gained influence in postwar Czechoslovakia, the press and government officials began to blame American authorities and the United Nations for the slow pace of repatriations. *Národní osvobození* reported in October 1947 that 13-year-old Hana Š. from Lidice was living with German foster parents who refused to relinquish her. American military authorities shielded intransigent German foster parents, the newspaper claimed. When the conflict continued with no foreseeable resolution, Czech repatriation officials took matters into their own hands. "Our people decided to abduct the girl," the paper reported. "And so Hanička finally returned to the Czech land of her birth. This solution was dramatic, but what a tragedy! In 1947 Czechs must kidnap Czech children from German families, who were stolen in 1942 from Lidice! This abduction was made necessary by the American authorities, who guard the children kidnapped during the war by the Nazis."[13]

Over the course of the next ten years, dozens of citizens in Germany and Czechoslovakia participated in the hunt for lost children, reporting sightings of the Lidice children across Central Europe. Marie Jirásková, from Kolín, wrote to the national committee of Lidice after reading an announcement about the search in the newspaper. In Kolín, she had lived next to a couple of avowed Nazis during the war. In 1943 a small girl, 3–4 years old, appeared in the household, "dark-eyed, curly, dark hair, altogether weak. They declared that she was adopted." But Jirásková was immediately suspicious. "Several things immediately occurred to me. How exactly did a girl from Halle get to Kolín? Because when the 'mother' was not present, the child spoke very good Czech, and precisely without the characteristic accent of all the Germans who speak Czech. And why was the child adopted so soon after the Lidice tragedy?"[14]

Arnošt Cetkovský of Jihlava also reported a furtive encounter with the kidnapped children of Lidice. In August of 1942, Cetkovský claimed, he heard a rumor that Lidice children were living in the local public elementary school. He went to the school, which was notoriously "used for the Germanization of Czech children." The building was heavily guarded, but he could hear Czech and German voices through an open window. He approached the window and yelled, "Little girls, are you from Lidice?" A girl replied "Yes!" and another echoed "Me too!" But before he could ask for their names, a German soldier appeared, and he was forced to make a quick getaway. Five days later, the children had disappeared.[15]

Both sightings were products of overactive imagination. A police investigation concluded that while some Czech-speaking children had been living in the school in Jihlava, they were children of Nazis. The adopted girl in Kolín had learned Czech from the children of her neighbors, not in Lidice.[16]

Lidice sightings were widespread in part because the massacre had become such an important symbol of Nazi brutality and Czech victimization under Nazi rule. But the search for the children of Lidice was also a captivating melodrama of lost identity. As European societies struggled to reinvent themselves after World War II, stories of confused identities engaged the public's imagination. Lost children dramatically personified both the danger and possibility of wartime imposture, precisely because such children were often unaware of their own origins.

Czech writer Zdeňka Bezděková even dramatized the plight of lost children in a popular children's book. Her novel *They Called Me Leni (Řikali mi Leni)* was first published in 1948 and later translated into English, German, Dutch, Slovene, Swedish, Japanese, Ukrainian, Slovak, and Sorbian. It was reprinted eight times in Czech (most recently in 2001). In the preface Bezděková wrote that she had been inspired by a newspaper report about real-life lost children. "In 1947 I read a newspaper report about a little Czech girl who returned to her home country after having lived for many years with a German family. She was one of a number of children who were abducted from their home country by the Germans during World War II and placed with Nazi families to be reeducated. I pondered over her sad fate and the fate of all these stolen children, and I decided to write this story."[17]

Leni Freiwald, the story's heroine, was born Alena Sýkorová. In 1946, Alena lives in Herrnstadt, Germany, with a Nazi family—completely unaware of her Czech origins. Bit by bit, Leni is confronted with mysterious clues about her true identity. She overhears her adoptive mother and grandmother fighting about her behind closed doors. A classmate calls her a "foreign Czech bastard." Eventually she discovers a suitcase in the attic, filled with traces of her past—a peasant doll, a white hat, a pair of stockings with the initials AS embroidered into them. Finally recognizing her Czech origins, Leni runs away to a local UNRRA office and declares "I have a mother in Czechoslovakia!" With the help of a sympathetic teacher and a friendly UNRRA social worker, Leni's mother is finally located, and she is restored to her native family, language, and nation. The story ends on a sentimental note, however, as Leni acknowledges what she has lost: "For the first time, I felt love. But I couldn't say anything. I didn't know how to say Mummy in Czech."[18]

The travails of displaced Czech children were also dramatized for the big screen, and for an American audience. *The Search*, a 1948 film starring Montgomery Clift, was directed by Austrian-American Jewish director Fred Zinnemann. Nominated for five Academy Awards, the film was a box-office hit, winning the 1948 Academy Award for best screenplay. *The Search* was based on Zinnemann's research at an actual UNRRA DP children's camp, where he shadowed American UNRRA social worker Susan Pettiss. Scenes were filmed in UNNRA's Rosenheim Transit Center in Bavaria, and 400 refugee children featured as extras.

The mysterious young protaganist of *The Search* is introduced in an UNRRA office. Social workers question him about his origins, but he cannot even recall his own name. His only response to UNRRA workers' persistent questions is "Ich weiss nicht" ("I don't know"). We later learn that this particular lost child is Karel Malík, the child of middle-class Czech parents. He has miraculously survived Auschwitz and has a tattoo on his forearm, although we later learn that he is not Jewish. The choice of a Czech child to dramatize the fate of Europe's lost children was not coincidental, although only a small minority of children in UNRRA camps (let alone Auschwitz survivors) would have been non-Jewish Czech children. Since at least World War I, Czechs had been widely perceived as the most "western" and "cultured" Central Europeans. Given lingering anti-Semitism in the United States and Europe after World War II, a middle-class Czech child made for a more sympathetic protagonist than a Jewish child or even the more exotic Poles or Ukrainians who populated Europe's refugee camps.[19]

Against the iconic backdrop of German cities in ruins, we follow Karel's mother as she traverses Europe on foot in a heroic struggle to piece together her family. She works in an UNRRA children's home, where she discovers an outlet for her maternal instincts caring for other lost children. In the meantime, a young American officer named Ralph Stevenson (Steve) befriends Karel. With Steve's help, Karel learns English. He is outfitted with a mini officer's uniform, American shoes, and the name Jimmy. Steve eventually decides to adopt Karel and take him home to the United States. But in the film's sentimental climax, Karel and his mother are reunited in a chance encounter. The happy ending restores Karel to his maternal home and to his national homeland. *The Search* ultimately affirms the dominant solutions to the problem of postwar displacement: return to family and nation.[20]

Real-life family reunions were major media events in postwar Czechoslovakia. The few children located in Germany and repatriated to Czechoslovakia were greeted like celebrities. Seven-year-old Hana Spotová returned home on April 2, 1947, on a train with 31 other Czech children who had been displaced in Germany. As the train crawled into Prague's Wilson Station, it was met by "an unusually excited and tense crowd of simple men and women, among whom mingled the khaki uniforms of the employees and representatives of UNRRA and our soldiers," reported *Obrana lidu*. The crowd was thick with filmmakers, photojournalists, and newspaper reporters, who "feverishly prepared to capture the extraordinary moment of reunion of parents with their children who were robbed from them by the barbarous German regime."[21] Finally the moment arrived when "a tearful Mrs. Spotová embraced her seven-year-old daughter, who had been dragged away by the Gestapo when she was two years old."[22]

In reality, orphans returning to distant kin or institutions often found themselves in precarious circumstances. In December 1945, officials in the Ministry of Social Welfare expressed alarm about the "unhappy living conditions of the young repatriants and the danger threatening their moral and physical health."[23] Some Czech officials even worried that the fame of the Lidice children was being exploited. In September 1945, the Ministry of Interior alerted the Ministry of Social Welfare that "the recovered children from Lidice, especially those whose mothers died in the Auschwitz or Ravensbrück concentration camps . . . are entirely dependent on their relatives and other strangers . . . they are being abused in the true sense of the word, because their guardians seek to exploit their popularity."[24]

The massive campaign to repatriate lost children coincided with and complicated the expulsion of Czechoslvakia's German citizens. In December 1945, Czechoslovak officials ordered local branches of the Czech Provincial Commission in Moravia to search German children's homes and foster families in order to prevent Czech children from being deported. After a thorough search, however, Czech social workers reported that they had recovered only 20–30 Czech children in German institutions. Most were children of mixed marriages who had been abandoned or orphaned and then placed with German families by Nazi welfare authorities. Unconvinced, government officials again ordered a sweep of all German internment camps by Czech social workers in January 1946, in order to ensure that kidnapped children of "Czech blood" were not accidentally expelled. An April 1946 memo from the Interior Ministry explained, "It is a well-known reality that there is a large number of missing children who became victims of Nazi terror and were given to German families to be raised after the execution or the torture of their parents— Lidice and other cases. It is therefore not only a matter of service and duty for the relevant institutions, but a moral, patriotic duty, that nothing is neglected that could lead to the rectification of these tragic realities."[25] Meanwhile, the Ministry of Social Welfare asked editors of all major Czech newspapers to publicize the hunt for Czech children among German expellees, advising, "It is in the sovereign interest of our nation that not a single Czech or Slovak child is transferred to German territory and thereby lost to us."[26] But the search once again turned up only a handful of children from mixed marriages. One such child was removed from her German grandmother (who was deported) and placed with a Czech uncle.[27]

In reality it was difficult for Czechoslovak authorities to distinguish between the "German" children that they sought to deport and the "Germanized" children that they hoped to save for the Czech nation. Four years of Nazi occupation had not made the task easier. As George Kennan, the American diplomat, noted of one Bohemian town shortly after the invasion, "It became difficult to tell where the Czech left off and the German began."[28] In July 1945, the Czech Provincial Commission for Child Welfare in Bohemia sent an urgent memo to the Ministry of the Interior, asking how the agency should distinguish between German children and Czech children. Children of mixed marriages, in particular, forced officials to choose between two conflicting nationalist goals: an ambition to cleanse the Bohemian Lands of every last trace of Germandom, and a populationist goal to preserve every last drop of "Czech blood" for the "small" Czech nation. As historian Benjamin Frommer has cogently argued, "The national consensus to 'cleanse' [očistit] the state broke down over the fate of interethnic families."[29]

Czech soldiers, local security forces, and militias began their campaign to rid the Bohemian Lands of its Germans soon after the allied victory, expelling over 700,000 Germans by the end of 1945. Most had lived in the Bohemian Lands for generations. At the Potsdam Conference in July of 1945, the Allies sanctioned the expulsions that were already underway. Two million more

Germans were stripped of their citizenship and shipped westward during the so-called organized transfers that began in January of 1946, with the blessing of the international community. On August 2, 1945, President Eduard Beneš issued Presidential Decree 33, which officially deprived Germans and Magyars of their Czechoslovak citizenship and property rights. Nationality was legally determined based on the records of the 1930 Czechoslovak census (which had been preserved, and were never anonymous).[30] Individuals who had "never acted against the Czech or Slovak nations and who actively contributed to the struggle for their liberation" could file a petition to retain their citizenship rights. But many Czechs felt that even anti-fascist Germans could not be trusted. In May of 1944, a Czech informant reported the widespread opinion that "not a single of our Germans can stay here, no, not even the Socialists, Sudeten Germans are all alike ... We need to be certain that at least our children will have some rest from the Germans."[31] Decree Nr. 33 also broke with longstanding patriarchal traditions in Czechoslovak law. In interwar Czechoslovakia, married women had automatically acquired the citizenship of their husbands, and legitimate children carried the nationality of their fathers. Decree Nr. 33 however required that the nationality and citizenship of both women and children be evaluated "independently." In recognition of paternal rights, however, the decree simultaneously mandated that applications for citizenship filed by German women married to Czech men be judged "benevolently."[32]

At the same time that the expulsions were carried out, Czech officials were busy repatriating 692,000 Czech citizens from abroad, mostly foreign workers who had either voluntarily or forcibly labored in Germany during the war. Of this number, around 200,000 were so-called re-emigrants—Czechs or Slovaks and their descendants who had emigrated and now reclaimed their Czechoslovak citizenship with the encouragement of the government in Prague.[33] Re-emigrants could hardly replace the labor power of three million Germans, however. The Czech government therefore launched an ambitious program to resettle the evacuated borderland regions with Czechs and Slovaks from the interior.

Northern Bohemia had been a critical site of industrial production during the First Republic. The postwar Czechoslovak economy could not afford to allow German factories and businesses to shut down. Between 500,000 and 650,000 new Czech settlers arrived in the borderlands in the summer of 1945 alone, nearly matching the number of Germans expelled during that time. The simultaneous process of expulsion and resettlement fostered a gold-rush culture in which local officials and settlers in search of property competed to seize the homes, businesses, furniture, livestock, and land of German expellees. Government officials aimed to resettle 2.5 million Czechs and Slovaks in the borderlands by 1949. But the ambitions of the Settlement Office in Prague to recruit industrial workers, farmers, and miners clashed with the dreams of Czech newcomers, who aspired to become pub owners and landlords.[34]

The Communist-dominated Ministry of Interior in Prague officially regulated decisions about citizenship and property. But on the ground, local and district national committees handled the internment and expulsion of Germans, redistribution of German property, and applications for the restitution of citizenship. Local, district, and provincial national committees had been established by decree in December 1944. In 1945, approximately 40 percent of local national committee members and many of their leaders were Communist party members. Initially intended to be temporary, the national committees consolidated their hold on local government after the war, filling the vacuum of power left by departing Nazis. They were empowered to prosecute so-called "crimes against national honor" and to issue "certificates of national reliability" that were now essential to get a job, attend school, find housing, or receive welfare benefits. While the Interior Ministry officially crafted citizenship laws, local national committees also enjoyed considerable latitude to interpret and implement these decrees.[35]

Serious conflicts soon erupted between state officials in Prague's central ministries, local national committee members, new settlers in the borderlands, and so-called "old settlers" who had lived in the borderlands before 1938.[36] While property often drove these disputes, they manifested in debates about children of mixed marriages. German and Czech speakers had long intermarried in the Bohemian Lands. In spite of Nazi racial laws, intermarriage continued throughout the Second World War. One-fifth of marriages in the Protectorate in 1939 were between German citizens and Czech subjects. After 1941, with the Protectorate under the rule of Reinhard Heydrich, the SS exerted greater influence over Germanization and citizenship policies. But intermarriage remained legal, as long as the Czech partner submitted to a racial examination. In fact, intermarriage was only formally banned by Czechoslovak authorities in October 1945. Of course, the very term "mixed marriage" is problematic, as it assumes that each partner actually had a distinctive national identity to begin with, and that nationality is immutable. Many so-called "mixed" couples would not have described themselves in these terms.[37]

Rumors that internment camps and trains bound for Germany were crowded with Czech-speaking children provoked alarm across the political spectrum. Only a week after the promulgation of Decree Nr. 33, the Ministry of the

Interior ordered "the forced evacuation of families with children of mixed marriage be temporarily stopped" until further regulations could be issued. But district committees continued to deport intermarried couples and their children.[38] In the face of ongoing confusion, the Czech Provincial Commission for Youth Welfare demanded that the Ministry of the Interior make "a principled, responsible, and singular decision . . . as to how to determine the nationality and legal standing of these minor children . . . children from mixed marriages are very numerous, and because the evacuation of Germans is progressing steadily, it is necessary to decide quickly." The Provincial Commission, for its part, proposed that "in the greater interests of the nation . . . every child in whose veins Czech blood flows, even if only from one parent, should be considered a Czech child and educated as a Czech."[39] In spite of the Interior Ministry's repeated ordinances on the subject, decisions about who was Czech and who was German were governed by inconsistency and opportunism locally. In April 1946, the Ministry of Social Welfare issued a directive to local National Councils, in an attempt to clarify matters. "It is necessary to emphasize that when determining the origins of children one must strictly insure that this action [expulsion] is only applied to children for whom it is safely determined that they are of the German nationality, meaning that both parents were Germans."[40]

Ongoing debates about the boundaries of the Czech nation challenged a binary conception of national identity, whereby every citizen was either Czech or German. Officials instead measured nationality on a spectrum: individual children and families could be more or less German or Czech. In early 1946, for example, officials in the Ministry of Social Welfare debated whether or not to allow the repatriation of a group of 38 "Czech" families from Gorzowo, in Poland. They were descendants of Bohemians who had migrated to Austrian Galicia to work in factories between 1905 and 1910. In the meantime they had assimilated to the local German-speaking community in Poland, where the children attended German schools. "National relations in the family are very ambiguous. It is certainly true that the fathers of the families speak excellent Czech, but their wives and children speak no Czech at all with few exceptions," reported Czech officials.[41] Such cases were problematic in the context of postwar nationalist absolutism. It was not enough to simply determine if an individual or a family was Czech or German. The question was whether they were Czech *enough*, and what to do when some family members seemed more Czech than others.

Children were central to the debate around mixed marriages in postwar Czechoslovakia. The problem faced by Czech policymakers was how to cleanse

Czech society of Germandom while simultaneously retaining the maximum number of children for the Czech nation. One obvious solution was simply to dissolve nationally entangled families. Child welfare officials in Ústí nad Labem, the site of some of the most violent expulsions, recommended in July 1945 that "parents [in mixed marriages] be offered the opportunity to divorce, so that their children can be saved."[42] A year later, the Czech Provincial Commission for Child Welfare requested the government's permission to forcibly remove children of mixed marriages from their German parents. Even as they vigorously denounced Nazi officials for the kidnapping and denationalization of children, postwar Czech nationalists thus promoted the separation of nationally mixed families in the name of their own national interests.[43]

Proposals to forcibly dissolve mixed families were extreme, but were seriously entertained by government officials, the press, and private citizens. In 1946, Josef Břecka, an enterprising Czech middle school teacher, offered his unsolicited advice to government officials. In a lengthy memo, he proposed that children of mixed marriage be forcibly separated from their German parents. Expelling "Germanized" Czech children, in his view, amounted to nothing less than a concession of defeat in the Czech-German battle for demographic supremacy. For Břecka, populationist goals outweighed the potential political threat posed by such families. "The latest news from Germany shows that there is a very large population among the youngest generation. We however are increasing that population even more, through the expulsion of children from mixed marriages and Germanized regions. Isn't that an extreme form of recklessness?" These children could be saved for the Czech nation if they were quickly resettled in the Czech interior and re-Czechified. Meanwhile, "The Germanizing parts of the family ... must be prevented from exercising any influence on the family ... Even if they are not guilty, they must be sentenced to forced labor and only permitted to visit [the family] for short periods of time."[44]

Not everyone agreed, but Břecka's proposal was circulated to several government ministries, where officials seriously debated its merits. While the Ministry of Foreign Affairs endorsed the plan, officials in the State Statistical Office were more skeptical. It was not the separation of parents and children that troubled them, however. Rather, the Statistical Office accused Břecka of upholding the "Nazi theory of nationality, which considers nationality a corporeal and material fact," and countered with its own, less forgiving plan. "So-called Germanized Czechs, or individuals whose ancestors were Czechs, are Germans. A Czech man or woman who joined the German nationality through marriage or German influence and thereby deserted us does not deserve any sentimental accommodation. It is not in the interest of the Czech nation to expand its ranks with the German nation's trash. The few thousand German children we expel will not add much to the German nation's many millions, but for our Czech nation of a few million, those children would be a large germinating embryo of future collaborators and fifth columnists."[45]

Břecka's memorandum inspired vigorous debate because it cut to the heart of an ongoing dispute among Czech officials. Was it more important to increase population or to achieve national homogeneity? The two goals reflected different approaches to the so-called "German problem" and implied different attitudes toward children of mixed marriages. While concern for population growth was largely concentrated in the central government ministries in Prague, Czech citizens in mixed marriages appropriated populationist rhetoric, since they had a personal stake in keeping the boundaries of the Czech nation fluid. Meanwhile, other Czechs, especially new settlers to the borderland areas, pressed for the expulsion of every last trace of Germandom from Czechoslovak soil. Their view of transnational romance as a form of national treason was anchored in law. The 1945 "Small Decree," which punished so-called "offenses against national honor," criminalized wartime romantic liaisons with Germans. Individuals (mostly women) convicted of sleeping with the national enemy could be subject to prison sentences and fines.[46]

*　　*　　*

Pronatalism took hold across Europe and in the United States after the war, and Czechoslovakia was no exception. In contrast to most other European lands, however, the population of Czechoslovakia had actually increased under Nazi occupation. Czechoslovakia had been spared military casualties, and food rations were more generous in the occupied Protectorate than elsewhere in the Nazi empire. In addition, Czech women had been subjected to a barrage of pronatalist propaganda since the beginning of Nazi occupation. Many young Czech women became pregnant as a strategy to avoid conscription for labor in German war factories. "We have to thank the Nazis for a remarkable increase in the birthrate. There have never been so many pregnant women to be seen in Prague or in the countryside—the sole protection against mandatory labor," observed one Czech informant in late 1943.[47] The number of Czech births increased from 103,642 in 1938 to 153,953 in 1944, the highest rate since 1932. In 1962 German demographer Albert Eissner estimated that the Czech population had enjoyed a net increase of 236,000 people by the end of the war.[48]

Regardless of the causes of wartime population growth, the expulsion of three million Germans intensified pressure to accelerate the baby boom. Concerns about population led to the formation of a new interministerial Commission on Population Questions by the Czechoslovak Ministry of Health in June 1946. The commission aimed to coordinate major state and voluntary organizations involved with population policy.[49] In December of 1946, the Ministry of Social Welfare drafted a proposal for wide-ranging legislation to increase population and decrease infant mortality. The Ministry's recommendations included birth premiums, marriage loans, subsidized housing for large families, more generous maternity leave, the expansion of government-supported nurseries, and stricter abortion laws. The Ministry also planned for the creation of a new state-sponsored Population Institute to study population and demography.[50] In 1948, shortly after the Communist takeover, several of these proposals were implemented.[51] The perceived population crisis also drew press attention. In May 1946, the editors of *Lidová demokracie* maintained, "It is clear that in the next 20 or 30 years the Republic is going to face a serious problem, how to compensate for our diminishing population . . . It is a question of compensating for the three million German citizens who are leaving us, so that the work of rebuilding the Republic isn't paralyzed."[52]

The population question was immediately linked to children, to ongoing debates about ethnic cleansing, and to discussions about the economic and demographic transformation of the borderlands. Oppositional voices within Czechoslovak society began to question the totality of the expulsions, focusing in particular on children. At the level of government ministries in Prague, populationist concerns triumphed, but regulations concerning citizenship left a great deal to local interpretation. In March 1946 the Ministry of Foreign Affairs specified that in carrying out the expulsions, local officials should "make it a clear priority to preserve as many people as possible for the Czechoslovak nation in whom Czech or Slovak blood flows."[53] The Ministry of Social Welfare expressed similar concerns about the health and welfare of children of mixed marriage. An Interior Ministry ordinance from May 17, 1945 had stipulated that all Germans in postwar Czechoslovakia, including children, should receive the same rations allocated to Jews by the Nazis during the war. Local authorities included many children of mixed marriages in this starvation regime. Officials in the Ministry of Social Welfare objected that this policy endangered the health of Czech children, protesting, "As a small nation we cannot afford to deprive ourselves of the souls of any Czech children."[54]

The Interior Ministry shared these concerns. In December of 1945, the Ministry issued a memorandum stipulating that Czech women married to German men and their husbands should not be deported. But the ultimate status of nationally entangled families remained vague. It was May 1946 before the Ministry finally exempted all intermarried Germans who had not engaged in "anti-state activities" from expulsion and other punitive measures, as long as the marriage had been contracted before May 21, 1938. In theory, after May of 1946, intermarried Germans and their children were not to be subjected to any of the measures inflicted on other Germans. These included confiscation of property, eviction from apartments, and the requirement to wear armbands with the letter "N." They were legally entitled to "Czech" rations and pay, and again permitted to ride public transportation.[55]

In practice, however, these regulations did little to change the treatment of mixed families. At the local level, District National Committees simply ignored government instructions. The Interior Ministry received numerous reports that hundreds of Czech individuals were expelled to Germany with their spouses in June of 1946, well after such expulsions should have ceased. The Settlement Office in Prague lamented, "There are unfortunately a number of districts that either ignore or reject the directives of the government." One transport to Germany on June 11, 1946 reportedly included 120 children under the age of six, and nearly half of them could not speak a word of German. "During the entire transport the Czech language dominated, as though it was a transfer of Czechs and not Germans." The Settlement Office warned that this was a great loss for the Czech nation, as these children would soon expand the ranks of Germandom, becoming "the enemies of the Czech nation, when they could have been safely saved."[56] As late as July 1948, tensions between the central ministries in Prague and local national committees persisted, as the Interior Ministry continued to issue regulations that local authorities blatantly ignored.[57]

As Benjamin Frommer has demonstrated, not all mixed couples were treated equally, however. German women married to Czech men fared far better than German men married to Czech women. Presidential Decree Nr. 33 immediately enabled all German women married to Czech men to apply for the reinstatement of their Czechoslovak citizenship and stipulated that such applications were to be treated "benevolently" by local authorities. But German men married to Czech women first gained the right to apply for citizenship in January 1947.[58] There were several reasons for the double standard. The state was reluctant to interfere with traditions of patriarchal privilege, particularly the right of Czech men to pass their nationality on to their children. In addition, German men married to Czech women were considered more threatening to state security, since they were likely to have served in the Wehrmacht or other Nazi political organizations. German women, by contrast, were considered apolitical and less threatening by virtue of their gender.[59]

This policy provoked bitter protests from Czech women married to German men. Their appeals also relied on the assumption of traditional gender roles, however. Czech women invoked their status as financially and emotionally dependent wives and mothers, insisting that the ill treatment of their husbands threatened the livelihood of their Czech children. They stressed that they had raised their children to be good Czechs, resisting all Nazi attempts to Germanize them.[60] In an April 1946 petition on behalf of "Czech women and children of mixed marriages," a group of women appealed to the Ministerial Council: "Most of us are without a bread-winner . . . Not only have all of our financial resources been confiscated, but they have also confiscated our apartments, our furniture, our dishes, our linens, our clothing and the clothing of our children, so that we have nothing left to dress them in." This treatment was all the more unjust, they argued, given that they had loyally educated their children as Czechs during the Nazi occupation. "It brings us great suffering . . . that our efforts to educate good Czech children for the nation have been misunderstood and that our patriotic feelings have been ignored, even insulted and humiliated, and that we and our families are subjected to unending hardships."[61]

Czech women also insisted that they exercised a greater influence over the national orientation of their children than their German husbands. "The majority of us led our families in a pure Czech spirit even throughout the entire period of the occupation. On the other hand, marriages between Czech men and German women, which are today treated benevolently by decree, were led in a German spirit," Czech wives protested. In addition, intermarried women appropriated populationist rhetoric for their own ends. "We are searching the entire world for every last Czech child—why are we forgetting Czech children from mixed marriages? Give these Czech children from mixed marriages their homes and fathers back, and we will educate them to be the model sons and daughters of our nation."[62]

None of these women claimed that marriage was a private affair. Nor did they object to the overall logic of ethnic cleansing. Rather, intermarried Czech women made claims on the state by arguing that their families fell firmly on the Czech side of the Czech/German divide. By depicting themselves as victims of the Nazi regime and as faithful servants to the Czech nation in the home, they claimed a place among the ranks of Czech victims rather than German perpetrators. Rhetorically, they participated in the ethnic cleansing of their own families.

Some appeals on behalf of intermarried couples came from so-called old-settlers, *(starousedliky)* long-term Czech residents of the borderlands who had social and kinship ties to their German neighbors. A large demonstration of old-settlers in Ústí nad Labem on April 7, 1946, issued a petition demanding that German men married to Czech women be permitted to apply for the return of their citizenship.[63] Josef Klement, a lawyer and borderland activist in Žamberk, appealed to the Interior Ministry in 1945: "Whereas the Germans, as a large nation, attempted to entice and appropriate Czech souls everywhere ... our local national council tosses out and excludes Czech mothers and children, even babes-in-arms, as Germans, even though we are a small nation that is dependent on every single individual."[64]

While officials in the central Ministries and aggrieved couples couched their arguments in populationist terms, many new settlers in the borderlands demanded ethnic cleansing without exception. A petition from the village of Hoštek to the office of Klement Gottwald in December of 1947 proclaimed, "We, the settlers of the borderland village of Hoštek cannot approve of the return of German confiscated property to the hands of mixed couples ... We want our city of Hoštek and the entire borderland region to be CZECH ... Only after this transfer is completely and successfully finished will we be able to breathe and work freely."[65] In Ostrava in January 1948, a local branch of the Communist National Women's Front also protested the lenient treatment of intermarried couples. Above all, the group rejected initiatives to return property to individuals in mixed marriages. "The property of these Germans, traitors and collaborators ... was rightly confiscated ... and redistributed to people deemed worthy by the state ... What a great spiritual disappointment for those people who were allocated confiscated property that it may now be returned to our enemies through strange and complicated directives and decrees."[66]

Because nationality and citizenship were determined based on the 1930 census, thousands of citizens wrote to the Interior Ministry arguing that their 1930 or 1939 census forms had been falsified, begging for the reinstatement of their citizenship. Such requests were rejected as a general rule. But occasionally the state recognized particular kinds of service to the nation. Valentín Bolom, for example, was officially recognized as a Czech national after divorcing his German wife. He claimed that his wife Marie Meixner had declared him a German without his consent on the census of 1939. Against his will, he insisted, his wife had enrolled their daughter in a German school. "Because of disagreements over national questions and especially because of the applicant's opposition to the enrollment of his daughter at a German school, where she was enrolled by her mother, the marriage ended in divorce," his lawyer argued on his behalf. Whether or not national differences truly precipitated this divorce, Bolom was rewarded for the dissolution of his marriage with the reinstatement of his Czechoslovak citizenship.[67]

Czechoslovak citizens also deployed nationalist arguments as they attempted resolve custody disputes in their favor. Jaroslav Kouřik of Prague enlisted the support of American and Czechoslovak officials in his battle to win custody of his four children, Nera (13), Irena (11), Jiřina (10) and Jiří (6), who had been expelled to Germany with their German mother. He appealed to American military authorities, "My former wife named Anna Kouřiková, born Freiová, never cared for the children ... because of her loose life (liaisons with Gestapo members) the marriage was divorced ... I am sure I can give the children more than the mother."[68] Kouřiková was living in severe material distress in Germany, working as a farm laborer, and was living in two rooms with her four children and a German partner. The Czech courts awarded custody to Kouřik, and the children were forcibly separated from their mother and repatriated. The German Youth Welfare Office in Bavaria protested that Kouřiková was a "kind and motherly woman, who did well for her children," and cited the case as an example of the "autocratic" methods of American occupation authorities, to no avail.[69]

The struggle over national classification on Czechoslovak territory was clearly only half of the battle. Czechoslovak authorities also aimed to reshape their postwar population through repatriation policies. They sought to entice or compel certain members of the population to return to Czechoslovakia and rejected the requests of others to come home. Applications for repatriation often came from members of nationally entangled families who wished to join their spouses or children in Czechoslovakia. These petitioners included German men married to Czech women who had been abroad as POWs or members of the Wehrmacht, as well as individuals who had been expelled and wished to reunite with their families in Czechoslovakia. A 1946 directive from the Interior Ministry cautioned that individuals in mixed marriages should not be repatriated to Czechoslovakia if the "non-Czech elements [in the family] are dominant and there is no hope of changing this situation." The memo did not, however, provide specific criteria for determining whether the Czech or German partner in a given family "dominated." It did specify that Czechs and Slovaks in "German-dominated" marriages were obliged to divorce their German spouses in order to return to Czechoslovakia.[70] Another set of rules applied to orphans and unaccompanied children in Germany. Interior Ministry officials instructed UNRRA that unaccompanied children over the age of 14 could be repatriated only if they had sufficiently mastered the Czech or Slovak language. Orphans over the age of eight of were subject to an investigation to determine their nationality based on "objective characteristics," and only certified Czechs or Slovaks were permitted to return. Orphans under the age of eight, however, could be repatriated even if they were labeled Germans or Hungarians, since they could presumably be reeducated as Czechs in Czech orphanages or foster families.[71]

Inside Czechoslovakia, family members appealed to the Interior Ministry and to local national committees on behalf of their exiled family members. Not surprisingly, the decisive factor was typically whether or not there were under-age children who could be "saved" for the Czech nation. Once again, displacement, repatriation, and expulsion became a forum through which state officials and citizens determined not only the legal boundaries between Czechs and Germans, but also the boundaries between legitimate and illegitimate families. In Prostějov in 1946, for example, social worker Ladislav Vítasek, an employee of the City Health and Welfare Office, appealed to the Ministry of Interior on behalf of Helena Ludmilová, mother of Leopolda, Otomora and Helen. Vítasek requested the repatriation of Ludmilová's German husband, who had served in the Wehrmacht and recently returned to Germany from a Russian POW camp. Although Helena's husband was a German, Vítasek reported, "He spoke only Czech at home and all three of the children were raised solely in Czech." The childrens' teachers also testified, "The children have truly been raised to be good Czechs." But immediate action was necessary, as Helena was in desperate straits. Vítasek invoked the nation's long-term demographic interests on her behalf. "Everywhere it is continuously exalted that every child that is lost to us through the transfer is a great shame. . . . The mother of the children is herself living in a completely unbalanced mental state, because she is unsure what to do . . . As a wife she wants to be with her husband and her children . . . but on the other hand as a Czech she fights against it, she wants to stay here and she would also like to preserve her children for the Republic." The local family court in Prostějov ultimately supported Helena's appeal "in the interests of the three children, who can be retained for the Czech nation."[72]

Families were denied the right to reunify on Czech territory if they were not actually married, however—even if children were involved. Jiří Baudyš applied for the repatriation of his German girlfriend, who had been expelled from Czechoslovakia in July of 1946. She was about to give birth to his child. Baudyš hoped to marry her. "Because I want for my child to be raised as a Czech and to attend Czech school, I request my wife and child's return and the possibility to marry her . . . I know that today, in a period in which we are dependent on every newly born child . . . it wouldn't be right to allow a child who will have half Czech blood to vegetate and perhaps to die somewhere in a foreign country." His petition was typical in its instrumental use of nationalist and populationist rhetoric. It is also typical in its tacit acknowledgment that family reunification was not a right, but rather a reward for loyal national conduct. But mixed marriages had been illegal in Czechoslovakia since October 1945, and his request was denied.[73]

Jewish children were not seen as demographic assets to the Czechoslovak population after World War II. Many Jewish families were therefore denied the privilege of family reunification on Czechoslovak soil.[74] Out of a prewar population of some 354,342 Jews, approximately 30,000 Jews survived the war and returned to postwar Slovakia in November of 1946. In the Bohemian Lands, the Jewish population numbered only 24,395 in June 1948, including some 8,500 Jews who resettled in Czechoslovakia following the annexation of the Subcarpathian Rus by the Soviet Union in 1945.[75] In May of 1945, the Czechoslovak Interior Ministry sent a memo to the Jewish community in Prague, specifying that any Jew who had registered as a German on the 1930 census would not be considered a Czechoslovak citizen. These Jews were to "be regarded as German citizens" who were subject to measures that applied to Germans, "including amongst others the transfer."[76] In February of 1946 a representative of the United Nations in Prague reported with dismay that "Czechoslovak authorities are still making no distinction between Jews and pro-Nazi Sudeten Germans and are therefore insisting on their expatriation to Germany. Many Jews have fallen into distress."[77]

Leaders of the Jewish community in Prague were understandably outraged. In a letter to the Interior Ministry, they protested, "We wish to state that Jews who in the First Czechoslovak Republic . . . declared their nationality to be German . . . cannot be regarded as German citizens. Hitler's Reich never extended to the Jews German citizenship and it was certainly never the intention of the Czechoslovak legislators to force upon these people ex post this German citizenship."[78] In April 1946, the American JDC reported from Czechoslovakia that while Jews could now apply for reinstatement of their

Czechoslovak citizenship, "Very few have received a reply." In the meantime, no distinction was made between Jews and non-Jews in the expulsion of Germans.[79] It was only in September of 1946, with the expulsions well underway, that the Interior Ministry formally changed its policy. Henceforth, all Czechoslovak Jews were eligible for Czechoslovak citizenship provided that they now professed "to belong to the Czech, Slovak or another Slavic nationality and never acted against the Czech or Slovak nation."[80]

In practice, however, Jewish requests for citizenship, repatriation and the return of their property continued to be delayed or rejected by local officials, on the grounds that the applicants had contributed to Germanization. Out of 16,000 individual Jewish petitions for the restitution of property, by the end of 1947, only 3,000 were granted.[81] Anti-Semitism manifested itself in more violent ways as well. In Bratislava in August 1948, not long after the Communist seizure of power, a pogrom erupted after a Jewish woman, Mrs. Frank, was accused of cutting into a line in front of a fruit vendor. Mrs. Frank had asked the vendor to put aside some apples for her while she left to do additional shopping. When she returned, a line had formed. Since the vendor had forgotten to pack Mrs. Frank's apples, she weighed and packed them while the queue waited. A pregnant woman in the line began to shout anti-Semitic slurs, resulting in a skirmish. Police arrived and took both women to the station. Meanwhile a crowd formed and began to spread rumors that a Jewish woman had attacked a pregnant woman who had delivered a stillborn child, that a Jewess had caused the death of a pregnant woman, and so on.

Early that evening a crowd gathered and proceeded to vandalize the Jewish hospital, the Jewish kitchen building, and a Jewish orphanage. The mob broke the windows of 50 private Jewish homes, the synagogue, and the Yeshiva. At the Jewish kitchen, rioters smashed the windows and all of the dishes, broke the tables and chairs, pulled chandeliers out of the sockets, and yanked the sinks and toilets out of the walls and floors. Only the threats of a Jewish doctor who guarded the building with a gun prevented a similar scene at the Jewish hospital. According to a JDC report, it took the police 45 minutes to reach the sites of vandalism. Telephone calls to the police station from the Jewish hospital went unanswered. In no case did the police arrive before the mob and intervene. The government eventually made 67 arrests in the case, and blamed the violence on "a small group of fascist elements and work-shy persons," but the incident, like other pogroms in postwar Eastern Europe, encouraged many of Czechoslovakia's remaining Jews to take flight.[82]

Meanwhile, local factory councils targeted Jewish-owned factories for nationalization, based on allegations that the owners had contributed to interwar Germanization. In blatant defiance of Ministry of Interior decrees, national councils confiscated Jewish property and denied restitution claims based on allegations that Jews had sent their children to German schools or spoke German at home. They justified these decisions based on a clause of Decree 108, which called for the confiscation of the property of anyone who had "supported Germanization" during "the period of heightened danger" to the Republic (from May 21, 1938).[83]

In a typical case, officials in the Ministry of National Defense refused Emmanuel Goldberger's application to repatriate to Czechoslovakia after the war, on the grounds that he was German. Goldberger considered himself Czech and had been active in the interwar Zionist movement. He had escaped a concentration camp in 1942 and then joined the Czechoslovak foreign legion. But Ministry of Defense officials concluded that Goldberger had only joined the foreign legion for opportunistic reasons, and that he professed to be a Czech only "in order to avoid racial persecution as a Jew" and "in order to remain hidden and avoid attention," rather than out of genuine patriotism. Goldberger had attended German schools as a child, "only spoke German at home and read German newspapers," officials asserted. He therefore remained a German who "could not be considered loyal from the perspective of state citizenship."[84] These examples suggest that the blatant state-sponsored anti-Semitism that would surface in the 1953 Slansky show trials, when 14 high-ranking Czechoslovak Communists (11 Jewish) were tried for treason—and 11 executed—cannot be considered mere Soviet orchestrations. The trials built on native Czechoslovak anti-Semitism that had not been diminished by the Holocaust.[85]

* * *

Both expulsion and repatriation in postwar Czechoslovakia were part of a larger project of ethnic cleansing in which children were targets and prizes. Ethnic cleansing was officially focused on territory, the creation of nationally homogenous states through physical removal of Germans from Czech space. But it was directed just as much at the Czechoslovak families who remained at home, or who had been displaced during the war. The twin processes of expulsion and repatriation forced individuals to self-cleanse, to choose between Czech and German family members, and to expunge national ambiguity from their own families and consciousness.

Several goals of postwar reconstruction conflicted in postwar Czechoslo-vakia. On one side, there was the pressing ideal of a homogenous Czechoslovak nation-state, in which all traces of Germanness were expunged in the name of national security and sovereignty. On the other, there was a long-term goal of increasing population, which demanded a more flexible ideal of the Czech nation. If populationist logic triumphed in Prague's central ministries, it was defeated in practice by the local practitioners and beneficiaries of ethnic cleansing. By the end of 1946 only 30,000 intermarried German men and perhaps 14,000 to 15,000 intermarried women remained in Czechoslovakia. Over 18,000 Czechoslovak Jews, meanwhile, immigrated to Palestine between 1948 and 1950. Between 14,000 and 18,000 remained at the end of 1950, less than 10 percent of the prewar Jewish population. By 1950, the vast majority of Jews and nationally entangled families had left Czechoslovakia, whether voluntarily or by force.[86]

Ethnic cleansing not only remade the population of Europe after World War II, it also remade families. After the Second World War, family reunification was touted across Europe as the recipe for individual and collective rehabilitation. In this framework, the homecoming of lost Czechoslovak children was linked to postwar justice, denazification, and the biological reconstruction of the Czechoslovak nation. But in the final analysis, not all families were considered equal. The ideal of reconstructing war-torn families often conflicted with the ambition to create a nationally homogenous state. Families that challenged or confused national categories had to be either cleansed internally or dissolved in postwar Czechoslovakia. The dissolution of families was ultimately as much a part of the postwar search for stability as the sentimental reunions celebrated by the press and humanitarian organizations.

The expulsion of millions of Germans from Eastern Europe after World War II is usually seen as the violent culmination of decades of nationalist conflict in Eastern Europe.[87] But it also reflected the horizontal context of wartime and postwar population displacement across Europe. Throughout interwar and wartime Europe, government officials crafted migration policies with an eye toward the creation of homogenous nation-states. This process climaxed after World War II, not only in the so-called "borderlands" of Central and Eastern Europe, but also in the nation-states of Western Europe and abroad (France, the United States, Canada, Australia) that rejected or recruited potential immigrants and displaced persons based on their race, ethnicity, and perceived assimilability. Both the politics of immigration and repatriation and the more violent waves of expulsion that accompanied the liberation of

Europe reflected the shared goal of creating nationally homogenous families and territories after 1945.

Western and East European governments faced similar apparent choices between national homogeneity and population growth, between promoting the reunification or dissolution of transnational families. But while the postwar decades would ultimately bring massive foreign labor into Great Britain, France, and West Germany, the borders of Eastern Europe soon closed to emigration. Freedom of movement would be harshly restricted for fifty years under Communist rule. Ironically, what had once been the most linguistically diverse regions in Europe became the most homogenous, while those that had supposedly been the most homogenous became more diverse—but with deep inequalities between foreign laborers and citizens.

The French government invited German children onto French territory, while the Czechoslovak government (at least initially) drove them out. On the surface, the decision to adopt the children of the German enemy seems to reflect a generous Republican tradition of assimilation that can be contrasted to the exclusive ethnic nationalisms of Eastern Europe. But in reality, the far-fetched French scheme to adopt children of French-German couples and Czechoslovak policies toward children of mixed marriage reflected a shared agenda. Both French and Czechoslovak authorities aimed to create nationally homogenous states in the name of national security after World War II. Both policies favored children, presumed to be the most assimilable members of the national body. And in both Eastern and Western Europe, postwar migration policies reflected prevailing racial, ethnic, and gender hierarchies, privileging the interests of nationalist policymakers in the name of children's "best interests."

7

Repatriation and the Cold War

In Yugoslavia in 1948, the Belgrade newspaper *Tanjug* publicized the tragic fate of Yugoslav children in postwar Austria. "In Austria at the present time there are large numbers of Yugoslav children who were taken by force from Yugoslavia during the war. Scattered throughout Austria, exposed to Germanization and education designed to make them hate their own country, these children are unscrupulously exploited as free manual labor," the paper reported. "Efforts by the Yugoslav government and Red Cross to find these children and bring them back to their native country are blocked by the occupation authorities in the Western Zones ... This state of affairs is also caused, in large part, by the IRO, which will stop at nothing in order to prevent the return of Yugoslav children to their native land."[1]

As *Tanjug's* rhetoric makes clear, Europe's lost children had become pawns in an escalating Cold War conflict by 1948. In the immediate wake of the Nazi defeat, struggles over the resettlement of refugee children were typically framed as a nationalist, demographic contest between Germany and its neighbors to the East and West. By 1948, however, disputes over the fate of displaced youth were increasingly translated into Cold War terms. The nationalist struggle between Nazis and Slavs was refashioned as a political battle between East and West, as the future of Europe itself was projected onto the bodies of refugee children. Cold War conflicts in liberated Europe not only pitted East against West, however. Debates about the future of displaced youth also cut across national lines. They pitted Czechs against Czechs, Poles against Poles, Germans against Germans, and created new and surprising political alliances. Aleta Brownlee, the Chief of UNRRA and IRO's child welfare division in the

American zone of Austria recalled that as Cold War divisions hardened, former Allied powers turned against one another, ex-enemies became friends, "West was set upon East, the Catholic Church against Communism." Some British and American officials shared the anti-Semitic and anti-Slavic prejudices of the Nazis. Since the vast majority of displaced children in Austria were from Eastern Europe, Brownlee recalled that at least one high-ranking British official took the position that the children should be kept in Germany, since "there are too many Slavs anyway."[2]

The diplomatic struggles that erupted over the repatriation of displaced children reflected the high political stakes of repatriation in postwar Europe. The great majority of Displaced Persons—both adults and children—were desperate to return home after the Second World War. During May and June of 1945 alone, 5.25 million Europeans made the journey home. But not everyone willingly boarded the repatriation trains, nor were they necessarily welcomed home with open arms. In February of 1945, Allied leaders signed the Yalta agreement, agreeing to the forcible repatriation of Soviet citizens in the Western zones of occupation. By the end of September 1945, 2,272,000 DPs had returned to the Soviet Union. Of the civilians and POWs who returned to the Soviet Union as of March 1, 1946, an estimated 6.5 percent were "referred to the NKVD" and 14.48 percent were conscripted into forced labor battalions immediately upon arrival, according to Soviet government statistics.[3]

Forced repatriations from the American and British zones subsided by the end of 1945 and officially ceased in 1947. Already in September of 1945, approximately 1,325,000 DPs from Eastern Europe who were unable or unwilling to return home crowded UNRRA camps. In July 1947, a so-called "hard core" of 650,000 East European DPs became the responsibility of the IRO, which focused on resettlement rather than repatriation, at least with respect to adults. Around the globe, governments were beginning to recruit DPs as a labor resource with which to rebuild their postwar economies. They often made special provisions for youth, who were seen as particularly desirable migrants and workers. The American DP Act of 1948, for example, promised to admit up to 3,000 European war orphans to the United States. Many young refugees from Eastern Europe set their sights on American shores.[4]

Unaccompanied children formed only a tiny part of the "hard-core" contingent of refugees who remained in Germany several years after liberation. But their fates were violently contested. In June of 1947, the IRO reported that out of 16,800 registered unaccompanied children in the British and American zones, approximately 6,871 had been repatriated (mostly to Eastern Europe), while 1,889 (mostly Jewish children) had been resettled abroad. Another 3,793 (including 2,400 Jewish children) "disappeared" (to Palestine or into the German economy), 1,138 celebrated their 18th birthdays and were released into the general population, and 1,073 were reunited with relatives in exile. The rest remained in the care of the IRO as their identities were verified and their custody disputed, a process that could take years.[5]

Repatriation was a central component of reconstruction in postwar Europe. In Belgium, France, and the Netherlands, the success of repatriation campaigns was linked to the legitimacy of new postwar governments. New postwar regimes aimed to prove their mettle through their ability to bring POWs and deportees home quickly and provide them with housing, medical care, and welfare benefits.[6] In Eastern Europe, the stakes were even higher. East European states had generally suffered much higher numbers of casualties during the Second World War. Devastated East European economies desperately needed repatriates to replace the dead and complete the physical and intellectual work of reconstruction (all the more once their governments deported millions of Germans). The refusal of displaced persons to return home represented nothing less than an act of treason to newly established Communist governments in the East. Following the consolidation of Communist power in 1948, the return of displaced POWs, forced laborers, and lost children became a highly politicized referendum on the legitimacy of Communist rule.

The citizens of Eastern Europe's new Socialist states could no longer vote freely at the ballot box. But until the borders between East and West were guarded with guns and barbed wire, they could vote with their feet—either by fleeing Communist regimes or choosing not to return home from exile in the West. In Germany alone, over three million citizens crossed from East to West before the Berlin Wall was constructed. One-half of the defectors were youth or children under the age of 25.[7] Socialist officials denounced adults who defected or who refused to repatriate as fascists and traitors, but it was more difficult to demonize children who refused to return home. East European authorities instead blamed allied military authorities, international organizations, German officials, and Catholic priests for allegedly brainwashing and sequestering displaced youth who refused repatriation (or ran away to the West) after the war.

In Poland, which was, in the words of one Polish military official "the greatest loser of children," the repatriation of displaced children was particularly contentious. Polish officials saw the Germanization of Polish children as part of a broader Nazi scheme for the wholesale extermination of the Polish nation. A 1948 memo from the Polish Ministry of Labor and Social Welfare elaborated, "Violating all human rights and trampling on the Rights of Nations, Germany organized the systematic robbery of children with the dual goal of strengthening their own nation's biological power and furthering the biological destruction of occupied nations. These were, according to their plans, sentenced to total annihilation."[8] Such rhetoric was intended to establish a false equivalence between Nazi policies toward Jews and Poles during World War II. By linking the displacement and denationalization of Polish children to a planned Nazi genocide against Poles, Polish authorities hoped to justify their demands for the forcible repatriation of Polish children from Germany after the war.

Approximately 75 percent of the unaccompanied children in UNRRA and IRO care were registered as non-Jewish Poles (though children's nationalities were frequently disputed).[9] These numbers reflected the relative "success" of Nazi plans to kidnap and deport Polish children from Eastern Europe. In Czechoslovakia, Nazi Germanization efforts had failed and were largely abandoned shortly after the Lidice massacre in 1942. But in Poland, the systematic Germanization of Polish children continued throughout the war. The number of children who ultimately fell victim to Germanization policies was hotly disputed, however. In 1948 Polish authorities in Warsaw alleged that over 200,000 Polish children remained in Nazi hands in the Western zones of occupation, but more reliable estimates suggest that the number was closer to between 20,000 and 50,000.[10]

The problem of numbers reflected the widespread persistence of national ambiguity in Central Europe. Some 43 percent of children initially identified as potential East European nationals by the IRO in the Hesse region in Germany were later classified as Volksdeutsche, for example.[11] Many children transferred to German orphanages and foster homes were Silesian, in which case their nationality was generally disputed. German authorities considered these children "Polonized Germans," while Polish authorities generally considered Silesian natives to be Poles or "Germanized Poles" who could be "rehabilitated" for the Polish nation. In 1945, for example, a confused Polish repatriation officer in Bavaria wrote to city officials in Królewska Huta in Silesia. He needed to determine whether 60 children, between the ages of 10 and 15, from the town were Polish or German. They had all been Polish citizens before 1939, he reported, but were "strongly Germanized and disoriented" now. Asking the children about their national loyalties was no use. "It is impossible to rely on the children themselves for clarification of this complicated and ambiguous issue," he reported. He hoped that the children's parents might determine once and for all "if they are currently of the Polish or German nationality."[12]

Immediately after the war, the Polish Red Cross began efforts to trace and repatriate Poland's lost children in cooperation with UNRRA. In 1947, the search intensified, when the Polish Ministry of Labor and Social Welfare launched a special Operation for the Revindication of Children *(Akcja rewindikacji dzieci)*, headed by Roman Hrabar. But by the end of 1950, Operation Revindication boasted meager results: only 3,404 unaccompanied children had been repatriated to Poland from occupied Germany since the end of the war: 1,195 from the American zone, 1,040 from the British Zone, 196 from the French zone, and 965 from the Soviet zone.[13]

Relations between the Polish government, Red Cross Representatives, and UNRRA were initially friendly. Stefan Tyska, a delegate of the Polish Red Cross attached to UNRRA Team 104g in Regensburg, reported in 1947, "UNRRA brought its full force and facilities to try and uncover the lost and missing children of the United Nations, assuming this to be its inherent responsibility. To UNRRA and to those who bring to the solution of this problem their good will and fullest efforts, we are thankful and appreciative." While Tyska was frustrated that repatriation progressed slowly, he blamed German resistance rather than Allied obstruction.[14] Between 1945 and 1947, Polish authorities still generally depicted conflicts over repatriation as a clash between unrepentant German Nazis and East European victims. In Austria, for example, Polish Red Cross officials complained that Austrian foster parents systematically gave out false information and even forged documents in order to hide Polish children. "With respect to the children who proved to be a good form of slave labor during the war . . . Austrian foster parents have spared no measure in order to keep these children with them," the Red Cross alleged. Many displaced Polish children initially refused to leave their German foster homes. But once they were safely en route to Vienna, the children reportedly confessed that they had endured hard labor on Austrian farms, and "only professed to love their German foster parents out of fear of punishment."[15]

In cases of serious conflict, Polish officials tended to be somewhat flexible between 1945 and 1947. The case of Janina and Mackowiak Kazmierz was typical. The children had been born in 1931 and 1932 respectively. They lost their father in 1936 and their mother in 1938, and were subsequently placed in a Polish orphanage. Nazi officials deemed the children Germanizable, changed their names to Johanna and Fritz Markert, and transferred them to a German orphanage in 1940. They were subsequently placed in the care of the Coppenraths, a childless German couple near Wiesbaden. After the war, the Coppenraths hoped to adopt the children. But in October 1946 they were repatriated to Poland against their will. After only a week in Poland, Janina/Johanna and Mackowiak/Fritz ran away from the Polish Red Cross Children's Center. They spent the next two months traversing Central Europe by foot in order to return to the Coppenraths. In a 1947 memo, officials in the Polish Ministry of Public Administration conceded that the children "are so attached to their foster parents that all efforts made by Polish representatives to awaken their Polish spirit and a desire to return to their homeland have been without success." The Ministry recommended that the children be allowed to remain in Germany, since it seemed doubtful that "they could develop normally" and "become valuable members of Polish society" if repatriated again. The Coppenraths subsequently adopted the children.[16]

This pragmatic approach changed dramatically in 1948, with the consolidation of Communist power in Poland and the replacement of UNRRA by the IRO. Increasingly, Polish Red Cross delegates and government officials insisted on the repatriation of all Polish minors, regardless of their age, whether or not they had living relatives in Poland, and irrespective of their personal wishes. They defended this policy in the name of the children's best interests. In March of 1948, for example, the Polish Red Cross in Austria insisted on the forcible repatriation of orphans from Austria, since "even if they are complete orphans, Polish children are obligated to return to their homeland, where they will certainly find better care in orphanages or in foster families than with Austrian families."[17]

Instead of blaming the Germans, moreover, Polish authorities increasingly denounced Western occupation authorities and the IRO for deliberately sequestering Polish children. The British Military Government was considered the worst offender. Based in part on Anna Freud's insistence that continuity of care was the single most important factor in a child's psychological well being, British officials typically ruled that it was in the "best interests" of Polish children to remain with their German foster parents. Polish Red Cross officials were fed up with the endless paperwork required to repatriate a child from the British zone, which included evidence of personal correspondence between parents or relatives and their children.[18] Particularly infuriating was the British demand for proof that a displaced child would enjoy the same material standard of living in Poland as in Germany or Austria. In the case of Eugeniusz Bartczak and Zofia Arden, for example, E. Dunkel, a child search officer with the IRO, demanded "original letters from the relatives in Poland indicating that they are willing and capable to give the children care equal to that which they are receiving in Germany."[19] Polish and British officials even contested the basic definition of an unaccompanied child. Twelve-year-old Sofia Pogoda, for example, was an orphan who had been raised by her paternal aunt in Silesia. In 1945, she fled advancing Russian troops to Germany with her aunt. In 1948 the Polish Red Cross attempted to remove the girl from her German aunt, in order to transfer her to the custody of a paternal aunt back in Poland. British military authorities rejected the request. Sofia was not legally an unaccompanied child, or even a Displaced Person, in their view. "The child is almost 13 years of age and does not wish to return to Poland. She is living with the aunt in the German economy . . . it is not within the jurisdiction of this Headquarters to order her removal to Poland."[20]

Surprisingly, however, repatriation was not much more expedient in the Soviet Zone. In 1947, Roman Hrabar noted that the search, identification, and repatriation of Polish children from the Soviet zone was being conducted "sporadically," and lacked "the character of a planned or organized program."[21] Soviet authorities were intent on bringing displaced Soviet children home, but they were indifferent about the repatriation of Polish and other allied children from the Soviet zone of Germany. Polish authorities estimated after the war that there were at least 14,000 unaccompanied Polish children in the Soviet zone of occupation, but only 965 had been repatriated to Poland by 1950. Many of these children probably disappeared into the Western zones of occupation.[22] Instead of blaming Soviet officials, however, Polish Red Cross delegates declared that Soviet occupation authorities were "neutral" on the issue of repatriation. They continued to attribute the slow pace of repatriation from the Soviet zone to local German obstruction.[23]

Polish Communists meanwhile escalated their attacks against the Western Allies, accusing them of deliberately hijacking Polish children. Jakub Prawin, the head of the Polish Military Mission in Berlin, issued a virulent letter of protest to the military governors of the American, British, and French Zones in late December 1948. It was an affront to democracy itself, he argued, that Polish children continued to languish in German homes. "Whatever be the interpretation of the democratic way of life that the German people should enjoy, it certainly could never be democratic as long as thousands and thousands of foreign children are absconded from their home and country and are being brought up as Germans . . . My Country . . . can no more subdue the voices of thousands of mothers expecting that something essential be done to . . . give them back their babies."[24] Prawin, like Polish Red Cross Delegates and other government authorities, blamed Western obstruction for the abysmal rate of repatriation. But in reality the struggle over displaced children often pit Poles against Poles, as Polish officials allied with the Communist government in Warsaw clashed with Polish refugees in Germany who refused repatriation for political, social, religious or pragmatic reasons.

Even Polish refugees who were not politically hostile to repatriation were typically less worried about the Germanization of their children than representatives of the Polish government in Warsaw. In 1947, for example, the Committee for the Care of Polish Children in Berlin organized summer camps in Poland for 600 refugee children in Germany. These camps, the organization reported, had successfully "awakened Polish loyalties" in exiled children and improved their Polish language skills. The problem was that the children's own Polish parents insisted on speaking German at home. "A considerable number of the preschool children do not hear any Polish even in their own parental home," the Committee lamented. "When the tentacles of Germanization encroached even into the home during Hitler's regime, the colloquial language became German. The most difficult war for the committee to win is the war over the use of Polish at home."[25] Even more frustrating, Polish authorities privately confessed, was the problem of Polish parents who abandoned their children on German soil, even after the liberation. The Polish Red Cross in Germany reported that many single Polish women in Germany "attempt to rid themselves of their children, who are a burden to them." Most of these women, former forced laborers, left their children in the care of German families or institutions. They wanted to return to Poland and feared the social approbation (not to mention material difficulties) that awaited them as single mothers.[26]

In some cases, Polish parents later attempted to reclaim their children in Germany, reporting that they had surrendered them only under extreme duress. Around two million of the 7.7 million forced laborers and POWs in the Third Reich in 1944 were women. Before 1942, if a female forced laborer became pregnant in Germany, she was allowed to go home. But in the spring of 1943, Nazi authorities began to perform involuntary abortions on a large number of foreign workers. In the event that a forced laborer from the East became pregnant by a German man, a commission of racial and medical experts decided whether the newborn was "racially valuable." Infants deemed Germanizable were seized from their mothers and placed in Lebensborn homes. Those children rejected for Germanization meanwhile languished in institutions where they typically died of neglect or starvation.[27]

Other forced laborers were subject to less formal pressure to abandon their children. In 1943, Polish workers Wiktoria and Feliks Galuhn signed a document relinquishing custody of their newborn, Henryk Galuhn, to Karl and Annelise Leithauser in Germany. The Galuhns later requested the repatriation of their child to Poland. They attested that they had not been able to read the custody agreement, which was in German, and that they feared being sent to a concentration camp if they refused to relinquish their child. In 1949, as the custody battle dragged on, Wiktoria swore that "as a Pole I intend to educate my own child in a Polish spirit and in the Catholic faith." But British officials opposed the child's return to Poland, asserting that the infant "would have died but for the excellent care of the foster parents."[28]

In numerous other cases, however, Polish parents did not reclaim their children after the war. Erika Smigas was born on New Year's Day 1944 to Polish forced laborers. Her mother died in an allied bombing and her father entrusted the child to the Borgden family in Germany, and then settled abroad. Polish Red Cross officials attempted to remove Erika from her German foster parents and repatriate her to Poland, but IRO officer Clifford Kocq van Bruegel rejected the claim. "In this particular case there is no question of a 'lost' child. The father stayed with the Borgden family and himself left the child in their care. Erika is treated and considered as their own child and the whole family is extremely attached to the child . . . Her present home may not be luxurious, but we are convinced the child is suffering no hardship and receives the best care the foster parents can give her."[29]

By the late 1940s, a veritable civil war between the Warsaw Communist government and the Polish government-in-exile in London had erupted over the fate of displaced Polish children in Germany. This struggle concerned the education of refugee children as well as the question of their ultimate settlement. Exiled Polish parents and educators had spontaneously created a school system for Polish refugee children in Germany after the liberation. In the fall of 1945, some 38,000 students attended classes in 437 Polish elementary schools in the American, British, and French zones. But control of these schools was contested between the pro-Warsaw Head Office for Schools in Germany *(Central Skolnictwa Polskiego w Niemczech)* and the pro-London, anti-Communist Central Committee for Schools and Education *(Centralny Komitet dla Spraw Skolnych i Oświatowych)*. Both sides agreed that it was necessary to prevent Polish children from being Germanized. The aim of these schools, according to a pamphlet sent from London in 1945, was to save refugee children "for Poland and for Polishness."[30] But the political content of the curriculum was bitterly disputed. The anti-Communist Union of Polish Refugees in Germany protested in 1947 that schools for Polish refugee children were increasingly subjected to the authority of the government in Warsaw, (ironically, by UNRRA) objecting, "This is an attempt to give control to the Warsaw administration of the education of those Polish children whose parents refuse to recognize that very administration."[31]

Polish anti-Communists in Germany also vigorously obstructed the repatriation of Polish orphans to Communist Poland. In 1948 the Union of Polish War Refugees denounced the "forcible repatriation" of 600 Polish orphans to Poland. "The majority . . . were complete orphans, who could have benefitted from a democratic education in the United States. . . . Since there are already a million orphans and half-orphans in Poland, living in terrible conditions and not receiving a proper education, multiplying this number through forcible repatriation is neither felicitous nor advisable for the children." The Union maintained that the children themselves ardently opposed repatriation, and reported "tragic scenes" en route to Poland. Some children allegedly jumped from repatriation trains or ran away, while others immediately fled back to Germany upon their return to a "homeland" they didn't recognize.[32]

Communist officials, meanwhile, were outraged by schemes to resettle displaced East European youth in the United States, Canada, or Australia. In a 1948 memo to IRO, the Polish Red Cross asserted that Western governments were recruiting displaced Polish children as a source of slave labor. "We cannot stand by in silence while Polish children stolen from their country are once again threatened with denationalization . . . The IRO favors those agents who are looking for cheap labor for foreign industries . . . The recruitment of labor among refugees in foreign countries resembles a slave auction, even though slavery has been abolished since Lincoln."[33]

But even as they made insistent demands for the return of displaced children and youth, Polish officials (like other European governments) wanted to ensure that the right *kind* of lost children returned to Poland. There was little interest among Communist authorities in repatriating Jewish youth, for example. In October 1947 the Polish *Gazeta Ludowa* even accused the German government of attempting to dump biologically inferior children in Poland. The report complained that a considerable number of children repatriated to Poland were "deformed children. . . . Examinations performed prove that the majority of children are handicapped mentally, speak only German, and were born in Germany of illegitimate parents . . . There exists a justified suspicion that . . . the Germans are simply take advantage of this opportunity to throw off onto Poland elements troublesome for them . . . the care of such children is very expensive."[34]

UNNRA and IRO social workers found themselves caught in the crossfire, mediating between East and West, Communists and Catholics, foster parents and biological parents, military authorities and local populations. Contrary to East European protests, however, UN workers generally favored the repatriation of displaced children to Eastern Europe, even after the Communist seizure of power. But displaced children and their families also had a say in the matter, complicating the situation on the ground. Even as the political stakes of these Cold War custody battles intensified, moreover, Polish Communists, UNRRA social workers, and American and British occupation authorities were united in one respect. They all claimed to uphold children's "best interests," and they all defined those interests in psychological, as well as material and moral terms. They disagreed sharply, however, about whether repatriation to Eastern Europe or resettlement abroad was the recipe for psychological stability in the aftermath of wartime displacement.

By the time unaccompanied children landed in IRO care, many retained only distant memories of their families and country of origins. This was certainly true of the 148 Polish children who found themselves at the center of an escalating diplomatic conflict in 1948 to 1949.[35] On July 30, 1941, shortly after Hitler's invasion of the Soviet Union, Polish and Soviet diplomats had signed an agreement that reestablished the Polish state, provided for the release of Polish citizens in the Soviet Union, including anti-Communist Poles imprisoned in Siberia, and enabled the formation of a Polish army on Soviet soil, led by General Wladyslaw Anders. In March 1942, Anders evacuated 74,000 Polish troops, including approximately 41,000 civilians, many children, to Iran. These children were soon scattered in DP camps throughout Iran, Palestine, India, and Africa. At the war's end, 148 Polish children and youth landed in Tanganyika, Africa, under the care and supervision of the Polish government-in-exile in London and the Polish resettlement corps in the United Kingdom. Following the liquidation of the African camp, the IRO transferred the children to Salerno, Italy. In 1948 the Canadian Catholic Immigrant Society offered to resettle the youth in Canada, triggering an international crisis.

The position of the Polish government, predictably, was that anything but the repatriation of these children sanctioned Hitler's crimes against the Polish nation. Consistent with its beliefs about the psychological importance of a stable national identity, IRO officials generally endorsed this view. IRO

Director-General J. Donald Kingsley explained before the UN General Assembly in November 1949, "In ordinary circumstances, the ideal solution for a displaced person is return to the homeland. There, he finds a familiar form of social organization and hears a familiar tongue . . . In his homeland, he has the full rights of citizenship. Here he has his roots." At the same time, IRO policy clearly forbade the forcible repatriation of any person against his or her will. Even in the case of minors, IRO regulations specified, "The recommendation made for the repatriation or settlement of the child should not be contrary to the wishes of the child. Such wishes shall be assessed in the light of the age of the child and of all the circumstances. They shall be taken into account only if they have been expressed freely, and provided they are based on considerations which, in the case of a person over 17 years of age, would be considered as valid objections." And all of the Polish youth in Tanganyika stubbornly refused to return to Poland. Moreover, of the 148 youth concerned, 81 were over 16 years old and only 24 were under 13. Only 28 had a living parent in Poland.[36]

It was not, however, against the IRO mandate to attempt to convince DPs to repatriate of their own "free will," or to bribe them with rations. In August 1949, the IRO sent a team of officials, including a Polish repatriation officer named Pierre Krysz, on a three-week mission to the Children's Centre in Salerno. Krysz interviewed each child in order to better understand his or her reasons for refusing repatriation. To his dismay, the children did not share the IRO or Polish government's understanding of their "best interests." Krysz and Child Tracing Officer Charlotte Babinski instead noted that the young refugees displayed what they perceived as a pathological "indifference" to their families and homeland. "A number of children and youth, larger than it is reasonable to expect in an institutional group, displayed disinterest or indifference in having parents traced or clues on relatives followed up. One young man deliberately lied about his mother's Christian name, and later admitted the falsehood, saying he feared pressure might be put on him to return to Poland," reported Babinski.[37] Krysz concurred, lamenting, "the complete disinterest [of the children] in parental or family care is striking in most of the cases."[38]

Krysz and Babinski attributed these attitudes to indoctrination by the children's anti-Communist teachers. But the children's own testimony suggests that they did not share the IRO's faith in the healing powers of nation and family. Many had been separated from their families and homes for almost ten years. Their relatives in Poland, and Poland itself, were distant memories. The appeal of a fresh start, educational opportunities in Canada, their own political and religious convictions, and the solidarity of the group itself were more meaningful than family ties or nationalist sentiments. In other cases, the children's own relatives dissuaded them from returning to Poland.[39]

Bogdan Sypincki, whose mother lived in Poland, informed Krysz that he "wants to finish his studies, and not in Poland, and does not want to become a Communist." Eugenia Zurawska, age 14, insisted that she would prefer to live in an orphanage in Canada than rejoin her father, "because he remarried and has three step-children and because she 'thinks' that her father could not give her an adequate education," Krysz noted critically. Boleslaw Kacpura's elder sister in Poland warned him not to return home because she was unable to support him. He refused repatriation on the grounds that he "does not want to starve." In each case, Krysz concluded that the children had "no valid objections" to repatriation. Yet the responses of these youth to his questions reveal that they were typically planning rationally for their futures.

Meanwhile, the IRO faced heavy political fire from all sides. On the one hand, the Catholic and anti-Communist activists who planned the resettlement accused the IRO of unduly pressuring the children to repatriate. In an urgent telegram to IRO headquarters on August 6, 1949, Monsignor Meystowicz, assigned by the Vatican to accompany the children, protested that "this continued pressure and harassment can only be interpreted as forcible repatriation."[40] The Count E. H. Czapski, an anti-Communist Pole who chaired the Board of Guardians charged with caring for the orphans in Italy, wrote a passionate letter of protest to IRO headquarters: "The young people concerned have lost everything as a result of Soviet aggression—their country, family, and fortune. Saved almost miraculously . . . do you believe that they would voluntarily return to live under Soviet domination? Perhaps you are also ignoring the fact that close to 1,000 Polish children are buried in Tehran's only cemetery, those who were able to leave Russia but did not survive their experiences in 'the Soviet paradise.'"[41]

In the United States, meanwhile, anti-Communists mounted protests against the repatriation of East European children to the Soviet bloc. *The New York Times* weighed in on the issue in September 1948. "A shocking and alarming proposal has been made by the United States, British, Netherlands, and Brazilian delegates to the United Nations Economic and Social Council that all 'unaccompanied children' under 16 years of age in the displaced persons camps of Europe be returned to their countries of origins." The *Times* opposed this "callous solution" on humanitarian grounds, arguing that most of the young refugees had no desire to return to their homelands, and no families to return to. The United States had a moral obligation to open its "minds and hearts" to East European youth "without discrimination," as they had earned the right to "decide for themselves" where they would settle.[42]

While the *New York Times* editorial made no explicit reference to the Cold War tensions underlying the custody battle, a letter from anti-Communist activists published shortly afterwards made the political stakes explicit: "UNRRA, despite its excellent relief work, was too often made to serve the purposes of the Soviet Union and its satellites, especially as regards repatriation of displaced persons . . . Are the Communist states today any better than concentration camps on a national scale? Recent reports confirm earlier information that in some of the Soviet occupied lands, thousands of orphaned children wander from village to village, begging for food and clothing . . . But far worse than this, those who are returned . . . would be taught hatred for the ideals we hold dear and they would be militarized in preparation for the Communist conquest of the world." Representatives of several American anti-Communist organizations signed the letter, including Common Cause, the Committee Against Mass Expulsion, the Refugee Defense Committee, and the Worker's Defense League.[43]

The IRO was bombarded with even more intense criticism in favor of repatriating the children, however. Not surprisingly, the Polish Red Cross, the Polish Government, and other Communist sympathizers delivered the most fiery rhetoric. In a letter to the IRO, the Democratic Women's Association of East Germany claimed that the children's refusal to repatriate reflected the defective state of their characters, a consequence of displacement itself: "These young people were torn from their homes as children and put in a completely new environment, far from their country and their parents. It was impossible there to create for them a new home such as growing young people need for their development, and so they became beings without roots." Rehabilitating these children—and European democracy—required returning the youth to their nation and families: "Now, four years after the end of the war, it is the duty of all people of democratic thought and feeling to repair the wrongs done by the Fascist murderers and criminals. That certainly includes the return to their old home of all those Hitler had uprooted from their native land. These young people, too, although they may have spent the last few years in Africa, are Polish by nationality, tradition, and character, belong to the Polish people, and will always by homeless in a foreign country."[44] Polish Communists also used the affair to question the democratic credentials of the West. The Polish journal *Repatriant* protested, "In the course of recent years, this is not the first case of theft of Polish children who should be returned to their country. . . . Does such an attitude conform to the humanitarian principles promoted in the West?"[45]

Pressure to repatriate the children did not simply flow from the pens of Communists, however. In a letter to the President of the United Nations General Assembly, the International Save the Children Union insisted that returning displaced children with their nations and families of origin was a matter of human rights. Save the Children leaders declared, "We feel obligated to inform you how concerned we are . . . about the subject of children removed or separated from their parents, whatever the reason. . . . The Declaration of the Rights of Child, promulgated in 1923 by our union, demands respect for the intangible rights and duties of parents with respect to their children, and the same is true of the Universal Declaration of Human Rights."[46]

In spite of such protests, the first group of children set sail for Canada on August 29, 1949, and the rest followed shortly after. The IRO injunction against forcible repatriation (and the intensification of anti-Communist sentiment in the West) ultimately prevailed over competing claims of nation and family. Afterwards, in a speech to the U.N. General Assembly, Donald Kingsley defended the resettlement. He expressed the hope that it reflected a new kind of postwar migration, that of a more democratic and humanitarian world: "In the long history of mankind, there have been many mass migrations of people, some of them also overseas. Most, however, had their motivation in evil or fanaticism, were executed in violence or necessity . . . Never before has there been such a movement as this, motivated by good will, executed in generosity, and adding, surely, to the hopes of millions for a peaceful life."[47]

Similar struggles raged over the repatriation or resettlement of Yugoslav children displaced to Austria. One particularly explosive controversy centered on a group of 49 boys between the ages of 8 and 17. Most of the boys came from farmers' families in Bosnia and Dalmatia. The children had been placed in the care of Roman Catholic nuns by Croatian authorities or by their parents in 1942. In October of 1944, they were evacuated as part of a Nazi-run school from Zagreb to Ramsau in Austria, a village located in the British occupation zone. They remained there after the war, living in the picturesque Hotel Almfrieden, an alpine lodge perched high on a plateau with snow-covered glaciers behind it. The children were all told by the Nazis that their parents had been killed by partisans, and were being prepared to train for the priesthood. But UNRRA investigations ascertained that 44 out of the 49 boys actually still had living parents in Yugoslavia.

The Yugoslav government demanded that the children be immediately repatriated, even if their parents had not been located. But British military officials and Catholic authorities were equally passionate in their opposition to repatriation, and the children themselves refused to return home. Aleta Brownlee of UNRRA was convinced that British authorities deliberately obstructed the repatriation of Yugoslav children out of anti-Communist sympathies. In November of 1946, she noted, "It is my firm belief and allegation that repatriation is not encouraged in the British zone but that only lip service is given to it."[48] At the Weidmansdorf DP camp, she found that the Assistant to the Principle Welfare Officer was "unequivocally opposed to repatriation" and considered Yugoslavs who did return home to be traitors. In fact, many Nazi collaborators were residing in the camp, biding their time until (they hoped) British, American, Austria, and Yugoslav forces would unite to overthrow Tito. British Colonel Logan-Gray, director of DP operations in the British Zone, also unequivocally opposed the repatriation of Yugoslav children, reasoning that "every Yugoslav and Soviet child that you return will be one against us later on."[49]

Representatives of UNRRA, however, strongly favored repatriation. Aleta Brownlee herself personally visited Yugoslavia to investigate social conditions and welfare institutions for children. She reported positive developments. "Yugoslavia has a government which is purposeful and which is planning intelligently not only for economic recovery but also for a better life for its people. Therefore, children who live with their own families can be assured decent housing, education, and necessary medical care . . . There is no reason why all Yugoslav children in Austria should not be repatriated as quickly as possible. To prolong further their separation from their people and their country is cruel, and to accede to permanent separation condones German atrocity," she concluded.[50]

But Catholic officials refused to relinquish the children. The conflict came to a head in late November 1946. On November 25th, a conference was held to decide the children's fate, attended by representatives of the British Red Cross, Brownlee, the Yugoslav Red Cross and The Yugoslav Ministry of Welfare. A delegate from the Yugoslav Red Cross insisted, "These children are Yugoslavs . . . The Catholic Church has nothing to say about it. The Roman Catholic Church cannot decide whether children are Yugoslav or some other nationality."[51] The next day a meeting took place between representatives of the British occupation authorities and Father Methodius Kelava and Sister Anka, who had cared for the children since 1944. By now representatives of the British government had also reluctantly agreed to the children's repatriation. But Kelava continued to express the Church's opposition. "The parents are poor and cannot take proper care of the children . . . The Holy See is interested in this affair, especially with relation to the very difficult position of the

Catholic Church in Yugoslavia," he maintained. Kelava even deployed the new language of human rights to make his case, pleading, "Our right is a moral right, our right is a human right, and we hope that the British government will give us every possible support to take these children to Italy."[52]

His protests were fruitless. Early the next day UNRRA trucks arrived at the Hotel Almfrieden to transfer the children to an UNRRA home at Leoben. Upon seeing the trucks, however, forty out of the forty-nine children, dressed in overcoats and equipped with backpacks full of provisions, fled into the woods. Over the next few days all but two trickled back, alone or in groups of two and three, hungry and thirsty, their new suits disheveled and stained with mud and grass.[53]

Once the children returned to Leoben, UNRRA social workers sought to gradually soften their attitudes toward repatriation. Syma Klok was the UNRRA child welfare officer responsible for the children's reeducation. In a 1947 memo, Klok reported that preparing the boys for their return to Yugoslavia was a tremendous challenge. "This group had been educated and trained for more than five years along the lines that their parents were dead, that the present government in Yugoslavia was bad, and that they should not return. Our job was to reeducate these children within a period of two months so that they should accept repatriation willingly. It was a fantastic task." When asked why he had run away, for example, one boy replied, "We thought that we should be hanged when we arrived [in Yugoslavia]." Another insisted that he wanted to be a priest and that in Yugoslavia, "priests are being shot." Others objected that their parents were too poor to support them. "Hours were spent on individual children . . . endeavoring to revive their love for their family and country, their attitude to which was so warped as a result of their previous teaching," Klok recalled. One by one, the children gradually volunteered to return.[54]

The boys were greeted as celebrities when they finally repatriated. "When we passed over the border into Croatia, they shouted at the top of their voices 'Look Mrs. Klok, Croatia! We are no longer foreigners, we are at home!'" Klok reported. In Zagreb, hundreds of people waved flags at the train station as the children's train arrived. Parades of children in Young Pioneer uniforms, an orchestra, and nationalist songs rounded out the festivities. In Sokolowic, the eldest child in the group, once a hard-core opponent of repatriation, gave a speech to the assembled crowd, declaring, "We are glad to be home again after such a long time." As Klok listened to the boy she felt happy and proud. "How different this boy spoke compared with a short time ago. He has now experienced the advantages of repatriation." The boy's transformation served as living validation of UNRRA's pedagogy of renationalization.

Klok's narrative was typical of U.N. workers' accounts of their journeys on repatriation trains to Eastern Europe. It affirmed the core values of UNRRA and IRO—that children were best served by return to their nation of origins. These reports and letters from Eastern Europe were also intended to encourage the youth remaining in Austrian and German DP camps to board the repatriation trains. The most successful propaganda for repatriation came from those who had themselves made the journey successfully. Josip Music reported to his friend Jamus Zdenko in early January 1947, "Now we have arrived in Zagreb. We never expected that they would receive us so well . . . We got enough to eat. They said that we would become young Tito Pioneers and we look forward to that." Another boy boasted of good provisions and encouraged his friends to join him, writing, "The first day at home we ate so much pork and bacon that afterwards I had a bad time." Young Ante bragged to his friend Mate, "I'm better off here than you there. If you can, follow me."[55]

But family reunions were not always so joyful. In 1950, for example, the Yugoslav government demanded the repatriation of a group of 100 children living in Austria, allegedly stolen by the Nazis. In reality, many of these children had been sent across the border by their own parents to live with foster parents or relatives in Austria. The Yugoslav government had expelled others as ethnic Germans in 1945, and now, five years later, reclaimed them as Yugoslav nationals.[56] Several parents opposed the repatriation of their own children. One Slovene mother wrote, "Dear ____ You wrote me about Michko, that I should like to have him home. What will he do there as I cannot get ration cards . . . He also does not know Slovene and they would beat him here like a bull. Is he maybe a great engineer that he is needed so much here in Yugoslavia? . . . After all he is not so important that the Government cannot do without him. I request that he remain with you and be diligent."[57]

In other cases the children's parents were themselves living in exile. The IRO typically opposed repatriation under these circumstances, privileging family reunion over repatriation when the two goals conflicted. But Yugoslav officials held that even children whose parents remained in Germany or Austria should return to their homeland. As far as they were concerned, parents who refused to return to Yugoslavia were morally and politically suspect. Yugoslav repatriation officer Ivo Bajin insisted in December 1948, "Such people . . . should return to Yugoslavia and join their children there. If they did not wish to [repatriate] . . . it shows that they were probably war criminals or collaborators who had reason to fear the justice of their country." Brownlee replied that the position of the IRO was that a child belongs "first to his parents and then to his country."[58]

Bajin clearly hoped to use displaced children as bait with which to lure adult defectors home, a tactic also deployed by the Soviet government. One such case concerned 120 children of White Russian émigrés and Serbian mothers in Yugoslavia, who attended a boarding school in Belgrade during the war. In September of 1944, the Germans evacuated the school to a small town near Linz in Austria. In November of that year, the children moved on to Annaberg in the Erzgebirge of Saxony, but most of the children's parents remained in DP camps in Austria. Soviet authorities repatriated the children from the Soviet zone of Germany to the USSR without their parents' consent.[59] Some of the children clearly believed that they would never see their parents again. On the eve of her repatriation, Alla wrote, "We will be transported to Russia . . . [We were told that] if our parents want, they will get the address of their children and can be sent to Russia to join their children . . . Dear Parents, for God's sake, don't be anxious . . . it is all the same for me, and you have to live how you will . . . I am weeping bitterly, because I think I shall never see you again."[60] Brownlee recalled visiting the Soviet Headquarters in the Imperial Hotel in Vienna in order to plead for the children's return. After a year of careful negotiation, the children were finally returned to their parents in Austria. Soviet authorities later claimed that they believed that the children's parents were dead.[61]

Until 1950, American occupation authorities in Germany typically accepted the recommendations of UNRRA or the IRO for the repatriation or resettlement of unaccompanied children. But on October 5, 1950, the U.S. High Commissioner in Germany signed law Nr. 11, changing the way conflicts about repatriation and resettlement were arbitrated in the U.S. zone. Henceforth, the final decision concerning the placement of unaccompanied children in the U.S. Zone would be made exclusively by the District Courts of the U.S. High Commissioner. The District Courts held a custody hearing in each case, attended by representatives of the IRO, the child's closest living "blood relation," the child's (German) foster parents, a representative of the German Jugendamt, and a court-appointed guardian charged with representing the child's "best interests." Significantly, representatives of the child's country of origins were not invited to the hearings, but could be included at the discretion of the court.[62]

Law Nr. 11 was officially instituted to protect the "best interests" of unaccompanied children, but it clearly reflected deepening Cold War antagonisms. Specifically, American occupation authorities were dismayed by the IRO's favorable stance toward the repatriation of unaccompanied children to the Eastern Bloc. Local Germans were also becoming more incensed and vocal about the removal of Allied children from German foster homes. In a context in which West Germans were being transformed from the vanquished enemies of the United States into Cold War allies, maintaining peaceful relationships with Germans had become a greater priority for American authorities. At a conference in Geneva in July 1951, an official from the U.S. Children's Board explained, "In the early days, many actions have been taken by IRO, in an excess of zeal, involving the taking of children out of German homes by force, that . . . stirred up considerable resentment against IRO among the (German) people . . . Law Nr. 11 was . . . passed to counteract . . . that resentment and to impose a rigid safeguard against a recurrence of such actions." IRO officials were understandably dismayed by Law Nr. 11, which seriously limited the organization's own authority over the fortunes of displaced youth.[63]

Not surprisingly, Law Nr. 11 drastically reduced the number of unaccompanied children who returned to Eastern Europe from the U.S. occupation zone. Out of a sample of approximately 150 cases (taken by the author) adjudicated by the American courts in Germany, only six children actually returned to the Eastern bloc. The majority of children were resettled in the United States under the aegis of the 1948 DP Act. Those few children who were repatriated were very young, and had typically been claimed directly by their mothers or a close relative. In cases in which East European governments claimed orphans, or when the children themselves refused repatriation, the court almost always opted for resettlement in the United States.

Transcripts of the court's proceedings reveal the ways in which American courts redefined "the best interests of the child" in Cold War terms. Hannelore Pospisil, for example, was the child of an unmarried couple of ambiguous national origins in Czechoslovakia. The Nazis had placed her in foster care during the war. After the war she was expelled from Czechoslovakia with her German foster parents. Her mother, who remained in Czechoslovakia and remarried a Czech man, claimed that Hannelore had been taken from her by force and requested her daughter's repatriation to Czechoslovakia after the war. But by 1951, Hannelore was thirteen years old, and did not want to return to her birth mother. The American judge who heard the case refused to send the girl back to her homeland. In his decision, he proclaimed, "In deciding what will be a happy home for a child it is clear that the kind of country in which that home is located is relevant. It is, therefore, our duty to give thoughtful consideration to the kind of country Czechoslovakia is now. It is concededly a Communist dictatorship . . . In those countries no one can call their soul their own." As precedent for his ruling, he cited a 1936 divorce case in New Jersey in which the court awarded custody to the children's father because their mother was allegedly a Communist. This mother, the New Jersey Court had ruled, could not be allowed to "instill into the minds of the children, against the will of their father, doctrines (Communistic, Atheistic) looked upon with abhorrence by the vast majority of people."[64]

American authorities in the State Department objected to this decision, or at least to the judge's polemical rhetoric, noting that "the effect of this decision is to bar the return of children to Iron Curtain countries unless the court is satisfied that the child is capable of deciding, and does decide that it wants to return."[65] But this objection did not change the nature or even the tone of the court's subsequent rulings. The case of Josef Ochota was typical. In Ochota's hearing, Judge Leo Goodman questioned the boy before the court. Josef had been living in a Hitler Youth home in Czechoslovakia when he was evacuated to the West as Soviet troops advanced toward Germany. Several years later, his mother in Czechoslovakia located him and requested his repatriation. But like Hannelore, Josef refused to go home. When the judge asked Josef why he did not want to return to his mother, he replied, "I am [sic] away from her for 5 years, and it is not true I have been taken from my mother. She herself put me in a kind of home." He had clearly been influenced by the other youth he had met in an IRO children's home. "Those boys who had come over from Czechoslovakia told me everything, how bad things were over there and how bad education was over there," he testified. The IRO and representatives of the Czech government recommended that the boy be repatriated anyway, while the German Jugendamt, the boy's guardian, and Josef himself argued for resettlement. Josef got his wish and was allowed to immigrate to the United States. In his decision Goodman explained, "It has been the policy of this Court not to forcibly repatriate or resettle people who have a mind of their own. This is a policy that is followed in all civilized communities of the world . . . I do not want it to be said that this court is in the business of kidnapping children. On the other hand it will never be said that this Court has compelled people of maturity to be forcibly sent where they do not want to go."[66]

In Ochota's case and many others like it, the anti-Communist convictions of American judges and occupation authorities clashed with their proclaimed ideals of family reunification. In a few exceptional cases concerning small children, family reunification triumphed. In the highly politicized case of Johanna Bobrowitsch, for example, Judge Goodman ultimately sent the child back to the Soviet Union. Johanna was only eight years old in 1951. She had been born in Krakow on Christmas Day in 1943 to Sinaida Bobrowitsch. Shortly after her birth, Johanna was placed in a German nursery home, which was then evacuated to the West as Soviet forces closed in on the city. Johanna lived in a series of children's homes in Bavaria before she was finally identified as a Polish national and transferred to UNRRA's care in May of 1946. She remained in UNRRA/IRO hands for several years while social workers unsuccessfully attempted to trace her mother. Finally in September of 1950, Sinaida Bobrowitsch contacted the IRO in search of her lost daughter. "From the depth of my heart I beg you to use all the means available to you so that I should be able to press my natural daughter to my motherly breast as soon as possible," she appealed. After a lengthy effort to verify the identities of both mother and child (which included a professional handwriting analysis of Sinaida's letters), the District Court finally concluded that Sinaida, now living in Lwow in the USSR, was indeed the child's birth mother.

In this exceptional case, Judge Leo Goodman ordered the repatriation of the child to the USSR, in spite of his personal reservations. "In order to be reunited with its mother the child must of necessity be returned to a country whose regime cannot be acquitted of unfriendliness to the spirit of democracy," he elaborated. But could the American courts "properly deny this mother her child, because we condemn the regime under which she lives?" He decided that it would not be in the child's best interests, or in the interests of American citizens abroad. "The child is eight years old now. It has lived an institutional and nomadic existence as an orphan and a ward of charity since the day of its birth and that is the future which is in store for her here, if her mother's claim should be denied." He concluded that retaining the child in Germany would set a dangerous precedent, "permitting a court to bar an individual who is temporarily within its jurisdiction from returning to his mother country simply because we are opposed to the political philosophy which prevails therein . . . We cannot subordinate justice to politics."[67]

The decision was probably also influenced by intense Soviet lobbying and publicity surrounding the case. During one of the early hearings, two Soviet officers stormed into the courtroom and demanded to make a political speech in favor of the child's repatriation. The judge denied them the right to speak unless they filled out an official Notice of Appearance. The Soviet officers refused, because they did not want to acknowledge the validity of the American court's jurisdiction. They instead staged a press conference at their headquarters at the Hotel Astoria, where they announced, "Soviet authorities regard it to be absolutely unwarranted that Soviet children are brought to the United States or other countries by force or given to foreign persons as servants . . . No decree of an American Court will be honored by the Soviet authorities." Boris Nalivaiko, the Russian Consul General in Berlin, alleged at the conference that the IRO was in the business of "selling children" and declared the intention of the Russian government to repatriate all exiled Russian children "even if they live on the moon."[68] The Soviet press also publicized the case at home. On November 11, 1951, a lengthy article entitled "Dealers of Children in Judicial Robes" appeared in *Trud*, proclaiming, "Soviet Children languishing in American bondage must be returned to their motherland. No American or British court can decide the fate of Soviet children and keep them in foreign lands! The savage high-handed acts of the American authorities have aroused indignation not only of parents whose children are in captivity but also of the entire Soviet public."[69]

In general, American judges framed the decision to resettle East European refugee children in the United States as a realization of both family values and democratic ideals. Orphans repatriated to the East, American judges maintained, were sentenced to a dreary childhood in Soviet or Polish orphanages, whereas in America they would find a loving adoptive family. In the case of Dieter Strojew, a child abandoned in Germany at birth by his Russian mother, Judge Goodman elaborated that "what this boy needs for his proper and wholesome development is the affection and care of worthy parents . . . In order to make this possible he should be removed without delay from the institutional life he has been leading since his birth. No evidence has been presented and no assurance given to this court that this institutional life would not be continued in Russia." Although the IRO recommended that Dieter be repatriated to the USSR, Goodman opted for resettlement in the United States. He justified his decision in a lengthy disquisition in which he elaborated the differences between the "totalitarian" East and democratic United States. "Upon his resettlement in the United States the boy will grow up in a country which safeguards the well-being of its citizens . . . not as exploited or regimented servants of a totalitarian state . . . In the United States the boy will grow up in a country where the guarantees of individual liberty are not empty phrases, but are living rights which may be enforced by each citizen against the State. . . . Surely it cannot be said that such an environment with these opportunities and these rights would be inimical to his wholesome development."[70]

Through Law Nr. 11, American occupation officials put Communism itself on trial in occupied Germany. It was a remarkable shift from the immediate postwar moment, when the Allies had colluded in the forcible repatriation of Soviet citizens to their homelands. Displaced persons who refused to return to Eastern Europe remained in Germany at a high economic and political cost to the Allies and to intergovernmental organizations. But in the context of the escalating Cold War, displaced children also represented valuable symbolic capital. American occupation officials ultimately used their cases to publicly affirm the supremacy of the American way of life (and the American system of foster care), even as the decisions of American judges undermined their own official rhetoric of family reunification.

Between 1945 and 1951, the fate of displaced children shifted with political tides in a Europe under reconstruction. Once primarily objects of intense competition between German, French, and East European nationalists for population growth and national sovereignty, refugee children from Eastern Europe became pawns in a Cold War struggle between East and West. These conflicts over repatriation reflected the profound significance of perceived national "rights" to children in postwar Europe, even as these rights were embedded in new European and international norms, laws, and institutions. Disputes over the fate of refugee youth were not necessarily bipolar in nature, however. Between East and West there were many actors, each with their own agenda for the rehabilitation of refugee families: international organizations, the Catholic Church, and displaced persons themselves. There was no winner in the struggle for Europe's children after World War II, but the battle itself became a forum for defining democracy and family in the aftermath of Nazi rule and the shadows of Communism.

From Divided Families
to a Divided Europe

In November of 1947, Else Prolsdorff located her long-lost son Hans-Joachim Freyschmidt after 16 years of separation. Hans-Joachim, a 17-year-old former Hitler Youth, turned up after the war in a home for displaced children in Czechoslovakia directed by the Czech Christian pacifist Přemysl Pitter. According to *Revue,* a West German tabloid, Else's "Odyssey of Maternal Love" had begun with a violent domestic dispute in 1930: the night her husband Robert hit her for the first time—and the first time she felt her child move in her womb.

Robert Prolsdorff allegedly came home drunk that night, and made advances at Else, who refused him. He became enraged and began to beat her. After their child was born he promised to change his ways, but continued to drink and sleep around. One night Robert flew into a rage and threw Else out of the house. He tore their son from her arms and hit her in the face, screaming, "The child is staying here! You will never see him again!" Else fled to her parents' home "a broken woman. He had taken everything that she had, and that everything was her child," *Revue* recounted. She tried unsuccessfully to retrieve Hans-Joachim, even attempting to kidnap him. Soon afterward Else met a Dutch man and remarried, and the couple moved to Utrecht. She eventually returned to Germany and again attempted to claim her son, but the Nazis were now in power. Officials at the Jugendamt rejected her appeal for custody on racial grounds. "It is simply impossible," a Nazi official informed her. "A pure German child" could not be raised as a Dutchman.

Only in 1946, after Else had moved to South Africa and the Third Reich had collapsed, did she finally receive word of Hans-Joachim's whereabouts.

At the end of the war her son was in a Hitler Youth training camp in Czechoslovakia, with a group of "raucous, fanatical Nazis, who had sworn allegiance to Hitler." Hans-Joachim was interned by the Russians, but released and transferred to Pitter's care after falling ill with tuberculosis. But Else's quest to reunite with her son was now hindered at every turn by vengeful Czech officials, who refused her requests for a visa. One woman took her application, crumpled it up, and threw it furiously to the floor. "Since you were born a German get a visa somewhere else. You won't get one from me!" she yelled. Else screamed back, "They are killing my child! Don't you have a soul, or only hatred?" She got the visa, but missed her plane. After several days of sleepless travel, Prolsdorff finally arrived, disheveled and anxious, at the gates of a picturesque villa outside of Prague. She was met by Pitter, and requested to see her son immediately. But Pitter greeted her with tragic news: her son had "closed his eyes forever" only three days earlier.[1]

Else's story, as recounted (and sentimentalized) by *Revue* in 1955, was particularly well suited to the Cold War context of postwar West Germany. Many Germans in the 1950s ranked themselves first in the hierarchy of victims after the Second World War, as they claimed to have been misled by Nazi leaders, and then violated in turn by Russian soldiers, allied occupiers, and vengeful East European nationalists.[2] *Revue* portrayed Else as a heroic victim of domestic violence and of both the Nazi and Czechoslovak states. This victim status, moreover, was defined in terms of her suffering as a mother. Her story pitted the universal values of family solidarity against the evil of the Nazi regime and of Czechoslovak authorities. This lesson was particularly well suited to 1955, the year in which the Federal Republic of Germany joined NATO. It rhetorically integrated West Germany into the ranks of Western nations that defined democracy in terms of a particular brand of family values.

Hans-Joachim's own life and death, meanwhile, was transformed into another Cold War morality tale. In the final years of his short life, Freyschmidt became a model subject in Přemysl Pitter's brazen postwar pedagogical experiment. Between 1945 and 1951, Pitter, a Czech Christian pacifist, pedagogical reformer, and anti-Communist, promoted "reconciliation" in Czechoslovakia by housing German, Jewish, and Czech refugee children together in collective children's homes.[3] By reconciling refugee children, Pitter aimed to prove that German, Jewish, and Czech adults could peacefully coexist in Central Europe. In a 1947 newsletter for residents of the children's castles, Pitter eulogized Freyschmidt. "In the semi-consciousness of his final days, Jochen often repeated that he had to write a book for German youth about reconciliation between the youth of both of our lands. Now he has left this great task of reconciliation to us. We should write a living book of brotherhood . . . Jochen's pure, noble soul will help us from above. Let us remain bound to him and to one another in this spirit!"

Přemysl Pitter was in many respects an exceptional figure in postwar Europe. He promoted the coexistence of Czechs, Germans, and Jews at a moment when retribution was the order of the day. He was also one of few Czech public figures to loudly protest the expulsion of Germans from Czechoslovakia immediately after the war. But in other ways, Pitter was typical of the legions of humanitarian workers and educators who mobilized to rehabilitate European children after the war. Through the reeducation of refugee children, Pitter sought to advance a particular Christian and anti-Communist vision for the reconstruction of Central Europe. His vision was decisively rejected in Czechoslovakia in the 1940s but would resonate powerfully in Bavaria in the 1950s.

Neither pacifism nor reconciliation was a popular cause in Europe after World War II. Military authorities, intergovernmental organizations, victims, and vigilantes instead focused on bringing perpetrators to justice. Prosecutors at Nuremberg aimed to hold Nazis accountable for war crimes. In Czechoslovakia, people's courts put 135,000 citizens on trial for so-called "crimes against national honor," which could include anything from sending Jewish neighbors to their death to speaking German too loudly in the street.[4] Retribution was a popular spectacle across liberated Europe. In France, Italy, and Germany, women suspected of engaging in social or sexual relations with the enemy suffered public violence and humiliation. Millions of German women were victims of rape at the hands of Russian (and other occupying) soldiers, who often saw sexual violence as a legitimate form of revenge on the German people.[5] East European Jews returning from exile in the Soviet Union and from Nazi concentration camps also saw little hope for reconciliation with their neighbors, who often greeted them with outright hostility or violence.[6] And the perceived impossibility of national coexistence propelled the expulsion and expropriation of millions of Germans from Eastern Europe after the war.

Pitter's unusual pedagogy of reconciliation was deeply linked to his anti-Communist vision for the reconstruction of Czechoslovakia. The Communist party quickly established a stronghold in liberated Czechoslovakia. The western powers had largely been discredited in the eyes of many Czechs since the 1938 Munich agreement. In the name of "peace in our time," the Allies had delivered the Sudetenland to Hitler. Many Czechs lost faith in the West and looked to the USSR for support during and after the Second World War. A full 38 percent of the Czechoslovak electorate voted for the Communist party in Czechoslovakia's free parliamentary elections in May 1946, and another 12.1 percent voted for the Social Democrats. In Bohemia and Moravia, the Communists received 40 percent of the vote. It was a decisive victory that helped legitimate the Communist takeover two years later.[7]

Pitter was deeply disturbed by these trends. As long as Czechs feared and hated their German neighbors, he reasoned, they were bound to look to the Soviet Union for support. He began to articulate a kind of anti-Communist multinationalism even before the Second World War ended, insisting that Czechs and Germans were joined by history, culture, economics, and fate. "The Germans were and will stay our neighbors, and whether we like it or not, we are mutually dependent and economically in their hands. The maintenance of an 'iron curtain' in an age of jet-propelled airplanes is not possible in the long run, and such isolation from the West and dependence on the East will be to the detriment of our nation," he predicted. "As long as Czechs hate Germans, they will seek help and support from the Russians. . . . We must seek a path which will enable us not to fear Germans and shield ourselves from them."[8]

But Pitter had not always been so averse to communism. He was born in Prague to middle-class parents in 1895. The First World War transformed Pitter into a devout Christian and pacifist. He became a member of the International Movement for Christian Communism, a radical wing of the Christian Social movement, as well as the International Fellowship for Reconciliation. In interwar Czechoslovakia Pitter embarked on a mission to educate the proletarian children of Prague's Žižkov neighborhood. By 1933, Pitter and his lifelong companion and colleague, Swiss teacher and pedagogical theorist Olga Fierz, had opened a day-care center for Prague's working-class children called the Milíčův Dům. The home was intended to offer supervision and moral education to the children of working mothers. The Milíčův Dům, like many other collectivist pedagogical experiments in interwar Europe, was founded on the philosophy that fragile families required the support of the state and voluntary organizations. "When parents are not able to meet their responsibilities sufficiently due to moral, economic, or social circumstances, voluntary welfare organizations must step in," Pitter maintained.[9]

During the Second World War, Pitter welcomed Prague's Jewish children into the Milíčův Dům. Most of these children were ultimately deported to Terezín after 1941 and very few returned home. But after Prague was liberated in May 1945, the Czech National Council approached Pitter and asked him to take charge of the rehabilitation of Jewish children liberated from German concentration camps and the Terezín ghetto. He was offered three villas outside of Prague, all expropriated from German nobles: Olešovice, Kamenice, and Lojovice. He later acquired a fourth home at Střín. The first group of 260 children soon arrived from concentration camps in Germany in Red Cross ambulances.[10]

Meanwhile, the expulsion of Germans from Czechoslovakia was underway. A week after the armistice, Pitter received an anonymous phone call, asking him to come to the assistance of a family in the Flora district of Prague, where Nazis had occupied many Jewish homes during the war. More than a thousand German women and children were packed into a local school, waiting to be deported. Fierz described the scene: "The sick and the well, grown-ups and children, all lay together like limp flies caught in the frost. One of the internees, a German doctor in a dirty smock, pointed hopelessly to a room in which he had been able to isolate the babies. There they lay, with wrinkled faces, on the school desks; just skin and bones, like dried-up old men. They didn't get any milk, for it had been ordered that Germans should have only the rations they had allowed the Jews."[11]

In August of that year, the Czechoslovak Ministry for Social Welfare assigned Pitter to inspect internment camps for Germans. He discovered appalling conditions. There were approximately thirty camps in greater Prague for Germans and collaborators, housing close to 10,000 adults and 1,500 children. The most infamous was the Sokol stadium, where "hopeless invalids and children lay around in the summer heat, vermin-ridden, in unspeakable filth," Fierz recalled. In August 1945, the Czechoslovak Ministry of the Interior ordered that all children under the age of 14 should be released from internment camps. But the directive was widely ignored. As of September 1945, some 10,000 children under the age of 14 were still interned in Czechoslovakia.[12]

The Ministry of Social Welfare assigned Pitter to care for children who were released. But since many interned women refused to part from their children, those transferred to Pitter's care were typically orphans or refugees who had been separated from their parents in the chaos of the war. More than 800 children ultimately passed through Pitter's castles. Of this number, 266 were Jews. Another 103 were children from mixed marriages, 35 were Czech children of collaborators, 55 were of "uncertain" national origins, and 214 were Germans, including many former Hitler youth such as Hans-Joachim. But in a context in which bilingualism and national indifference remained widespread, it was not simple to categorize children by nationality. "We could not always easily judge which children should be allowed to attend the Czech public schools and which were to be expelled as Germans," Fierz recalled. "Later it became clear that in some cases we had made mistakes."[13]

Pitter sought to balance individualist and collectivist ideals after the war. In a 1946 memo to the Ministry for Social Welfare, he explained, "It is a bad kind of collectivism that suppresses individuality . . . just as it is bad individualism and liberalism that does not subordinate the success of the individual to the public good. The creators of the new order must remember both elements and learn to bring them together in harmony."[14] He demanded state support for orphans and children born out of wedlock, as well as state bonuses for large families. In line with widespread pronatalist ideals, he proposed that childless individuals be required to pay a special tax. He combined his familialist vision with strong collectivist values. Children without siblings, he insisted, should be required to attend day care centers so that they experienced some form of collective socialization. All children were to attend summer camps from the age of three onward. Pitter also wanted the new Czechoslovak government to impose strict limits on the amount of wealth or property a single individual or family could accumulate.[15]

Reconciliation, as Pitter envisioned it, was a two-way process. It required Nazis to atone for their sins, but it also required victims of the Third Reich to forgive their persecutors. Since there were few individuals with more to forgive, Jewish children occupied a special place in Pitter's pedagogy of reconciliation. When Jewish youth arrived at the gates of Pitter's castles, they exhibited traits that were familiar to humanitarian workers across postwar Europe. They were mistrustful. They seemed hostile and entitled. Having slaved for the Nazis for years, they refused to work. But according to their teacher Antonín Moravec (known as Toník), after only a few months, the Jewish youth in Pitter's care "willingly and happily prepared the home for the interned German children . . . While adults are busy building new walls of hatred amongst themselves, our youth in the homes long ago found the way to take them down."[16]

Toník's anecdote reflected a general pattern. Pitter and Fierz transformed their Jewish wards into models of Christian brotherhood. It was a formula that left little room for unheroic thoughts and actions among Jewish youth, and reflected a general suppression of (Jewish) revenge as an acceptable response to the Holocaust. In a 1953 radio sermon, Pitter preached, "Girls and boys whose parents had been tortured to death or asphyxiated in gas-chambers, these Jewish lassies and lads . . . had no thoughts of revenge. They were capable of looking upon the children of their tormenters as upon innocent victims, whilst we, the so-called Christians, let them starve. Let us get rid today of all thoughts

of vengeance and retaliations!"[17] Such parables of Jewish-German reconciliation reflected a broader tendency to transform Holocaust victims into symbols
of Christian martyrdom in Europe and America.[18] Already in 1946, Pitter
was reporting in his newsletter, "These [Jewish] children had more of the spirit
of Christ than many Christians."[19]

Local Czechs failed to rise to their level, Pitter and Fierz lamented. Czechs
in the neighborhoods surroundings Pitter's castles frequently griped to authorities about the German voices they heard coming from the children's homes.
They denounced Pitter in newspapers, complaining that his German and Jewish wards drank full-fat milk while Czech children endured rationing, shortages, and watered-down substitutes. Czech police even conducted a midnight
raid on Pitter's castles, searching for Nazi collaborators and black market supplies under the children's bunks. In June of 1946, the Communist newspaper
Rudé právo printed an article alleging, "In the castle at Lojovice, to the great
indignation of the local population, Přemysl Pitter is housing German children, who even have German nurses in such numbers that there is one nurse
for every two children ... It is appalling that 60 Germans are living in a pretty
building that could be used to restore the health of our own children."[20]

There is plenty of evidence that survivors of concentration camps harbored
fantasies of revenge. Some certainly acted on these fantasies.[21] But Jewish
youth in Pitter's care seem to have at least partially internalized their role as
models for the Czech population. In October 1945, Jewish children in Střín
and Olešovice protested, "Before it was Jews suffering in concentration camps,
now there are Germans in the same conditions, except that they don't await
death in gas chambers.... We who returned from the concentration camps as
the only living members of our families ... who could rightly feel malice and
hatred toward Germans, we don't act this way ... If we really want peace, we
cannot have hatred within ourselves."[22]

While Jewish children were cast as symbols of Christian brotherhood, Pitter
and Fierz extended their pedagogy of reconciliation to former Nazis such as
Hans-Joachim. Dobroslava Štepankóva, a teacher in Pitter's castles, reported
that German children were in poor shape after the German defeat. They "were
educated to worship nation and the Führer. Now all that lay in ashes. There is
nothing to believe in, nothing to love ... They are apathetic about what comes
next." In Pitter's homes, Hitler Youth were taught to worship God instead of
Hitler. "There is only one medicine for the whole world, including Germany,
and that is a return to God," Štepankóva argued.[23] One fifteen-year-old boy
chronicled his own rehabilitation in 1947. "Nobody can deny that we hated

everything that called itself Czech. We saw the Czech nation only through our fear and made no distinctions. They took us to Střín. The first ones we met were the Jewish boys . . . We remembered back to Terezín [where Hitler youth were interned after the war], where it was precisely some Jews who terrorized us the most . . . But they fed us, gave us clothing, we bathed, slept in comfortable beds. Our faith in God was reawakened. Soon we learned to see the Czech nation with different eyes. My hatred disappeared."[24]

The Communists consolidated their monopoly on political power in Czechoslovakia in March 1948. For almost two years, Pitter continued to operate his Milíčův Dům. But in December 1949, the Milíčův Dům was forced to close its doors by Communist authorities. In August 1951 Pitter became a refugee himself, crossing the border from Czechoslovakia to Germany in flight from Communism. In a 1951 interview on the BBC he claimed that the Communist assault on the family drove him into exile. "One day I was ordered to speak to a meeting of parents about the institutions for children and youth that are being established all over the country in order to make it possible for mothers to go to work . . . I quoted the popular Russian Communist pedagogue Makarenko who wrote that 'ordered family life is the basis of socialist society,' and I added that the very best institution cannot be regarded as the ideal, which is the family where the mother can devote herself to her children," he recounted.[25] Parents applauded, and Communist party members in the room interpreted the speech as an affront. Local Communists forced Pitter to resign, the police searched his home, and he was interrogated. Fearing arrest, he fled to Germany.

In 1952, Pitter accepted a position as a preacher in the Valka refugee camp outside of Nuremberg in Bavaria, the largest camp in Germany for "hardcore" Cold War refugees from Eastern Europe. Valka also happened to house many former Nazi collaborators. Ironically, these collaborators, along with the Sudeten German and Silesian expellees in the camp, often rose to positions of power in the camp by virtue of their knowledge of the German language and of East European politics. They subsequently played an important role in making decisions in asylum cases as Czech refugees from Communism began to pour over the border after 1948.[26]

In the Valka camp, which housed 4,300 refugees in October 1951, Pitter became a regular speaker on Radio Free Europe and the BBC. Like many anti-Communists in Europe and America, he defined the concept of totalitarianism in terms of its alleged destruction of the family. On Mother's Day 1954, Pitter declared in a BBC talk that "the Communist thoroughly takes care that children are not left over to the influence of their parents." Working outside the home, Pitter argued, degraded women, reducing them to whores. "When woman is not a priestess anymore, she becomes a harlot. Some idealists imagined the Communist idea was a way to liberate and uplift women. But this proved to be a deceiving illusion. What has woman been liberated from in the countries ruled by Communists? From that which is her deepest longing and a task given her by God and nature."[27]

In his postwar speeches, Pitter promoted a messianic anti-Communism and familialism that seems like a jarring postscript to his career in Czechoslovakia. He had, after all, spent twenty years of his life running day care centers and collective homes for refugee children and children of working mothers. He never once objected to women's employment outside the home, which had been a fact of life for most working-class women in Czechoslovakia between the wars. Now any separation of mother and child represented a totalitarian attack on the family and an abrogation of God's will.

Pitter's changing politics reflected a deeper transformation in the political and pedagogical climate of postwar Europe. In the context of the early Cold War, anti-Communists demonized both Nazism and East European Communist regimes in terms of their alleged destruction of the family. By defining totalitarianism in terms of an assault on the family, German anti-Communists conveniently rescued ordinary Germans and East Europeans from guilt by association with the Nazi regime. Any parent could identify as a victim of the totalitarian state: Czech, Pole, German, or Jew. Women were allegedly required to send their children to state-run nursery schools in order to insure "the undisturbed indoctrination of the child with the Communist world view," claimed activist Käte Fiedler in 1955. In a 1955 West German government publication, Hans Köhler likewise asserted that in the East, "wherever possible mothers have no more opportunities to devote themselves to their children."[28] Pitter deployed similar rhetoric in his BBC sermons. "The Totalitarian State appropriates to itself total rights upon man. There will soon be no time at all left for private life. The Communists know quite well that quiet family life is a danger to them."[29]

In the United States, the popular press reported that the family had ceased to exist in Eastern Europe. In a 1950 article in the *Saturday Evening Post* entitled "Communism's Child Hostages," Joseph Wechsberg traced the sad fate of the Czech children of Lidice. Having survived the Lidice massacre and exile in Germany, he claimed, they returned to Czechoslovakia only to be brainwashed by the Communist regime. "Today the children in the people's democracies in Central, Eastern and Southeastern Europe are being turned into unthinking robots," he declared. "It is the same pattern which the Nazis introduced successfully when they began to take the children away from their families. Once again there are millions of parents in Eastern Europe who have to look on, in despair and helplessness, as their own children are taken away from them."[30]

These images of Socialist society and education were refracted through the mirrors of the Cold War. Historically, collective education had no inherent ideological or political content. In interwar Europe, Socialists, Catholics, fascists, nationalists, Republicans, and Communists had all appropriated collectivist pedagogies for their own purposes. In spite of Alexandra Kollontai's revolutionary prediction that the family was "doomed to disappear" under Communism, the nuclear family was alive and well in postwar Eastern Europe.[31] By the late 1930s, the Soviet government, for example, was engaged in an active campaign to increase the birthrate, repress abortion, and prevent divorce, not least because the liberalizing reforms of the 1920s had been unpopular.[32]

Postwar East European governments were equally uninterested in "destroying" the traditional family. Even as they legislated greater legal equality for women and encouraged them to enter the work force, the family was still seen as the fundamental unit of Socialist societies. Nor were women relieved of their responsibilities for child care and housework by the strong arm of the Socialist state. The construction of child care institutions proceeded at a glacial pace, as postwar East European governments invested in increasing industrial capacity rather than building day care centers. As of 1955 in East Germany, fewer than one in ten infants was in a nursery and only one in three preschoolers attended a kindergarten. It was not until the 1970s that the majority of young children had places in state-run day care centers. The shortage of spots in child-care centers was a constant complaint of working women in East Germany.[33]

The family was not dissolved in Eastern Europe, but defending the family from the alleged totalitarian menace became a powerful rallying cry in West Germany in the 1950s, particularly among the Christian Democratic Union/Christian Socialist Union politicians who dominated the political scene in Bavaria.[34] This was the milieu in which Pitter found himself after the Second World War, and he harnessed the familialist rhetoric of the CDU/CSU to his own political agenda. "Not from a political point of view, but in the name of God Himself and Jesus Christ we must protest against this bringing of womanhood into disgrace and degradation! The very fact that Communism is revolting against laws of God and nature gives us great hope. For nothing can last against God and nature," Pitter proclaimed in his 1954 Mother's Day sermon.[35]

Pitter linked the collective setting of the refugee camp to the moral and psychological degradation of European youth—and of European civilization at large. He portrayed the young male inmates of Valka, in particular, as demasculinized victims who had been deprived of the essential accessories of male citizenship: the privacy of a stable home, support of a wife and children, and productive employment. Alcoholism, sexual promiscuity, and criminality allegedly plagued itinerant young men without sovereign homes and dependent wives and children. Pitter grimly predicted that "time will show that the dictators of our century have done greater evil through moral destruction than through physical attacks and murders." Emasculated men in refugee camps, he concluded, were "as much the victims of war and terror as those killed on the battlefields and physically destroyed in concentration camps."[36]

From his pulpit in the Valka refugee camp, Pitter continued to exhort Czechs to break their ties with Russia and to make peace with their German neighbors throughout the 1950s. He even spoke of German-Czech coexistence as part of a divine plan, and of the expulsions as an abrogation of God's will. "The first step is the recognition of our common, indivisible Heimat, in which God blessed us to cohabitate . . . It is God's will that we reach out our hands to one another and without reproach begin a new life."[37]

For Pitter, only national reconciliation could save both the Czech nation and the sovereign family, which stood in for democracy itself in his rhetoric. This family was to be free from state "interference" and presided over by a male breadwinner and a stay-at-home mother. In Bavaria in the 1950s, the collectivist ideals that had animated Pitter's own interwar pedagogy in Czechoslovakia were no longer compatible with his Christian and anti-Communist values. Ultimately, Pitter's pedagogy of reconciliation aimed to replace one form of polarization with another. Divisions and enmities that existed between Germans, Czechs, and Jews, he hoped, would be superceded by a more trenchant division between East and West. In this vision for postwar Europe, Czech, German and Jewish children would finally learn to get along—and Czechoslovakia would take its rightful place on the Western side of the Iron Curtain.

Individuals like Pitter participated in the construction of a new international order in postwar Europe. They seamlessly translated older nationalist conflicts between Germans and Slavs into a zero-sum-game struggle between

East and West. Even as Pitter formulated an image of children as models of reconciliation, he used them as a wedge with which to contrive new political divisions at the dawn of the Cold War. Pitter's children's castles were only one of many sites of pedagogical experimentation in liberated in Europe, one of many sites in which ideals of family and of Europe's political future developed in tandem. More than mere orphanages or refugee camps, these laboratories of rehabilitation were simultaneously laboratories of European reconstruction.

*   *   *

The political stakes of activism on behalf of lost children in postwar Europe were frequently transparent, but the success of these efforts is less easily measured. After several years in the field, many humanitarian workers were doubtful that they had accomplished anything at all. In 1949, Jacques Cohn of the OSE recalled, "We thought that it would be easy for us to educate all of our children . . . with the grand ideas of justice and humanity." But after five years of work with Jewish youth in postwar France, his idealism had been dampened by experience. "Today . . . we must admit that we have not changed the world, that no OSE child has done much of anything great up until now, and perhaps they never will," he despaired.[38] Cohn's ambivalence was symptomatic of a basic tension that defined postwar reconstruction efforts. Efforts to rehabilitate European youth, in particular, simultaneously reflected dystopian fears about the total collapse of European civilization and utopian visions of regeneration. As they assessed their own impact, child welfare experts themselves lurched between optimism and despair.

Refugee children also experienced extreme highs and lows as they reconstructed their postwar lives. Ruth Kluger recalls that immediately after her escape from a Nazi death march, she was exhilarated by freedom. As she arrived in Bavaria, posing as a Volksdeutsche refugee from Eastern Europe, she reflected, "I was still carried along by a dizzy sense of happiness . . . the very opposite of what the genuine German refugees experienced. For they had lost everything, that is, all their property, while we hoped to have gained everything, that is, the rest of our lives."[39] But a few years later, as she attempted to establish a new life in New York, she sunk into a deep depression. She was plagued by a deep sense of shame, what would be labeled "survivor guilt" by psychoanalysts in the 1960s.[40] Ruth's guilty feelings were compounded by her gender. "There were times when it seemed that instead of being liberated, I had crawled away like a cockroach from the exterminator. . . . At a time when women were constantly put in their supposed place, it was natural for a young refugee to question her own value. In my family the women had survived, not the men. And that meant that the more valuable human beings had lost their lives."[41]

Even those children reunited with their parents faced a painful adjustment to so-called normalcy. After seven years of separation, Edith Milton rejoined her mother in New York at the age of 14. Edith had been evacuated from Nazi Germany to the United Kingdom on a Kindertransport. During their years of separation, she had constructed an elaborate fantasy about her mother. Her flesh-and-blood mother failed to live up to this fantasy. The long-awaited reunion between mother and daughter was as emotionally disturbing as the initial shock of separation, she later recalled. "Meeting this odd duck of a woman who seemed to work at being as far removed from my invented, ideal Mother as anyone in the same species could get, certainly seemed to me by far the most disastrous thing that had ever happened to me." Edith, like Ruth, suffered from depression as she settled into her new life in the United States. "The weather of despair always hangs at the edge of my memory of my first two years in America; it threatened to cover the world of the refugees among whom . . . I now lived."[42]

In a letter to Judith Samuel of the OSE, written in the 1980s, Elie Wiesel recognized that the young survivors of Buchenwald had been nearly impossible to reach. "At that time, the survivors had nothing to say to the living. Europe and the world celebrated the victory over Hitler's Germany and its accomplices without us. Walled into the solitude of a childhood that had been mutilated, stolen, jeered at, we wanted to live apart . . . We didn't want any of your help, or your understanding, or your psychological tests, or your charity." But despite these obstacles, Wiesel believed that OSE educators had accomplished something significant. "With a little time, we found ourselves on the same side," he recalled. "To what do we owe that miracle? How can it be explained? The fact is that all of the children could have turned to violence or opted for nihilism: you knew how to lead them to trust and reconciliation."[43]

The psychological scars of wartime experiences (as well as the psychological impact of postwar pedagogy) often surfaced only years or decades after the war. Many concentration camp survivors, in particular, remained relatively free of traumatic symptoms for several years, during which their energies were consumed by the basic challenge of reestablishing their lives. Once settled in, and forced to abandon the hope that missing family members would someday return, however, some sunk into despair.[44]

But as Europe's lost children became adults, there were also pleasant surprises. A twenty-year follow-up study of the children of the Hampstead nurseries in Britain concluded that the worst fears of Anna Freud and John Bowlby were never realized, for example. Young children evacuated from London without their mothers in 1940 did not become juvenile delinquents or "affectless characters" after all. "In spite of the disruptions of war which meant separation from their mothers and adjustment to a new and quite different environment, they did develop into normal adults without psychic crippling effects and without any therapeutic intervention," the study concluded.[45]

Children of Jewish refugees who immigrated to the United States, with or without their parents, also fared better than anyone might have predicted. As adults they boasted higher than average educational and professional achievements, as well as marital stability and self-reported happiness. Many young German-Jewish refugees, particularly those who had escaped Nazi Germany before the war, experienced emigration as a great adventure rather than a form of trauma. After the war, even in the shadow of catastrophic losses, they made themselves at home in far-flung locales with considerable zest and pride.[46]

Ruth Kluger attaches no redemptive moral to her own story, but she does reject one recurring narrative about children's lives during World War II, namely, the presumption that she had no childhood at all. "This too, was childhood," she reflects. "I grew up, I learned something, as every child does who grows up . . . I would have learned different and better things under other, more normal circumstances . . . I would give a lot if I could look back on a different childhood. But it was what it was. And, I repeat, this, too, was childhood."[47]

*　　*　　*

The impact of the Psychological Marshall Plan on Europe's lost children is now cloaked in the fog of memory. The recollections of former refugee children have themselves been shaped by the culture of memorialization that has developed around World War II and the Holocaust since the 1970s. Their memories have also been molded by the trajectories of displaced children's adult lives. Memories of childhood are inseparable from our adult self-perceptions and experiences, which we tend to project backward, consciously or unconsciously straining to construct coherent life stories.

The theories developed in Europe's laboratories of rehabilitation left more concrete traces on postwar political culture, however. In 1940, following the first British campaign to evacuate children from London, British children's writer Amabel Williams-Ellis proclaimed, "Wars, whatever we may think of them, can teach something to those of us who are ready to learn . . . This war, owing to the dangers from bombing from the air, has taught us—of all things—a great deal about children. Not only about the state of health and degree of cleanliness and 'civilization' and so on . . . but about how children . . . will behave in unusual circumstances, and through that we find that we have learnt some fundamental truths about all children."[48] These "fundamental human truths" trickled up and spread outward from Europe's foster homes, refugee camps, and orphanages after World War II. They went on to inform child-rearing practices, welfare and migration policies, and international norms of human rights in the era of European reconstruction.

In 1951, the United Nations ratified its Convention and Protocol Relating to the Status of Refugees, which came into force in 1954. Building on the perceived lessons of the Second World War, the final act of the U.N. Conference on the Status of Refugees explicitly declared family unity to be "an essential right of the refugee" and urged governments to take special measures to protect this unity, particularly "in cases where the head of the family has fulfilled the necessary conditions for admission to a particular country."[49] The U.N.'s founding document on refugee rights thus reflected the newfound conviction that the separation of families represented a violation of human rights and a threat to children's welfare. But the Convention was also founded on the assumption of a male political refugee accompanied by a dependent wife and children. At the same time that U.N. delegates upheld family unity as a human right, they reinforced the subordinate place of women and children within family units.

The United Nations' 1959 Declaration of the Rights of the Child also reflected the tidal shift in ideas about children's needs and rights over the course of the twentieth century. In 1924, the League of Nations had adopted the Geneva Declaration of the Rights of the Child, authored by the Save the Children Fund's founder Eglantyne Jebb. The 1924 Declaration reflected the dominant concerns of interwar humanitarian organizations and child welfare experts. It focused, above all, on guaranteeing the basic material needs of children in times of crisis. "The child that is hungry must be fed; the child that is sick must be nursed; the child that is backward must be helped; the delinquent child must be reclaimed; and the orphan and the waif must be sheltered and succored," it declared.[50]

Thirty-five years later, the United Nations' Declaration of Children's Rights reflected a dramatically expanded conception of children's rights, with a strong focus on family unity and psychological welfare. "The child, for the full and harmonious development of his personality, needs love and understanding," the 1959 Declaration insisted. "He shall, wherever possible, grow up in the care and under the responsibility of his parents, and, in any case, in an atmosphere of affection and of moral and material security; a child of tender years shall not, save in exceptional circumstances, be separated from his mother."[51]

Over the course of thirty-five years, children had gained a "right" to love and affection and a "right" to remain with their mothers. Emotional dislocation within the family was now considered as menacing to children's well being as political and social upheaval outside the family. In the 1950s and 1960s, policymakers and psychologists eagerly applied these insights to children suffering from neglect, divorce, and abuse outside the theaters of war. Bruno Bettelheim, for example, famously developed theories of childhood schizophrenia based on his observations of children whose parents had died in concentration camps. Bettelheim made direct comparisons between victims of neglectful parenting and victims of the Nazi state, writing in 1952, "The process of rehabilitating a person remains the same regardless of whether their personality was destroyed through the despotic machinery of a political regime or because this individual was rejected and abandoned by his parents."[52]

While rejecting the familialist solutions advocated by American psychoanalysts, Ernst Papanek spent the postwar years applying what he had learned about the psychological consequences of displacement to African-American juvenile delinquents at the Brooklyn Training School for Girls and the Wiltwyck School for boys in New York, which he directed until 1958.[53] French psychologist André Rey, meanwhile, placed victims of wartime displacement and children of divorce on the same plane, advocating similar therapeutic treatment for both: "One may compare the child victims of war with any children anywhere who have suffered from family disruption or are orphans. The same mechanism is responsible in both cases for the disturbance of psychological and spiritual health."[54] By equating emotional neglect within the family to the consequences of war and racial persecution, psychologists both intensified pressure on parents (particularly mothers) to perform their roles flawlessly, and deemphasized the political dimensions of children's wartime experiences in Europe.

The Second World War also profoundly shaped the practice of international adoption in the decades that followed. International adoption was itself a major legacy of World War II. In the 1940s, growing humanitarian interest in Europe's war orphans coincided with a shift away from the institutional care of children and the liberalization of adoption laws in Europe and the United States. The International Social Service (ISS) became the leading international adoption agency in the decades following the war. The agency built on its wartime experiences in Europe as it transferred an unprecedented number of children from Asia to adoptive families in the United States and Europe during the Korean and Vietnam wars.[55] In 1956 alone, the ISS facilitated 3,500 inter-country adoptions. This was a tiny number by today's standards (between 1999 and 2009, more than 218,000 children were adopted from abroad by American families), but enough to confirm that international adoption was a growing trend rather than a postwar anomaly.[56]

In recognition of this trend, the United Nations and the ISS organized a major conference in Geneva on international adoption in January 1957. Convention delegates adopted 11 basic principles, which they intended to serve as international guidelines for ethical international adoptions. Several of these principles reflected the perceived lessons of the Second World War and its aftermath. Like UNNRA workers in Europe after World War II, delegates saw a confused national identity as a recipe for psychological dysfunction, warning, "It is hazardous to transplant a child outside of his cultural milieu."[57] In light of the risks, international adoption was justified only in exceptional cases in which "adoption in another country offers . . . the only chance for a normal family life." Viable candidates included illegitimate children in countries "where illegitimacy is considered a flaw of the child," children born to adulterous or incestuous couples, children born to parents "of poor or doubtful morality, living in communities which believe that the behavior of the parents will be reflected in the character of the child"; and finally, "children born to a parent of a different race than that of the milieu in which they live."[58]

The final criterion emerged with specific reference to children born to African-American soldiers and German women during the postwar occupation of Germany, and was subsequently applied to children of GIs and Japanese and Korean women. Based on the conviction that children of mixed race would be rejected by the "backward" and "closed" societies of Germany and East Asia, social service agencies and the press in the United States construed the transfer of biracial children to Jim Crow America as a selfless humanitarian gesture.[59] In short, even as international child welfare advocates insisted that international adoption should be a last resort, they defined the parameters of "normal family life" narrowly enough to guarantee a steady supply of children on the international adoption market.

The 1957 convention on international adoption also explicitly defined children's "best interests" in psychological rather than material terms, advising, "The psychological factors determining the well-being of the child and the family should outweigh the material and social factors." This too was presented as a lesson of World War II. During and after the Second World War, the

UN handbook maintained, "Children were too quickly conferred to adoptive families, in particular to families in the United States, because of the material advantages at play. In a number of cases the child's own parents did not understand the significance of abandoning their parental rights; they sometimes even had the illusion that the adoption would facilitate their own emigration [to the United States]."[60]

Theories developed through the observation of displaced children informed popular and official perceptions of children's best interests well beyond the offices of adoption agencies, shaping the broader culture of child-rearing after the war. When wartime and postwar humanitarian workers described the separation of children from their biological parents as a universal recipe for trauma, they strengthened the privileged legal and social status of the patriarchal family and encouraged policies that anchored women in the home. In February 1946, Barbara Bosanquet of the Save the Children Fund in Britain asserted that the war and evacuations had demonstrated, above all, "that the mother of a family should not do full-time outside work." When women went to work in war factories, she insisted, "The effect on the children was in many cases tragic; and the real cause of the tragedy lay in the lack of realization by the Government and the community that parenthood is the single most important human function and that it should be so supported and honored that no other job is put before it."[61]

After rising dramatically during the Second World War, women's employment plunged to prewar levels in most of Europe and in the United States, and even sank below interwar levels in West Germany, from 36.1 percent in 1939 to 31.3 percent in 1950. In the United States, women's labor force participation shot up from 25 percent to 36 percent during the Second World War, but would not return to wartime levels again until the early 1960s.[62] In postwar Western Europe, and particularly in the United States and the U.K., the claim that the traditional family best serves children's psychological development bolstered arguments against women's paid employment and state-supported childcare.

More recently, psychoanalytic theories developed by Anna Freud and John Bowlby during World War II have enjoyed a renaissance among middle-class parents in the United States. Advocates of "attachment parenting" have promoted a style of intensive parenting designed to foster emotional attachment between parents and their babies. Mothers have been called upon to abandon bottles in favor of the breast, strollers in favor of slings, cribs in favor of co-sleeping, and diapers in favor of a practice called "elimination communication," in which parents use signals and timing to intuit a child's need to eliminate waste. Needless to say, these practices require the near constant vigilance of a stay-at-home caregiver. The historically and culturally specific origins of attachment parenting are rarely mentioned in contemporary discussions of childrearing. These theories are instead typically presented as self-evident facts about children's emotional and developmental needs. Proponents of attachment parenting often (selectively) cite anthropological studies of non-western cultures, to support the claim that such practices are both natural and timeless.[63]

*   *   *

In liberated Europe, advocates of an earlier incarnation of attachment parenting also claimed to have unlocked universal and timeless secrets of child development. But their prescriptions for the rehabilitation of European youth did not go unchallenged. Debates about children's "best interests" were, from the beginning, highly politicized, pitting continental pedagogues steeped in collectivist traditions against British and American child welfare experts faithful to "individualist" psychoanalytic principles.

Gradually, however, conflict often gave way to compromise. Collectivist and individualist visions for the rehabilitation of European youth—and for the reconstruction of Europe—became deeply enmeshed. American and British humanitarian workers gradually absorbed many of the nationalist ideals that they encountered in Central and Eastern Europe into their own evolving notions of children's best interests. They came, above all, to insist that children needed a stable national identity as well as a stable family to develop as healthy individuals. Some postwar social workers and political activists even equated family and nation, portraying them as interchangeable sources of psychological and political stability. Edith Sterba, a social worker who counseled Jewish refugee children in Detroit after World War II, thus compared the loss of a national homeland to loss of the mother's breast. "Loss of the mother country is very often experienced as oral loss . . . loss of the homeland is experienced as identical with the trauma of weaning," she argued in a 1940 article on "Homelessness and the Breast."[64] More typically, child welfare experts and government officials represented the national community as a substitute family for orphaned children. The imagined equivalence between nation and family was particularly compelling to postwar Zionists, but also underpinned East European demands for the repatriation of displaced orphans after the war.

Apparent tensions between individualist and collectivist conceptions of democracy were at the very heart of European reconstruction. These tensions were expressed in very mundane, but highly charged decisions about the education and care of children—in debates about whether children's homes or foster families were best for children's development, for example. And yet shared assumptions often lurked beneath the surface of rhetorical oppositions between "individualist" and "collectivist" (and nationalist and internationalist) visions for European reconstruction. Refugee children were not, in the end, targeted as abstract individuals. They were targeted as members of groups: as Polish, Jewish, German, or French children, girls or boys. Nor can the limitations of postwar individualism simply be blamed on the "politicization" of humanitarian activism. These limitations were intrinsic to the very logic of postwar relief efforts. They reflected underlying tensions between overlapping humanitarian and human rights regimes as they developed in twentieth century Europe.

In the 1940s, contemporary notions of human rights were still in their infancy. The rhetoric of human rights was (and remains) highly flexible. It was mobilized on both sides of the Iron Curtain, for and against the repatriation of refugee children to Eastern Europe, for example. During the postwar reconstruction of Europe, a still inchoate concept of "human rights" coexisted and clashed with older traditions of humanitarian relief. A hierarchical logic has historically underpinned humanitarian activism, particularly as it developed in colonial and post-colonial contexts. Humanitarian rhetoric specifically reinforced an unequal relationship between "the compassionate and the suffering" that is at odds with the presumed universalism and egalitarianism of human rights discourses.[65]

Child-savers in twentieth-century Europe not only consolidated hierarchies between the donors and recipients of humanitarian aid, and between "modern" and "backward" societies. They also reinforced unequal relationships between men and women, children and adults. Children and women in postwar Europe were rarely targeted for humanitarian protection simply because of their presumed equality or their shared humanity. Rather, they received assistance because of their perceived vulnerability and innocence.[66]

This innocence was particularly important in the context of the Second World War. Civilian populations across Europe had been morally compromised to an unprecedented extent under Nazi occupation. Children sometimes appeared to be the only "innocent victims" left standing in 1945. Even here

there were doubts. Children, after all, yelled anti-Semitic slurs at Ruth Kluger in Vienna and hurled stones at Thomas Buergenthal in Poland. And the boundaries between childhood and adulthood, victims and perpetrators, were highly porous. Was a 16-year-old German boy (such as Günter Grass) conscripted by the Waffen-SS in 1944 a child? Was he an innocent victim?[67]

Answering such questions was itself a central task of postwar reconstruction. United Nations workers and postwar governments were charged with classifying Europeans into different categories of humans, each entitled to different kinds of rights and opportunities. They divided children from adults, Germans from Czechs, Poles from Russians, Jews from Christians, victims from perpetrators. Even as they spoke a universal language of human rights, these decisions profoundly shaped access to basic necessities, including food, shelter, opportunities to emigrate, and citizenship rights. Children—seen as more assimilable than their parents, and therefore as more desirable immigrants and citizens—often enjoyed more rights and opportunities than adults.

Humanitarian workers also participated in the construction of divisions between East and West, particularly as they adjudicated custody battles over East European children. But it should not be forgotten that the future of Europe was remarkably open between 1945 and 1948. The division between East and West that would structure European politics for the next fifty years was not predetermined. There were, of course, profound differences between Eastern and Western European experiences of war, occupation, and liberation. The Nazi regime's messianic anti-Communism, combined with a racial ideology that portrayed Jews and Slavs as subhuman, guaranteed that the war on the Eastern Front was far more deadly to both soldiers and civilians. Eastern Europe was the physical site of the Nazi genocide, an open secret that relied on the complicity of local populations. Nazi racial policies intensified conflicts between different linguistic and religious groups in the East, setting the stage for the violent population transfers that followed the war. And the fact that the Red Army liberated and occupied most of Eastern Europe set many parameters of reconstruction.[68]

And yet several basic assumptions underpinning the project of postwar reconstruction transcended the East-West divide. In both Eastern and Western Europe, policymakers saw children as a form of national property. In both East and West, World War II also strengthened the conviction that only homogenous nation-states could guarantee peace and stability in Europe. This conviction justified East European policies of expulsion and ethnic cleansing as well as the racial hierarchies that underpinned West European migration policies after World War II. An overriding concern with crafting homogenous nation-states ultimately undercut the humanitarian rhetoric of family reunification, particularly in the case of transnational families. French officials thus encouraged German mothers of French occupation children to abandon their children to the French state, while Czech authorities urged German-Czech couples to dissolve their marriages, emigrate, or cleanse their families of national ambiguity.

In this context, lost children became central figures in wide-ranging debates about the boundaries of citizenship and the meaning of democracy after World War II. These boundaries were ultimately drawn differently in the United States, Great Britain, Germany, France, Czechoslovakia, and Poland. But across Europe, the displacement of millions of people during World War II was both lamented as a humanitarian crisis and seized as an opportunity to remake populations. The history of Europe's lost children thus reveals a story of shared challenges and priorities in liberated Europe, as policymakers in the East and West mobilized to reconstruct families, replenish populations, create homogenous nation-states, and prevent future outbreaks of German imperialism. Children were essential to all of these goals.

The history of displaced families not only confounds the presumed oppositions between Western and Eastern Europe. It also challenges a tendency to analyze the experiences of different refugee groups in isolation from one another.[69] Jewish displaced persons, German expellees, and East European refugees all had disparate wartime and postwar experiences. In occupied Germany and Austria, they were subject to different legal regimes and unequal access to food and other welfare benefits. They were often physically segregated, and treated with varying degrees of sympathy (or hostility) by local Germans, military authorities, and United Nations' officials. But as the story of Přemysl Pitter suggests, different groups of refugees also interacted in daily life, traded resources, defined themselves and were defined in relation to one another. In spite of distinctive wartime experiences, they adopted similar strategies to cope with displacement, investing hope in the national community and in children as a source of future stability and regeneration.[70]

Juxtaposing the history of German, Jewish, and East European refugees after World War II highlights the broader tensions between universalism and particularism that shaped European reconstruction. Jewish refugees, in particular, were widely seen as the paradigmatic group in need of human rights after World War II.[71] But postwar European governments simultaneously denied the specific, genocidal nature of Nazi policies toward Jews, as they promoted patriotic memories of nations united in suffering and resistance under Nazi rule. The psychoanalytic principles adopted by humanitarian workers also obscured the distinctive experiences of Jewish children in universalist theories of child development. And the dominant solutions to the problem of wartime displacement—return to nation and family—were of little use to Jewish survivors who had neither a home nor (until 1948) a nation to which they could "return." Jewish organizations, advocates, and refugees did not passively accept universalist narratives about their wartime experiences, however. Contrary to the myth of postwar "silence" about the Holocaust, Jews outspokenly asserted the specificity of their experiences of genocide during the Second World War. And they demanded distinctive solutions to the problem of homelessness after the war, not only through Zionism, but also though their efforts on behalf of Jewish children.[72]

The example of Jewish refugees reflects a broader reality of the postwar moment. Universal and particularist values and claims were entangled at the heart of the concepts such as "human rights," "humanitarianism," and "democracy" that structured postwar European reconstruction. Humanitarian workers may have refashioned nationalist ideals in a more universalist language of psychological health, human rights, and children's best interests after World War II. But nationalist principles, particularly the priorities of guaranteeing national sovereignty and homogeneity, were more central than ever to European hopes for stability after the Second World War.

The story of refugee children, in particular, demonstrates that the histories of humanitarianism and of ethnic cleansing in twentieth-century Europe are neither unrelated nor contradictory. By privileging the young, European and American policymakers and citizens consistently cloaked racial and national hierarchies—some of which could be less openly articulated in the "democratizing" context of postwar Europe—in a rhetoric of humanitarian assistance. If the twentieth century was the "Century of the Child," as Swedish pedagogue Ellen Key proclaimed in 1900, this was the product of chauvinism as much as humanitarianism. From the Armenian Genocide to the Kindertransports to the postwar resettlement of European refugees, children were not only saved (to the extent that they *were* saved) from violence, racial persecution, and purgatory in refugee camps because they were seen as innocent and vulnerable. They were saved because they represented the biological future of nations. And they were saved to the extent that people believed that they could assimilate, and thereby serve the dreams of policymakers to construct homogenous nation-states.

In times of crisis and destruction, people often seek something to believe in and to survive for. Children embodied Europeans' most ambitious hopes and their deepest fears about the future in 1945. Policymakers and international organizations successfully harnessed these hopes and fears to their own agendas for reconstruction. Europe's separated families, its orphans and lost children, became vessels for building a post-fascist order. But lost children were not empty vessels, even in Europe's so-called Zero Hour. They often had their own dreams for the future, plans that sometimes conflicted with those of the social workers, diplomats, and relatives who sought custody of their future.

An unprecedented number of Europeans left home during the Second World War. After the war, most sought to return home. They hoped to find stability there, a refuge from the upheaval of war and displacement, and perhaps from politics itself. But it was not possible for many Europeans to return home in 1945, at least not to the societies or families they had left behind. Nor could the family be a tranquil refuge from mass politics. The problem was not only that children and parents had grown apart, that homes had been looted or bombed, and that neighbors and relatives had been murdered. The significance of the family itself had changed, as had basic ideas about what constitutes a happy home. The family was more politicized than ever in 1945, as it seemed to hold the key to European peace and to the future of democracy. The Second World War did not simply transform Europe's geography, demography, and political landscape. Wartime displacement transformed both children and childhood, remaking home and homeland as we know it.

Archival Sources and Abbreviations

Austria

Österreichisches Staatsarchiv, Vienna (OestA)
    Archiv der Republik
        Bundesministerium des Innern, 12-U
        Bundesministerium für soziale Verwaltung (BmfsV)

Czech Republic

Archiv Přemysl Pitter, Prague (PP)
Národní archiv, Prague (NA)
    Ministerstvo práce a sociální péče—repatriace (MPSP-R)
    Ministerstvo práce a sociální péče (MPSP)
    Ministerstvo vnitra-nová registratura (MV-NR)
    Ministerstvo zahraničních věcí—výstřižkový archiv (MZV-VA)
    Národní jednota severočeská (NJS)
    Úřad předsednictva vlády (ÚPV-bez.)
    Zemské ústředí péče o mládež v Čechách (ČZK)
Jewish Museum in Prague
    Sbírka Terezín

France

Archives nationales, Paris
    International Refugee Organization (43/AJ)
    Commissariat Général du Plan (80/AJ)

Police générale (7/F)
Affaires militaires, Rapatriement (9/F)
Archives des Affaires Étrangères, Paris (MAE)
Guerre 1939–1945
Espagne, Europe 1918–1940
Allemagne, Z-Europe
Societé des Nations
Direction des personnes deplacées et réfugiés du Haut-
Commissariat de la République française en Allemagne (PDR)
Centre de documentation juive contemporaine (CDJC)
Kap-Fi (Fond Kaplan-Finaly Affair)
WIZO—Union of French-Jewish Women for Palestine

Germany

Bundesarchiv Berlin
NS 19/345
Suchdienst für vermißte Deutsche- DO 105
Bundesarchiv Koblenz
B 106
B 150

Netherlands

International Institute for Social History (IISH)
Ernst Papanek Collection

Poland

Archiwum akt nowych, Warsaw
Delegatura Polski Czerwony Krzyż na Niemcy (PCK—Niemcy)
Delegatura Polski Czerwony Krzyż na Strefę Amerykaska w Niemczech
Generalny Pełnomocnik Rzadu RP do Spraw Repatriacji w Warszawie
Ministerstwo Pracy i Opieki Społecznej
Polski Czerwony Krzyż. Zarząd Główny w Warszawie (PCK)
Polska Misja Wojskowa przy Sojuszniczej Radzie Kontroli w Berlinie

United States

Archives of the American Joint Distribution Committee (JDC)
Belgium, 1945–1954
Czechoslovakia, 1945–1954

Poland, 1945–1954
France, 1945–1954
Austria, 1945–1954
Displaced Persons: Children, 1945–1954
German Jewish Children's Aid, 1933–1944
U.S. Committee for the Care of European Children, 1933–1944
Center for Jewish History (CJH), YIVO, New York.
German Jewish Children's Aid/European Jewish Children's Aid
(RG 249, GJCA/EJCA)
Leo Schwarz Papers
DP Camps—Austria (RG 294.4)
Harvard Divinity School, Andover Theological Seminary
Unitarian Service Committee (USC)
Hoover Archive, Stanford University (HA)
American Relief Administration (ARA)
Aleta Brownlee Papers
National Archives and Records Administration (NARA), College Park, MD
Records of the U.S. High Commissioner for Germany, 1944–1955
Records of the Displaced Persons Commission, 1948–1952
Piłsudski Institute, New York
Uchodźcy Polscy w Niemczech po 1945
Social Welfare History Archive (SWHA), University of Minnesota
International Social Service (ISS)
United States Holocaust Memorial, Museum and Archive (USHMMA)
American Friends Service Committee (AFSC)
Centralny Komitet Żydow w Polsce. Wydział Oświaty (CKŻP)
Oeuvre de secours aux enfants (OSE)
United Nations Archive, New York (UN)
United Nations Relief and Rehabilitation Administration (UNRRA)

Notes

Introduction

1. Report on Interview, Subject—Davidowicz, Ruth-Karin, born 31.5.1938—German Jew; Final Report of Interview, Subject: Davidowicz, Ruth-Karin, 31.5.38, File 365, Reel 8.17, German-Jewish Children's Aid, YIVO, Center for Jewish History (CJH), New York.

2. Memo to Mr A. C. Dunn, Policy on Unaccompanied Children. Dated May 27, 1949, 43/AJ/926, AN (Archives nationales, Paris).

3. For memoirs of such experiences, see Susan T. Pettiss with Lynne Taylor, *After the Shooting Stopped: The Story of an UNRRA Welfare Worker in Germany, 1945–47* (Victoria, BC, 2004); Kathryn Hulme, *The Wild Place* (Boston, 1953); Aleta Brownlee, "Whose Children?" Box 9, Aleta Brownlee Papers, Hoover Archive (HA), Stanford University.

4. William I. Hitchcock, *The Bitter Road to Freedom: A New History of the Liberation of Europe* (New York, 2008), 182–183.

5. For statistics on homelessness, see Thérèse Brosse, *War-Handicapped Children: Report on the European Situation* (Paris, 1950), 22; Elizabeth D. Heineman, *What Difference Does a Husband Make? Women and Marital Status in Nazi and Postwar Germany* (Berkeley, 1999), 79. On social conditions in liberated Germany, see Richard Bessel, *Germany 1945: From War to Peace* (New York, 2009).

6. Bird-eye View of Child Welfare Services in Vienna, July 12, 1946, Folder 1, Carton 1, Brownlee Papers, HA.

7. Alice Bailey, *The Problems of the Children in the World Today* (New York, 1946), 9–10.

8. Marion Kaplan, *Between Dignity and Despair: Jewish Life in Nazi Germany* (Oxford, 1998), 54–73.

9. Ruth Kluger, *Still Alive: A Holocaust Girlhood Remembered* (New York, 2001), 52.

10. Ibid., 54.

11. Ibid., 97.

12. For statistics see Brosse, *War-Handicapped Children*, 22; Tony Judt, *Postwar: A History of Europe Since 1945* (New York, 2005), 22.

13. Sprawozdanie z pracy wychowawcej za rok 1945–46, sig. 303-IX-974, Centralny Komitet Żydow w Polsce, Wydział Oświaty (CKŻP), RG.1708M, United States Holocaust Memorial, Museum, and Archive (USHMMA).

14. On repatriation in Japan, see Lori Watt, *When Empire Comes Home: Repatriation and Reintegration in Postwar Japan* (Cambridge, Mass., 2009); On UNRRA activity in China, Korea, and the Philippines, see George Woodbridge, *UNRRA: The History of the United Nations Relief and Rehabilitation Administration*, vol. II (New York, 1950), 371–465, 492.

15. Malcolm Proudfoot, *European Refugees, 1939–52: A Study in Forced Population Movement* (London, 1957), 159, 228, 259; Bessel, *Germany 1945*, 256. On UNRRA's nationality statistics, see Andrew Janco, "The Soviet Refugee in Postwar Europe and the Cold War, 1945–61" (Ph.D diss., University of Chicago, 2011).

16. Jacques Vernant, *The Refugee in the Postwar World* (New Haven, 1953), 101, 180.

17. Proudfoot, *European Refugees*, 266–267.

18. Bergen-Belsen, June 27, 1946, Papanek Europe Tour, F-13, Papanek Collection, International Institute for Social History (IISH), Amsterdam.

19. Policies Regarding Reestablishment of Children, April 25, 1949, 43/AJ/926, AN.

20. Letters to the IRO, 43/AJ/926, AN.

21. Simone Marcus-Jeisler, "Réponse à l'enquête sur les effets psychologiques de la guerre sur les enfants et jeunes en France," *Sauvegarde* 8 (February 1947): 12.

22. Letter from Morris C. Troper to Eleanor Roosevelt, June 7, 1941, Folder F-12, Papanek, IISH.

23. Kaplan, *Between Dignity and Despair*, 116, 118.

24. On the evacuation of children during World War II, see Laura Lee Downs, "'A Very British Revolution?' L'évacuation des enfants citadins vers les campagnes anglaises, 1939–45," *Vingtième siècle* 89 (January–March 2006): 47–49; Rebecca Manley, *To the Tashkent Station: Evacuation and Survival in the Soviet Union at War* (Ithaca, 2009); Julia Torrie, *For Their Own Good: Civilian Evacuations in Germany and France* (New York, 2010).

25. Herbert, *Hitler's Foreign Workers*, 269.

26. Ibid., 268–273.

27. Ulrich Herbert, *Hitler's Foreign Workers: Enforced Foreign Labor under the Third Reich*, trans. William Templer (Cambridge, UK, 1997), 323; numbers, 281.

28. Darstellung des Flüchtlingsproblems, Ministry of Interior, April 30, 1952. Carton 9, Bundesministerium des Innern (BMI), 12u-34, Archiv der Republik (AdR), Österreichisches Staatsarchiv (OestA).

29. Isabel Heinemann, *"Rasse, Siedlung, deutsches Blut": Die Rasse und Siedlungshauptamt der SS und die rassenpolitische Neuordnung Europas* (Göttingen, 2003), 508–509.

30. Deborah Dwork, *Children with a Star: Jewish Youth in Nazi Europe* (New Haven, 1993), 274–275; For detailed survival estimates see also Herman D. Stein, "Welfare and Child Care Needs of European Jewry," *Jewish Social Service Quarterly* 25 (March 1948): 298, 301.

31. The number of Poles deported to the USSR between 1939 and 1941 is disputed. Older estimates typically settled around 1.5 million, while revised estimates put the number at 315,000–319,000. The number of Jews deported is also unclear—around 200,000 returned to Eastern Europe after the war, but a much higher number may have been initially deported. For a discussion of this debate, see Katherine Jolluck, *Exile and Identity: Polish Women in the Soviet Union During World War II* (Stanford, 1999), 9–11.

32. Atina Grossmann, *Jews, Germans, and Allies: Close Encounters in Occupied Germany* (Princeton, 2007), 160.

33. All of these numbers are approximate. Proudfoot, *European Refugees*, 267. On the Jewish baby boom, see Grossmann, *Jews, Germans, and Allies*, 184–236. On Zionist youth, see Avinoam Patt, *Finding Home and Homeland: Jewish Youth and Zionism in the Aftermath of the Holocaust* (Detroit, 2009), 98, 211 for numbers.

34. On the allied fixation with "processing" refugees, see Hitchcock, *The Bitter Road to Freedom*, 253–255.

35. Mark Wyman, *DPs: Europe's Displaced Persons, 1945–1951* (Ithaca, 1998), 49.

36. For disputed Polish numbers Heinemann, *Rasse, Siedlung, deutsches Blut*, 508–509. On hidden children, see Daniella Doron, "In the Best Interest of the Child: Family, Youth, and Identity in Postwar France, 1944–1954," (Ph.D diss., New York University, 2009), 49.

37. Ivan Jablonka, *Ni père, ni mère. Histoire des enfants de l'Assistance publique 1874–1939* (Paris, 2006). On child labor and migration, see also Klaus Bade, *Migration in European History* (Oxford, 2003), 5.

38. On the shift between the "old" and "new" regimes of childhood, see Laura Lee Downs, *Histoire des colonies de vacances de 1880 à nos jours* (Paris, 2009). On changing ideals of childhood and child welfare in the nineteenth century, see Anna Davin, *Growing up Poor: Home, School, and Street in London, 1870–1914* (London, 1997); Lydia Murdoch, *Imagined Orphans: Poor Families, Child*

Welfare, and Contested Citizenship in London (New Brunswick, 2006); Edward Ross Dickinson, *The Politics of German Child Welfare from the Empire to the Federal Republic* (Cambridge, MA, 1996).

39. Wilma A. Dunaway, *The African-American Family in Slavery and Emancipation* (New York, 2003), 273; Brenda E. Stevenson, *Life in Black and White: Family and Community in the Slave South* (New York, 1996), 160–161.

40. Thomas C. Holt, *Children of Fire: A History of African Americans* (New York, 2010), Chapter 4.

41. David Kertzer, *The Kidnapping of Edgardo Mortara* (New York, 1997).

42. On British child emigration schemes see Kathleen Paul, "Changing Childhoods: Child Emigration Since 1945," in *Child Welfare and Social Action in the Nineteenth and Twentieth Centuries,* ed. Jon Lawrence and Pat Starkey (Liverpool, 2001), 122–124; Geoffrey Sherington, "Fairbridge Child Migrants," in *Child Welfare and Social Action,* 53–81; Patrick A. Dunae, "Gender, Generations and Social Class: The Fairbridge Society and British Child Migration to Canada, 1930–60," in *Child Welfare and Social Action,* 82–100; Wendy Webster, "Transnational Journeys and Domestic Histories," *Journal of Social History* 39 (Spring 2006): 651–666.

43. Linda Gordon, *The Great Arizona Orphan Abduction* (Cambridge, Mass., 2001).

44. International Migration Service, Memorandum on the Work of the American Branch, April 1928, 2, Folder 11, Social Welfare History Archive (SWHA), Collection 109, University of Minnesota.

45. Edward Fuller, "The New Universalism," *The World's Children* 26 (January 1946): 9, Reel 6, *The Western Aid and the Global Economy,* series one. The Save the Children Fund Archive, London. Accessed at the Center for Research Libraries, Chicago.

46. No author, *Today's Children, Tomorrow's Hope: The Story of Children in the Occupied Lands* (London, 1945), 3.

47. On the place of the family in the reconstruction of postwar Europe, see Robert Moeller, *Protecting Motherhood. Women and the Politics of Postwar West Germany* (Berkeley, 1993); Heineman, *What Difference Does a Husband Make;* Dagmar Herzog, *Sex After Fascism: Memory and Morality in Twentieth Century Germany* (Princeton, 2005); Heide Fehrenbach, *Race After Hitler: Black Occupation Children in Postwar Germany and America* (Princeton, 2005); Donna Harsch, *Revenge of the Domestic: Women, the Family and Communism in the German Democratic Republic* (Princeton, 2007); On the "return to normalcy," see Richard Bessel and Dirk Schumann, eds. *Life After Death: Approaches to a Cultural and Social History of Europe During the 1940s and 1950s* (New York, 2003). On the family in Cold War America, Elaine Tyler May, *Homeward Bound: American Families in the Cold War Era* (New York, 1988).

48. For a critique of the ahistorical use of "trauma" in histories of childhood, see Nicholas Stargardt, *Witnesses of War: Children's Lives under the Nazis* (London, 2005).

49. Anna Freud and Dorothy T. Burlingham, *War and Children* (London, 1943), 45.

50. On the alleged triumph of individual over collective rights in postwar West European politics and human rights activism, see Judt, *Postwar*, 564–565; Paul Lauren, *The Evolution of International Human Rights* (Philadelphia, 1996); Mark Mazower, "The Strange Triumph of Human Rights, 1933–1950," *The Historical Journal* 47 (June 2004): 386–388; A. W. Brian Simpson, *Human Rights and the End of Empire: Britain and the Genesis of the European Convention* (Oxford, 2001), 157–220; Elizabeth Borgwardt, *A New Deal for the World: America's Vision for Human Rights* (Cambridge, Mass., 2005).

51. Mark Mazower, *Dark Continent: Europe's Twentieth Century* (New York, 1999), 191. For an account that emphasizes the ongoing resonance of collective rights after World War II, see Eric Weitz, "From the Vienna to the Paris System: International Politics and the Entangled Histories of Human Rights, Forced Deportations, and Civilizing Missions," *American Historical Review* 113 (December 2008): 1313–1343.

52. See especially Mark Mazower, *No Enchanted Palace: The End of Empire and the Ideological Origins of the United Nations* (Princeton, 2009).

53. Judt, *Postwar*, 18.

54. Saul Friedländer, *When Memory Comes* (New York, 1979), 94.

55. Doron, "In the Best Interest," 22.

56. Bessel, *Germany 1945*, 272. On impersonation among Soviet refugees, see Janco, "The Soviet Refugee."

57. Johanna Müller to the German Red Cross, March 6, 1953, B 150/213 Heft 1, Bundesarchiv Koblenz.

Chapter 1. The Quintessential Victims of War

1. Survey of the Needs of the Spanish Refugees and the Relief Projects to Help them in France, 1945, bMs 16035-2, Unitarian Service Committee Archive (USC), Andover Theological Seminary, Harvard Divinity School.

2. France—St. Goin—Parrainages, 1948, bms 16035, USC.

3. J. M. Alvarez, "When I grow up," 1947, bMs 16035-9, USC.

4. Howard Kershner, *Quaker Service in Modern War* (New York, 1950), 156.

5. Lindsay H. Noble, Colonies d'enfants, July 17, 1941, Folder 57, Box 61, Reel 73, American Friends Service Committee (AFSC), United States Holocaust Museum, Memorial, and Archive (USHMMA).

6. Charles Joy, A Preliminary Study of Post-War Work in France for the Unitarian Service Committee, June 24, 1944, 6, bms16035-1, USC.

7. *Relief of European Populations,* Hearing before the Committee on Ways and Means, House of Representatives, January 12, 1920, part 2 (Washington, 1920), 68.

8. Francesca Wilson, *In the Margins of Chaos: Recollections of Relief Work in and Between Three Wars* (New York, 1945), 10–11.

9. Wilson, *In the Margins of Chaos,* 12.

10. On the Red Cross, see David P. Forsythe, *The Humanitarians: The International Committee of the Red Cross* (New York, 2005).

11. Klaus Bade, *Migration in European History* (Oxford, 2003), 142. Mae M. Ngai, *Impossible Subjects: Illegal Aliens and the Making of Modern America* (Princeton, 2004), 59.

12. John Torpey, "The Great War and the Creation of the Modern Passport System," in Jane Caplan and John Torpey, eds., *Documenting Individual Identity: The Development of State Practices in the Modern World* (Princeton, 2001), 256–270.

13. Jean Claude Farcy, *Les camps de concentration française de la première guerre mondiale* (Paris, 1995), 51–63.

14. Gerard Noiriel, *The French Melting Pot: Immigration, Citizenship, and National Identity* (Minneapolis, 1996), 61; Bade, *Migration in European History,* 176.

15. Claudena M. Skran, *Refugees in Interwar Europe: The Emergence of a Regime* (New York, 1995), 4, 40; John Hope Simpson, *The Refugee Problem: Report of a Survey* (London, 1939), 561; Annemarie Sammartino, *The Impossible Border: Germany and the East, 1914–1922* (Ithaca, NY, 2010).

16. For a more in-depth discussion of the Armenian Genocide, Ronald Grigor Suny, "Truth in Telling: Reconciling Realities in the Genocide of the Ottoman Armenians," *American Historical Review* 114 (October 2009): 930–946; Vahakn Dadrian, *The History of the Armenian Genocide: Ethnic Conflict from the Balkans to Anatolia to the Caucases* (New York, 2004); Michael Marrus, *The Unwanted: European Refugees in the Twentieth Century* (New York, 1985), 75; Maud Mandel, *In the Aftermath of Genocide: Armenians and Jews in Twentieth Century France* (Durham, NC, 2003), 22–25.

17. Skran, *Refugees in Interwar Europe,* 65–101.

18. For first-hand accounts of children's experiences, see Donald E. Miller and Lorna Touryan Miller, *Survivors: An Oral History of the Armenian Genocide* (Berkeley, 1993), quotations, 110, 108. See also Keith David Watenpaugh, "'A pious wish devoid of all practicability:' Interwar Humanitarianism, The League of Nations and the Rescue of Trafficked Women and Children in the Eastern Mediterranean, 1920–1927," *American Historical Review* 115 (December 2010).

19. I thank Eric Weitz for alerting me about the League's mission in Armenia. For in-depth accounts, See Vahram L. Shemmassian, "The League of Nations and the Reclamation of Armenian Genocide Survivors," in Richard G. Hovannisian, ed. *Looking Backward, Moving Forward: Confronting the Armenian Genocide* (New Brunswick, NJ, 2003), 81–110; Dzovinar Kévonian, *Réfugiés et diplomatie humanitaire: les acteurs européens et la scène proche orient pendant l'entre-deux guerres* (Paris, 2004), 144–159; Watenpaugh, 'A pious wish.'

20. Kévonian, *Réfugiés et diplomatie humanitaire,* 144; Shemassian, "The League of Nations," 82.

21. Deportation of Women and Children in Turkey, Asia Minor, and Neighboring Territories. September 22, 1921, Folder 1829, Societé des Nations (SDN), Archives des Affaires Étrangers (MAE), Paris.

22. Ibid.

23. Karen Jeppe, Déportations des femmes et des enfants en Turquie et en Asie Mineure, May 22, 1922, Folder 1829, SDN, MAE.

24. Cited in Miller and Miller, *Survivors,* 124.

25. Jeppe, Déportations des femmes.

26. W. A. Kennedy, Report on the Work of the Commission of Enquiry with Regard to the Deportation of Women and Children, Folder 1829, SDN, MAE.

27. Letter from Miss Emma D. Cushman, July 16, 1921, Folder 1829, SDN, MAE.

28. League of Nations, *The League of Nations and the Deportations of Christians in Turkey* (Geneva, 1921), 20.

29. Karen Jeppe, Rapport du president de la commission de la societé des nations pour la protection des femmes et des enfants dans la Proche-Orient, July 1923– July 1924, 9 August 1924, 11, Folder 1830, SDN, MAE.

30. Miller and Miller, *Survivors,* 126.

31. Cited in Watenpaugh, "A pious wish," 25. See Watenpaugh for a more complete discussion of the Turkish response to the League's Rescue effort.

32. Note pour Monsieur Clauzel, 26 May 1925; Aristide Briand to General Sarrail, Affaire Karen Jeppe, 6 June 1925, Folder 1830, SDN, MAE.

33. Note de M. Robert de Caix, 29 August 1925, Folder 1830, SDN, MAE.

34. Shemmassian, "The League of Nations," 94, 104.

35. Karen Jeppe, Rapport de la Commission pour la protection des femmes et des enfants dans le Proche-Orient, 1 July 1926–1930 June 1927, Folder 1830, SDN, MAE.

36. Jeppe, Rapport du president de la commission, 10–11, Folder 1830, SDN, MAE.

37. Überleitung von Flüchtlingskindern von Wien aufs Land, April 27, 1918, Carton 15, Bundesministerium für soziale Verwaltung (BmfsV), Archiv der Republik (AdR), Österreichisches Staatsarchiv (OestA).

38. Aktionen "Kind in's Ausland" im Monate August 1920, Carton 1666, BmfSV, AdR, OestA.

39. Bericht über den vom 25 bis 27 Februar stattgefundenen Kongress der Kinder-hilfswerke der vom Kriege betroffenen Länder, 6, Carton 1664, Staatsamt für soziale Verwaltung, Volksgesundheit, 1920, Kind, AdR, OestA.

40. Richard Goldstein, "Miep Gies, Protector of Anne Frank, dies at 100," *New York Times,* January 11, 2010. For quotations, "Youth," http://www.miepgies.nl, (accessed January 12, 2010).

41. Laura Lee Downs, *Childhood in the Promised Lands: Working-Class Movements and the Colonies de Vacances in France, 1880–1960* (Durham, NC, 2002), 137.

42. "Les enfants français en Hollande," *Débats,* February 26, 1919, 15/F/23, Archives nationales, Paris (AN).

43. Dominique Marshall, "The Construction of Children as an Object of International Relations: The Declaration of Children's Rights and the Child Welfare Committee of the League of Nations, 1900–1924," *The International Journal of Children's Rights* 7, nr. 2 (1999): 103–147.

44. A Summary of the Period March 1919 to June 30, 1922, 36, 51, Folder 3, Box 624, American Relief Administration (ARA), Hoover Archive (HA), Stanford University.

45. No author, "The Children's Graveyard," *The Record of the Save the Children Fund* 1, nr. 11, April 15, 1921, 167.

46. Report from M. L. Thomas, Box 615, Folder 2, ARA, HA.

47. Maureen Healy, *Vienna and the Fall of the Habsburg Empire: Total War and Everyday Life in World War I* (Cambridge, 2004), 31–86, statistics, 41.

48. Wilson, *In the Margins of Chaos,* 114.

49. Comparison between Vienna and other capitals, Folder 3, Box 654; Vital Statistics, October 19, 1920; A Review of the Work of the American Relief Administration in Austria, November 1, 1921, 4, Folder 9, Box 632, ARA, HA.

50. European Self-help in Relief, Folder 9, Box 632, ARA, HA.

51. Herbert Hoover, "First Year–to August 1919," October 4, 1920, Folder 7, Box 631, ARA, HA.

52. Herbert Hoover, Children's Relief and Democracy, interview with I. F. Marcosson in the *Saturday Evening Post* of April 30, 1921, Folder 7, Box 631, ARA, HA.

53. Dr. Clemens Pirquet, Founder of the NEM and Peldisi Systems, November 3, 1921, Folder 2, Box 632, ARA, HA.

54. Wilson, *In the Margins of Chaos,* 127–128.

55. Mrs. Philip Snowden, "The Cry of the Children," *The Record of the Save the Children Fund* 1, nr. 5, January 15, 1921, 68.

56. On orientalism and Eastern Europe, see Larry Wolff, *Inventing Eastern Europe: The Map of Civilization on the Mind of the Enlightenment* (Stanford, 1994); Maria Todorova, *Imagining the Balkans* (Oxford, 1997).

57. No author, "Czecho-Slovakia," *The Record of the Save the Children Fund* 1, nr. 1, October 1, 1920, 4.

58. N. Leach, Survey Report Ruthenia, Prague, July 18, 1920, 2, Folder 1, Box 669, ARA, HA.

59. W. P. Fuller, General Report, Warsaw, Poland, January 17, 1920, Folder 10, Box 702, ARA, HA.

60. Lina Fuller to W. P. Fuller, January 21, 1920, Folder 10, Box 702, ARA, HA.

61. N. Leach, Report on Conditions Relative to E.C.F. in Bucharest, Wien, September 5, 1919, Folder 9, Box 632, ARA, HA.

62. H. May, Report on Future of Kitchens in the Košice District, January 18, 1921, Box 669, ARA, HA.

63. Troubles, Abuse, and a Conclusion, January 7, 1920, Folder 3, Box 705, ARA, HA.

64. Ngai, *Impossible Subjects*, 27.

65. On immigration in interwar France, see Mary D. Lewis, *Boundaries of the Republic: Migrant Rights and the Limits of Universalism in France, 1918–40* (Stanford, 2007); Clifford Rosenberg, *Policing Paris: the Origins of Modern Immigration Control Between the Wars* (Ithaca, 2006); Elisa Camiscioli, *Reproducing the French Race: Immigration, Intimacy, and Embodiment in the Early Twentieth Century* (Durham, NC, 2009); Gérard Noiriel, *The French Melting Pot: Immigration, Citizenship, and National Identity* (Minneapolis, 1996).

66. International Migration Service, Memorandum on the Work of the American Branch, April 1928, 2, Folder 11, Box 15, SW109, Social Welfare History Archive (SWHA), University of Minnesota.

67. General Project of the International Migration Service, May 1944, Folder 19, Oswego Project, Reports & Statistics, Folder 11, Box 15, SW109, SWHA.

68. Surveying the International Social Service after 25 Years, 1951, Folder 17, Box 16, SW109, SWHA.

69. On fears of juvenile delinquency after World War I, see Richard Bessel, *Germany after the First World War* (Oxford, 1993); Healy, *Vienna and the Fall*.

70. George Warren, The Widening Horizon in our Service to Foreign-Born Families, June 15 1931, 3, Folder 28, Box 615, SW109, SWHA.

71. Preliminary Memorandum on the Recruitment and Placement of Foreign Workers, May 1930, 2, Folder 36, Box 15, SW109, SWHA.

72. Kenneth Rich and Mary Brant, Maintenance Orders in Separated Families as Seen by the Immigrants Protective League in Chicago, 1927, 2–5, Folder 3, Box 15, SW109, SWHA.

73. Ibid., 8.

74. Antony Roman, Report on the Present Situation of Poland, 5, Folder 21, Box 36, SW109, SWHA.

75. Adam Nagorski to George Warren, February 4, 1939, Folder 21, Box 36, SW109, SWHA.

76. Report by Miss Joan Kossak, September 1926, 2, Folder 21, Box 36, SW109, SWHA.

77. Rich and Brant, Maintenance Orders, 17.

78. The American branch had handled 23,350 cases by 1939. Memorandum to New York Foundation, May 13, 1940, Folder 11, Box 15, SW109, SWHA.

79. Ruth Larned, The Tangled Threads of Migrant Family Problems, June 13, 1930, 159, Folder 5, Box 15, SW109, SWHA.

80. Resumé des points principals discutés pendant la réunion des directeurs et directrices des colonies enfantines, November 5, 1942, Folder 1, Box 57, Reel 68, AFSC, USHMMA.

81. Marrus, The Unwanted, 190–193.

82. Ministry of the Interior to Ministry of Foreign Affairs, November 11, 1940, Document 19, Guerre 1939–1945, Vichy 275, Archives des Affaires Étrangères, Paris (MAE).

83. Célia Keren, "Sauver les enfants d'Espagne! L'accueil en France des enfants de la guerre' (1936–40)," (MA Thesis, EHESS, Paris, 2008), 29–33.

84. Dorothy Legaretta, The Guernica Generation (Reno, Nev., 1984), 36–39.

85. Falange española tradicionalista y de las J.O.N.S., Secretaria General, Servicio Exterior, "Informe sobre la labor desarollada hasta le fecha para la repatriacion de menores españoles expatriados," 3, published in Ricard Vinyes, et. al., eds. Los niños perdidos del franquismo (Barcelona, 2002), 205.

86. For Soviet numbers, see Daniel Kowalsky, Stalin and the Spanish Civil War (New York, 2004), 15.

87. Keren, "Sauver les enfants," 9.

88. "Suffering France," 6–7, Folder 9, Box 34, Reel 37, AFSC, USHMMA.

89. Legaretta, The Guernica Generation, 71.

90. Traduction d'un article paru dans la New Republic 19 mars 1939, 199, Espagne 188, Europe 1918–1940, Archives des Affaires Étrangères, Paris (MAE).

91. Legaretta, The Guernica Generation, 62–63.

92. Ibid., 62.

93. Legaretta, The Guernica Generation, 167–168.

94. Eduardo Pons Prades, Los niños republicanos (Madrid, 2005), 117.

95. Legaretta, The Guernica Generation, 169–171, 270.

96. Rapatriement d'enfants espagnols à Saint-Sébastien, March 25, 1937, Espagne 268, Europe 1918–1940, MAE.

97. Contra la séquestration d'enfants espagnols, Protestation des femmes françaises, *Diario Vasco,* March 20, 1937, Espagne 268, Europe 1918–1940, MAE.

98. Rapatriement des enfants espagnols, May 15, 1939, Espagne 269, MAE.

99. Démarche de Mgr. Antoniutti, August 23, 1937, Espagne 268, Europe 1918–1940, MAE.

100. Nécessité de repatrier les enfants espagnols réclamés par leurs familles, June 25, 1937, Espagne 268, Europe 1918–1940, MAE.

101. Le Préfet de l'Ain to the Ministry of Interior, November 23, 1937, Espagne 268, Europe 1918–1940, MAE.

102. A.s. de la jeune Cecila Vera Gandul, February 23, 1939, Espagne 269, Europe 1918–1940, MAE.

103. Rapatriement de la nommée Ferrer de nationalité espagnole, January 28, 1942, Document 123, Espagne 283, Guerre 1939–1945, Vichy, Z- Europe, MAE.

104. Rapatriement des enfants espagnols réfugiés à l'étranger, December 4, 1940, Document 59, Espagne 283, Guerre 1939–1945, Vichy, Z- Europe, MAE.

105. Rapatriement des enfants espagnols hébergés dans le département de l'Isère, September 14, 1938, Espagne 269, Europe 1918–40, MAE.

106. Letter to le Préfet du Tarn, Albi, January 30, 1938, Espagne 268, Europe 1918–1940, MAE.

107. Letter from Comité d'accueil aux enfants d'espagne to Venancio Pinado-Saez, January 14, 1939, Espagne 268, Europe 1918–1940, MAE.

108. Ministry of Interior to Ministry of Foreign Affairs, February 20, 1939, Espagne 269, Europe 1918–1940, MAE.

109. Legaretta, *The Guernica Genration,* 209.

110. Ministry of Interior to Minister of Foreign Affairs, October 4, 1940, Document 30, Espagne 283, Guerre 1939–1945, Vichy, Z-Europe, MAE.

111. Ministry of the Interior to Ministry of Foreign Affairs, November 11, 1940, Document 19, Guerre 1939–1945, Vichy 275, MAE; Vinyes, et. al. *Los niños perdidos,* 77.

112. Alicia Alted, "Le retour en Espagne des enfants evacués pendant la guerre civile espagnole: la délégation extraordinaire au rapatriement des mineurs (1938–1954), in Centre d'histoire de l'Europe du vingtième siècle, ed. *Enfants de la guerre civile espagnol: vécus et representations de la génération née entre 1925 et 1940* (Paris, 1999), 53.

113. Vinyes, et. al. *Los niños perdidos,* 75.

114. Eduardo Pons Prades, *Los niños republicanos,* 233–240.

115. Vinyes et. al., *Los niños perdidos,* 167.

116. Alted, "Le retour en Espagne," 58. These numbers only included children evacuated and repatriated through official channels.

117. Ibid., 71–75.

118. Vinyes, et. al. *Los niños perdidos,* 166.

119. Colonies scolaires d'enfants en Espagne et à l'étranger, August 19, 1937, Espagne 268, Europe 1918–1940, MAE.

120. Legaretta, *The Guernica Generation,* 75.

121. Alfred Brauner, *Les repercussions pyschiques de la guerre moderne sur l'enfance* (Paris, 1946), 39.

Chapter 2. Saving the Children

1. Ruth Kluger, *Still Alive: A Holocaust Girlhood Remembered* (New York, 2001), 29.

2. Ibid., 41.

3. Ibid., 60. On the experiences of Jewish children under Nazi rule, see Deborah Dwork, *Children with a Star* (New Haven, 1991); Marion Kaplan, *Between Dignity and Despair: Jewish Life in Nazi Germany* (Oxford, 1998), 94–118; Nicholas Stargardt, *Witnesses of War: Children's Lives Under the Nazis* (London, 2005).

4. Marion Kaplan, *Between Dignity and Despair: Jewish Life in Nazi Germany* (Oxford, 1998), 70–73, 119–144.

5. Kluger, *Still Alive,* 57.

6. Kaplan, *Between Dignity and Despair,* 118.

7. Kluger, *Still Alive,* 58.

8. Ibid., 26. Marion Kaplan has found that women often took the initiative in planning for emigration and in convincing their husbands to leave Germany. See Kaplan, *Between Dignity and Despair,* 63–70

9. Kaplan, *Between Dignity and Despair,* 116–118.

10. For numbers, see Clauda Curio, *Verfolgung, Flucht, Rettung: Die Kindertransporte 1938/39 nach Grossbritanien* (Berlin, 2006), 99.

11. Laura Lee Downs, "'A Very British Revolution?' L'évacuation des enfants citadins vers les campagnes anglaises, 1939–45," *Vingtième siècle* 89 (January–March 2006): 47–49. Quotation from Tom Harrison, *War Begins at Home* (London, 1940), 299–300.

12. Laura Lee Downs, *Childhood in the Promised Land: Working-Class Movements and the Colonies de Vacances in France, 1880–1960* (Durham, NC, 2002).

13. Downs, "'A Very British Revolution?'" 47–49.

14. Ritchie Calder, "The School Child," in Margaret Cole and Richard Padley, eds. *Evacuation Survey: A Report to the Fabian Society* (London, 1940), 147.

15. Anna Freud and Dorothy Burlingham, *Infants without Families. Reports on the Hampstead Nurseries, 1939–45* (New York, 1973), 161.

16. Ibid., 171.

17. Ibid., 178, 185.

18. John Bowlby, "Psychological Aspects," in *Evacuation Survey,* 190.

19. John Bowlby, *Maternal Care and Mental Health* (Geneva, 1952), 12.

20. Ibid., 68.

21. See Michal Shapira, *The War Inside: Child Psychoanalysis and Remaking the Self in Britain, 1930–1960,* Chapter 7, unpublished manuscript.

22. Denise Riley, *War in the Nursery: Theories of the Child and the Mother* (London, 1983), 85–110.

23. Susan Isaacs, ed. *The Cambridge Evacuation Survey: A Wartime Study in Social Welfare and Education* (London, 1941), 181.

24. Downs, "'A Very British Revolution?'" 54–55.

25. Bowlby, *Maternal Care,* 45.

26. Isaacs, ed. *Cambridge Evacuation Survey,* 9.

27. Curio, *Verfolgung, Flucht, Rettung;* Kaplan, *Between Dignity and Despair,* 116–118. On Youth Aliyah, see Erica B. Simmons, *Hadassah and the Zionist Project* (New York, 2006), 115–152.

28. Elsa Castendyck, Review of the European-Jewish Children's Aid, New York City, December 1943, 4–6, Folder 584, RG 249, YIVO, Center for Jewish History (CJH), New York.

29. Cited in Curio, *Verfolgung, Flucht, Rettung,* 46, numbers, 99.

30. Claudia Curio, "'Invisible Children': The Selection and Integration Strategies of Relief Organizations," *Shofar: An Interdisciplinary Journal of Jewish Studies* 23 (Fall 2004): 41–56.

31. Letter from GJCA to Reichsvertretung der Juden in Deutschland, February 20, 1936, Folder 64, RG 249, YIVO, CJH.

32. Migration of Children, File U.S. Committee, American Friends Service Committee Archive, Philadelphia.

33. No author, *Judisches Nachrichtenblatt,* May 9, 1939, 7. Cited in Curio, "Invisible Children," 49.

34. Findings of the Study Regarding Unaccompanied Children, Folder 35; Lotte Marcuse, Report of the European-Jewish Children's Aid, March 2, 1949, File 585, both in RG 249, YIVO, CJH.

35. Cited in Wolfgang Benz, "Emigration as Rescue and Trauma: The Historical Context of the Kindertransport," *Shofar* 23 (Fall 2004): 5.

36. Kaplan, *Between Dignity and Despair,* 116–118.

37. Unterbringung eines 13 jähr. Knaben in Amerika, May 12, 1934, AR 33–44, Folder 233, German-Jewish Children's Aid, JDC.

38. Interview cited in Rebekka Göpfert, *Der jüdische Kindertransport von Deutschland nach England 1938/39* (Frankfurt/Main, 1999), 120–121.

39. No Author, *Children Knocking At Our Gates,* German-Jewish Children's Aid, New York, May 1937. AR 33–44. Folder 234, German-Jewish Children's Aid, JDC.

40. Castendyck, Review of the European-Jewish Children's Aid, 10.

41. Testimony of Mrs. Alice Waters, *Admission of German Refugee Children. Joint Hearings before a Subcommittee of the Committee on Immigration,* April 20, 21, 22, and 24, 1939 (Washington, 1939), 197–198.

42. Judith Tydor Baumel, "The Jewish Refugee Children from Europe in the Eyes of the American Press and Public Opinion, 1934–45," *Holocaust and Genocide Studies* 5 (Fall 1990): 293–312.

43. Castendyck, Review of the European-Jewish Children's Aid, 43.

44. Lotte Marcuse to Mr. Siegfried Thorn, November 18, 1941, Folder 296, RG 249, YIVO, CJH.

45. For more on the reception and development of psychoanalysis in America, see Nathan Hale, *The Rise and Crisis of Psychoanalysis in the United States: Freud and the Americans, 1917–1985* (New York, 1995), 74–101; John H. Ehrenreich, *The Altruistic Imagination: A History of Social Work and Social Policy in the United States* (Ithaca, 1985), 60–65; James H. Capshew, *Psychologists on the March: Science, Practice, and Professional Identity in America 1929–1969* (Cambridge, 1999); Edith Kurzweil, *The Freudians: A Comparative Perspective* (New Haven, 1989), 23–27, 127–151.

46. Ehrenreich, *The Altruistic Imagination,* 60–65; Paul Lerner, *Hysterical Men: War, Psychiatry, and the Politics of Trauma in Germany, 1890–1930* (Ithaca, 2003), 24–30.

47. Cited in Ehrenrich, *The Altruistic Imagination,* 73.

48. Elsa Castendyck, "Origin and Services of the United States Commission for the Care of European Children," *The Child* 6 (July 1941): 6, Box 1, bMs 16029, Unitarian Service Committee Archive (USC).

49. Lotte Marcuse to Mr. Siegfried Thorn, November 18, 1941, Folder 296, RG 249, YIVO, CJH.

50. Lydia Murdoch, *Imagined Orphans: Poor Families, Child Welfare, and Contested Citizenship in London* (New Brunswick, 2006); Ivan Jablonka, *Ni père, ni mère: histoire des enfants de l'Assistance publique (1874–1939)* (Paris, 2006).

51. Letter to Miss Ostry, Montreal, Canada from Lotte Marcuse, July 18, 1941, Folder 302, YIVO, CJH.

52. Main Problems Concerning Employment and Vocational Training, 1948, 2, 43/AJ/593, Archives Nationales, Paris (AN).

53. Barbara Levy Simon, *The Empowerment Tradition in American Social Work: A History* (New York, 1994), 125.

54. Letter from Lotte Marcuse to Hanna Steiner, March 25, 1940, Folder 305, YIVO, CJH.

55. Hans Jürgenson, 1 Monat in Amerika, December 10, 1934, Folder 63, RG 249, YIVO, CJH. For an analysis of letters between family members during the Kindertransport, see Michael Geyer, "Virtue in Despair: A Family History

from the Days of the Kindertransports," *History & Memory* 17 (Spring/ Summer 2005): 323–365.

56. Deborah Portnoy, "The Adolescent Immigrant," *The Jewish Social Service Quarterly* 25 (December 1948): 272.

57. What's Happened to the Refugee Children, 5–6, June 1938, Folder 131, RG 249, YIVO, CJH.

58. Portnoy, "The Adolescent Immigrant," 269.

59. Letter from Lotte Marcuse to Hanna Steiner, March 25, 1940, Folder 305, YIVO, CJH.

60. Castendyck, Review of the European-Jewish Children's Aid, 18.

61. Letter from Jack Feller, Carton 7, Aleta Brownlee Papers, Hoover Archive (HA), Stanford University.

62. Letter from Doris Cybulski, April 19, 1950, Folder 406, RG 249, YIVO, CJH.

63. Ella Zwerdling and Grace Polansky, "Foster Home Placement of Refugee Children," *Journal of Social Casework* 30 (July 1949), 278; On problems with family reunification and placement in Holland, see Diane Wolf, *Beyond Anne Frank: Hidden Children and Postwar Families in Holland* (Berkeley, 2007). For more on the experiences of Jewish refugee children in the United States, see Beth B. Cohen, *Case Closed: Holocaust Survivors in Postwar America* (New Brunswick, 2007). On the reactions of the American Jewish community to Holocaust survivors see Hasia R. Diner, *We Remember with Reverence and Love: American Jews and the Myth of Silence after the Holocaust, 1945–62* (New York, 2009), 150–215.

64. Gertrude Dubinsky, Philadelphia, Folder 131, 1936, RG 249, YIVO, CJH.

65. Castendyck, Review of the European-Jewish Children's Aid, 47.

66. Deborah Portnoy, Los Angeles, 7/30/45, Folder 43, RG 249, YIVO, CJH.

67. Castendyck, Review of the European-Jewish Children's Aid, 43.

68. What's Happened to the Refugee Children, 8.

69. Castendyck, Review of the European-Jewish Children's Aid, 8–9, 44–46.

70. Hasia R. Diner, *The Jews of the United States, 1654–2000* (Berkeley, 2004), 285.

71. Letter from GJCA to Reichsvertretung der Juden in Deutschland, February 20, 1936, Folder 64, RG 249, YIVO, CJH.

72. H. Meyerowitz, Kaufer, Tusia, April 27, 1948, Folder 43, RG 249, YIVO, CJH.

73. Lotte Marcuse, Evaluation Schedules, May 28, 1945, Folder 584, RG 249, YIVO, CJH.

74. What's Happened to the Refugee Children, 9–10.

75. Marcel Kovarsky, "Case Work with Refugee Children," *The Jewish Social Service Quarterly* 24 (June 1948): 402–407. See also Morris H. Price, "Discussion on Adolescent Refugees," *The Jewish Social Science Quarterly* 24 (September 1947): 149.

76. Curio, *Verfolgung, Flucht, Rettung,* 154–155; On American anti-Semitism and the DP Act, see Haim Genizi, *America's Fair Share: The Admission and Resettlement of Displaced Persons, 1945–52* (Detroit, 1993), 66–111. On the the hierarchy of children over adults in British refugee policy, see Tony Kushner, *The Holocaust and the Liberal Imagination: A Social and Cultural History* (Oxford, 1994); On the place of children in Holocaust memory, Mark M. Anderson, "The Child Victim as Witness to the Holocaust: An American Story?" *Jewish Social Studies* 14 (Fall 2007): 1–22.

77. Hannelore Brenner-Wonschick, *Die Mädchen von Zimmer 28: Freundschaft, Hoffnung, und Überleben in Theresienstadt* (Munich, 2004), 60.

78. Stargardt, *Witnesses of War,* 420.

79. Kluger, *Still Alive,* 70.

80. Stargardt, *Witnesses of War,* 201.

81. Cited in Thelma Gruenbaum, *Nešarim: Child Survivors of Terezín* (London, 2004), 44.

82. Gruenbaum, *Nešarim,* 49

83. Brenner-Wonschick, *Die Mädchen von Zimmer 28,* 291.

84. Herbert Fischl, "This is Not a Gang, or Making a Movie in Our Town," in R. Elizabeth Novak, ed. *We are Children Just the Same: Vedem, the Secret Magazine by the Boys of Terezín* (Philadelphia, 1995), 128.

85. Kinder im Ghetto, September 12, 1943, inventarní čislo (i.č.) 300, Péče o mládež, Terezín, Jewish Museum of Prague.

86. Jana Reněe Friesová, *Fortress of My Youth: Memoir of a Terezín Survivor,* trans. Elinor Morrisby and Ladislav Rosendorf (Madison, 2002), 95.

87. Brenner-Wonschick, *Die Mädchen von Zimmer 28,* 209.

88. Egon Redlich, *The Terezin Diary of Gonda Redlich,* ed. Saul S. Friedmann, trans. Laurence Kutler (Lexington, 1992), 121. For more on children's art in Terezín, see Nicholas Stargardt, "Children's Art of the Holocaust," *Past & Present* 161, nr. 1 (1998): 191–235.

89. Stargardt, *Witnesses of War,* 208.

90. Deborah Dwork, *Children with a Star* (New Haven, 1991), 126. Stargardt, *Witnesses of War,* 205–210; Friesová, *Fortress of My Youth,* 101–102.

91. On Zionism in interwar Czechoslovakia, see Tatjana Liechtenstein, "Making Jews at Home: Zionism and the Construction of Jewish Nationality in Interwar Czechoslovakia," *East European Jewish Affairs* 36 (June 2006): 49–71.

92. Gruenbaum, *Nešarim,* 157–158; Saul S. Friedmann, "Introduction," in Redlich, *The Terezin Diary,* xii–xiii; Stargardt, "Children's Art," 211; Freisová, *Fortress of My Youth,* 98.

93. Dr. Maximilien Adler, "Utopie als Wirklichkeit," 2, in *Péče o mládež. Zprávy k. 1 výročí činnosti domovů v L417,* i.č. 304/1, Sbírka Terezín, Jewish Museum

in Prague. Contributions to the volume are ordered alphabetically rather than with page numbers.

94. On Korczak, see Barbara Engekling and Jacek Leociak, *The Warsaw Ghetto: A Guide to the Perished City,* trans. Emma Harris (New Haven, 2009), 317–321, quotation, 321.

95. Rosa Engländer, "Unsere Aufgabe, unser Weg," 1, *Péče o mládež,* g. See also Pepek Stiassný, no title, 1–3, *Péče o mládež,* dd.

96. "Report by Franta, 1942," cited in Gruenbaum, *Nešarim,* 27–32.

97. Dr. G. Bäuml, "Über positive Erziehung," 1, *Péče o mládež,* b.

98. Dr. Franz Kahn, "Der Paradox der jüdischen Erziehung," 2, *Péče o mládež,* o.

99. For Zionist perspectives on the education of youth in Terezín, see Dr. Desider Friedmann, "Die jüdische Schule," 1–2; Leo Janowitz, no title, 1; Dr. Franz Kahn, "Die Paradox der jüdischen Erziehung," 1–2; Prof. Israel Kestenbaum, "Jüdische Erziehung," 1–2, all in *Péčeo mládež.*

100. Ota (Gideon) Klein, "O tak zvané politické výchově mládeže," 1, *Péče o mládež,* r.

101. Redlich, *The Terezin Diary,* 77, 91.

102. Klein, "O tak zvané politické výchově," 2.

103. Redlich, *The Terezin Diary,* 121.

104. Jarka, "Úvodník," *Bonaco,* nr. 1 (1943), 2.

105. Sojka, "Mladý člověk v Terezíně," *Bonaco,* nr. 4 (1943), 2–3.

106. Kluger, *Still Alive,* 86.

107. Edith Ornstein, "Das Leben der Frau in Theresienstadt," 9, i.č. 159, Ústředí práce, pracovní nasazení, Terezín, Jewish Museum in Prague.

108. Brenner-Wonschick, *Die Mädchen von Zimmer 28,* 152–154.

109. Brenner-Wonschick, *Die Mädchen von Zimmer 28,* 315.

110. An additional 1,600 children under age 15 who evaded deportation were liberated in 1945.

111. "From the Deposition of Zeev Shek before the Commission for the Concentration Camp of Terezín, June 29, 1946," in *We Are Children Just the Same,* 30.

Chapter 3. A "Psychological Marshall Plan"

1. Howard Kershner, American Friends Service Committee in France, December 31, 1940, 3, American Friends Service Committee Archives (AFSC), Reel 73, Box 61, Folder 55, United States Holocaust Museum, Memorial and Archive (USHMMA).

2. Paul Lerner, *Hysterical Men: War, Psychiatry, and the Politics of Trauma in Germany, 1890–1930* (Ithaca, 2003), 24–30; Allen Young, *A Harmony of Illusions: Inventing Post-Traumatic Stress Disorder* (Princeton, 1995), 43–85.

3. As of June 30, 1947, UNNRA and had handled 22,058 cases of unaccompanied children. See Office of Statistics and Operational Reports, Unaccompanied Children in Austria and Germany, April 29, 1948, 43/AJ/604, AN. Another 6,000 unaccompanied children were repatriated or resettled by the IRO between 1948 and 1951.

4. Monnetier, June 2, 1946, Papanek Europe Tour, F-13, Ernst Papanek Collection, International Institute for Social History (IISH), Amsterdam.

5. UNRRA, "Psychological Problems of Displaced Persons," June 1945, JRU Cooperation with Other Relief Organizations, Wiener Library, 1.

6. Georges Heuyer, "Psychopathologie de l'enfance victime de la guerre," *Sauvegarde* 17 (January 1948), 3.

7. For an helpful overview of American psychoanalysis in the 1940s, see Nathan Hale, *The Rise and Crisis of Psychoanalysis in the United States: Freud and the Americans, 1917–1985* (New York, 1995); On British psychoanalysis, see Laura Lee Downs, "'A Very British Revolution?'" L'évacuation des enfants urbains vers les campagnes anglaises, 1939–1945," *Vingtième siècle* 89 (January–March 2006): 47–60; Denise Riley, *War in the Nursery: Theories of the Child and the Mother* (London, 1983); Michal Shapira, "The War Inside: Child Psychoanalysis and Remaking the Self in Britain, 1930–60," (Ph.D diss., Rutgers University, 2009).

8. Francesca M. Wilson, *In the Margins of Chaos: Recollections of Relief Work in and Between Three Wars* (New York, 1945), 293; Elizabeth Borgwardt, *A New Deal for the World. America's Vision for Human Rights* (Cambridge, MA, 2005), 119; G. Daniel Cohen, "Between Relief and Politics: Refugee Humanitarianism in Occupied Germany, 1945–46," *Journal of Contemporary History* 43 (July 2008): 438.

9. Ben Shepard, "'Becoming Planning Minded': The Theory and Practice of Relief, 1940–45," *Journal of Contemporary History* 43 (July 2008): 410; Jessica Rheinisch, "Introduction: Relief in the Aftermath of War," *Journal of Contemporary History* 43 (July 2008): 371–404.

10. On high modernism, see James C. Scott, *Seeing Like a State: How Certain Schemes to Improve the Human Condition Have Failed* (Yale, 1998); Amir Weiner, ed. *Landscaping the Human Garden: Twentieth-Century Population Management in a Comparative Perspective* (Stanford, 2003).

11. Borgwardt, *A New Deal for the World,* 119.

12. Wilson, *In the Margins of Chaos,* 293.

13. Cohen, "Between Relief and Politics," 439.

14. Ibid., 437; Shepard, "'Becoming Planning Minded'," 411; Hitchcock, *The Bitter Road to Freedom,* 220.

15. George Woodbridge, *UNRRA: The History of the United Nations Relief and Rehabilitation Administration* (New York, 1950), 417, 418.

16. Wilson, *In the Margins of Chaos*, 304.
17. Aleta Brownlee, "Whose Children?" 7, Folder 1, Box 9, Aleta Brownlee Collection, Folder 1, Box 9, Hoover Archive (HA), Stanford University.
18. Susan T. Pettiss with Lynn Taylor, *After the Shooting Stopped: The Story of an UNRRA Welfare Worker in Germany, 1945–47* (Victoria, BC, 2004), 8.
19. Wilson, *In the Margins of Chaos*, 306, 304.
20. Pettiss, *After the Shooting Stopped*, 8.
21. Brownlee, "Whose Children," 2.
22. On the concept of totalitarianism, see Hannah Arendt, *The Origins of Totalitarianism* (New York, 1951).
23. For an approach emphasizing the individualist strain in Nazi ideology and policy, see Moritz Föllmer, "Was Nazism Collectivistic? Redefining the Individual in Berlin, 1933–45," *Journal of Modern History* 82 (March 2010): 61–100.
24. USC Child & Youth Programs, Helen Fogg—Child Care Program Prospectus 1951, 2, bMS-16036-3, Unitarian Service Committee Archive (USC), Andover Theological Library (ATL), Cambridge, MA.
25. Eric Fromm, "Theoretische Entwürfe über Autorität und Familie," in *Studien über Autroität und Familie* (Paris, 1936), 85.
26. Joseph Goldstein, Anna Freud, et. al, *Beyond the Best Interests of the Child* (New York, 1973).
27. Erika Mann, *School for Barbarians* (New York, 1938), 29.
28. Bertolt Brecht, "Der Spitzel," in *Furcht und Elend des III Reiches* (New York, 1945), 61–70. Translated by Eric Bentley as *The Master Race* (New York, 1944), 71–84.
29. Alfred Brauner, *Ces enfants ont vécu la guerre* (Paris, 1946), 182. On the mythic narrative of the child informant Pavel Morozov in the Soviet Union, see Catriona Kelly, *Comrade Pavlik: The Rise and Fall of a Soviet Boy Hero* (London, 2005).
30. On the relationship between imagined public and private spheres and citizenship in liberal and republican thought, see Isabel Hull, *Sexuality, State and Civil Society in Germany, 1700–1815* (Ithaca, 1996); Carole Pateman, *The Sexual Contract* (Palo Alto, CA, 1988).
31. On the "return to normality," see Richard Bessel and Dirk Schumann, "Introduction: Violence, Normality, and the Construction of Postwar Europe," in idem. eds., *Life After Death: Approaches to a Cultural and Social History of Europe During the 1940s and 1950s* (New York, 2003), 1–15.
32. Jean Henshaw, Report on International Children's Center, Prien, April 28, 1947. S-0437-0012, United Nations Archive (UN), New York.
33. Charlotte Helman, "La rapatriement des enfants de Bergen-Belsen," in Marie-Anne Matard-Bonucci and Edouard Lynch, eds. *La libération des camps et le retour des déportés* (Paris, 1995), 157.

34. Kathryn Hulme, *The Wild Place* (Boston, 1953), 124.

35. Atina Grossmann, *Jews, Germans, and Allies: Close Encounters in Occupied Germany* (Princeton, 2007), 184–236; Herman Stein, "Welfare and Child Care Needs of European Jewry," *Jewish Social Service Quarterly* 25 (March 1948): 302.

36. Louise W. Holborn, *The International Refugee Organization: A Specialized Agency of the United Nations. Its History and Work* (New York, 1956), 501.

37. Gunnar Dybwad, "Child Care in Germany," Unitarian Service Committee Pamphlet, 1951, bMs 16036-4, USC.

38. Frances Burns, "Germans say war didn't upset their nerves, but blood pressure and ulcers contradict them," *Boston Daily Globe,* October 1, 1949, bMs 16036-4, USC.

39. Prospectus 1951, 1, bMS-16036-3, USC.

40. Report #2, Helen Fogg—Germany, Institute 1950, bMs 16036-4, USC.

41. UNRRA, "Psychological Problems of Displaced Persons," 2.

42. Thérèse Brosse, *War-Handicapped Children: Report on the European Situation* (Paris, 1950), 12, 24.

43. Dorothy Macardle, *Children of Europe: A Study of the Childen of Liberated Countries, their Wartime Experiences, their Reactions, and their Needs* (Boston, 1951), 270.

44. On debates over familialist and collectivist solutions for Jewish children and youth, see Daniella Doron, "In the Best Interest of the Child: Family, Youth, and Identity in Postwar France, 1944–1954," (Ph.D diss., New York University, 2009).

45. On the OSE and hidden children in France during and after the war, see Shannon Fogg, *The Politics of Everyday Life in Vichy France: Foreigners, Undesirables, and Strangers* (New York, 2009), 151–187; Sabine Zeitoun, *L'Oeuvre de secours aux enfants sous l'Occupation en France, du légalisme à la résistance, 1940–44* (Paris, 1990); Katy Hazan, *Le Sauvetage des enfants juifs pendant l'Occupation, dans les maisons de l'OSE* (Paris, 2008); Vivette Samuel, *Sauver les enfants* (Paris, 1995); Doron, "In the Best Interest"; Katy Hazan, *Les orphelins de la Shoah: les maisons de l'espoir (1944–1960)* (Paris, 2000).

46. On the formation of the Central Committee, see David Engel, "The Reconstruction of Jewish Communal Institutions in Postwar Poland: The Origins of the Central Committee of Polish Jews, 1944–45," *East European Politics and Societies* 10 (December 1995): 85–107; Avinoam Patt, *Finding Home and Homeland: Jewish Youth and Zionism in the Aftermath of the Holocaust* (Detroit, 2009), 72–74.

47. Sprawozdanie z Wydziału Opieki nad Dzieckiem, February 5, 1946; Sprawozdanie z działności Centralnego Wydziału Opieki nad Dzieckiem,

July 20, 1946, 303-IX-9; Sprawozdanie z Pracy Wydziału Szkolnego za rok kalendarzowy 1946, 303-IX-10, RG-15.078M, USHMMA.

48. Ernst Papanek, "The Child as Refugee. My Experiences with Fugitive Children in Europe," *The Nervous Child* 2 nr. 4 (1943): 302, Folder Ernst Papanek, Papanek Collection, International Institute for Social History (IISH).

49. Ernst Papanek, "The Montmorency Period of the Child-Care Program of the OSE," in *Fight for the Health of the Jewish People (50 Years of OSE)* (New York, 1968), 119, Folder D13, Papanek Collection, IISH; Papanek, "The Child as Refugee," 307.

50. On individualism and collectivism in the Austrian school reform movement see John Boyer, *Culture and Political Crisis in Vienna* (Chicago, 1995), 46–55, 174–186; Malachi Hacohen, *Karl Popper—The Formative Years, 1902–1945: Politics and Philosophy in Interwar Vienna* (Cambridge, 2000), 107–116.

51. Ernst Papanek, "Contributions of Individual Psychology to Social Work," *American Journal of Individual Psychology* 11, nr. 2 (1955): 146.

52. Ernst Papanek (with Edward Linn), *Out of the Fire* (New York, 1975), 221–222.

53. Papanek, "The Child as Refugee," 302.

54. No author, *OSE France—Homes d'enfants 1946* (Paris, 1946); OSE—Union 1946/1947 its Work and Program, Paris, May 12, 1947, 1, Box 26, Reel 1, OSE, USHMMA.

55. On the Buchenwald boys, see Doron, "In the Best Interest," 239–268; Katy Hazan and Éric Ghozian, eds. *A la vie! Les enfants de Buchenwald, du shtetl à l'OSE* (Paris, 2005); Judith Hemmendinger, *Survivors: Children of the Holocaust* (Bethesda, 1986).

56. Jacques Bloch, "L'assistance aux enfants juifs, son organisation et ses problèmes," September 18, 1946, 2, Box 26, Reel 1, OSE, USHMMA.

57. "La situation des populations juives indigentes à la liberation de la France," 4, Box 26, Reel 1, OSE, USHMMA.

58. Sprawozdanie Wzdziału Opieki nad Dzieckiem CKZWP za rok 1946, 303-IX-9, RG-15.078M, CKŻP, USHMMA.

59. Organizacja pracy wzchowawczej w Domu Dziecka, December 12, 1947, 303-IX-67, RG-15.078M, USHMMA; *Lendemains OSE, par les jeunes, pour les jeunes,* January 1947 (Paris, 2000), 16.

60. On restitution in postwar France, see Maud S. Mandel, *In the Aftermath of Genocide: Armenians and Jews in Twentieth-Century France* (Durham, NC, 2003), 52–86; Leora Auslander, "Coming Home? Jews in Postwar Paris," *Journal of Contemporary History* 40 (April 2005): 237–259.

61. "La situation des populations juives indigentes à la liberation de la France," 5–6, Box 26, Reel 1, OSE, USHMMA.

62. Eleonora Heit, letter to CKŻP, November 9, 1948, 303-IX-83, RG.15–078M, USHMMA.

63. Wytyczne, Warsaw, July 10, 1945, 303-IX-3, RG-15.078M, USHMMA.

64. Sprawozdanie z działności Poradni Pyschologicznej za rok 1946, 303-IX-134, RG-15.078M, USHMMA.

65. Organizacja pracy; Sprawozdanie z działnoci Poradni Pyschologicznej za rok 1946, 303-IX-134, both in RG.15–078M, USHMMA.

66. *Lendemains,* January 1947, 12.

67. Ibid., 13.

68. Ernst Jablonski (Jouhy), "Le problème pédagogique des jeunes de buchenwald," in *Les enfants de Buchenwald* ed. Eugene Minkowski (Geneva, 1946), 63.

69. *Lendemains,* January 1947, 16–17.

70. Ibid., 13–15.

71. Ibid., 18

72. *Lendemains,* February 1947, 13.

73. Organizacja pracy.

74. See Mark Mazower, *Dark Continent: Europe's Twentieth Century* (New York, 2000); Tony Judt, *Postwar: A History of Europe Since 1945* (New York, 2005).

75. Thomas Buergenthal, *A Lucky Child* (London, 2009), 134–143.

76. No author, *Des enfants dans leur maison* (Sèvres, 1951), 5.

77. Ibid., 9.

78. Laura Lee Downs, *Childhood in the Promised Land: Working-Class Movements and the Colonies de Vacances in France, 1880–1960* (Durham, NC, 2002).

79. On collectivist modes of education in Europe between the wars, Catriona Kelly, *Children's World: Growing up in Russia, 1890–1991* (New Haven, 2007); Edward Ross Dickinson, *The Politics of German Child Welfare from the Empire to the Federal Republic* (Cambridge, Mass., 1996); Downs, *Childhood;* Zahra, *Kidnapped Souls: National Indifference and the Battle for Children in the Bohemian Lands, 1945–48* (Ithaca, 2008).

80. Myra Kaplan, "L'expérience familiale et l'expérience collective," *Lendemains,* May–June 1947, 4–6.

81. Complaint of Yugoslav Leaders, November 14, 1945, S-0437-0016, United Nations Archive (UN).

82. Yvonne de Jong, Quels sont les principaux problèmes concernant les enfants réfugiés? 43/AJ/599, AN.

83. Current Problems Relating to Children in the German Field of Operations, April, 1946, 5, S-401-3-10, UN.

84. On gendered experiences of the Holocaust and displacement during World War II and after, see Grossmann, *Germans, Jews, and Allies;* Gisela Bock, ed. *Genozid und Geschlecht. Jüdische Frauen im nationalsozialistischen Lagersystem*

(Frankfurt/Main, 2005); Katherine R. Jolluck, *Exile and Identity: Polish Women in the Soviet Union during World War II* (Pittsburgh, 2002).

85. Uwagi do sprawozdania z transportu XXV, Katowice, January 7, 1947, Folder 316, Generalny Pełnomocnik Rzadu RP do Spraw Repatriacji w Warszawie, Archiwum Akt Nowych (AAN), Warsaw.

86. Pieter Lagrou, *The Legacy of Nazi Occupation. Patriotic Memory and National Recovery in Western Europe, 1945–61* (New York, 2000), 144–156; Megan Koreman, *Expectation of Justice: France, 1944–46* (Durham, NC, 1999), 84–85.

87. Rapport sur l'activité sociale du Gau Berlin vis à vis des femmes françaises enceintes, September 25, 1947, Folder PDR 5/10, Bureau des Archives de l'Occupation française en Allemagne et en Autriche, Colmar (MAE-Colmar).

88. Edith Ornstein, "Die arbeitende Frau in Theresienstadt," Lecture, 1944, 4–6, 12, inventarní čislo 159, Terezín Collection, Jewish Museum in Prague.

89. Progress Report of the Working Party on Special Needs of Women and Girls, 8–11, 9/F/ 3292, AN.

90. Report on Visits to Child Welfare Centers of UNRRA, June 1946, 5, File F-13, Papanek Collection, IISH.

91. Vinita Lewis, Field Visit to Aglasterhausen Children, September 8, 1948, 5–6, 43/AJ/599, AN.

92. Joseph Weill, Remarques sur le rôle des organisations privés et assistance sur l'oeuvre de reconstruction de l'après guerre, 3, Box 23, Reel 22, OSE, USHMMA.

93. Similar tropes can also be seen in colonial psychiatry. See Richard C. Keller, *Colonial Madness: Psychiatry in French North Africa* (Chicago, 2007); Lynette Jackson, *Surfacing Up: Psychiatry and Social Order in Colonial Zimbabwe* (Ithaca, 2005). On the developmental logic underpinning psychoanalysis, see Carolyn Steedman, *Strange Dislocations: Childhood and the idea of Human Interiority* (Cambridge, Mass., 1995); John R. Morss, *The Biologising of Childhood* (New York, 1990).

94. J. Wolf-Machoel, *La Réadaptation de la jeunesse et des déracinés de guerre* (Boudry, 1945), 27–29.

95. For French debates on wartime and postwar juvenile delinquency, see Sarah Fishman, *The Battle for Children: World War II, Youth Crime, and Juvenile Justice in Twentieth Century France* (Cambridge, Mass., 2002); Robert Jobs, *Riding the New Wave: Youth and the Rejuvenation of France after the Second World War* (Stanford, 2007), 141–185.

96. Simone Marcus-Jeisler, "Réponse a l'enquête sur les effets psychologiques de la guerre sur les enfants et jeunes en France," *Sauvegarde* 8 (February 1947): 6. On anxieties about the return of French POWs after World War II, see Kristen Stromberg Childers, *Fathers, Families, and the State in France,*

1914–45 (Ithaca, 2003), 136–140. On conflicts accompanying the return of POWs in Germany, Robert C. Moeller, *Protecting Motherhood: Women and the Family in the Politics of Postwar West Germany* (Berkeley, 1993), 28–31; Frank Biess, *Homecomings: Returning POWs and the Legacies of Defeat in Postwar Germany* (Princeton, 2006).

97. Jeisler, "Réponse a l'enquête," 10.

98. Gwendolen Chesters, Some Findings on the Needs of Displaced Children, June 25, 1948, Paper presented at meeting of directors of children's villages, Trogen, Switzerland, July 4–11, 1948. http://unesdoc.unesco.org (Accessed May 12, 2010).

99. Robert Job, "Our Pupils in France," *OSE Mail* 4 (August 1949), 53–55, 43/ AJ/1268, AN.

100. Report on International Children's Center, Prien, April 28, 1947, S-0437-0012, UN.

101. Hemmendinger, *Survivors,* 21.

102. Monsieur Jouhy, 1947, Box 20, Reel 20, OSE, USHMMA.

103. UNRRA, "Psychological Problems of Displaced Persons," 35.

104. Robert Job, "Our Pupils in France," *OSE Mail* 4 (August 1949), 53–55, 43/ AJ/1268, AN.

105. UNRRA, "Psychological Problems of Displaced Persons," 3–4, 38.

106. Robert Collis, *The Lost and Found: The Story of Eva and Laszlo, Two Children of War-Torn Europe* (New York, 1953), 5.

107. Ibid., 71.

Chapter 4. Renationalizing Displaced Children

1. On the ideological origins of the UN Convention and Declaration, see Mark Mazower, *No Enchanted Palace: The End of Empire and the Ideological Origins of the United Nations* (Princeton, 2009).

2. See Robert van Krieken, "The 'stolen generations' and cultural genocide: the forced removal of Australian Indigenous children from their families and its implications for the sociology of childhood," *Childhood* 6 (August 1999): 297–311; Isabel Heinemann, "Until the Last Drop of Good Blood": the Kidnapping of "Racially Valuable" Children and Nazi Racial Policy in Occupied Eastern Europe," in A. Dirk Moses, ed. *Genocide and Settler Society: Frontier Violence and Stolen Children in Australian History* (New York, 2004), 244–267. On debates about transnational and transracial adoption in other contexts, see Linda Gordon, *The Great Arizona Orphan Abduction* (Cambridge, Mass., 1999); Heide Fehrenbach, *Race After Hitler: Black Occupation Children in Postwar Germany and America* (Princeton, 2005).

3. Policy on Unaccompanied Children, May 27, 1949, 43/AJ/926, AN.

4. John Cooper, *Raphael Lemkin and the Struggle for the Genocide Convention* (New York, 2008), 157–158.

5. Raphael Lemkin, *Axis Rule in Occupied Europe: Laws of Occupation—Analysis of Government—Proposals for Redress* (Washington, D.C., 1944), 79.

6. Mazower, *No Enchanted Palace,* 104–149.

7. Cited in Cooper, *Raphael Lemkin,* 158.

8. Mazower, *No Enchanted Palace,* 19–22, 28–65, 104–148, quotation, 8. Samuel Moyn also argues persuasively that the concept of human rights in the 1940s was not intended to challenge the sanctity of the nation-state. Samuel Moyn, *The Last Utopia: Human Rights in History* (Cambridge, MA, 2010), 44-84.

9. Mazower, *No Enchanted Palace,* 149–189.

10. Susan T. Pettiss with Lynne Taylor, *After the Shooting Stopped: The Story of an UNRRA Welfare Worker in Germany, 1945–47* (Victoria, BC, 2004), 5–6.

11. Joseph Weill, Remarques sur le rôle des organisations privés, 1, Box 23, Reel 22, OSE, United States Holocaust Memorial, Museum and Archive (USHMMA).

12. Brochure, "Children Without a Country to Become World Citizens." 43/ AJ/597, Archives nationales, Paris (AN).

13. Thérèse Brosse, *War-Handicapped Children: Report on the European Situation* (Paris, 1950), 96, 12.

14. Akira Iriye, *Global Community: The Role of International Organizations in the Making of the Contemporary World* (Berkeley, 2002), 40–52. See also Elizabeth Borgwardt, *A New Deal for the World: America's Vision for Human Rights* (Cambridge, MA, 2005).

15. For numbers, see Ewa Morawska, "Intended and Unintended Consequences of Forced Migrations: A Neglected Aspect of East Europe's Twentieth Century History," *International Migration Review* 34 (June 2000): 1049–1087; Joseph B. Schechtmann, *Postwar Population Transfers in Europe, 1945–1955* (Philadelphia, 1962), vii.

16. On retaliation against female fraternizers, Fabrice Virgili, *Shorn Women: Gender and Punishment in Liberation France* (New York, 2002); Perry Biddiscombe, "The Anti-Fraternization Movement in the U.S. Occupation Zones of Germany and Austria, 1945–48," *Journal of Social History* 34 (Spring 2001): 611–47; Benjamin Frommer, *National Cleansing: Retribution Against Nazi Collaborators in Postwar Czechoslovakia* (New York, 2005).

17. On the nationalization of DPs and refugees, Avinoam Patt, *Finding Home and Homeland: Jewish Youth and Zionism in the Aftermath of the Holocaust* (Detroit, 2009); G. Daniel Cohen, "The Politics of Recognition: Jewish Refugees in Relief Polices and Human Rights Debates, 1945–50," *Immigrants and Minorities* 24 (July 2006): 125–143; Pamela Ballinger, "Borders of the Nation, Borders of Citizenship: Repatriation and the Definition of National

Identity after World War II," *Comparative Studies in Society and History* 49 (July 2007): 713–741; Liisa Malkki, *Purity and Exile: Violence, Memory, and National Cosmology among Hutu Refugees in Tanzania* (Chicago, 1995).

18. Hannah Arendt, *The Origins of Totalitarianism* (New York, 1951), 292.

19. On DP internationalism, see Anna Holian, "Displacement and the Postwar Reconstruction of Education: Displaced Persons at the UNRRA University of Munich," *Contemporary European History* 17 (May 2008): 167–195.

20. James P. Rice, AJDC, Steiermark and Upper Austria, October 4, 1945, RG 294.4, DP Camps—Austria, Reel 1, Folder 5, YIVO, Center for Jewish History (CJH)—New York; Richard Bessel, *Germany 1945: From War to Peace* (New York, 2009), 266.

21. On the Harrison Report, see Grossmann, *Jews, Germans, and Allies: Close Encounters in Occupied Germany* (Princeton, 2007), 140–142. In the British zone Jews were not separated from other refugees of their nationality. See Hagit Lavsky, *New Beginnings: Jewish Survivors in Bergen-Belsen and the British Zone of Germany, 1945–50* (Detroit, 2002).

22. Pettiss, *After the Shooting Stopped*, 62.

23. On children as nationalist property in East Central Europe before 1945, see Tara Zahra, *Kidnapped Souls: National Indifference and the Battle for Children in the Bohemian Lands, 1900–48* (Ithaca, 2008).

24. On national ambiguity in Eastern Europe see Chad Bryant, *Prague in Black: Nazi Rule and Czech Nationalism* (Cambridge, MA, 2007); Pieter M. Judson, *Guardians of the Nation: Activists on the Language Frontier of Imperial Austria* (Cambridge, MA, 2006); Timothy Snyder, *The Reconstruction of Nations: Poland, Ukraine, Lithuania, Belarus, 1569–1999* (New Haven, 2003); Tara Zahra, "Imagined Noncommunities: National Indifference as a Category of Historical Analysis," *Slavic Review* 69 (Spring 2010): 93–119.

25. An St.A.40/Jugendamt, 46, January 13, 1941, Folder 10, Reel 7, Stadtverwaltung Litzmannstadt, USHMMA.

26. Beschluss, Amtsgericht Litzmannstadt, Folder 12, Reel 7, Stadtverwaltung Litzmannstadt, USHMMA.

27. *Trials of War Criminals Before the Nürnberg Military Tribunals* vol. 4 (Washington, 1950), 1007.

28. N. St. M IV C-35 j/43 g. An den SS Standartenführer Dr. Brandt von Deutsche Staatsminister für Böhmen und Mähren, June 13, 1944. NS 19/345, Bundesarchiv Berlin. For more on Nazi Germanization policies in the Bohemian Lands, see Zahra, *Kidnapped Souls*, chapters 6–8; Chad Bryant, *Prague in Black: Nazi Rule and Czech Nationalism* (Cambridge, MA, 2007).

29. Dorothy Macardle, *Children of Europe: A Study of the Children of Liberated Countries, Their Wartime Experiences, Their Reactions, and Their Needs* (Boston, 1951), 54–56.

30. Isabel Heinemann, *"Rasse, Siedlung, deutsches Blut": Die Rasse und Sied-lungshauptamt der SS und die rassenpolitische Neuordnung Europas* (Göttingen, 2003), 508–509.

31. Memorandum concernant le problème de la revendication et du rapatriement des enfants polonais, 1948, 43/AJ/798, AN.

32. Mark Mazower, "The Strange Triumph of Human Rights, 1933–1950," *The Historical Journal* 47 (Spring 2004): 386–388.

33. Displaced Orphan Children in Europe, November 13, 1946, 43/AJ/45, AN.

34. Jevgenija Migla, Comments on the guardianship problem of unaccompanied children, March 5, 1948, 43/AJ/926, AN.

35. Report on International Children's Center, Prien, April 28, 1947, S-0437-0012, United Nations Archive (UN).

36. Thérèse Brosse, *Homeless Children* (Paris, 1950), 24.

37. W. R. Corti, "A few thoughts on the children's village," *News Bulletin of the Pestalozzi Children's Village* (May 1948), 9, 43/AJ/599, AN.

38. Brosse, *War-Handicapped Children*, 21–22.

39. H. Weitz, Child Searching in the French Zone, Innsbruck, April 1, 1947, Box 1, Aleta Brownlee Papers, Hoover Archive (HA), Stanford University.

40. W. C. Huyssoon, "Who is this Child," File 11, S-0437-0013, UN.

41. Ballinger, "Borders of the Nation," 713–741.

42. Removal of Children (Polish) from the St. Joseph's Kinderheim, October 14, 1946, File 16, S-0437-0013, UN.

43. In the Matter of the Resettlement of Therese Strasinkaite aka Tamara Sharkov, Box 15, District Courts: Children's Resettlement Case Files, 1949–54, 278/350/902/49/3, National Archives and Research Administration, College Park (NARA).

44. Case 52-RR-1, Josette Claude Phellipeau, Box 21, District Courts: Children's Resettlement Case Files, 1949–54, 278/350/902/49/3, NARA. For a fiction-alized account of a similar "anthropological investigation," see Hans-Ulrich Treichel, *Lost,* trans. Carol Brown Janeway (New York, 2001).

45. Jean Henshaw, Report on International Children's Center, Prien, April 28, 1947, S-0437-0012, UN.

46. Yvonne de Jong, Quels sont les principaux problèmes concernant les enfants réfugiés? June 1948, 43/AJ/599, AN.

47. Daily Log of October 19th, 21st, from District Child Search Officer Eileen Davidson, S-0437-0014, UN.

48. Provisional order nr. 75 and the British Zone Policy, November 9, 1948, 43/AJ/599, AN.

49. Similar arguments shaped German debates about the future of children born to African-American soldiers and German women in occupied Germany. See Fehrenbach, *Race After Hitler.*

50. Eileen Davidson, Removal from German families of Allied Children, February 21, 1948, 7, 43/AJ/599, AN.

51. Aleta Brownlee, "Whose Children?" 262–264, Box 9, Folder 1, Brownlee Papers, Hoover Archive (HA).

52. Davidson, Removal from German Families, 11–12.

53. Brownlee, "Whose Children?" 160.

54. Ibid., 14.

55. Michael Marrus, *The Unwanted: European Refugees in the Twentieth Century* (New York, 1985), 313–317; Tony Judt, *Postwar: A History of Europe Since 1945* (New York, 2005), 22; On anti-Semitism in postwar Poland, Jan Gross, *Fear: Anti-Semitism in Poland After Auschwitz* (Princeton, 2006).

56. Thomas Buergenthal, *A Lucky Child* (London, 2009), 142–143.

57. Patt, *Finding Home and Homeland*, 68–106.

58. Memo from Dr. Hirshzorn to Prezydium CKŻP, November 13, 1946, 303-IX-714, RG-15.078M, Centralny Komitet Żydów w Polsce, Wydział Oświaty (CKŻP), USHMMA.

59. Sprawozdanie Wzdziału Opieki nad Dzieckiem CKZWP za rok 1946, 303-IX-9, RG-15.078M, CKŻP, USHMMA.

60. Kalman Wolnerman, Repatriacji z Niemiec, June 2, 1947, 303-IX-692, RG-15.078M, CKŻP, USHMMA.

61. Letter from Pepi Neufeld to the Polish Red Cross, November 18, 1947, 303-IX-694, RG-15078M, CKŻP, USHMMA.

62. Letter from Cornelia Heise (UNRRA) to Pepi Neufeld, December 5, 1947, 303-IX-693; Letter from CKŻP to Kalman Wolnerman, September 19, 1947, 303-IX-694, RG-15078M, CKŻP, USHMMA.

63. For details on the conflict, see see Margaret Myers Feinstein, *Holocaust Survivors in Postwar Germany, 1945–57* (New York, 2010), 159–198, quotation, 173.

64. Minutes of Jewish Child Care Committee held at UNRRA US Zone Headquarters, Heidelberg, March 13, 1947, S-0437-0012, UN; Jewish Children, February 22, 1947, S-0437-0015, UN.

65. Documentation of Jewish children proposed for emigration to Palestine, March 17, 1948, 43/AJ/604, AN.

66. Marie Syrkin, *The State of the Jews* (Washington, DC, 1980), 26–27.

67. On the debate about the extent of Zionist sentiment among Jewish DPs, see especially Patt, *Finding Home and Homeland;* Zeev W. Mankowitz, *Life Between Memory and Hope: the Survivors of the Holocaust in Occupied Germany* (Cambridge, UK, 2002); Grossmann, *Jews, Germans, and Allies,* 158–159, 178–181, 249–251.

68. Feuereisen, Edith, March 9, 1946, 16, Folder 564, RG 249, YIVO, Center for Jewish History (CJH).

69. Patt, *Finding Home and Homeland,* 66–67; 161–162, quotation, 162.

70. Robert Collis, *The Lost and Found: The Story of Eva and Laszlo, Two Children of War-Torn Europe* (New York, 1953), 4.

71. On the myth of Jewish silence after the Holocaust, see Daniella Doron, "In the Best Interest of the Child: Family, Youth, and Identity Among Postwar French Jews, 1944–54," (Ph.D diss., New York University, 2009); Maud Mandel, *In the Aftermath of Genocide: Armenians and Jews in Twentieth Century France* (Durham, NC, 2003); Hasia R. Diner, *We Remember with Reverence and Love: American Jews and the Myth of Silence after the Holocaust, 1945–62* (New York, 2009).

72. Michael Marrus, "The Vatican and the Custody of Child Survivors after the Holocaust," *Holocaust and Genocide Studies* 21 (Winter 2007): 388.

73. Summary—Memorandum in Yiddish from the Central Zionist Coordination Committee in Poland, April 12, 1946; Meeting on Poland, September 22, 1947, both in 45/54 #741 Poland, Children: General, JDC Archive, NYC. On Jewish children in postwar Poland, see Joanna B. Michlic, "Who Am I? Jewish Children's Search for Identity in Postwar Poland, 1945–49," *Polin* 20 (2007): 98–121. On efforts to recuperate hidden children in Holland, see Diane Wolf, *Beyond Anne Frank: Jewish Families in Postwar Holland* (Berkeley, 2007). On custody disputes in postwar France, see Doron, "In the Best Interest," 99–152.

74. Ciekawe Wypadki, CKŻP, 303-IX-671, RG-15.078M, CKŻP, USHMMA.

75. Wykaz dzieci, ktore nalezy odebrać od opienkunów Polaków, March 29, 1946, 303-IX-663, RG-15.078M, CKŻP, USHMMA.

76. Correspondence avec l'AJDC, WIZO, Centre de documentation juive contemporaine (CDJC), Paris.

77. Marrus, "The Vatican," 385.

78. Ibid., 392.

79. On the Finaly affair, see Joyce Block Lazarus, *In the Shadow of Vichy: The Finaly Affair* (New York, 2008); Catherine Poujol, *Les enfants cachés: L'affaire Finaly* (Paris, 2006); Katy Hazan, *Les orphelins de la Shoah* (Paris, 2000), 92–100; Doron, "In the Best Interest," 132–149.

80. Copie de la lettre de Mlle Brun à Mme Fischer, Novembre 1945, Kap-Fi, Box 2, CDJC.

81. On the role of the Vatican and the custody of child survivors, see Marrus, "The Vatican," 378–403.

82. "L'un des enfants Finaly serait mort," *Combat,* March 21, 1953, Box 3, Kap-Fi, CDJC.

83. Sous dossier Courrièrs non-datés, Letter from Alexandre Kogan to Grand Rabbi Kaplan, Box 1, Kap-FI, CDJC.

84. Lazarus, *In the Shadow,* 37.

85. Maurice Carr to Grand Rabbi Jacob Kaplan, February 8, 1953, Box 1, Kap-Fi, CDJC.

86. Discours de Maurice Garçon, June 22, 1953, Box 1, Kap-Fi, CDJC.

87. Mythe de l'attachement maternal de Mlle Brun, February 12, 1953, Box 1, Kap-Fi, CDJC.

88. "La mère spirituelle au-dessus des lois?" *Franc-tireur,* February 11, 1953, Box 3, Kap-Fi, CDJC.

89. "Un déclaration des avocats de Mlle Brun," *La Croix,* February 13, 1953, Box 3, Kap-Fi, CDJC.

90. Paul Levy, "Il est impossible d'arracher à mademoiselle Brun Robert et Gérald Finaly," *Aux écoutes,* May 2, 1953, Box 3, Kap-Fi, CDJC.

91. Discours Kaplan, March 31, 1953, Ce qui est en jeu dans l'affaire Finaly. Box 4, Kap-Fi, CDJC.

92. Letter to Grand Rabbi Jacob Kaplan, June 6, 1953, Box 1, Kap-Fi, CDJC.

93. Paul Benichou, "Réflexions sur 'l'Affaire,'" *Le Monde,* March 1 & 2, 1953, Box 3, Kap-Fi, CDJC.

94. Letter to Gérard and Robert, published in *La Semaine Juive,* February 26, 1953, 1–2. Box 3, Kap-Fi, CDJC.

95. Letters from Gérard and Robert, Paris, June 30, 1953, Box 1, Kap-Fi, CDJC.

96. Felix Goldschmidt, Rapport strictement confidentiel, July 27, 1953, 1–2, Box 1, Kap-Fi, CDJC.

97. Letter from Robert Finaly to M. and Mme Weil, July 29, 1954, Box 1, Kap-Fi, CDJC.

98. Note pour Monsieur le Ministre, Febuary 16, 1953, 7/F/16088, AN. On the conversion of hidden children, see also Deborah Dwork, *Children with a Star: Jewish Youth in Nazi Europe* (New Haven, 1993), 96–109.

99. M. Vigne à M. Rousseau, December 23, 1948, 7/F/16088, AN.

100. Letter from Paulette Zujdman to Rousseau, February 17, 1948, 7/F/16088, AN.

101. Doron, "In the Best Interest," 20. On republican narratives of French national heroism and suffering during the war, see Henry Rousso, *The Vichy Syndrome: History and Memory in France Since 1944* trans. Arthur Goldhammer (Boston, 1991); Pieter Lagrou, *The Legacy of Nazi Occupation: Patriotic Memory and National Recovery in Western Europe, 1945–1965* (New York, 2000); Megan Koreman, *The Expectation of Justice: France, 1944–1946* (Durham, NC, 1999).

102. Letter from Léon Weiss to Monsieur Delahoche, July 30, 1948, 7/F/16088, AN.

103. Sarah Kofman, *Rue Ordener, Rue Labat,* trans. Ann Smock (Lincoln, 1996), 47.

104. Ibid., 57.

105. Ibid., 58–61.
106. On the status of Jews as both exceptional and paradigmatic refugees after World War II, see Cohen, "The Politics of Recognition," 125–143.
107. Arendt, *Origins*, 299.

Chapter 5. Children as Spoils of War in France

1. Conférence de presse de M. Pierre Pfimlin, April 5, 1946, 80/AJ/75, Archives nationales, Paris (AN).
2. For a detailed history of children born to French-German couples during and after World War II, see Fabrice Virgili, *Naître ennemi: les enfants de couples franco-allemandes* (Paris, 2009).
3. Entrée en france des enfants nés en Allemagne, undated, Direction des personnes déplacées et réfugiés—Enfants (PDR) 5/274, Archives des Affaires étrangères, Bureau des Archives de l'Occupation française en Allemagne et en Autriche (MAE-Colmar).
4. On Nazi population policy and empire, see Mark Mazower, *Hitler's Empire: How the Nazis Ruled Europe* (New York, 2008); Adam Tooze, *The Wages of Destruction: The Making and Breaking of the Nazi Economy* (New York, 2008); Götz Aly, *"Final Solution": Nazi Population Policy and the Murder of the European Jews*, trans. Belinda Cooper and Allison Brown (London, 1999).
5. Michael Marrus, *The Unwanted: European Refugees in the Twentieth Century* (New York, 1985), 313–317; Tony Judt, *Postwar: A History of Europe Since 1945* (New York, 2005), 22.
6. Cited in Paul-André Rosenthal, *L'Intelligence démographique: Sciences et politique de populations en France (1930–1960)* (Paris, 2003), 110.
7. On French debates about the children of rape during World War I, see Ruth Harris, "The 'Child of the Barbarian,'" *Past & Present* 141, nr. 1 (1993): 170–206; Stèphane Audoin-Rouzeau, *L'enfant de l'ennemi* (Paris, 1995).
8. Alfred Zeil, Rapport sur les questions de nationalité, February 23, 1918, 4, 30/AJ/96, AN.
9. Harris, "The 'Child of the Barbarian,'" 195–196. On the myths and realities of German occupation in France and Belgium during World War I, see Johne Horne and Alan Kramer, *German Atrocities 1914: A History of Denial* (New Haven, 2001); Isabel Hull, *Absolute Destruction: Military Culture and the Practices of War in Imperial Germany* (Ithaca, 2004), 207–214.
10. Richard Bessel, *Germany 1945: From War to Peace* (New York, 2009), 116–117, 158.
11. Rapport sur le fonctionnement des "Centres de Jeunesse et de Santé en Allemagne" pendant l'année 1946, January 30, 1947, PDR 5/285, MAE-Colmar.

12. Réfugiés politiques d'orgine allemande ou autrichienne, October 2, 1945, Volume 110, Allemagne, Z-Europe, MAE.

13. Daniella Doron, "In the Best Interest of the Child: Family, Youth and Identity Among Postwar French Jews" (Ph.D diss., New York University, 2009), 32, 80–81.

14. Rosenthal, *L'intelligence démographique*, 107.

15. On Mauco and postwar population policy in France, see Karen Adler, *Jews and Gender in Liberation France* (Cambridge, 2003), 106–143. On DP migration to postwar France, see G. Daniel Cohen, "The West and the Displaced: The Postwar Roots of Political Refugees," (Ph.D diss., New York University, 2000).

16. Georges Mauco, *Projet pour une prémiere organisation de l'immigration* (Paris, 1946), Cited in Rosenthal, *L'intelligence démographique*, 310.

17. Rosenthal, *L'intelligence démographique*, 109.

18. Robert Debré et Alfred Sauvy, *Des Français pour la France (le problème de la population)* (Paris, 1946), 228.

19. Comité International pour l'Étude des Questions Européen, "Les Resultats de la Guerre de 1939 à 1945 en ce qui concerne la population de l'Allemagne," April 13, 1946, Volume 105, Allemagne, Z-Europe, MAE.

20. La situation démographique de l'Allemagne, 1946–48, Volume 109, Allemagne, Z-Europe, MAE.

21. Problème démographique allemand, March 10, 1946, Volume 105, Allemagne, Z-Europe, MAE.

22. Ibid.

23. Déclaration faite à Moscou le 15 mars 1947 par M. Georges Bidault, Volume 109, Allemagne, Z-Europe, MAE.

24. Réaction de la presse allemande au sujet de l'émigration et des transferts de population, April 27, 1947, Volume 107, Allemagne, Z-Europe, MAE.

25. Prüfung der Möglichkeiten und Auswirkungen einer Auswanderung grösseren Maßstabes, July 25, 1947, Volume 108, Allemagne, Z-Europe, MAE.

26. See Atina Grossmann, *Jews, Germans, and Allies: Close Encounters in Occupied Germany* (Princeton, 2007), 131–184; Rainer Schulze, "Growing Discontent: Relations between Native and Refugee Populations in a Rural District in Western Germany after the Second World War," in Robert Moeller, ed. *West Germany under Reconstruction: Politics, Society, and Culture in the Federal Republic* (Ann Arbor, 1997), 53–72; Philipp Ther, "The Integration of Expellees in Germany and Poland after World War Two: A Historical Reassessment" *Slavic Review* 55 (Winter 1996): 779–805.

27. Konrad Theiss, *Colonization Abroad: A Solution to the Problem of the German Expellees* (Stuttgart, 1948), 7.

28. Lt. Colonel Breveté Schott, *Chômage et Emigration* (Baden-Baden, 1947).

29. Letter from the American Unitarian Association to Henri Bonnet, March 30, 1947, Volume 107, Allemagne, Z-Europe, MAE.

30. Raymond Bousquet, Politique démographique française, October 21, 1946, 80/AJ/75, AN.

31. Enfants allemands au Danemark, February 24, 1947, Direction Generale des Affaires Administratives et Sociales, Volume 110, Allemagne, Z-Europe, MAE.

32. Henri Fesquet, "Les enfants nés en Allemagne pendant la guerre," *Le Monde,* August 8, 1946, PDR 5/238, MAE-Colmar.

33. Recherche en Allemagne des enfants resortissants des nations unies, February 16, 1946, PDR 5/284, MAE-Colmar.

34. Rapport du Service Sociale du 28 avril au 26 mai 1945, Stuttgart, May 26, 1945, PDR 5/284, MAE-Colmar.

35. Note relative au rapatriement des enfants, August 5, 1946, PDR 5/238, MAE-Colmar.

36. Ivan Jablonka, *Ni père, ni mère: histoire des enfants de l'Assistance publique, 1870–1939* (Paris, 2006), 29–31.

37. A. François Poncet à Mme Ingeborg Haug, May 16, 1950, PDR 5/222, MAE-Colmar.

38. Ministry of Public Health to the Central Tracing Bureau, September 25, 1946, PDR 5/271, MAE-Colmar. On reforms to French adoption laws see Adler, *Jews and Gender,* 61–62.

39. Conférence de presse de M. Pierre Pfimlin, April 5, 1946, 80/AJ/75, AN.

40. Julius Schwoerer, Die Rechtstellung des in Deutschland geborenen unehelichen Kindes einer deutschen Mutter und eines französischen vaters, Freiburg 1946, PDR 5/276, MAE-Colmar. On the history of paternity laws in France, see Rachel Fuchs, *Contested Paternity: Constructing Families in Modern France* (Baltimore, MD, 2008).

41. DPOW/P(46)84 Final, Autorité Allié de Contrôle, Directoire Prisonniers de Guerre et Personnes Déplacées, October 1, 1946, PDR 5/62, MAE-Colmar; Recherches d'enfants nés de père français, January 29, 1948, PDR 5/233, MAE-Colmar.

42. Perry Biddiscombe, "The Anti-Fraternization Movement in the U.S. Occupation Zones of Germany and Austria, 1945–48," *Journal of Social History* 34 (Spring 2001): 630, "Pregnant Frauleins are Warned" *Stars and Stripes,* April 8, 1946, cited by Biddiscombe, 636; On children of African-American soldiers and German women see Heide Fehrenbach, *Race After Hitler: Black Occupation Children in Postwar Germany* (Princeton, 2005).

43. Fehrenbach, *Race after Hitler,* 30, 68–73.

44. Fehrenbach, *Race after Hitler,* 31–45, 65–69, quotation 41.

45. Rapport à l'intention de Monsieur Poignant, July 3, 1946, PDR 5/215, MAE-Colmar.

46. Alimentation des Français séjournant en Z.F.O., April 8, 1948, PDR 5/273, MAE-Colmar.

47. Nicholas Stargardt, *Witnesses of War: Children's Lives Under the Nazis* (New York, 2005), 328.

48. See Virgili, *Naître ennemi;* Biddiscombe, "The Anti-Fraternization Movement": Fabrice Virgili, *Shorn Women: Gender and Punishment in Liberation France* (New York, 2002); Fehrenbach, *Race After Hitler;* Maria Höhn, *GIs and Frauleins: The German-American Encounter in 1950s West Germany* (Chapel Hill, 2002).

49. Steffens/Boyer, Au gouvernement militaire, October 30, 1946, PDR 5/272, MAE-Colmar.

50. Hildegard Steiner à Monsieur le maire de Cruzy, March 26, 1947, PDR 5/272, MAE-Colmar.

51. Letter from Anna in Kaifenheim, March 21, 1947, PDR 5/272, MAE-Colmar.

52. Letter from Maria in Pommern, March 3, 1947, PDR 5/272, MAE-Colmar.

53. Gerdes-Lirola, March 27, 1946, PDR 5/273, MAE-Colmar.

54. Rapport du Service Sociale du 28 avril au 26 mai 1945, May 26, 1945, PDR 5/284, MAE-Colmar.

55. Activités, prévisions et besoins de la Section "Enfance" de la Division PDR, December 30, 1946, PDR 5/242, MAE-Colmar.

56. Enfants naturels reconnus et abandonnés, December 28, 1949, PDR 5/278, MAE-Colmar.

57. René Bourcier, born 1932, PDR 5/242, MAE-Colmar.

58. Klara Herron, November 18, 1949, PDR 5/375, MAE-Colmar.

59. Recherche et rapatriement d'enfants nés en Allemagne de père français, June 6, 1946, PDR 5/370, MAE-Colmar.

60. Compte rendu d'activité du service recherches enfants depuis sa creation, 1949, PDR 5/285, MAE-Colmar.

61. Debré and Sauvy, *Des Français pour la France,* 125–126.

62. Recherche et rapatiements d'enfants Français, February 15, 1947, PDR 5/213; Recherche et rapatriements d'enfants français, Plan 1947, January 24, 1947, PDR 5/242, MAE-Colmar.

63. Recherches et rapatriement d'enfants des Nations-Unies, May 23, 1947, PDR 5/238, MAE-Colmar.

64. Enfants abandonnés d'origine nord africaine, July 18, 1947, PDR 5/239, MAE-Colmar.

65. Fehrenbach, *Race after Hitler,* 94, 142.

66. Fehrenbach, *Race after Hitler,* 132–168, quotation, 142.

67. Ibid., 53–55, 83–86. On the racial discourses surrounding the occupation of the Rhineland, Julia Roos, "Women's Rights, Nationalist Anxiety, and the "Moral" Agenda in the Early Weimar Republic: Revisiting the "Black Horror"

Campaign against France's African Occupation Troops," *Central European History* 42 (September 2009): 473–508.

68. On the relationship between racial and cultural hierarchy in French colonial and migration policies, see Todd Shepard, *The Invention of Decolonization: the Algerian War and the Remaking of France* (Ithaca, 2006); Elisa Camiscioli, *Reproducing the French Race: Immigration, Intimacy and Embodiment in the Early Twentieth Century* (Durham, NC, 2009); Mary D. Lewis, *The Boundaries of the Republic: Migrant Rights and the Limits of Universalism in France, 1918–1940* (Stanford, CA, 2007); Alice Conklin, *A Mission to Civilize: Republican Idea of Empire in France and West Africa, 1895–1930* (Stanford, 1997).

69. Debré et Sauvy, *Des Français pour la France,* 229.

70. Louis Chevalier, *Le problème démographique Nord-Africain* (Paris, 1947), 209.

71. Le Service Sociale I.M.S. en Afrique du Nord en 1946, 20050590, article 11, Centre des archives contemporaines (CAC), Fontainebleau.

72. Le Ministre de la Santé Publique et de la Population à Monsieur le Général Koenig, February 21, 1948, PDR 5/239, MAE-Colmar.

73. Enfants abandonnés d'origine Nord-africaine, August 25, 1947, PDR 5/239, MAE-Colmar.

74. Adoptions des enfants abandonnés, August 1950, PDR 5/62, MAE-Colmar.

75. Entrée en france des enfants nés en Allemagne, undated, PDR 5/274, MAE-Colmar.

76. Abandon d'enfants d'origine française, July 18, 1950, PDR 5/62, MAE-Colmar.

77. Rosenthal, *L'intelligence démographique,* 202.

78. Abandon d'enfants d'origine française, August 31, 1950, PDR 5/62, MAE-Colmar.

79. Adoptions des enfants abandonnés, August 1950, PDR 5/62, MAE-Colmar.

80. Abandons d'enfants, December 10, 1949, PDR 5/63, MAE-Colmar.

81. On efforts to distinguish postwar population, welfare, colonial, and migration policies from Nazi racism, see for example, Rita Chin, Heide Fehrenbach, Atina Grossmann, and Geoff Eley, eds. *After the Racial State: Difference and Democracy in Germany and Europe* (Ann Arbor, 2009); A. W. Brian Simpson, *Human Rights and the End of Empire: Britain and the Genesis of the European Convention* (Oxford, 2001); Fehrenbach, *Race after Hitler;* Shepard, *The Invention of Decolonization;* Paul Gilroy, *There Ain't No Black in the Union Jack: The Cultural Politics of Race and Nation* (Chicago, 1991).

82. Tara Zahra, *Kidnapped Souls: National Indifference and the Battle for Children in the Bohemian Lands, 1900–48* (Ithaca, 2008), ch. 6–8; Mazower, *Hitler's Empire;* Elizabeth Harvey, *Women and the Nazi East: Agents and Witnesses of Germanization* (New Haven, 2003).

83. On postwar Australian emigration schemes, see Kathleen Paul, "Changing Childhoods: Child Emigration Since 1945," in *Child Welfare and Social Action*

in the Nineteenth and Twentieth Centuries, ed. Jon Lawrence and Pat Starkey (Liverpool, 2001), 123–124.

84. Kathryn Hulme, *The Wild Place* (Boston, 1953), 237.

85. Fremdsprachige Flüchtlinge in Österreich, 12u-49, Memo to International Committee of the Red Cross, January 13, 1950, Carton 10, BMI, 12u-34, Archiv der Republik (AdR), Österreichisches Staatsarchiv (OestA).

86. See Tara Zahra, "'Prisoners of the Postwar'": Expellees, Displaced Persons, and Jews in Austria after World War II," *Austrian History Yearbook* 41 (2010): 191–215.

87. Haim Genizi, *America's Fair Share: The Admission and Resettlement of Displaced Persons, 1945–52* (Detroit, 1993), 22–23.

88. Ibid., quotation 80, 66–111.

Chapter 6. Ethnic Cleansing and the Family in Chzechoslovakia

1. Protokoll der Frau Klara Werner, Carton 849, Ministerstvo ochrana práce a sociální péče-repatriace (MPSP-R), Národní archiv, Prague (NA).

2. Jolana Macková and Ivan Ulrych, *Osudy lidických dětí* (Lidice, 2003).

3. On the history of ethnic cleansing in Eastern Europe, see in particular Benjamin Frommer, *National Cleansing: Retribution against Nazi Collaborators in Postwar Czechoslovakia* (Cambridge, UK, 2005); Eagle Glassheim, "National Mythologies and Ethnic Cleansing: The Expulsion of Czechoslovak Germans in 1945," *Central European History*, vol. 33, no. 4 (November, 2000): 463–48; Philipp Ther and Ana Siljak, eds. *Redrawing Nations: Ethnic Cleansing in East-Central Europe, 1944–1948.* Cold War Book Series No. 4. (Lanham, MD, 2001); Norman Naimark, *Fires of Hatred: Ethnic Cleansing in Twentieth-Century Europe* (Cambridge, MA, 2001).

4. On mixed marriages and the expulsions in Czechoslovakia, see Benjamin Frommer, "Expulsion or Integration: Unmixing Interethnic Marriage in Postwar Czechoslovakia," *East European Politics and Societies* 14 (March 2000): 381–410.

5. These numbers are all approximate, as estimates of the numbers of displaced depend on the sources and are contested. Philipp Ther, "A Century of Forced Migration: The Origins and Consequences of 'Ethnic Cleansing,' in *Redrawing Nations,* 54–57. On postwar population transfers, see also Peter Gatrell, "World Wars and Population Displacement in Europe in the Twentieth Century," *Contemporary European History* 16 (November 2007): 415–426; Naimark, *Fires of Hatred*; Agnes Tóth, *Migrationen in Ungarn, 1945–1948: Vetreibung der Ungarndeutschen, Binnenwanderungen und slowakisch-ungarisch Bevölkerungsaustausch* (Munich, 2001); Timothy Snyder, *The Reconstruction of Nations: Poland, Ukraine, Lithuania, Belarus, 1569–1999* (New Haven, 2003).

6. On "patriotic memories" of occupation in Europe see Pieter Lagrou, *The Legacy of Nazi Occupation: Patriotic Memory and National Recovery in Western Europe, 1945–61* (New York, 2000).

7. Ohledně pátrání po lidických dětech, January 8, 1946, Carton 849, MPSP-R, NA.

8. Wo Sind die Kinder von Lidice?, Carton 849, MPSP-R, NA.

9. No author, *Pohřešované československé děti* (Prague, 1946), Carton 846, MPSP-R, NA. See also No author, *Lidické děti* (Prague, 1945), Carton 849, MPSP-R, NA.

10. "Po stopách uloupených čs. dětí," *Národní osvobození,* February 23, 1947, 3. Carton 409, Ministerstvo zahraničních veci—výstřižkový archiv (MZV-VA), NA.

11. "Po stopách zavlečených dětí," *Lidové noviny,* January 13, 1949. Carton 409, MZV-VA, NA.

12. "Zavlečené děti musí otročit Němcům," *Svobodné noviny,* March 16, 1947, Carton 409, MZV-VA, NA.

13. "Neuvěřitelná případ," *Národní osvobození,* October 12, 1947, Carton 409, MZV-VA, NA.

14. Letter from Marie Jirásková, November 9, 1945, Carton 845, MPSP-R, NA.

15. Obec Lidice, dotaz po dětech, November 5, 1945, Carton 849, MPSP-R, NA.

16. Pátrání po lidických dětech, May 29, 1946, Carton 849, MPSP-R, NA.

17. Zdeňka Bezděková, *They Called me Leni* trans. Stuart R. Amor (New York, 1973), 6.

18. Bezděková, *They Called me Leni,* 82.

19. On images of Czechs as western and modern, see Andrea Orzoff, *Battle for the Castle: The Myth of Czechoslovakia in Europe, 1914–48* (Oxford, 2009).

20. On *The Search,* see Anna Holian, "Framing Displacement: Americans, Europeans, and the Problem of Displaced Children in *The Search* (1948)," Paper delivered at the European Social Science History Conference, Lisbon, Portugal, February 27, 2008; Jim G. Tobias and Nicola Schlichting, *Heimat auf Zeit: Jüdische Kinder in Rosenheim, 1946–47* (Nuremberg, 2006), 76–77; Sharif Gemie and Louise Rees, "Reconstructing Identities in the Post-War World: Refugees, UNRRA, and Fred Zinnemann's *The Search,*" unpublished manuscript.

21. "Návrat uloupených dětí do vlast," *Obrana lidu,* April 3, 1947, Carton 409, MZV-VA, NA.

22. "Slzy radosti vítaly nalezené děti," *Právo lidu,* April 3, 1947, Carton 409, MZV-VA, NA.

23. Péče o mladistvé repatrianty, December 19, 1945, Carton 270, MPSP-R, NA.

24. Nalezené lidické děti, péče o sirotky, September 18, 1945, Carton 848, MPSP-R, NA.

25. Zjišťování a přešetřování dětí neznámého původu při provádění odsunu Němců, April 18, 1946, Carton 153, Zemské ústředí péče o mládež v Čechách (ČZK), NA.

26. Pozor na české děti při odsun Němců, February 7, 1946, Carton 846, MPSP-R, NA.

27. 3017–46 II B kr. March 7, 1946. Carton 153, ČZK, NA.

28. Cited in Jeremy King, *Budweisers into Czechs and Germans: A Local History of Bohemian Politics, 1848–1948* (Princeton, 2002), 176.

29. Frommer, "Expulsion or Integration," 381.

30. On the Czechoslovak census of 1930, see Tara Zahra, *Kidnapped Souls: National Indifference and the Battle for Children in the Bohemian Lands, 1900–48* (Ithaca, 2008), 106-41.

31. Frommer, "Expulsion or Integration," 387-88. Quotation, Zprávy z domova, 5 May 1944, 3. Sig. 91/7, Fond 37, Vojenský ústřední archiv, Prague.

32. Frommer, "Expulsion or Integration," 387-88. For quotations and text of Decree Nr. 33, see Ústavní dekret prezidenta republiky ze dne 2. srpna 1945 o úpravě československého státního občanství osob národnosti německé a maďarské, 33/1945 Sb., in Karel Jech and Karel Kaplan, eds., *Dekrety prezidenta republiky 1940-45: Dokumenty* (Brno, 1995), 345-46.

33. Jaroslav Vaculík, *Poválečná repatriace československých tzv. přemístěných osob* (Brno, 2004), 26; Inventař, MPSP-R, 13, NA. On re-emigration, see also Jaroslav Vaculík, *Poválečná reemigrace a usídlování zahraničních krajanů* (Brno, 2002).

34. On resettlement, see David Gerlach, "For Nation and Gain: Economy, Ethnicity, and Politics in the Czech Borderlands, 1945–48" (Ph.D diss., University of Pittsburgh, 2007); Frommer, "Expulsion or Integration," 381–410; Andreas Wiedemann, *"Komm mit uns das Grenzland aufbauen!" Ansiedlung und neue Strukturen in den ehemaligen Sudetengebieten, 1945–52* (Essen, 2007); František Čapka, Lubomír Slezák and Jaroslav Vaculík, eds. *Nové osídlení pohraničí českých zemí po druhé světově válce* (Brno, 2005).

35. For more on the establishment and composition of national committees, see Gerlach, "For Nation and Gain," 46–58.

36. On tensions between old and new settlers and between central government and national committees, see David Gerlach, "Working with the Enemy: Labor Politics in the Czech Borderlands, 1945–48," *Austrian History Yearbook* 38 (2007):179–207; Wiedemann, *Komm mit uns,* 289–319; Frommer, "Expulsion or Integration," 392–393, 397–398.

37. Frommer, "Expulsion or Integration," 382–390; Gerlach, "For Nation and Gain," 182–185; Wiedemann, *Komm mit uns,* 310–316. On mixed marriage in the Protectorate, see Chad Bryant, *Prague in Black: Nazi Rule and Czech Nationalism* (Cambridge, MA, 2007), 55–56, 136, 166.

38. Frommer, "Expulsion or Integration," 391.
39. Národnost dětí ze smíšených rodičů, July 9, 1945, Carton 1421, Ministerstvo vnitra-nová registratura (MV-NR), NA.
40. Dr. Fiala, Ministerstvo ochrana práce a sociální péče, July 3, 1946, Carton 846, MPSP-R, NA.
41. Repatriace z Gorzowa, January 24, 1946, Carton 412, MPSP-R, NA.
42. Národnost dětí ze smíšených rodičů, July 9, 1945, Carton 1421, MV-NR, NA.
43. Dětí ze smíšených manželství, April 12, 1946, sig. 1364/2, Carton 1032, Úřad předsednictva vláda (ÚPV-bez), NA.
44. Josef Břecka, Opis k č.j. 11560-II-2947/46, March 12, 1946, sig. 1364/2, Carton 1032, ÚPV-bez, NA.
45. Napravení germanisace, Návrh Josefa Břecky, April 15, 1946, sig. 1364/2, Carton 1032, ÚPV-bez, NA.
46. On the Small Decree, see Frommer, *National Cleansing*, 186–250.
47. Zpráva o poměrech ve vlasti, October 6, 1943, sig. 91/6, Fond 37, Vojenský ústřední archiv (VÚA).
48. Detlef Brandes, *Die Tschechen unter deutschem Protektorat* vol. 2 (Munich, 1975), 48; No author, *V dětech je národ věčný. Zpráva o činnosti zemského ústředí péče o mládež v Praze* (Prague, 1946), 23; Albin Eissner, "Die tschechoslowakische Bevölkerung im Zweiten Weltkrieg," *Aussenpolitik* 13 (1962): 334. For birthrates in interwar Czechoslovakia, see *Statistisches Jahrbuch der tschechoslowakischen Republik* 14 (1936), 17.
49. Zřizení ústřední komise pro otázky populační, June 25, 1946, Carton 618, sig. 1113, MPSP-R, NA.
50. Navrh vhodných opatření pro zvyšení populace, December 24, 1946, Carton 618, MPSP-R, NA.
51. Zákon ze dne 25. března 1948 o státní podpory novomanželům, č. 56/1948; Zákon ze dne 25. března 1948 o zálohování výživného dětem, č. 57/1948, both in *Sbírka zákonů a nařizení státu československu* (Prague, 1948).
52. "Problem populační začina být u nás velmi vážný," *Lidová demokracie,* May 4, 1946, Carton 310, MZV-VA, NA.
53. Pátrání po dětech-otázka národnosti, March 16, 1946, Carton 846, MPSP-R, NA; For the Ministry of Foreign Affairs response, Smíšená manželství a napravení germanisace-návrh Josefa Břecky, May 13, 1946, sig. 1364/2, Carton 1032, ÚPV-bez, NA.
54. Národnost, výdej potravných lístků spotřebitelům ze smišeného manželství, October 1, 1945, Carton 1421, MV-NR, NA.
55. Směrnice o ulévách pro některé osoby německé národnosti, May 27, 1946, sig. 1364/2, ÚPV-bez. Carton 1032, NA.
56. Směrnice o ulévách pro nekteré osoby německé národnosti- zavady, June 1946, sig. 663, Carton 1615, ÚPV-bez., NA.

57. Právní poměry osob žijicích v národnostně smíšených manželství, June 7,1948, sig. 1364/2, Carton 1032, ÚPV-bez, NA.

58. Vyhlaška ministra vnitra ze dne 20. prosince 1946 o lhutě k podávání o vrácení československého státního občanství manžely československých státních občanek, č. 254/1946, in *Sbírka zákonů a nařízení státu československsku* (Prague, 1946).

59. Frommer, "Expulsion or Integration," 388–89.

60. Prachatice-smišena manželství, odsun českých žen, April 25, 1946, sig. 1364/2, Carton 1032, ÚPV-bez., NA.

61. Petition to Ministerial Council, April 1946, sig. 1364/2, Carton 1032, ÚPV-bez., NA.

62. Ibid.

63. Petition to the office of the president, Ústí nad Labem, April 7, 1946, sig. 72, MPSP, NA.

64. Letter from Josef Klement to the Ministry of Interior, July 14, 1945, Carton 1421, MV-NR, NA.

65. Open letter to Klement Gottwald, December 11, 1947, Carton 1032, sig. 1364/2, NA.

66. Resoluce národní fronty žen, January 12, 1948, sig. 1364/2, Carton 1032, ÚPV-bez., NA.

67. Valentin Bolom, February 13, 1946; Ministry of Interior to Valentín Bolom, February 13, 1946, both in Carton 1421, MV-NR, NA.

68. Translation, testimony of Jaroslav Kouřik, undated, probably September 1947, Carton 846, MPSP-R, NA.

69. Land Commissioner for Bavaria, Political Affairs Division, Children's Case Files 1946–1952, Sig. 466/250/72/12/07, Box 6, National Archives and Records Administration (NARA).

70. Jaroslav Němec, no date (1946), Carton 8245, MV-NR, NA.

71. Směrnice pro repatriaci sirotků, April 28, 1947, Carton 847, MPSP-R, NA.

72. Ladislav Vítasek, November 26, 1946, MV-NR, Carton 1421, NA.

73. Jíři Baudyš, February 24, 1947, Carton 8279, MV-NR, NA.

74. On Jews in postwar Czechoslovakia, see Peter Brod, "Židé v poválečném Československsku," in *Židé v novodobých dějinách*, ed. Václav Veber (Prague, 1997), 147–162; Peter Brod, "Die Juden in der Nachkriegstschechoslowakei," in *Judenemanzipation—Antisemitismus—Verfolgung in Deutschland, Österreich-Ungarn, den böhmischen Ländern und in der Slowakei*, ed. Jörg K. Hoensch et. al. (Essen, 1999), 211–228; Helena Krejčová, "Židovská očekávání a zklamání po roce 1945," in *Češi a Němci: Ztracené dějiny?* ed. Eva Malířová, (Prague, 1995), 245–248; Alena Heitlinger, *In the Shadows of the Holocaust & Communism. Czech and Slovak Jews since 1945* (New Brunswick, 2006); Jana Svobodová, "Erscheinungsformen des Antisemitismus in den Böhmischen

Ländern 1948–1992," in *Judenemanzipation—Antisemitismus—Verfolgung,* 229–248.

75. Katerina Čapková, Michal Frankl, and Peter Brod, "Czechoslovakia," in *The YIVO Encyclopedia of Jews in Eastern Europe,* vol. 1 (New Haven, 2005), 380–381.

76. Transfer of People of Jewish Origin, May 29, 1945, 43/AJ/64, Archives nationales (AN).

77. Document WR 178/3/48, February 5, 1946, 43/AJ/64, AN. For more on the treatment of Jews as "unwanted elements" in the postwar Czech borderlands, see David Gerlach, "Beyond Expulsion: The Emergence of 'Unwanted Elements' in the Postwar Czech Borderlands, 1945–50," *East European Politics and Societies* 24 (May 2010): 278–279, 284–285.

78. Transfer of persons of Jewish Origin and Faith, July 25, 1946, 43/AJ/64, AN.

79. Max Gottschalk, The Jews in Czechoslovakia, April 1946, Folder 201 (Czechoslovakia), JDC Archive, New York.

80. Otázka židovské národnosti, April 13, 1948, Carton 8245, MV-NR, NA.

81. Krejčová, "Židovská očekávání," 247.

82. Report from Bratislava, August 23, 1948, 45/54, Folder 199 (Czechoslovakia), JDC Archive, New York.

83. Decree 108, part 1, section 1, paragraph 1, number 3. Published in Karek Jech and Karel Kaplan, *Dekrety prezidenta Republiky 1940–1945: dokumenty,* vol. 2 (Brno, 1995), 848.

84. Ministerstvo národní obrany, Goldberger Emmanuel- Setření národnosti, November 5, 1946, Carton 1421, MV-NR, NA.

85. On popular opinion and the the Slansky trials, see Keven McDermott, "A 'polyphony of voices'?: Czech popular opinion and the Slansky affair," *Slavic Review* 67 (2008): 840–865.

86. Čapková, Frankl, and Brod, "Czechoslovakia," 380–381; Frommer, "Expulsion or Integration," 407.

87. See for example Philipp Ther, *Deutsche und polnische Vertreibene: Gesellschaft und Vertriebenenpolitik in SBZ/DDR und in Polen 1945–1956* (Göttingen, 1998); Detlef Brandes, *Der Weg zur Vetreibung, 1938–1945: Pläne und Entscheidungen zum "Transfer" der Deutschen aus der Tschechoslowakei und aus Polen* (Munich, 2001).

Chapter 7. Repatriation and the Cold War

1. Article from the bulletin of "Tanjug" October 26, 1949, Repatriation of Yugoslav Children in Austria blocked by the IRO. See also (in the same carton), "Les enfants Yougoslaves retenus par force en Autriche," *Tanjug,* Belgrade, January 7, 1948, 43/AJ/601, Archives nationales, Paris (AN).

2. Aleta Brownlee, UNRRA Mission to Austria. Child Welfare in the Displaced Persons Camps, 6, Programme, Box 5, Aleta Brownlee Papers, Hoover Archive (HA), Stanford University.

3. Figures from the inspection and filtration of repatriates, GARF, f. 9526, op. 3, d. 175, op. 4, d. 1, 1.62, 1.223. I thank Andrew Janco for providing me with these statistics.

4. Louise W. Holborn, *The International Refugee Organization: A Specialized Agency of the United Nations. Its History and Work* (New York, 1956), 511.

5. Unaccompanied Children in Austria and Germany, April 29, 1948, AJ/43/604, AN.

6. On the political stakes of repatriation in Western Europe see Pieter Lagrou, *The Legacy of Nazi Occupation: Patriotic Memory and National Recovery in Western Europe, 1945–61* (New York, 2000), 81–128; Megan Koreman, *The Expectation of Justice: France 1944–46* (Durham, NC, 1999), 79–91.

7. Edith Sheffer, *Burned Bridge: How East and West Germans Made the Iron Curtain* (Oxford, forthcoming), Chapter Six.

8. Memorial w sprawie rewindykacji dzieci zrabowanych w Polsce, Folder 372, Ministerstwo Pracy i Opieki Społecznej, Archiwm Akt Nowych, Warsaw (AAN).

9. Problem rewindykacji dzieci polskich z 3 zachodnich stref okup. Niemiec, December 31, 1948, Folder 251, Fond 284, Polski Czerwóny Krzyż, AAN.

10. "Poland Asserts British Zone Holds Children," *New York Herald Tribune*, Paris Edition, June 11, 1948, AJ/43/604, AN. For a reliable estimate of the number of children kidnapped from Poland, see Isabel Heinemann, *"Rasse, Siedlung, deutsches Blut": Die Rasse und Siedlungshauptamt der SS und die rassenpolitische Neuordnung Europas* (Göttingen, 2003), 508–509.

11. Office of the U.S. High Commissioner, Memo to Eric Hughes from Peter Stanne, September 21, 1951, Folder Legislation—Unaccompanied Children, RG 466, 250/68/15/3, National Archives and Records Administration, College Park (NARA).

12. Do Zarzadu Miejskiego Królewska Huta, 1945, Folder 313, Generalny Pełnomocnik Rzadu RP do Spraw Repatriacji w Warszawie, AAN.

13. Dane statystyczne z rewindikacji dzieci, July 11, 1950, Folder 33, Delegatura Polski Czerwony Krzyż na Niemcy, AAN.

14. Stefan Tyska, Impressions based on experience obtained while being attached by the Polish Red Cross to UNRRA Team 104g, April 14, 1947, Folder 36, Delegatura PCK na Strefę Ameryka ska w Niemczech, AAN.

15. Notatka o rewindikacji i repatriacji dzieci polskich w Austrii, November 30, 1948; Rewindykacja dzieci polskich w Austrii, June 27, 1947, Folder 26, Delegatura Polski Czerwony Kryż Na Austrię, AAN.

16. Mackowiak Kazmierz i Janina-repatriacja z Niemec , November 28, 1947, Ministerstwo Pracy i Opieki Społecznej, AAN.

17. Rewindkacji dzieci, March 15, 1948, Folder 101, Polski Czerwóny Krzyż, AAN.

18. For Polish Red Cross grievances about IRO and Allied military authorities, see Trudności w rewindikacji dzieci polskich ze Niemiec, December 21, 1948; Problem rewindikacji dzieci polskich z 3 zachodnich stref okupacynach Niemiec, December 31, 1948, Folder 31; Trudności napotykane przez Delegature Główna PCK na Niemcy w akcji rewindikacji dzieci, August 1948, Folder 30, Delegatura Polski Czerwony Krzyż na Niemcy, AAN.

19. Bartczak Eugeniusz and Arden Zofia, August 25, 1947, Folder 31, Delegatura Polski Czerwony Krzyż na Niemcy, AAN.

20. Child Pogoda Sofia, From British military official AC Todd to Polish Red Cross, Folder 31, Delegatura Polski Czerwony Krzyż na Niemcy, AAN.

21. Akcja Poszukiwania i rewindikacja dzieci w Strefie Sowieckiej, 1947, Folder 30, Delegatura Polski Czerwony Krzyż na Niemcy, AAN.

22. Roman Hrabar, Akcja rewindikacji dzieci, December 18, 1947, Folder 30, Delegatura Polski Czerwony Krzyż na Niemcy, AAN.

23. Notatka o rewindikacji I repatriacji dzieci polskich w Austrii, November 30, 1948, Folder 26, Delegatura Polski Czerwony Kryż na Austrię; Notatka sluzbowa, February 17, 1949, Folder 31, Delegatura Polski Czerwony Krzyż na Niemcy, AAN.

24. Letter from Major Prawin to General Brian H. Robertson, December 9, 1948, Folder 31, Delegatura Polski Czerwony Krzyż na Niemcy, AAN.

25. Sprawozdanie z prac Komitet Opieki nad Dzieckiem Polskim w Berlinie za okres od dnia 1 kwietna 1947r do dnia 1 października 1947r, December 20, 1947, Folder 317, Generalny Pełnomocnik Rzadu RP do Spraw Repatriacji w Warszawie, AAN.

26. Trudności napotykane przez Delegature Główna PCK na Niemcy w akcji rewindikacji dzieci, no date, Folder 30, Delegatura Polski Czerwony Krzyż na Niemcy, AAN.

27. Ulrich Herbert, *Hitler's Foreign Workers: Enforced Foreign Labor under the Third Reich,* trans. William Templer (Cambridge, UK, 1997), 268–273.

28. Sprawa Nr. 4, Galuhn Henryk, Oswiadczenie, August 18, 1949, Folder 31, Delegatura Polski Czerwony Krzyż na Niemcy, AAN.

29. Smigas, Erika, September 9, 1948; Objasnienia i komentarze do załączonych dowodów pisemnych o trudnościach stwarzanych przez władze IRO/CCG na terenie Strefy Brytyskiej Niemiec, Folder 31, Delegatura Polski Czerwony Krzyż na Niemcy, AAN.

30. Instrukcja w sprawie organizacji skolnictwa i oświaty polskiej w Niemczech, London 1945, 1, Folder 70, Fond Uchodźcy Polscy w Niemczech po 1945,

Piłsudski Institute of America (PI), New York. On Polish DP schools, see Anna D. Jaroszyńska-Kirchman, *The Exile Mission: the Polish Political Diaspora and Polish Americans, 1939–1956* (Athens, OH, 2004), 86.

31. Memorandum, London 1947, Folder 3, Polish Displaced Persons in Germany, Fond Uchodźcy Polscy w Niemczech po 1945, PI.

32. 600 sierot polskich przymusowo repatriowanych, January 10, 1948, Wladomosci Prasowe Z.P.U.W, nr. 9, Folder 34, Fond Uchodźcy Polscy, PI.

33. Memorandum concernant le problème de la revendication et du rapatriement des enfants polonais, March 5, 1948, 43/AJ/798, AN.

34. Suspicious German Action, Abandonning of Handicapped Children, *Gazeta Ludowa,* October 16, 1947, 43/AJ/608, AN.

35. For the complete story of these children, see Lynne Taylor, *Polish Orphans of Tengeru: The Dramatic Story of their Long Journey to Canada, 1941-49* (Toronto, 2009).

36. Statement of J. Donald Kingsley Before the Third Committee of the General Assembly of the United Nations, November 10, 1949, 43/AJ/604, AN.

37. Narrative Report on Special Registration Assignment at the IRO Children's Center, Salerno, Italy, August 15, 1949, 43/AJ/604, AN.

38. Polish Children from East-Africa, August 10, 1949, 43/AJ/604, AN.

39. Policies Regarding Re-Establishment of Children, April 25, 1949, 43/AJ/926, AN.

40. Telegram, Monsignor Meystowicz Bremen to IRO Geneva, August 6, 1949, 43/AJ/604, AN.

41. Memo from E. H. Czapski, August 8, 1949, 43/AJ/604, AN.

42. "Displaced Children," *New York Times,* September 5, 1948.

43. "Repatriating Children," *New York Times,* September 15, 1948. See also Martin Sherry, "Repatriating Children," *New York Times,* October 1, 1948.

44. Demokratischer Frauenbund Deutschlands, October 20, 1949, 43/AJ/604, AN.

45. Extrait du journal "Repatriant" nr. 132 (182), 43/AJ/604, AN.

46. Union Internationale de Protection de l'Enfance, Letter to Carlos P. Romulo, President of the General Assembly of the UN, January 24, 1950, 43/AJ/602, AN.

47. Statement of J. Donald Kingsley, 43/AJ/604, AN.

48. Report on the British Zone—Child Welfare Supervisor, 2, February 21, 1945–November 19, 1946, Aleta Brownlee Papers, Carton 1, HA.

49. Ibid., 3–5.

50. Aleta Brownlee to Deputy Chief of UNRRA Mission to Austria, Charles S. Miller, Field Visit to Yugoslavia—October, 1946, November 7, 1946, Folder 2, Carton 1, Brownlee Papers, HA. On favorable UNRRA impressions of Yugoslavia, see also William Hitchcock, *The Bitter Road to Freedom: A New History of the Liberation of Europe* (New York, 2009), 241.

51. Conference, November 25, 1946, Folder 2, Carton 1, Brownlee Papers, HA.

52. Conference with Father Methodius Kelava and Sister Anka, p. 1–2, November 26, 1946, Folder 2, Carton 1, Brownlee Papers, HA.

53. Aleta Brownlee, "Whose Children?" 138–139, Folder 1, Carton 9, Brownlee Papers, HA.

54. Report by Mrs. Syma Klok on the Repatriation of Forty-Nine Children from Leoben UNRRA Children's Home to Yugoslavia on 8 January 1947, Box 1, Brownlee Papers, HA.

55. Brownlee, "Whose Children?" 367.

56. On German expellees reclaimed for repatriation as Yugoslavs, see Memo from Aleta Brownlee to Major J. Pockar, February 2, 1948, 43/AJ/599, AN.

57. Excerpts from letters from parents or relatives in Yugoslavia to foster families or children in Austria, February 15, 1950, 43/AJ/603, AN.

58. Report on an Interview between Aleta Brownlee and Ivan Bajin, December 8, 1948, Box 8, Brownlee Papers, HA.

59. Annaberg School Children, May 17, 1946, Box 5, Brownlee Papers, HA.

60. Translation of a letter, January 21, 1946, Folder 2, Box 1, Brownlee Papers, HA.

61. Aleta Brownlee, "Whose Children?" 165–167.

62. Law Nr. 11, Repatriation and Resettlement of Unaccompanied Displaced Children October 5, 1950, Folder Legislation—Unaccompanied Children, RG 466, 250/68/15/3, NARA.

63. Children's Bureau-Conference in Geneva, Switzerland, re HICOG Law Nr. 11, July 13, 1951, Folder 64, Unaccompanied Children (Soviet), RG 466, 250/68/15/3; HICOG Law Nr. 11, Memo from Ingeborg Olsen to Theodora Allen, April 16, 1951, Box 131, 278/350/902/49/3, NARA.

64. U.S. District Court of the Allied High Commission for Germany, Case 51-7-15, Resettlement or Repatriation of Hannelore Pospisil, Folder 64, Unaccompanied Children (Soviet), RG 466, 250/68/15/3, NARA.

65. U.S. Court of Appeals Decision Affecting the Resettlement or Repatriation of an Unaccompanied Displaced Child, November 1, 1951, Folder 64, Unaccompanied Children (Soviet), RG 466, 250/68/15/3, NARA.

66. U.S. Court of the Allied High Commission for Germany in the Matter of the Repatriation or Resettlement of Josef Ochota, Case No. R. 51-8-1, District Courts: Children's Resettlement Case Files, 1949–1954, Box 1, 278/350/902/49/3, NARA.

67. U.S. District Court in the Matter of Resettlement of Johanna Bobrowitsch, Decision 51-8-21 R, December 2, 1952, District Courts: Children's Resettlement Case Files, 1949–1954, Box 4, 278/350/902/49/3, NARA.

68. Press Conference of Russian Delegation; Soviet Statement, November 13, 1951; Hearing in the Case of Johanna Bobrowitsch, November 13, 1951; Soviet Control Commission in Germany to John McCloy, January 10, 1952,

all in Folder 64, Unaccompanied Children (Soviet), RG 466, 250/68/15/3, NARA.

69. Issue of Soviet Children in Germany Revived, November 17, 1951, Folder 64, Unaccompanied Children (Soviet), RG 466, 250/68/15/3, NARA.

70. U.S. District Court in the Matter of Repatriation of Dieter Strojew, Action 51-8-80, Box 12, District Court Resettlement Case Files, 1949–1954, 278/350/902/49/3, NARA.

Chapter 8. From Divided Families to a Divided Europe

1. "Odysee der Mütterliebe," *Revue,* November 12, 1955, 31–38.

2. Robert G. Moeller, *War Stories: The Search for a Usable Past in the Federal Republic of Germany* (Berkeley, 2001).

3. On Pitter, see Tomáš Pasák, "Přemysl Pitters Initiative bei der Rettung deutscher Kinder im Jahre 1945 und seine ablehnende Haltung gegenüber der inhumanen Behandlung der Deutschen in den tschechischen Internie-rungslagern," in *Der Weg in die Katastrophe: Deutsch-tschechoslowakische Bezie-hungen 1938–47* ed. Detlef Brandes and Václav Kural (Essen, 1994), 201–213; Milena Šimsová, "Přemysl Pitter (1895–1976). Edice dokumenty," *Historické listy* 2 (1992): 31–34; Pavel Kosatik, *Sám proti zlu. Život Přemysla Pittra (1895–1976)* (Prague, 2009).

4. Benjamin Frommer, *National Cleansing: Retribution against Nazi Collaborators in Postwar Czechoslovakia* (Cambridge, UK, 2005), 2.

5. On the rape of German women after World War II, see Atina Grossmann, "A Question of Silence: The Rape of German Women by Occupation Sol-diers," in Robert G. Moeller, ed., *West Germany under Reconstruction: Politics, Society and Culture in the Adenauer Era* (Ann Arbor, 1997), 33–52; Norman Naimark, *The Russians in Germany: A History of the Soviet Zone of Occupation, 1945–49* (Cambridge, MA, 1995), 69–140. On rape by French soldiers, Richard Bessel, *Germany 1945: From War to Peace* (New York, 2009), 116–117; On reprisals against women suspected of collaboration, see Fabrice Virgili, *Shorn Women: Gender and Punishment in Liberation France* (New York, 2002); Perry Biddiscombe, "Dangerous Liaisons: The Anti-Fraternization Movement in the U.S. Occupation Zones of Germany and Austria, 1945–48," *Journal of Social History* 34 (March 2001): 611–647.

6. Jan Gross, *Fear: Anti-Semitism in Poland after Auschwitz* (Princeton, 2007).

7. Melissa Feinberg, *Elusive Equality: Gender, Citizenship and the Limits of Democracy in Czechoslovakia, 1918–50* (Pittsburgh, 2006), 195; Frommer, *National Cleansing,* 216. Bradley Abrams, *The Struggle for the Soul of a Nation: Czech Culture and the Rise of Communism* (Lanham, MD, 2004). Only 30.37 percent of Slovaks cast votes for the Communist party in May 1946, by

contrast. See James Felak, *After Hitler, Before Stalin: Catholics, Communists and Democrats in Slovakia, 1945–48* (Pittsburgh, 2009), 59–60.

8. Přemysl Pitter, "Dovětek k mému kulturnímu a sociálnímu programu," 2–3, undated—written during the Second World War, Box 15, Archive Přemysl Pitter, Prague (PP).

9. Přemysl Pitter, "In der Jugend von heute wachsen die Menschen heran, welche die Geschichte von morgen machen werden!" Pamphlet, Prague 1932, Box 15, PP.

10. Ústřední národní výbor, referat pro školství, vědy a umění, September 13, 1950, Box 16, PP.

11. Olga Fierz, "Rescue of German Children," *Reconciliation,* March 1960, 53–54.

12. Olga Fierz, "The Four Castles of Kindness," *Reconciliation,* May 1960, 88–91. On conditions in Czechoslovak internment camps between 1945 and 1948, see also Tomáš Staněk, *Internierung und Zwangsarbeit: Das Lagersystem in den böhmischen Ländern, 1945–48* (Munich, 2007), 159–164, for numbers, 159, 164.

13. Olga Fierz, *Kinderschicksale in den Wirren der Nachkriegszeit* (Prague, 2000), 109.

14. Přemysl Pitter, Kulturní a socialní program, 1946, 2, Box 15, PP.

15. Přemysl Pitter, Dovětek k mému kulturnímu a sociálnímu programu, 3–16, Carton 15, PP.

16. Antonín Moravec, "Naši chlapci," *Posel,* May 1947, nr. 7, 12, Carton 19, PP; See also Fierz, *Kinderschicksale,* 48–49.

17. Přemysl Pitter, Talk for BBC for October 11, 1953, Carton 72, PP.

18. Mark M. Anderson, "The Child Victim as Witness to the Holocaust: An American Story?" *Jewish Social Studies* 14 (Fall 2007): 1–22; Peter Novick, *The Holocaust and American Life* (New York, 2000); Joan B. Wolf, *Harnessing the Holocaust: The Politics of Memory in France* (Stanford, 2004).

19. Přemysl Pitter, *Posel,* April 1946, Carton 19, PP.

20. Přemysl Pitter, *Posel,* June 1946, 3, Carton 19, PP.

21. See for example Naomi Seidman, "Eli Wiesel and the Scandal of Jewish Rage," *Jewish Social Studies* 3 (Fall 1996): 1–19.

22. Projev, Židovská mládež z koncentračních táborů, Štřín a Olešovice, October 1945, Carton 18, PP.

23. Dobroslava Štepanková, "Ditě ve valce a po ní," *Posel,* May 1947, 15–16, Carton 19, PP. On Christian visions for the reeducation of West German youth, see also Mark Edward Ruff, *The Wayward Flock: Catholic Youth in Postwar West Germany, 1945–1965* (Chapel Hill, NC, 2004); Mark Roseman, "The Organic Society and the Massenmenschen: Integrating Young Labor in the Ruhr Mines, 1945–48," in *West Germany under Reconstruction,* 287–320.

24. Siegfried W., "Vzpomínka na Štřín," *Posel,* September 1947, Carton 19, PP.

25. BBC Interview with Přemysl Pitter, September 12, 1951, 1, Box 70, PP.

26. Přemysl Pitter, *Nad vřavou nenávisti. Vzpomincky a svědectví Přemysla Pittra a Olgy Fierzové* (Prague, 1996), 87.

27. Přemysl Pitter, BBC Sunday Talk for May 9, 1954, Box 72, PP.

28. Käte Fiedler, "Der Ideologische Drill der Jugend in der Sowjetzone," in *Die Jugend der Sowjetzone in Deutschland,* ed. Kampfgruppe gegen Unmenschlichkeit (Berlin, 1955), 36; Hans Köhler, "Erziehung zur Unfreiheit," in idem. *Jugend Zwischen Ost und West: Betrachtungen zur Eingliederung der jugendlichen Sowjetzonenflüchtlinge in das westdeutsche Wirtschafts- und Geistesleben,* ed. Harald v. Koenigswald (Troisdorf, 1956), 60.

29. Přemysl Pitter, "The Foundations of Family Life," BBC Talk, February 17, 1952, Box 70, PP.

30. Joseph Wechsberg, "Communism's Child Hostages," *Saturday Evening Post,* April 1, 1950, 123–126, Box 8, Aleta Brownlee Papers, Hoover Archive, Stanford University.

31. Alexandra Kollontai, "Communism and the Family," in Alix Holt, ed. *Alexandra Kollontai: Selected Writings* (New York, 1977), 259.

32. Wendy Goldman, *Women, the State and Revolution: Soviet Family Policy and Social Life, 1917–1936* (Cambridge, UK, 1993); On similarities between West and East European pronatalist policies, see David L. Hoffmann, "Mothers in the Motherland: Stalinist Pronatalism in its Pan-European Context," *Journal of Social History* 34 (Autumn 2000): 35–54

33. Donna Harsch, *Revenge of the Domestic: Women, the Family and Communism in the German Democratic Republic* (Princeton, 2007), 227–235, 297, statistics on day care, 227. See also Malgorzata Fidelis, "Equality through Protection: The Politics of Women's Employment in Postwar Poland, 1945–1956," *Slavic Review* 63 (Summer 2004): 301–324.

34. Robert G. Moeller, *Protecting Motherhood: Women and the Family in the Politics of Postwar West Germany* (Berkeley, 1993), 64–72.

35. Pitter, "The Foundations of Family Life."

36. Pitter, *Nad vřavou nenávisti,* 85–87.

37. Přemysl Pitter, "Die ausgestreckte Hand," *Glaube und Heimat,* nr. 3 (1956), 3, Box 52, PP.

38. Jacques Cohn, Education et réadaptation des enfants victimes de la guerre, *Oeuvre de Secours aux Enfants, Conférence Nationale 12–14 juin 1949,* 46, Box 4, Reel 10, OSE, United States Holocaust Memorial, Museum and Archive (USHMMA).

39. Kluger, *Still Alive,* 145.

40. For a geneaology of the concept of "survivor guilt" and analysis of challenges to it, see Ruth Leys, *From Guilt to Shame: Auschwitz and After* (Princeton, 2007), 17–83.

41. Kluger, *Still Alive,* 185.

42. Milton, *The Tiger in the Attic,* 196, 194.

43. Letter from Elie Wiesel to Judith Samuel, Box 22, Reel 23, OSE, USHMMA.

44. On delayed responses to trauma, see Leys, *From Guilt to Shame,* 28.

45. Ilse Hellman, "Hampstead Nursery Follow-Up Studies," *Psychoanalytic Study of the Child* 17 (1962), 159–175.

46. Gerhard Sonnert and Gerald Holton, *What Happened to the Children who Fled Nazi Persecution?* (New York, 2006). On Jewish-German experiences of emigration, Atina Grossmann, "German Jews as Provincial Cosmopolitans: Reflections from the Upper West Side," *Leo Baeck Institute Yearbook* 53 (January 2008): 157–168.

47. Ruth Kluger, *Still Alive: A Holocaust Girlhood Remembered* (New York, 2001), 122.

48. Amabel Williams-Ellis, "Foreword," in St. Loe Strachey, ed. *Borrrowed Children: A Popular Account of Some Evacuation Problems and their Remedies* (New York, 1940), ix.

49. "Convention and Protocol Relating to the Status of Refugees," http://www .unhcr.org, 12, (Accessed March 12, 2010).

50. "Geneva Declaration of the Rights of the Child of 1924," http://www .un-documents.net, (accessed March 21, 2010).

51. "United Nations' Declaration of Children's Rights," 1959, http://www.un.org, (accessed March 21, 2010).

52. Bruno Bettelheim, "Schizophrenia as a Reaction to Extreme Situations," in idem. *Surviving and Other Essays* (New York, 1952), 113.

53. Ernst Papanek (with Edward Linn), *Out of the Fire* (New York, 1975).

54. Thérèse Brosse, *Homeless Children: Report of the Proceedings of the Conference of Directors of Children's Communities* (Geneva, 1948), 49.

55. See Catherine Ceniza Choy, "Race at the Center: the History of American Cold War Asian Adoption," *The Journal of American-East Asian Relations* 16 (Fall 2009): 1–20; Heide Fehrenbach, *Race after Hitler: Black Occupation Children in Postwar Germany and America* (Princeton, 2005); Ellen Herman, *Kinship By Design: A History of Adoption in the Modern United States* (Chicago, 2008); Sara K. Dorow, *Transnational Adoption: A Cultural Economy of Race, Gender, and Kinship* (New York, 2006).

56. For current statistics, see "Adoptions to the United States," http://www .adoption.state.gov (accessed April 28, 2010). For 1956 numbers, United Nations, *Adoption entre Pays. Rapport d'un groupe d'experts européens* (Geneva, 1957).

57. *Adoption entre Pays,* 9.

58. *Adoption entre Pays,* 37–38.

59. Choy, "Race at the Center," 4–8. As Heide Fehrenbach has shown, these adoptions set the stage for a debate over whether Germany or America was a more racist society after World War II. Fehrenbach, *Race after Hitler.*

60. *Adoption entre Pays,* 17.

61. Barbara S. Bosanquet, "The Hand that Rocks the Cradle," *The World's Children: The Official Organ of the Save the Children Fund and the Declaration of Geneva,* February 26, 1946, 23. Bosanquet's comment may have been intended to support the postwar British campaign for "mother's wages," family allocations paid directly to mothers. On mother's wages, Susan Pedersen, *Eleanor Rathbone and the Politics of Conscience* (New Haven, 2004).

62. Rosalynn Baxandall and Linda Gordon, eds. *America's Working Women: A Documentary History, 1600–Present* (New York, 1995), 245; Walter Müller, Angelika Williams, and Johann Handl, eds. *Strukturwandel der Frauenarbeit 1880–1980* (Frankfurt, 1983), 35; A. T. Mallier and M. J. Rosser, *Women and the Economy: A Comparative Study of Britain and the USA* (New York, 1987), 1995; Sylvie Schweitzer, *Les femmes ont toujours travaillé: une histoire de leurs metiers, XIXe et XXe siècle* (Paris, 2002), 82–83.

63. See, for example Judith Warner, *Perfect Madness: Motherhood in the Age of Anxiety* (New York, 2005); Susan Douglas and Meredith Michaels, *The Mommy Myth: The Idealization of Motherhood and How it has Undermined all Women* (New York, 2005); Jill Lepore, "Baby Food," *The New Yorker,* January 16, 2009; Judith Warner, "Ban the Breast Pump," *The New York Times,* April 2, 2009; Hanna Rosin, "The Case Against Breastfeeding," *The Atlantic,* April 2009; Tina Kelley, "Toilet Training at 6 Months? Better Take a Seat," *New York Times,* October 9, 2005; Jennifer Bleyer, "The Latest in Strollers? Mom and Dad," *New York Times,* March 10, 2010.

64. Edith Sterba, "Emotional Problems of Displaced Children," *Journal of Social Casework* 30 (May 1949): 175–177.

65. Samuel Moyn, *The Last Utopia: A Recent History of Human Rights* (Cambridge, Mass., 2010), Chapter 1; Lynn Festa, *Sentimental Figures of Empire in Eighteenth-Century Britain and France* (Baltimore, 2006).

66. On the innocent child as an object of humanitarianism, see Carolyn Steedman, *Strange Dislocations: Childhood and the Idea of Human Interiority* (Cambridge, MA, 1995), 112–130; Hugh Cunningham, *The Children of the Poor: Representations of Childhood Since the 17th Century* (Oxford, 1991); Laura Briggs, "Mother, Child, Race, Nation: The Visual Iconography of Rescue and the Politics of Transracial and Transnational Adoption," *Gender and History* 15 (August 2003): 179–200; Seth Koven, *Slumming: Sexual and Social Politics in Victorian London* (Princeton, 2004), 88–138; Anderson, "The Child Victim," 1–22.

67. Nicholas Stargardt, *Witnesses of War: Children's Lives Under the Nazis* (New York, 2005).

68. Tony Judt, *Postwar: A History of Europe Since 1945* (New York, 2005), 18.

69. The literature on each of these groups is extensive. On Jews, Zeev W. Mankowitz, *Life Between Memory and Hope: The Survivors of the Holocaust in Occupied Germany* (New York, 2002); Hagit Lavsky, *New Beginnings: Holocaust Survivors in Bergen-Belsen and the British Zone of Germany, 1945–50* (Detroit, 2002); Ruth Gay, *Safe Among the Germans: Liberated Jews after World War II* (New Haven, 2002); Atina Grossmann, *Jews, Germans, and Allies: Close Encounters in Occupied Germany* (Princeton, 2007); Michael Brenner, *After the Holocaust: Rebuilding Jewish Lives in Postwar Germany* (Princeton, 1997); Avinoam Patt, *Finding Home and Homeland: Jewish Youth and Zionism in the Aftermath of the Holocaust* (Detroit, 2009). On East European refugees, Ilrike Goeken-Haidl, *Der Weg zurück: Die Repatriierung sowjetischer Zwangsarbeiter während und nach dem Zweiten Weltkrieg* (Essen, 2006); Katharine Jolluck, *Exile and Identity: Polish Women in the Soviet Union during World War II* (Pittsburgh, 2002); Anna M. Holian, *Between National Socialism and Soviet Communism: The Narration of Community among Displaced Persons in Germany, 1945–1951* (Ann Arbor, forthcoming); On expellees, see Rainer Schulze, ed. *Zwischen Heimat und Zuhause: deutsche Flüchtlinge und Vertriebene in West Deutschland, 1945–2000* (Osnabrück, 2001); Philipp Ther, *Deutsche und polnische Vertriebene: Gesellschaft und Vertriebenenpolitik in SBZ/DDR und in Polen, 1945–56* (Göttingen, 1998).

70. For attempts to bring the history of expellees, Jewish, and non-Jewish DPs into a single story, see Tara Zahra, "Prisoners of the Postwar: Expellees, Refugees, and Citizenship in Postwar Austria," *Austrian History Yearbook* 41 (2010), 191–215; Adam Seipp, "Refugee Town: Rural West Germany, 1945–52," *Journal of Contemporary History* 44 (October 2009): 675–95.

71. On the paradigmatic and exceptional status of Jews, see G. Daniel Cohen, "The Politics of Recognition: Jewish Refugees in Relief Polices and Human Rights Debates, 1945–50," *Immigrants and Minorities* 24 (July 2006): 125–43.

72. See Daniella Doron, "In the Best Interest of the Child: Family, Youth, and Identity in Postwar France, 1944–1954," (Ph.D diss., New York University, 2009).

Index